THE NATURE OF EVIL

BY THE SAME AUTHOR

THE PROBLEM OF IMMORTALITY:
Studies in Personality and Value

THE NATURE OF EVIL

BY

RADOSLAV A. TSANOFF, PH.D.

PROFESSOR OF PHILOSOPHY, THE RICE INSTITUTE

New York

THE MACMILLAN COMPANY

1931

KRAUS REPRINT CO.

New York

1971

Set up and electrotyped. Published January, 1931

L.C. 31-1840

Reprinted with the permission of the author
KRAUS REPRINT CO.
A U.S. Division of Kraus-Thomson Organization Limited

Printed in Germany

TO

MY FATHER AND MOTHER

PREFACE

If we conceive of philosophy as man's cosmic orientation, contemporary thought reveals two strains rich in philosophical significance. On the one hand is the radical reinterpretation of cosmological ideas necessitated by the experimental and theoretical advance of physical science. By stimulating metaphysical interest in scientists and scientific discipline in metaphysicians, this advance has led to a healthy rapprochement between the two. On the other hand is the insistent demand for a philosophy of value that will be more than a conciliatory epilogue to stark naturalism: for an adequate account of value and of its rôle in nature. Both of these strains in modern thought concern intimately the problem of man's cosmic status: what is man, and how is nature mindful of him and of his values? Thus both natural science and man's own self-criticism are making contemporary philosophy increasingly significant and alive.

The critical constructive thought of today and of tomorrow cannot neglect the record of the facts of nature supplied in the amazing advance of the physical and biological sciences. But nature is not limited to what telescope and microscope and test-tube reveal: the career and the character of nature are disclosed likewise in the lives and thoughts of men, in man's devotions and ideals, illusions and tragic frustrations: these are all facts relevant to what we may be allowed to call the Higher Behaviorism. The resolve not to ignore them may save us from a too precipitate and narrow 'naturalism' in cosmology, and surely the study of them leads us into the laboratory of the science and the philosophy of value.

In an earlier volume entitled *The Problem of Immortality: Studies in Personality and Value* the endeavor was made to examine man's conception of himself as more than a mere episode in the cosmic process, man's assured confidence in the permanent reality of his values and of himself as the bearer of them, and thus to understand the significance of man's claims to a certain kind of destiny. In this work we turn as it were to the other side of the picture. If the idea of immortality is the peak of man's aspiration, the tragic sense of evil is the abyss that ever threatens to engulf him and his ambitions, or at any rate to sober his self-esteem. It imposes a reconsideration of the values to which man commits his faith in himself and in nature. Pessimism and theodicy both reveal man's character: his grievous sense of his overwhelming problem, and his tireless effort to overcome it. The characteristic worth of man is thus essentially bound up with this tragic enterprise, and upon the adequate conception of the nature of evil hangs the whole philosophy of value.

The aim of this short preface has been to suggest the philosophical why and wherefore of this book rather than to give a preliminary tabulated statement of its contents. For the latter the reader is referred to the detailed Table of Contents which follows. As will be observed, a theme of such wide human interest reaches beyond the strict field of technical philosophy into the domains of religion and literature.

My obligations are as various as the contacts in which the complexity of my theme has involved me. An effort has been made to make due and accurate acknowledgment in the Notes, at the end of the volume. Parts of this work have been published separately, and I am grateful for permission to include here material that first appeared in the pages of the *Rice Institute Pamphlet* and the *Philosophical Review*. The final chapter is being used as a contribution to a cooperative volume on *Contemporary Tendencies in American Idealism.* I wish also to thank the Cambridge University Press for allowing me to quote from Mr. Geoffrey L. Bickersteth's translation of the poems of Leopardi. Shorter quotations from other works have been acknowledged in the Notes. Passages from foreign writers have been quoted in English, with reference to the original in the Notes and also cross-reference to the English translation cited. In the case of quoted poetry, the original text is given in the Notes. If no English version is cited in a note, the translation of the respective passage in the text, prose or poetry, is one for which I must be held responsible.

My colleague Professor Charles W. Morris has very kindly assisted me in the reading of the proofs. During the entire course of this work I have had the constant help of my wife.

RADOSLAV A. TSANOFF.

HOUSTON, TEXAS,
November, 1930.

TABLE OF CONTENTS

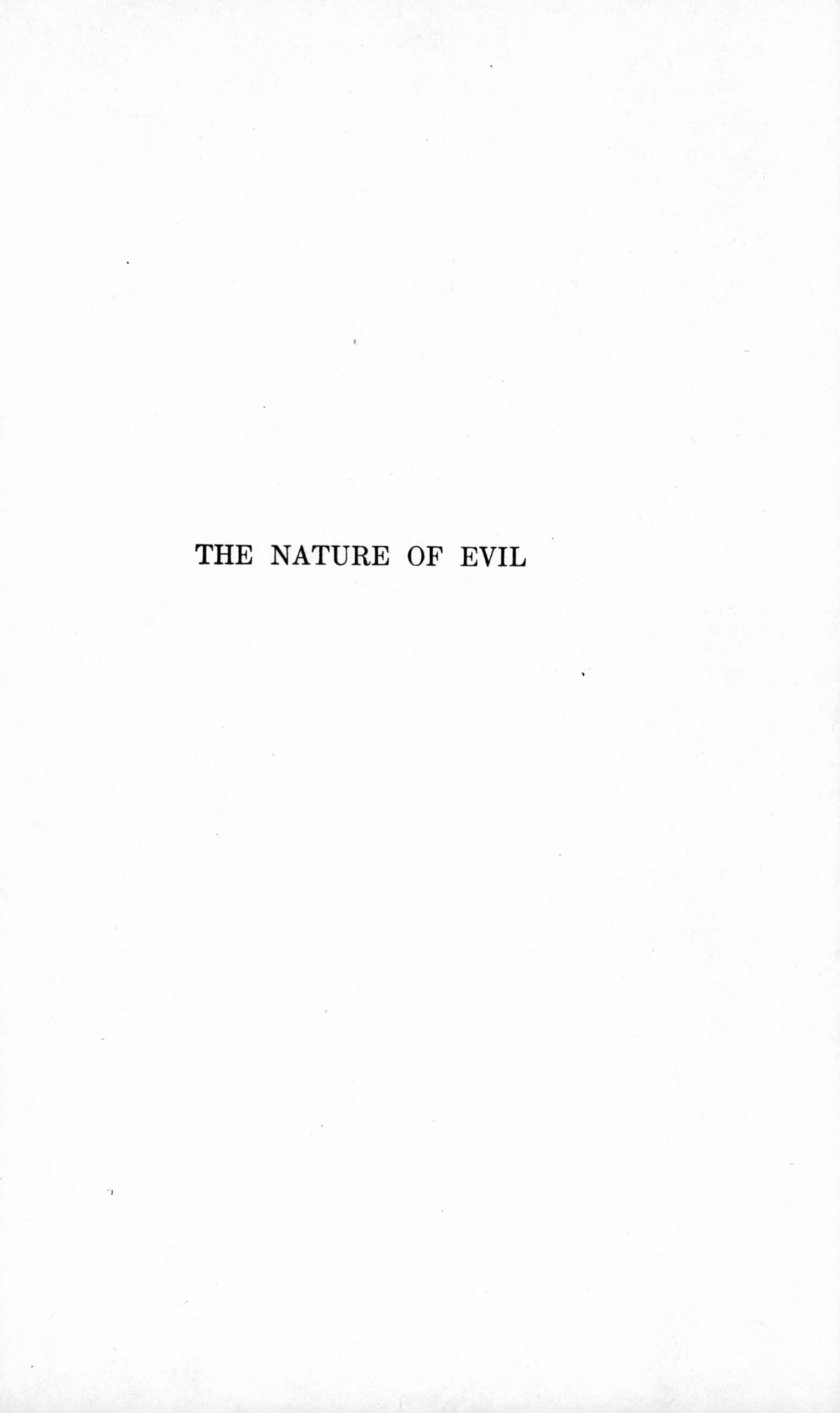

THE NATURE OF EVIL

THE NATURE OF EVIL

CHAPTER I

THE PROBLEM OF EVIL IN THE GREAT RELIGIONS

I

A precise definition of Pessimism cannot be offered at the outset, and it might prejudice our inquiry were we to attempt it; for the more carefully we survey our field, the greater will appear the variety of views which are styled pessimistic. The antonym superlative, Optimism, has been championed by so many theologians and philosophers with theological commitments and predilections that we should not be surprised if a common stock of axioms and a largely predestined type of reasoning has made likewise for more consistent uniformity in definition and in conclusion. Even here, though a dozen theodicies should declare that this is the best of all possible worlds, the sentence, eulogistic in some systems, is in others of a decidedly apologetic tone. Should we now, by way of distinction, follow a contemporary and define a pessimist as one who *fears* that this is the best possible world, we would only be brought to realize how astonishing is the range of negation. Orthodoxy may not be quite one, but heresy is surely legion. The *Aye* of docile acquiescence is a drilled choir chant, but like the thousand-voiced tumult of a troubled multitude is the *Nay* of discontent, disdain, and despair. Layer beneath layer of truth lies in the first words of *Anna Karenina:* "All happy families are more or less like each other; but every unhappy family is unhappy in its own particular way."

The initial step in understanding the problem of evil is to understand what makes it a problem.

Consider, in the first place, the point of view of consistent materialism. Suppose we assume that physical science is the only reliable source of metaphysical categories; suppose we declare, not merely that, of every process in nature, *a* mechanistic account is available, but that no other type of account is admissible. Such a point of view is essentially impersonal and therefore cannot comprehend the meaning of value; for it, both evil and good would be sounding brass and tinkling cymbal, words without meaning or misapplied labels. If nature, and human nature in it, is merely and nothing but a causal nexus in space and time, then (even allowing for the mystery, how this vast mechanism could come to know itself as a mechanism or could in any way theorize about itself) all we could undertake to do, or recognize as worth undertaking, in serious science or philosophy, would be the description and analysis and causal explanation of conditions and events,—not in any sense their evaluation.

A consistent materialistic-mechanistic philosopher may undertake to give us the real, that is to say causal, account of what is vulgarly known as 'evaluation,' approval or disapproval, but could he *as a materialist* evaluate or admit value-judgments or value-categories? He may investigate and record the manifold behavior of individuals who allege that they feel or confer praise or blame, but can he consistently admit in his system the ideas 'praiseworthy' and 'blameworthy'? That the materialist himself, like the rest of us, not only approves and disapproves, not only has preferences but undertakes to defend them, is only his own personal concession to sanity.

The critique of materialistic philosophy is not a part of our present undertaking.[1] Suffice it here to recognize that a problem of evil, the judgment of anything as good or bad, evaluation of any sort, cannot be an integral part of a mechanistic system. Whatever the nature of value in detail, or whatever our ultimate definition of it, it is clear that to attach any serious meaning to value or evaluation requires a philosophy that affords other than mechanistic categories, requires metaphysical respect for intelligence and personality and spiritual activity, requires the firm recognition of that truth to which Green has given perhaps the classical expression: "Our ultimate standard of worth is an ideal of *personal* worth. All other values are relative to value for, of, or in a person." [2]

While consistent materialism, being impersonalistic, cannot take either good or evil seriously, there is a temperament afflicted with happiness and characterized sometimes by a natural incapacity, more often by a passionate or an assumed refusal to admit the reality of evil. "In some individuals," William James wrote, "optimism may become quasi-pathological. The capacity for even a transient sadness or a momentary humility seems cut off for them as by a kind of congenital anaesthesia." [3] Calling such an attitude towards life abnormal will not dispose of it; we are bound to probe further into the significance of such luxury in woe as, for instance, is confessed by Marie Bashkirtseff: "Can you believe it? I find everything good and pleasant, even my tears, my grief. I enjoy weeping, I enjoy my despair, I enjoy being exasperated and sad." [4] But the question, "Can you believe it?" seems a little revealing: it suggests defiance beneath the enthusiasm, or at any rate discloses, running through the docile acquiescence and indeed sustaining it, one worry, one evil: the evil of worrying over evil. So we may well shake our heads in doubt. If evil is really an unreality, an illusion, why should one be so thrilled over one's unresponsiveness to it? Perhaps the pure type of this docile optimism is very rare or has seldom been recorded adequately, but it is of interest nevertheless to consider the significance of all the cherished and cultivated cheerfulness and cosmic expansive emotionalism. There is unintended sinister significance in the lines of Walt Whitman, the poetic seer of this cult of the Everlasting Yea:

> I think I could turn and live with animals, they are so placid and self-contained;
> I stand and look at them long and long.
> They do not sweat and whine about their condition;
> They do not lie awake in the dark and weep for their sins;
> They do not make me sick discussing their duty to God . . .[5]

James does not quote the last line, which is scarcely of the 'Everlasting Yea.' But what indeed is the meaning of the entire passage in its eulogy of animal, unthinking placidity? This optimism would be spontaneous all-perception of good, and it has become habitual and wholehearted, but still it is *willed* because it demands and feeds on enthusiastic reassurance. Thought disturbs man's rhapsody of bliss, and so Whitman "could turn and live with animals," or would contemplate perfection "observing a spear of summer grass."

This is only one of the strains in Whitman's joyous chant, but it expresses, perhaps unwittingly, the truth which we shall find uttered in the earliest myths of mankind: thought makes a man sensible of dissatisfaction and pain, it rouses in man desires, demands, dreams and ideals to which he cannot attain. And in this sense of manifold frustration all the countless woes of man lie in germ. Evil and the problem of evil seem to arise from an experienced clash and disaccord of the actuality with the ideal, whatever this may be. The consciousness of this frustration may be so intense as to lead to a settled conviction that the clash and disaccord are irremediable, that frustration is the primal and the final fact of life. This conviction, if reasoned, provides the texture of pessimistic philosophy, which may go to such an extreme painful sense of despised actuality that the cherished ideal is pronounced illusory, the world is conceived in terms which consistently preclude the reality of positive worth. Evil, in such a philosophy of despair, becomes the fundamental reality. But when this type of mind comes to itself, it finds confronting it—a problem of good! If in theological optimism it is difficult to show why there should be any need of salvation in God's own world, the extreme pessimist's perplexity is no less: in a world essentially and irremediably bad, irrational, and meaningless, how could there be, not only salvation, but even the demand for it: how could such a world include the disdain of it, to wit, pessimistic philosophy? This is the pessimist's problem of good.

When the consciousness of frustration is dominated, not only by a practical demand, but also by a theoretical conviction that actuality should and must accord with the ideal, then we have the several varieties of reasoned optimism, claiming that the alleged clash or disaccord is exaggerated, and that in any case it is not ultimate, that harmony is primal and fundamental and will somehow be final in the universe. The question, Why should there be such disaccord at all? becomes pressing for the theologian whose definition of the Creator precludes the belief that any such clash is part of the divine experience. For such a mind the problem of evil demands a theodicy: exculpation of God for the presence of evil. Consistently it should likewise demand the metaphysical depreciation, if not the excogitation, of evil. This excess of logic is exhibited by lay minds in behalf of theology, but not usually by theologians, for the theological view of life is bound to include a perception of its evil and of man's need of redemption.

This initial glance at the movement of thought shows a willy-nilly tendency from the two extremes towards the middle. Optimism and pessimism represent views of life which are not described with literal accuracy by these superlative terms. We shall not, however, resort pedantically to a manufactured terminology—bonism, meliorism, malism, peiorism—for even these labels will not cover all the significant alternatives. Instead we shall use the words optimism and pessimism to refer to estimates of the world and of human life which are dominantly approving or condemnatory. Philosophically a double problem of evil results. The pessimist asks: What is the ultimate nature of this evil and miserable world, and is there any way out of its woe? The optimist: Why should this fundamentally good and perfect world include any evil, and how can we acquiesce in it loyally and wholeheartedly?

II

The fundamental available alternatives are suggested by the questions: Are good and evil coördinate and both ultimate; or are they both somehow mixed in a world in which it is futile to look for any ultimate rhyme or reason; or is one subordinate to the other, though forever related to it in perennial antithesis, each one requiring the other; or is one subordinate to the other in the sense of being episodic, transitory, actual perhaps, but extinguishable and ultimately unreal? With regard to evil in particular: is it somehow involved as evil in the very stuff and substance of the one ultimate reality; or, dualistically, is it a principle of being coördinate with the principle of perfection and opposed to it; or is evil a permanent characteristic of finite existence; or are we responsible for the experience of evil, whether owing to our immoderate zeal, which leads both intellect and desire to overreach themselves, or else whether owing to our limited knowledge which enslaves us to illusion, or to our hazardously unlimited freewill which plunges us in sin? These questions, and the answers to them, sometimes distinctly perceived and reasoned out, but more often confused, or else intertwined and embroidered in the figured speech of mythology, or trimmed and fitted in theological doctrine, provide man's alternative estimates of life.

That evil *as evil* is rooted and dominant in the very heart of ultimate reality can be the claim only of a pandiabolism, blackest embittered despair. Philosophic pessimism scarcely reaches this extreme: Schopenhauer's Will-to-live is blind and irrational; Hartmann's Unconscious is metalogical; and Mainländer's pre-cosmic Will-to-die is pitiable and pitifully inconsiderate; but not one of them is strictly hateful. The pessimistic poet lets himself go more violently: pity for the woeful creature rouses in him hatred for the Creator of woe. Most wicked and miserable must be the Author of wicked misery. Burning lines from Alfred de Vigny come to mind, and the first and only written stanza of Leopardi's *Hymn to Ahriman,* and this blasphemy of despair from James Thomson's *City of Dreadful Night:*

> Who is most wretched in this dolorous place?
> I think myself; yet I would rather be
> My miserable self than He, than He
> Who formed such creatures to His own disgrace.
>
> The vilest thing must be less vile than Thou
> From whom it had its being, God and Lord!
> Creator of all woe and sin! abhorred,
> Malignant and implacable! I vow
>
> That not for all Thy power furled and unfurled,
> For all the temples to Thy glory built,
> Would I assume the ignominious guilt
> Of having made such men in such a world.

Logically distinguishable from this, but practically tantamount, though without the intense feeling of abhorrence expressed in the above lines, is the view of life which like a load of lead bore down the soul of Brahmanic India. Evil is inherent in finite existence; woe is irremediably bound up with life and with the attachment to life. Man is doomed to rebirth; doomed to expiate the sin and folly of unremembered past lives. To be sure, his present life, if good, will have its good results in some next life, but not at all assuredly in *the* next life. We reap today the harvest of unknown past sowing, to harvest in some unknown future the sowing of today. The thought of this unending nightmare of reincarnation roused in the heart but one longing: not to be. "In this sort of cycle of existence (samsara) what is the good of enjoyment of desires, when after a man has fed on them there is seen repeatedly his return here to earth? . . . In this cycle of existence I am like a frog in a waterless well." [6] Thus the one path of salvation for man was to cease existing: by absorption in the Infinite Brahman.

But if this whole world of finite existence is thus reckoned as a woeful blunder, is Brahman, then, the blunderer in having become manifest in this world of misery? There is comprehensible reluctance to undertake the explanation of this riddle, how or why Brahman should become so woefully individualized, and the Hindu theologian does not hold fast to the idea that the finite world is the self-outpouring and externalization of Brahman. A bolder insight leads the Upanishadic seer to proclaim all finite existence as unreal, a veil of illusion, Maya. Real, alas, is the soul which must expiate in the woes of transmigration its attachment to illusion, until it has been chastened and purified and enlightened, and in the end extinguished in absorption. So the immobile eye of the ascetic saint, waiting for the hour of release, looks with disdainful equanimity on this wretched riot of illusion.

Woe has thus its source in individual existence. Yet the perception of the identity of the individual soul with the Universal Soul was the quintessence of Upanishadic wisdom: "That which is the finest essence—this whole world has that as its soul. That is Reality. That is Atman (Soul). That art thou, Svetaketu." [7] To the Brahmanic list of illusions, the Buddhist added the soul, individual and universal. All alleged substantial reality is illusion, Maya, and the self-identical substantial soul is also illusory. There is a condition of individual existence; it is a process of combination, but it is also a process of change, and inevitably a process of dissolution. The passing illusion is not an illusion by contrast to something real and stable. All is passing, becoming, coming together, dissolving; nothing is fixed and permanent. Really no thing is: only a complex of activities obtains.

In this complex of activities, however, an impersonal law of retribution operates ruthlessly: in it, complexes of acts that make for attachment to individual existence result in successive rebirths; in it, complexes of acts that make for release from self-engrossment, result in the dissolving of self and the extinction of all that is involved in self. There is no stable reality, finite or infinite: there is stable cosmic order with which we must reckon and on which we can rely: it is the law of Karma.

Buddha saw error, lust, anger, pride, all evil and woe in attachment to self, finite individual existence, but he provided a cosmology and a gospel calculated to assure direct deliverance from self-engrossment. Misery is universal, and it arises from self-engrossment, and can be extinguished through emancipation from self-engrossment, by following the Buddhist path of life. The resulting state would be extinction of self, and of all the lusts of self, Arhatship, Nirvana.

There is grave confusion in this gospel of deliverance from

evil through erasure of personality. I have tried to point it out in my study of "The Buddhist Doctrine of Karma," in the seventh chapter of *The Problem of Immortality*. "Individuality, selfhood is rejected by the Buddhist because in the life of self the Buddhist saw error, evil, woe, lust, anger, and ignorance. Surely these are all in the life of self, and they are surely got rid of if existence is depersonalized. But efface and extinguish personality, and is it only evil and error that have vanished? Can you then have good, enlightenment, truth, sweetness and light? Evil and good, sorrow and joy, delusion and enlightenment, these are correlative, and they involve personal activity and self-consciousness. Already in Brahmanism we may observe this tendency to reduce moral evil to metaphysical limitation. . . . But if we thus baldly identify evil with individuality and finitude, then is not good wiped out entirely? For is not evil already imputed to the Infinite Being which becomes individualized and thus assumes finitude? But what becomes then of the distinction good-evil? . . . So Buddhism has undertaken a moral-religious judgment of life, which its treatment of self renders nugatory. The doctrine of Karma is essentially an impersonal, unmoral conception of the world process; and yet it is forced to do ethical service in the Buddhist religion. There is no self and no self's activity, and yet there must be moral action and moral destiny." [8]

That extinction of individuality should have been proposed as the true goal of existence, indicates clearly the profound pessimism of the Brahmanic-Buddhist philosophy of life. Brahmanism hoped for deliverance from evil through eventual absorption in Brahman; its pessimism was positive, but its path of salvation uncertain. More confirmed in his pessimism, more assured in his gospel of redemption was the Buddha. Buddhism brought cheer, for it brought promise of the utter and unqualified extinction of self and all its woes.

Salvation is in non-existence. So Gautama is the progenitor of Schopenhauer and Hartmann.

III

The evident influence of Brahmanism and Buddhism on Schopenhauer and Hartmann and their successors should not confirm us in the misleading tendency to regard modern philosophical pessimism as an exotic Oriental plant on European soil. While it is true that the religious and philosophical spirit of negation is not as characteristic of the West as of ancient India, calling the West optimistic is too offhand and does not dispose of our problem. Again, when in our survey of the history of morals we contrast the Hellenic world-affirmation with the Christian world-denial, we should not overlook the fact that while the Greek, unlike the Christian theologian, did not feel in duty bound to contemn this world, he did in fact perceive abundantly its evil and undertook to meet and to explain it. Consider the judgment of life in Graeco-Roman wisdom, from Theognis and Sophocles to Menander and Seneca, Pliny and Plutarch: a veritable proverb of life-disenchantment. Plutarch cites it on the authority of Aristotle as very ancient wisdom: Man's greatest boon is the brevity of his life. Not to be born at all were of all things the best; but, if born, then to die as soon as possible.[9] So Homer repeatedly bewails our vain and transitory life: "There is nothing more piteous than a man among all things that breathe and creep upon the earth. . . . This is the lot the Gods have spun for miserable men, that they should live in pain; yet themselves are sorrowless." [10]

Only the unthinking could fail to perceive the misery of existence, and indeed to the early Greek, man's thought and outreaching zeal seem to have been the roots of evil. But why? Because man does ill to think and aspire, or because the gods are envious of thinking and ambitious man? Very significant are the myths of the Promethean cycle.[11] When Zeus overcame the Titans, he denied man his due share of good fortune; Prometheus thereupon took up the cause of men and became their champion. He stole the celestial fire of Zeus and gave it to man, thus making possible human conquest of nature and civilized life. For this Prometheus was affixed by Zeus on a rock in Caucasus, "fast riveted in bonds beneath the sky," as Aeschylus has it.[12] Daily his liver, the organ of insatiate desire, was pecked by Zeus' eagle, and daily it grew again. Thus did Divinity punish the divine aspiration and achievement of the culture-hero. To the rest of us Zeus sent as a gift Pandora, divinely beautiful and with a mysterious box for her dowry. The pliable, sensuous, unreasonably curious Epimetheus, disregarding all warnings of his brother Prometheus, took Pandora and opened the casket. Out flew all the woes and torments and pests: only hope remained under the lid as a last refuge for unhappy man.

Here is profound legend, of which the story in Genesis is a parallel. Eating of the tree of knowledge, curiosity, the desire of man to rise above and depart from nature, the lure of the unattained, these forces which lift man from the brute to civilized existence, these are also the roots of all his woes and misery. Later thought will come to regard man's desire as sinful, his will as wilful, and his suffering as deserved.

In pre-Socratic thought the naturalistic preoccupation with cosmology causes evaluation to recede in the background, and the problem of evil receives scant attention. The Orphic bias of Pythagoreanism, however, leads it to a conception of human life as essentially a conflict between good and evil (myth of Dionysos Zagreus), and to a disdainful view of material, earthly existence. Heraclitus, "the Weeping Philosopher," who saw all things as in a flux, eternally changing, beginning, and passing away, compares the World-Fashioner to a child building sand houses only to brush them aside.[13] This shadow-like impermanence of human life Homer had expressed in comparing men to wind-blown leaves,[14] and Greek tragedy agrees with him: so Aeschylus in the *Agamemnon:*

> Ah! What is mortal life? When prosperous,
> A shadow can overturn it, and, when fallen,
> A throw o' the wet sponge blurs the picture out.
> This is more piteous than the ruin of pride.[15]

And Sophocles, in *Oedipus Rex:*

> O mortal tribes of men,
> How near to nothingness
> I count you while your lives remain!
> What man that lives has more of happiness
> Than to seem blest, and, seeming, fade in night?
> O Oedipus, in this thine hour of gloom,
> Musing on thee and thy relentless doom,
> I call none happy who beholds the light.[16]

In this unstable world, persistent and limitless is misfortune: thus Electra in the opening lines of Euripides' *Orestes*, reciting the woeful doom of the house of Atreus:

> Nothing there is so terrible to tell,
> Nor fleshly pang, nor visitation of God,
> But poor humanity may have to bear it.[17]

And even more poignantly Aeschylus in the *Libation Bearers:*

> Alas, that none of mortal men
> Can pass his life untouched by pain!
> Behold, one woe is here—
> Another loometh near.[18]

The prevalence of evil and of evil fortune, divine punishment of men for crimes committed unwittingly, undeserved suffering, and sinister doom, all served to render theodicy perplexing. Aeschylus is grimly aware of the problem: though himself not a Prometheus, he can understand and portray the Promethean temper. Sophocles, bound to see the light shining through the darkness, yet saw life too steadily to see it whole: the ills were too many and glaring. When Philoctetes hears that great Ajax is dead, while the mean, nimble, poor dastard Thersites lives, he exclaims:

> No evil yet was crushed,
> The Heavens will ever shield it. . . .
> When I praise
> Things god-like, I find evil in the Gods.[19]

"That," Lewis Campbell observes, "is the nearest approach in Sophocles to the occasional cynicism of Euripides."[20] Euripides was more sceptical and bolder in his reaction: while as a dramatist he used the old legends to stir the feelings of the multitude, his treatment of the sacred themes was so moulded "as to make it manifest to the more intelligent amongst his countrymen that these forms were morally untenable and inconsistent with the highest notion of the divine."[21]

The Socratic shift in Greek thought turned Greek attention to the problem of evil and emphasized the Greek tendency to seek an explanation of evil in the recalcitrancy of matter, thus inclining towards dualism, but preserving securely the infinite perfection of God. In Plato's philosophy the problem is imperative. If the real world is a rational system, if its essence and apex is infinite perfect Deity, then how could there be any evil in the cosmos? For Plato Perfect Rationality alone is perfectly real and the ultimate source of all reality; by comparison with it, material existence is but shadow-shape appearance. But matter is also a resistant to perfect rationality; it is the element of imperfection, error, and evil in the cosmos. Plato insists that "God and . . . the things of God are in every way perfect."[22] "That God being good is the author of evil to anyone is to be strenuously denied."[23] But while the souls created by God directly are purely rational and free of corruption, God either tolerates or else is confronted with the inferior creation of mortal souls which are joined to the immortal in a manner suggesting congenital depravity in the universe. The purely rational soul assumes a bodily vesture "by necessity," as we read in the *Timaeus;* [24] as a prisoner in his cell seeking freedom, so the soul in pursuit of knowledge seeks to regain its high estate. It feels itself divided; as in a chariot drawn by two horses that pull opposite ways,[25] it would attain to rational perfection, yet is dragged into the mire by blind passion and the lusts of the body. Ignorant man proceeds to his ruin under the illusion that he is pursuing his advantage; though no one desires evil directly, most of us are its thralls. "The soul . . . is dragged by the body into the region of the changeable, and wanders and is confused; the world spins round her, and she is like a drunkard when she touches change." [26]

Were it not for this lure and tug of the material, our life would be perfect. But how are we to explain the strength and the effectiveness of this lure, or the very initial presence of imperfection and the possibility of downfall in the divine universe? Bodily contamination, disease and dissolution, cannot destroy the soul; [27] the question arises, whether matter is the real evil, or only the medium and instrumentality through which the real evil is made manifest: itself being the soul's attachment to the body and all its cravings? But, if this attachment is "necessary," is God to be exculpated by a recourse to dualism? To be sure, from God the world receives all that it has of good, and the Divine Helmsman portrayed in the *Statesman* [28] acts directly in restoring the cosmos to order. But Fate and Innate Desire which reverse the divine cosmic motion, and the inferior deities who let go and abandon control,—are these agents of chaos and evil within or beyond the range of God's creative activity? The difficulties confronting Plato here are as serious as those which at a later age are to enmesh St. Augustine. Plato loyally maintains the essential perfection and justice of the rational universe, but his implied dualism does not quite save him from the lurking doubt whether the roots of evil do not after all reach below the phenomenal crust of material existence.

The strong ethical note in the Platonic metaphysics is replaced in Aristotle by a scientific analysis of the nature of existence. While prizing ideal rationality, he does not depreciate the reality of the material, and he would relate the two so as to avoid the dualistic tendency of Plato. In this universe matter is the necessary but inadequate vehicle through which perfect rationality is progressively made manifest. It is a condition for the attainment of perfection, but also an obstacle to perfect attainment. Since in all finite existence attainment is never complete but always involves potential unattained perfection, Aristotle, while clearly recognizing evil in this world, is more interested in observing it than in justifying it or in explaining it away.

The dominantly practical tone of Post-Aristotelian thought, which concentrated on the question of value and made philosophy more and more an *ars vivendi*, demanded of the Stoic, confident of the essential perfection and justice and cosmic supremacy of Divine Providence, a justification of evil, and led the Epicurean, clearly aware of unjustifiable evil in the world, to seek refuge in naturalism and atheism. Thus, in teleological and anti-teleological monism, Post-Aristotelian philosophy seeks to square itself with the problem of evil. To the Stoic, the universe is essentially God's world, and is thus perfect, and this truth could not be gainsaid by the presence of evil in the world. The Stoic first depreciates and discounts the gravity of evil, and then pronounces it necessary and justified as a foil and a spur to good. The wise man who perceives the essential rationality and Divine Providence dominant in all things sees that life is neither as evil nor needlessly evil as appears to those who lack understanding. Through the extirpation of passion man can attain self-possession and peace of soul and victorious disdain of the alleged evils to which sensual folly is heir. In the midst of apparent ruin, the Stoic sage remains calmly acquiescent, knowing that no real and final evil can touch the man devoted to reason and virtue, and that all other evils are either illusory or are else instrumental to a greater good.

In this firm conviction the Stoic partook of what life had to offer, content in advance and resolved not to grumble: life is as it is and we should accept it and beware of unseemly greed: "When we are invited to a banquet," Epictetus reminds us, "we take what is set before us; and were one to call upon his host to set fish upon the table or sweet things, he would be deemed absurd. Yet in a word, we ask the gods for what they do not give; and that, although they have given us so many things!" "True instruction is this:—to learn to wish that each thing should come to pass as it does. And how does it come to pass? As the Disposer has disposed it. Now He has disposed that there should be summer and winter, and plenty and dearth, and vice and virtue, and all such opposites, for the harmony of the whole." [29] And even more enthusiastic is the acquiescence of Marcus Aurelius: "Whatsoever is expedient unto thee, O World, is expedient unto me, nothing can either be unseasonable unto me, or out of date, which unto thee is seasonable. Whatsoever thy seasons bear, shall ever by me be esteemed as happy fruit and increase." [30] The difficulties inherent in this noble vindication of the cosmos cannot be discussed here; they were only accentuated in Christian theodicy with its explicit theism, and are writ large in the pages of St. Augustine and Pascal and Bayle and Leibniz.

This trust in Divine Providence was dismissed bluntly by

the Epicurean who stood his ground on undisguised and unwavering naturalism and rejected all teleology: "The nature of the world is by no means made by divine grace for us: so great are the flaws by which it stands beset." [31] The cosmos is really a stupendous dance of atoms in the void. No Divine Providence nor any Reason friendly or malicious governs the coupling and the dissipation of these material particles. Man's soul and body are passing combinations of irreducible bits of matter; lasting satisfaction is not to be had, nor can it be expected; immortality is a delusion; the evils in life should surprise us no more than its alleged goods; they are both but words in a world in which atoms whirling in empty space are alone real. So materialistic philosophy exhibits here its incapacity to recognize, much less to solve, the problem of evil. Epicurean cosmology could not provide for the values sought in Epicurean ethics.

Cyrenaic hedonism also, for all its concentration on happiness, had proved unreliable in affording serene assurance of the worth of existence. To Aristippus, at home and comfortable in whatever circumstances, the wise man was as a bee, extracting honey from the bitterest flower. But later Cyrenaics came to doubt the sweetness of the honey, and, finding it in any case rarer and harder to obtain than their master averred, saw no reason for attachment to life. Hegesias, in the third century B.C., gained in Alexandria the dismal epithet of "the advocate of death." Life, to be worth living, must be pleasurable; but the attainment of pleasure is exceptional and unstable, and, when attained, defeats itself by the weariness and satiety that follow in its train. The one goal worth seeking eludes him most who most pursues it, and thus ever-hoodwinked man has no good reason for preferring life to death. Hegesias' gloomy eloquence started an epidemic of suicides in Alexandria until his freedom of speech was curtailed by the king Ptolemy Soter.

Windelband points out the self-refutation of eudaemonological pessimism in this its first exponent: "If happiness, satisfaction of wishes, and enjoyment are to be the meaning and end of human life, it misses this end, and is to be rejected as worthless. Pessimism is the last but also the annihilating consequence of eudaemonism—its immanent criticism." [32]

With regard to the problem of evil, Greek thought is thus seen to exhibit an indecision of procedure due to a vacillation between monism and dualism, giving rise not only to different traditions, but to opposed motives in the same tradition. The fountain-head of perplexity appears to be Plato. On the one hand is the joyous acquiescence in nature, the belief that, through the dominance of reason, virtue and perfection are within the reach of man. On the other hand is a certain nostalgic sense of alienation, depreciation and distrust of nature, metaphysical as well as moral contempt of matter, asceticism, and a mystical reach after the beyond-rational which is decidedly sceptical in its implications. On the one hand, the Idea of the Good is Supreme Reality, and matter, imperfection, somehow *is not;* on the other, the conflict is somehow ingrained in the very stuff of Being, and "evils can never pass away." [33] Aristotle resists Plato's mystical depreciation of matter, but he is enabled to treat it as an integral moment and aspect of reality because of his objective scientific approach to his problem, because he lacks the Platonic tragic sense of imperfection in nature, and because, unlike Plato, he is never a stranger here below. The Stoic cosmology would overcome completely the antithesis of rational form and irrational matter by adopting the idea of a hierarchy of material existence; but the Stoic ethics, keenly sensible of the moral antithesis between reason and the passions, demands its overcoming in heroic ascetic apathy; while Stoic theodicy proclaims the course of material existence to be a pageant of Divine Providence precluding any evil, and at the same time attempts to justify evil as a spur to greater good. The Epicurean dismisses the Platonic difficulty by adopting a materialism which, unlike the Stoic, was anti-teleological: there is pain and pleasure in the world, but there can be no *problem* of evil. Things simply are.

Unlike the Stoic insistent fortitude and loyalty to the cosmos, and also against the Epicurean disdainful naturalism, the mystic-religious tradition of later antiquity manifests a more or less explicitly pessimistic attitude towards existence. According to Philo of Alexandria, evil is bound up with existence itself. By its union with the body, the soul inclines towards sin, and from this fatal leaning no one is ever free. Matter, the condition of finite existence, is also the ground and the medium of evil. The path of salvation is a path of asceticism and world-denial, the flight of the soul to perfection. The soul bent on redemption is not daunted by the evils that beset it: "The just endures death with courage and even with joy; he trusts in Providence and conserves to the full all his faculties.[34] But, for all Philo's insistent trust in Providence, the idea of radical evil persists: not the original sin of a morally neutral will, but evil inbred in the very nature of this finite world of change.[35] It were better had there been no matter, no world, but only the eternal perfect silence of the One. Gnostic, Neoplatonist, and Neopythagorean emphasized Plato's sense of nostalgic alienation, and the result was a manifold wail over the cosmic pity of it: that there should be a world at all was the essential tragedy, for from the very first the cosmic self-manifestation of God involves a downfall and a degradation. *The* original sin took place, not at the close of creation, but in the first verse of the first chapter. The first and essential blunder was not *in* existence, it was and is existence itself.

All these conflicting motives and demands reach their culmination in Plotinian Neoplatonism. Plotinus would not only explain, he would also vindicate the outpouring of the Eternal One in the cosmos. As fire warms and snow chills and light radiates and fragrance is diffused, so from the very plenitude of its perfection the Eternal One overflows and pours itself out. By the very fact of outpouring, though *The One* does not know itself as One or as Many, an awareness of Not-one arises. This is Thought, Spirit, Nous. And just as the One, while eternally itself, yet emanates in Spirit, so Spirit in turn, eternally itself, yet emanates in Soul, Psyche. And so in turn does Soul emanate in Body, Matter.

These are stages which we recognize in a process of progressively exhaustive outpouring which is continuous throughout. If it is perfection overabundantly overflowing, it should be perfect throughout, and no question of any imperfection or evil could arise. Yet there is evil. What is it, and how can it be? These questions lead us into the heart of the Plotinian theodicy, and we find ourselves enmeshed in serious perplexities.

Plotinus refuses to treat the process of emanation explicitly as progressive degradation of Reality. The Eternal One is perfect, but so is Spirit: perfect, to be sure, not as the One is perfect, but characteristically perfect as Spirit. And so is the Soul perfect as Soul, nor could we demand any other perfection of it. But does this mean that everything has its own characteristic perfection: human, equine, aquiline, plant-like, each in its way perfect as the Eternal One is perfect? And furthermore do you, do I, have our own individual characteristic perfection, distinguishable from the generically human as that in turn is from the equine? For, Plotinus says, "man, man as partial thing, cannot be required to have attained to the very summit of goodness: if he had, he would have ceased to be of the partial order." [36] The philosophy which condemns the finite individual for lacking the unqualified perfection of the Absolute cannot limit its condemnation to the material world. "We will be obliged to admit evil in the Supreme also, for there, too, Soul is less exalted than the Intellectual-Principle and That too has its Superior." [37]

In considering the difficulties confronting the Plotinian theodicy, we should not confuse Plotinus' temperament with that of the Gnostics or overlook his characteristic serenity in dealing with the actual. There is no tendency to cosmic lamentation in Plotinus. He is reluctant to blame the nature of the world: this audacity which he finds in the Gnostics seems to him due to lack of understanding.[38] Even Plato's milder "disparagement of the material world is not quite to his taste." [39] A sufficiently clear and comprehensive view of the world would serve to clear it of the evils which so impress the one-sided observer. One who has seen or listened to God can see reflections of Him even here and catch echoes of the divine harmony even in this discordant world of matter. What sort of world one perceives depends largely on the character of the perceiver. "A feeble contemplation makes a feeble object of contemplation." [40]

But while Plotinus is not a pessimist by temperament, his view of reality does impose grave burdens on his theodicy. With the Plotinian hierarchy of perfections on our hands, we travel an indistinct path between axiological abysses. Shall we say that each thing is perfect in its own way? Then how can we hold anything, even the Eternal One, more perfect than any other? Why may not man then stand up to God as the squirrel stood up to the mountain, in Emerson's *Fable:*

> If I cannot carry forests on my back,
> Neither can you crack a nut.

But how can we, then, admit imperfection at all, or rather, how can we avoid the Epicurean naturalism, according to which things are what they are, each with its respective nature, and there an end? In that case, for an apotheosis of things at random or else seriatim, a cosmic, expansive mood like Whitman's should suffice:

> The moth and the fish-eggs are in their place;
> The suns I see, and the suns I cannot see, are in their place;
> The palpable is in its place, and the impalpable is in its place. . . .
> I believe that a leaf of grass is no less than the journey-work of the stars,
> And the pismire is equally perfect, and a grain of sand, and the egg of the wren,
> And the tree-toad is a chef d'oeuvre for the highest,
> And the running blackberry would adorn the parlors of heaven. . . .[41]

Or shall we say, on the other hand, that a perfect horse is perfect as a horse, but its perfection is not as perfect as man's, nor man's in turn as perfect as God's perfection? But while this view is nowise inherently unreasonable in a cosmology such as that of Plotinus, it would scarcely deliver us from the problem of evil. For in this case all the so-called perfections of the finite world would, by comparison with God's perfection, prove undeserving of the title: the alleged hierarchy of perfections would be disclosed as a gradation of imperfections. Would we not, then, in spite of Plotinus' intention, be proceeding towards a Gnostic terminus, with the cosmic emanation process one of increasing degradation? "Plotinus denies and affirms metaphysical evil at the same time, denying it by insisting on the possibility of different kinds of perfection, affirming it by declaring these kinds to be at the same time degrees." [42] His perplexity is grave: how is he to 'accept the Universe' in a Stoic sense without accepting it in an Epicurean sense? And how is he, with his theory of emanationism, to face with moral vigor the actuality of evil, without proceeding to Gnostic condemnation of the world-process? If the goal of existence is the return of the Perfect One, how is the emanation from the One to be justified, with all the imperfections and evils that it involves? [43]

These difficulties are not quite resolved by referring the

evils of the world to Matter. Regarding Plotinus' estimate of matter, the *Enneads* allow considerable latitude of interpretation. From Zeller's point of view, Plotinus goes even beyond Plato in holding matter as "evil, indeed the primal evil; from it comes all evil in the material world, from the body the evil in the soul." [44] According to Dean Inge, those who, relying on a "few polemical passages," hold that Plotinus makes Matter the evil principle in the manner of Philo and the Neopythagoreans, misjudge "the whole tendency of his philosophy." [45] Even though matter is the cause of evil, it is not all evil. Were it by itself, chaotic and utterly without form or order, it would be evil unqualified. But it does not exist by itself. Despite the unfortunate tendency of popular Neoplatonism to acquiesce in the antithesis between God and Matter as providing a ready explanation of evil, Plotinus himself seems to have opposed the metaphysical dualism which would set matter over against the perfect Absolute as an independent reality. Matter is "the receptive principle by which alone the present world could be at all."[46] Its whole being is in its being acted upon by the higher. But in the philosophy of Plotinus matter is clearly not a merely cosmological concept. As Émile Bréhier puts it, in discussing Plotinus' book on the nature and origin of evil: "Plotinus identifies evil as a principle of religious pollution with the matter of the philosophers . . . a principle of rational explanation is transformed into a reality concerning the religious life of the soul." [47]

The primeval and ultimate evil, according to Plotinus, is not in man's will or in the soul's inclination: "We cannot be, ourselves, the source of Evil, we are not evil in ourselves; Evil was before we came to be; the Evil which holds men down binds them against their will. . . . The Measureless is evil primarily; . . . primarily, the darkness; secondarily, the darkened. Now Vice, being ignorance and a lack of measure in the Soul, is secondarily evil, not the Essential Evil, just as Virtue is not the Primal Good but is Likeness to The Good, or participation in it." [48] So *we* are evil in that we are attached to matter, but evil *is* first and last essentially in matter: "Thus the cause at once of the weakness of Soul and of all its evil is Matter. The evil of Matter precedes the weakness, the vice; it is Primal Evil. Even though the Soul submits to Matter and engenders to it; if it becomes evil within itself by its commerce with Matter, the cause is still the presence of Matter: the Soul would never have approached Matter but that the presence of matter is the occasion of its earth-life." [49]

If, however, the higher emanations are evil or imperfect only in so far as they incline or descend towards matter, whereas matter is inherently evil, what accounts for this radical collapse in the process of emanation? If emanation is continuous throughout, how could a theodicy be required,— or else, how could it be achieved? In dealing with evil, there is a tendency in Plotinus to define it as the necessarily 'last' of emanation: "Given that The Good is not the only existent thing, it is inevitable that, by the outgoing from it or, if the phrase be preferred, the continuous down-going or away-going from it, there should be produced a Last, something after which nothing more can be produced: this will be Evil. As necessarily as there is Something after the First, so necessarily there is a Last: this Last is Matter, the thing that has no residue of good in it: here is the necessity of Evil." [50]

Thus, if we hold to the all-perfection of the One and to the continuity of the emanation-process, and refuse to say that at the third rim of emanation evil somehow unaccountably appears, two alternatives seem open to us: either emanation proceeds in a moral sense and gradually from a plenitude of good and utter absence of evil towards complete extinction of good (Gnosticism again?); or else what is called 'evil' in matter is metaphysically rather than morally 'the last' or 'the ultimate least' of Being, to wit Non-Being, and in that case we cannot speak of any theodicy.

This dilemma is not altogether unlike that which appears to confront some present-day advocates of the theory of emergence, whom we may regard as the antipodes of Plotinus and his doctrine of emanation. Plotinus begins with a conception of the Divine First which cannot allow him to regard the 'descent' in emanation from Being to Non-Being as a degradation of the One in a moral sense. Thus, so long as we regard the world-process as one of emanation from Absolute Perfection, theodicy is either not in question or else is quite out of the question: if it is demanded at all, it cannot be executed. The advocate of emergence, on the other hand, begins with a mechanistic conception of the cosmic *terminus a quo*, and then notes fairly the successive factual rise of reality to ever 'higher' levels. This progressive emergence he records, but can he explain it without taking account of the Whole and reinterpreting the alleged process of emergence as one of progressive and ever more adequate self-manifestation, or better self-realization, of the Whole? "The spirit that moves over the deeps of seeming chaos, the divinity that streams like light through all, courses like life-blood through the whole, draws like an eternal magnet all to itself." [51] If the 'higher' is no more than the temporally 'later' or the more complex, the advocate of emergence may perhaps save his face as a 'scientist,' but can lay claim to discourse of God and good and other values at the close of his book only by straining terms and spraining logic, for these are either of nature, or else are unnatural.

> Yet nature is made better by no mean
> But nature makes that mean: so over that art
> Which you say adds to nature, is an art
> That nature makes. [52]

Thus with evil on our hands, the absolutist formula of initial, unqualified perfection requires revision; and on the other hand, if Münschhausen has indeed 'emerged,' it cannot have been by merely tugging at his bootstraps. There is drag in the universe, and there is likewise an urge; the drag and the urge appear to be conflicting factors, but they are factors of one cosmic process, and the true philosophy is one that can take account of them both. Plotinus and the advocate of emergence should both learn wisdom from the Gospel: "By their fruits ye shall know them,"—grapes and figs, but also thorns and thistles.

IV

The dualism God-Matter which Greek theodicy resisted was primarily metaphysical and only secondarily moral, and that is perhaps the chief reason why it could not be sustained. But if metaphysical dualism seems inevitably bound for the rocks, to a moral interpretation of the world dualism appears imperative. In a mind intensely moral but relatively untouched by metaphysics, dualism could maintain itself with greater assurance. So it is that the first principle in the Zoroastrian philosophy of life, which is not speculation but an act of heroism, is the principle of the essential duality of the cosmos.

To the Greek philosopher, God, by whatever name he was called, in the end signified ultimate and unqualified Reality. The moral antithesis good-evil, tagging after the metaphysical antithesis Being-Non-Being, had to do the best it could. The chief difficulties in Greek as in some modern theodicies, are traceable to this insistence on reducing a concretely moral to an abstractly metaphysical distinction.

The Zoroastrian began with the antithesis good-evil and deduced the rest from that. Good and evil could not issue from the same source; there is accordingly a duality of cosmic principles. More intent on preserving the moral than the metaphysical reputation of Deity, the Zoroastrian held fast to the goodness of Ahura-Mazda. The evil in this world is not his work: he neither caused it nor permitted it; his only relation to it is what yours and mine should be: unremitting opposition. The world is a battleground on which Ahura-Mazda and Ahriman, creating and counter-creating, strive for mastery. As truth and falsehood, purity and pollution are struggling for the mastery of man's soul, so health is battling with disease, and life with death, and grain with weeds, and life-giving rain with destructive storm, and light with darkness. No one so refused to blink at evil, no one perceived the universal conflict so thoroughly as the Zoroastrian. The moral struggle was nothing mysterious or exceptional or illustory to him; it was the outstanding and ever-present fact of all existence in which, from the God Ahura-Mazda clear down to the least item of goodness and life and light, the evil creation of Ahriman was being opposed in mortal combat. Here was a stirring sense of co-warriorship with God against the hosts of evil.

The struggle was not illusory, for Ahriman was real. Into the metaphysical problem of Ahriman's coördinateness with Ahura-Mazda, the Zoroastrian does not seem to have cared particularly to inquire. "Is Ahriman coeternal with Ahura-Mazda?" seems to have meant: "When did Ahriman start his dirty work?"—a question which was answered: "As soon as Ahura-Mazda began to create." Does this answer suggest possible Brahmanic ideas; does it mean that evil appears whenever finitude appears, that it is a function of finitude? Or didn't the Zoroastrian rather mean to say that evil, Ahriman and his work, could be nothing recent and exceptional, but that the struggle between good and evil was as old as existence itself? So evil is and has been right here; it is not to be prayed or excogitated out of existence; it is real enough and calls for real opposition.

Evil is real, but it does not deserve to be real. The moral intensity which begins with an insistence on the antithesis good-evil demands the assurance of its ultimate overcoming. The struggle is real but it is not futile. A day of days is coming when, under the leadership of Saoshyant, the hosts of Ahura-Mazda will utterly put to rout the vile cohorts of Ahriman. The world will then be consumed and refined in a universal conflagration; all things will then be pure and perfect, and evil will be no more.

V

The story of the Garden of Eden has probably Babylonian origins or kinship, and partakes of a common stock of primitive folklore in which it shares elements with Semitic and non-Semitic races. Its significance, as we have noted, resembles strikingly that of the Promethean myths. Man lost Paradise because he was lured into eating of the tree of knowledge of good and evil. As Pfleiderer has pointed out, "the original meaning of the story is simply this: The origin of the evils of human life is to be found in the transgression by the first men of the divine prohibition which had denied to them the higher knowledge, . . . the most elementary elevation of man above mere nature, the first dawning of the consciousness of supersensuous destiny which makes him higher than the beasts,—in fact, the first stirring of the impulse towards civilization." [53]

It was later theology which, imposing later views on this primitive legend, transformed its meaning. In the story itself Adam and Eve seem to have been banished from Eden because they had actually eaten of the tree of knowledge, and lest they should proceed further to eat of the tree of life and become immortal. Later thought laid stress on the disobedience of man and ascribed to that sin his subsequent woes.

The Greek, in one way or another, ascribed evil to a certain fatal flaw or imperfection in the constitution of reality, yet somehow not in its ultimate constitution; so he called it Matter. The Zoroastrian saw in evil the evidence of the operation of a cosmic principle opposed to God and everywhere at war with the good. Neither of these views was entertained in Israel. Excelling in moral vigor rather than in speculative genius, and bent more on perceiving evil and avoiding it than on explaining its ultimate origin, the Hebrew found a ready explanation of all things by attributing them to God as their source. God brings good and also evil: but he sends them to men wisely and justly. Israel from the start regarded man as standing in a contractual relation with his Maker. Fidelity to his laws God rewards with prosperity, and if evils beset men, the reason is not far to seek: it is due to men's remissness, disobedience, and sin towards God. When Israel came to think of Yahveh as author and director of the entire world-process, the elements of the standard theodicy were at hand. The first Psalm is an epitome of it and, should we compare the moral record of king and people during various reigns with their record in outward prosperity as chronicled in the Historical Books, we should see how firmly fixed was the idea that God brought success to his faithful people and punished them when they departed from his law. Most striking because of its sinister irony in conjunction with what follows is the statement of this view of life in the first three verses of the Book of Job: "There was a man in the land of Uz, whose name was Job; and that man was perfect and upright, and one that feared God, and turned away from evil. *And* there were born unto him seven sons and three daughters. His substance also was seven thousand sheep, and three thousand camels, and five hundred she-asses, and a very great household; so that this man was the greatest of all the children of the east."

Two points should here be kept clearly in mind: this contractual relation was limited to the here and now, and it was a relation of Yahveh to his people Israel. Now so long as the latter idea prevailed, the former was not likely to cause insuperable difficulties in theodicy. When however Israel was led, particularly by the prophet Jeremiah, away from the nationalistic towards a personal conception of religion, the inadequacy of the contractual idea to explain the facts of this life's experiences became apparent. For, while in the lives of peoples 'honesty is the best policy,' and one can with some assurance ascribe a country's stable well-being and prosperity to soundness of national character, in the lives of people we cannot apply the formula with equal confidence and, placidly attributing good fortune to goodness, rate every poor devil a devil.

The days of the Babylonian exile, which chronicled Israel's perception of the monotheistic idea and Israel's approach to the notion of personal and therefore universal as distinguished from nationalistic religion, provided the Hebrew mind with grave perplexities. In the sack of Jerusalem bad men as well as good had managed to escape personal disaster, and by the rivers of Babylon good men as well as bad bewailed their lot. Ascribe God's amazing patience with the wicked to his infinite loving-kindness; still, if he is one and supreme in power and justice and wisdom, how is the apparently undeserved suffering of the righteous to be explained? Before us is the masterpiece of Hebrew tragic genius, the Book of Job.

The obvious and complacent answer of orthodox tradition was that the suffering in question was not undeserved. This is the theme which Job's three friends play in a variety of keys, first in a reluctant obligato, with distant and compassionate intimation; then, failing to evoke the expected repentant antiphony in Job, crescendo, more and more bluntly and insistently: Eliphaz the Temanite resting his orthodox assurance on the rich harvest of a long life's experience, Bildad the Shuhite appealing to the verdict of immemorial tradition, and Zophar the Naamathite reaffirming and exhorting and confidently challenging experience. The kindliest of admonitions change into increasingly violent upbraiding, but end on a promissory note of restoration to prosperity, if only Job will repent and acknowledge his sin. This triple challenge to Job rests on alleged manifold evidence of experience, but ignores the very experience which has brought the three to the side of the former prince of the desert, now a mass of sores atop the ash-heap. "To lie for God is the most pernicious atheism."[54]

> Who ever perished, being innocent?
> Or where were the upright cut off? [55]

Who and where indeed? The poet is not content to observe that prosperous vice and longsuffering godliness do not invariably meet with appropriate reversal in accordance with orthodox specifications at the end of the chapter. Against the cruel complacence of orthodoxy, he masses with tragic intensity the anguished conviction of an upright man who, never arrogant or vain of his own perfection, and ever vigilantly on his guard lest he fall by the way unwittingly, is yet adamant in his assurance of lifelong unwavering devotion to the divine will. To this witness of Job's own conscience, the Prologue (whether or not we regard it as part of the original poet's work) adds God's own twice repeated testimony: "Hast thou considered my servant Job? for there is none like him in the earth, a perfect and an upright man, one that feareth God, and turneth away from evil."

The explanation of misery which the Prologue provides, that it is a testing of righteousness, is patently inadequate in a theistic system. Considering with Job that only too often

> The tents of robbers prosper,
> And they that provoke God are secure;
> Into whose hand God bringeth abundantly,[56]

and, on the other hand, remembering the friends' recital of the evil fortune of the wicked, while at the same time observing the trio of presumably righteous men without memory or anticipation of trouble, we may well doubt whether experimenting of the sort suggested in the Prologue is a settled policy of the Almighty. And furthermore, and more to the point, in view of the omniscience of God, we may inquire: For whose information are such tragic experiments conducted, and at whose expense?

The question which Satan asks ironically in the Prologue: "Doth Job fear God for nought?" is implied with tragic significance throughout the poem. Job's tragedy is not in the fact of his affliction, but rather in what his affliction means to his religion which is the heart of his being. Unable in the face of the plain facts of his own experience to regard his suffering as appropriate punishment for sin, and yet regarding his suffering as coming, together with all else, from God, he sees the former ground of his confidence in God's justice disappear, and no new ground in sight:

> For the thing which I fear cometh upon me,
> And that which I am afraid of cometh unto me.[57]

Hence his repeated plea to have it out with God: in his heart's anguish, it is his mind's demand for a new theodicy that does not outrage the facts of life. But the Voice out of the Whirlwind only overawes Job with the sense of his nothingness in the face of his problem. Undeserved suffering was a fact which Jewish theism could not comprehend: a yawning mystery in which man, face to face with his Maker, is humbled and abhors himself.

The Epilogue, reporting Job's restoration to prosperity,

so apparently in accord with his friends' orthodox promises and so out of accord with God's explicit condemnation of the trio, is probably a later addition to the poem, or else a concession in the nature of a happy ending, and in any case a flaw. But God's approval of Job, in conformity with the spirit of the poem, is conceivable only on the supposition that the answer to Satan's question is in the case of Job an affirmative answer. Job has really feared God for nought: here through all suffering and agony, doubly hard because not understood, he has remained loyal to God, but—or rather because—he has refused to ignore the facts of experience, or to force them into prefashioned moulds. "There is a service of God which is not work for reward: it is a heart-loyalty, a hunger after God's presence, which survives loss and chastisement; which in spite of contradictory seeming cleaves to what is Godlike as the needle seeks the pole; and which reaches up out of the darkness and hardness of this life to the light and the love beyond." [58]

Thus while the Book of Job offers no new formulated theodicy, it is a profoundly significant realization of the need of one, and a dramatic expression of the sort of spiritual attitude and temper of soul which alone could achieve it.

The poet of Job faced heroically the problem of evil. What he sees and exhibits might make many another a pessimist, but has not made him one. Compared with the buoyant optimism of the typical Israelite, who saw abundance of sin, but no occasion for being tragic about the cosmos, here is a world-view grim indeed. But it is a view heroic and defiant rather than hopeless. It is in a different strain of Jewish thought that we catch distinctly the note of weariness and cosmic disenchantment. This is the note of Ecclesiastes.

Job's dismay arises from intense and baffling suffering; the despondency of Ecclesiastes is due to surfeiting but yet unsatisfying pleasure. In Job is the tragic mystery of misery;

in Ecclesiastes, the tedious vanity of happiness. Here is a man of rich and varied experience, yet he finds his life to be poor monotony. The wisest in Jerusalem, he has found wisdom to be but madness and folly. He is a connoisseur in delight; he is rich and a man of property and power; he builds houses, pools of water, gardens and parks and orchards; at his beck are troops of manservants and maidservants, singers and musicians, to do his will and pleasure, to serve and entertain him. And seeing and having done all that is seen and done under the sun, behold, for him "Vanity of vanities, . . . all is vanity and a striving after wind. . . . That which hath been is that which shall be; and that which hath been done is that which shall be done: and there is no new thing under the sun." [59]

To be sure, he sees evils about him: injustice, wickedness, oppression. He concedes that some things are worse than others, and much of his thought is a play with comparisons: yet, be things better or worse, is there aught in life really good? How can good be good, or evil evil; how is wisdom to be preferred to folly, or anything to anything, or anything really cherished, if all things finally end in dust? "He finds nothing that makes it worth while to struggle for uprightness as the supreme end of life." [60] Ample variety of experiences he has had, but no variety of conclusion. "For that which befalleth the sons of men befalleth beasts; even one thing befalleth them: as the one dieth, so dieth the other; yea, they have all one breath; and man has no preëminence above the beasts: for all is vanity. All go unto one place; all are of the dust, and all turn to dust again." [61]

Despairing of lasting value in this pointless existence, and seeing no likely prospect of work, or device, or knowledge, or wisdom in Sheol, what is Ecclesiastes to do? He would eat his bread, and drink his wine, wear his garments white, oil his head, live joyfully with his wife, and make the best of a tedious bargain. But, adds the writer, or perhaps a later editor, Ecclesiastes would also keep in mind a certain grave *Perhaps* after the grave. Confronted with the possible alternative of a divine judgment in the hereafter, which he can neither anticipate nor evade with assurance, he would in any case fear God and keep his commandments. So the mind that had started a dirge of sceptical-cynical weariness ends, or is made to end, on a note of cautious piety. It is a politic conclusion of a calculating philosophy of life.

CHAPTER II

THE CHRISTIAN–MEDIEVAL TRADITION

I

The weary sense of universal vanity and the tragic anguish of unvindicated justice were transformed by the Christian gospel into intense vigilance and confident hope. God is in his heaven, a loving Father, and in and through Christ the stain of evil and the sting of death are removed and turned to God's greater glory in salvation. But the theological problem still remains: what, whence, and whither evil? St. Paul's treatment of these questions is meant to ascribe evil to man's wilful disobedience, to regard it as a departure from the way of the Lord into the selfish way of the flesh, and to see its consummation in death and damnation, or its extinction through the love of Christ in the life of the new man. "For as in Adam all die, so also in Christ shall all be made alive." [1] Here is the most intense abhorrence of the body and a yearning to be freed from the bonds of the flesh: "Wretched man that I am! who shall deliver me out of this body of death?" [2] But there is no despair of ultimate victory through Christ: "For I am persuaded that neither death, nor life, nor angels, nor principalities, nor things to come, nor powers, nor height, nor depth, nor any other creature shall be able to separate us from the love of God, which is in Christ Jesus our Lord." [3] In the very contempt of the flesh, and in the very evils of the world is the joyous certainty of final triumph which marks the saint's and the martyr's bliss: "For which cause I suffer also these things: yet I am not ashamed; for I know him whom I have believed, and I am persuaded that he is able to guard that which I have committed unto him against that day." [4] The eschatological sense of the speedily forthcoming end of all things was the assurance of a blissful prospect: even the original downfall gained sublime dignity as the medium in which the eternal divine plan of redemption was wrought out.

Between the revulsion and the ecstasy, Christian theology seeks a middle course that is yet in touch with both extremes. The orthodoxy that is to be is the more opposed to the incipient heresies just because it has so much in common with them. Heresy is mainly twofold: excess of revulsion and contempt for the world (leading consistently to despair of redemption), and excess of sanguine confidence in man's inherent capacity for good (depreciating the solemnity of redemption). The first type of heresy is Gnostic and Manichean; the second is notably Pelagian. Combating them both and steering between them is the orthodoxy of St. Augustine.

The Gnostic view of the world as an inverted hierarchy of divine self-degradation involved not only utter disgust for material existence but also a condemnation of the self-outpoured One, and, in good logic, nihilism to cap its pessimism. The Manicheans, combining the Persian dualism of good and evil with the Greek dualism of God and Matter, cast serious reflections on the all-primacy and omnipotence of God, and regarded man, not as the wilful, prodigal son of God, but rather as the devil-fashioned battleground on which God and the Devil are contending for dominion. Manicheanism took Satan too seriously, it appears, and man's sin and guilt not seriously enough. Adam, we are told, was created by Satan in his own image; and although, by depositing portions of stolen light in the first man for safekeeping, Satan prepared trouble for himself and made the redemption of man possible, yet the fact of man's dual nature remained. Man's wickedness is not wilfully acquired, but is rather inherent in his material nature as a son of darkness. The salvation of man demands the releasing of the rays of light from the darkness in which Satan ever seeks to imprison them.

The conflict between light and darkness was conceived by the Manicheans in crudely materialistic terms and led to some fantastic conclusions. The light rising from the dismal depths of the earth towards the sun and moon (radiant reservoirs of perfection) is held captive by the roots of plants, but bursts forth notwithstanding in flower and fruit. These the Manichean 'elects' may not pluck but, receiving them from the hands of others, should eat them and thus release and speed the divine light on its upward journey.[5] Meat, however, may not be eaten at all; for animal life is of the devil. The sexual propagation of life is likewise the devil's work. So the Manichean ideal of perfection demanded a rigorously limited diet, withdrawal from the kingdom of darkness, and chastity, or at any rate avoidance of parenthood.

Both Gnostic and Manichean emphasized mortification of the body; the ascetic bias which was gaining in the early Church found in them both strong confirmation. This ascetic abhorrence of the material was apt to develop into a studied contempt of material beauty wherever found and even into a cult of ugliness and filth. Loveliness, attractiveness, and all that is pleasant are of the devil. Do we say: Cleanliness is next to godliness? The hermit thought otherwise: godliness is marked rather by scorn for the body; the more famished, the more neglected, the more repulsive and macerated and vermin-infested the body, the more emphatic is the expression of the saint's holy contempt for it. So we are told that Justin Martyr and Tertullian could not tolerate the idea that Jesus the Lord was handsome to look upon, and represented him rather as the ugliest of men.[6] St. Augustine finds no special holiness in the ascetic neglect to wash, but he also, as he urges himself to take food as physic and to resist the manifold allurements of taste and touch, smell and color and sound, would at times even "desire that every air of the pleasant songs to which David's Psalter was often used be banished," for, "when it happens to me to be more moved by the singing than by what is sung, I confess myself to have sinned criminally."[7] To be sure Augustine's good sense comes to his rescue here, and in general we may say that this dismal view never quite prevailed; in the course of time Christian art was to reveal the manifold meaning of the beauty of holiness; yet the Gnostic and Manichean revulsion regarding matter expressed something not wholly alien to the early Christian; it was an extreme form of some real aspects of the Christian view of life.

Too great emphasis on the inherent evil of our material nature involved certain moral hazards. 'Human frailty' was apt to be used as an excuse for dissipation. The doughty virtue of the British monk Pelagius was outraged by the cowardly surrender which he found all too common. He refused to admit that man's will lacked the power to fulfil what man's duty required. "If I ought, I can." In the name of liberty he denounced libertinism. God is just and will punish us for our evil deeds; our wills could have refrained from the evil, and we are thus responsible and blameworthy: so much for the sterner side of the Pelagian doctrine. What impressed the age of Augustine was the sanguine hope which it entertained regarding man. Rejecting the teaching that man is innately corrupt, the Pelagians held that each infant is in the condition of Adam before the Fall, that man's will can turn away from evil and choose the good. While Christ proffers man a grace which was unavailable for Jew or Gentile prior to his coming, yet the Christian has the power of will freely to avail himself of this divine assistance. Adam's sin set a bad example, which the rest of us unhappily have been only too apt to follow. This example, however, holy men in all ages have freely resisted, and the blessed counter-example of Christ can stimulate us all freely to exert our wills and attain unto salvation. In the life of the Church our capacity for good is perfected and the evil example of Adam loses its influence. Here then was stalwart devotion to virtue, but also a sanguine view of man's lot and of his prospects.

St. Augustine attacks Manicheanism all the more vigorously because the heresy had claimed him for about ten years prior to his conversion; to root it out, therefore, was his first duty as a laborer in the Lord's vineyard. Holding fast to God's omnipotence, he rejects all dualism. There can be no evil power in the universe coördinate with sovereign Deity. And, since the world is the work of an almighty, all-wise, and infinitely just and good Creator, no essential flaw in nature imputable to God can be admitted. All that is positive and substantial in the universe is and manifests divine perfection. There is no duality of cosmic principles, nor a duality of souls in us, nor is the world-process one of self-degradation and self-dissipation of Deity.[8] Evil is nowise substantial in this world; there is nowhere and at no time an evil *nature*. Matter is not evil, nor body, nor the flesh: "Every nature, as far as it is nature, is good. . . . Take from waters their thickness and muddiness, and pure clear water remains; take from them the consistence of their parts, and no water will be left."[9] So with everything else in nature. On a dozen fronts Augustine maintains this position: that which is called evil is really nothing but corruption, perversion of nature. "When the will abandons the higher, and turns to what is lower, it becomes evil—not because that is evil to which it turns, but because the turning itself is perverse. Therefore it is not an inferior thing which has made the will evil, but it is itself which has become so by wickedly and inordinately desiring an inferior thing."[10] Not the beast, but wicked man alone, is beastly; a beast's nature is in man a vice.[11] The will is made evil by nothing else than a defection from God and from good, by inordinate and unnatural self-degradation in the literal sense of the term. Were it unwilling to become so, the will could not become evil; our sins, being not necessary but voluntary, are therefore justly punished.[12]

There is an optimistic note in this eulogy of uncorrupted nature and in this libertarian doctrine which Augustine was compelled later to modify or disavow in order to render his own maturer views more distinct. While he rejected evil as a cosmic principle, pronounced all things good in their proper order, and called evil a corruption and unnatural, his libertarianism and even his optimism were solemn rather than sanguine. He had defended the cosmos from the dualistic calumny of the Manicheans; was he now to yield to the Pelagian-Stoic complacency about sinful human nature? God forbid! This was to him an equally fatal though opposite abyss of error. "Your doctrines are amazing, they are new, they are false." [13] Maintaining against the Manicheans that all nature is appointed by God, Augustine now turns with equal resolution to maintain against the Pelagians that in all ages human nature must be sought after as ruined.[14] For, as it seemed to St. Augustine, Pelagianism not only ignored light-mindedly the gravity of the evil in which we are embroiled, but it was flagrantly unchristian. Is man an active contributor to his own salvation, and is 'grace' simply "a help towards good living . . . through the inspiring influence of a burning and shining charity?" [15] Thus conceived, the divine plan of redemption loses all solemnity, and indeed loses meaning. This cannot be Christianity.

How then is the actuality of evil in this world to be recognized, and man's ruined state and his utter need of divine redemption emphasized, without on that account implicating God as responsible for the evil in the world and disparaging either his omnipotence or his infinite wisdom or goodness?

The City of God is, among other things, a resolute portrayal of the wickedness and the countless miseries of our human estate. "For what flood of eloquence can suffice to detail the miseries of this life? . . . Its brevity . . . does not clear it of misery; neither ought it to be called happiness because it is a brief misery." [16] Evil is here in abundance, in God's own world, but God is not to blame for it. Who then is to blame? The initial defection of man's will from God is to blame, is Augustine's answer. If Adam's will had not been free, his choice would have lacked moral quality. So God could not deny to Adam the possibility of a good *or* an evil choice. "The first man had not that grace by which he should never will to be evil; but assuredly he had that in which if he willed to abide he would never be evil, and without which, moreover, he could not of free choice be good, but which, nevertheless, by free choice he would forsake." [17] In the exercise of this his freedom man actually made an evil choice, and in the fatal consequences of this evil choice the whole human race is involved. God "foreknew what man would do in unrighteousness; foreknew, however, but did not force him to this; but at the same time He knew what He Himself would do in righteousness concerning him." [18] So God did not compel, but only did not prevent the evil choice; foreseeing completely what he did not in any way predetermine, God justly foreordained the inevitable consequences: consequences utterly and eternally disastrous to man but for the infinite grace of God. Grace and salvation God owes to none, yet vouchsafes it: whether to all or only to some, is a point too long disputed to allow of being maintained unflinchingly.

Chapter and verse can be quoted for and against Gibbon's contention that "the real difference between (Augustine) and Calvin was invisible even to a theological microscope." [19] Similarly, with regard to Augustine's alleged final demolition of free will, we may well keep in mind his protests that it was not he, but the Pelagians who demolished free-will by exaggerating it.[20] By ourselves, we children of Adam can choose only evil, and we can choose the good only by the grace of God; enslave ourselves to lust and sin, that we can, but to liberate ourselves is beyond our power. "If the Son shall make you free, ye shall be free indeed." This divine gift of grace is altogether free; we are not entitled to it, and it is in no way given according to merit.[21] The holy endeavor of the elect is itself due to the gift of perseverance.[22] That God has vouchsafed this gift to some is due to his mercy; that He has not vouchsafed it to others, is due to his justice; if we should press the inquiry and ask: But why not to all? St. Augustine would seek refuge in the mystery of God's unsearchable judgments.[23] God is not a respecter of persons, he tells us,[24] and his words have sinister overtones. We should not relax complacently, nor yet should we despair; for, while the number of those predestined to the kingdom of God is certain and fixed, no one can presume on being certain that he is on God's blessed list.[25] So, after all, we are to "work out our own salvation with fear and trembling." [26]

God could not deny Adam the possibility of a good *or* evil choice. So, in Pfleiderer's summary, "evil is, according to Augustine, not mere weakness or sensual inclination; it is the fundamentally perverted direction of our will, which, instead of finding its centre in the love of God, rather in its self-love and love of the world deifies the creature, and withdraws from the Creator the honour which is due to Him: but a will thus poisoned to the very root by pride and selfishness, whose love is turned away from God to the transitory, can bring forth nothing truly good in detail; it is free to evil only, and destitute of all power for good; even its apparent virtues are in reality only splendid sins; any good it has can only come to it through God's redeeming grace, as it is conveyed by the means of grace in the hands of the Church." [27]

This masterpiece of theological ingenuity which, in one doctrine, emphasizes the actual evil in the world, yet exculpates the Creator of the world from any responsibility for it, but ascribes it rather to man's evil choice, therein also recognizing God's tragic respect for man's moral freedom: this theodicy sets its mark on all subsequent Christian thought, but is itself constituted of elements so incongruous that Augustine's successors have had to interpret and reinterpret and trim and fit and adjust. St. Augustine looms large in the thought of Pascal and Bayle, with whom we shall deal in our next two chapters, and we shall be content here only to point out the two Achilles' heels of this so sublime but also so vulnerable theodicy.

First of all, if we observe the moral tone which Augustine maintained in ascribing to man responsibility for the evil which his choice has brought into the world, then that disastrous choice could not be regarded as a matter of unaccountable chance. It was a choice representative of the chooser. But in that case, even granting Adam's immediate responsibility for the particular choice, the more ultimate question arises whether the Creator is nowise accountable for the sort of chooser that he had in his creature. The point is seen even more sharply if we ask: Was it impossible for God to create an Adam who could freely choose good as he did create one who freely chose evil? The dilemma which would follow the asking of this question is decidedly embarrassing to Augustinian orthodoxy. Furthermore, if Adam deserved the evil consequences of his freely chosen course, how is it with the rest of us? Can we also, as he hypothetically could, choose of our own free will either good or evil? But that alternative would surely betray us into the hands of the Pelagians. Or are we, as Augustine indeed maintains, utterly incapable of any good choice of our own, tainted as we are with the taint of original sin? Then, on this latter supposition, is the individual damnation of those of us who are not elected to grace, or at any rate do not attain unto it, a damnation morally justifiable? Are we to suffer eternally as individuals for a sinful nature for which no free choice of our own but rather a fatal racial inheritance was responsible?

Should we, in order to evade these difficulties, regard Adam and his evil choice not as referring to an individual and a particular event, but as truly representing humanity, then the same dilemmas simply spread out and cover the larger canvas: Either the moral freedom, involving the possible choice of evil *or good*, is admitted, in which case Pelagianism meets us at the turn of the road; or else man's allegedly free will in actuality always chooses evil, in which case the gravity of the former dilemma, hard enough with the one chooser Adam, is multiplied a thousandfold. It is hard for original sin and moral freedom to keep company in the same logical head. Furthermore the idea that newborn infants were sin-tainted and therefore bound for hell,—so many immortal little vipers, Jonathan Edwards was to call them,—unless redeemed by the grace of God, particularly if dying unbaptized, suggests some of the moral enormities confronting this type of theology.

Augustine recognizes that no explicit individual wickedness can be imputed to infants, yet he observes them as "they cry and struggle when they are baptized, and feel the sacred elements," [28] and in his *Confessions* he solemnly chronicles his own sundry childish "sins." At any rate he is bound to regard all children as tainted with original sin; they have no merit that entitles them to grace; and the best prospect he sees for such infants as quit the body without being baptized is "condemnation, but of the mildest character." [29] Later theology was, still more moderately, to accept the parental intention to baptize a child as a substitute for the actual rite. St. Bonaventura, in advocating a more consoling doctrine regarding the destiny of unbaptized infants than that of Augustine, maintains that in opposing the Pelagians, and "in order to lead them the more surely to the true middle position, (Augustine) pressed himself to the opposite extreme," further than his own doctrine really required.[30] Regarding the redeeming virtues of baptism, the African Christians in Augustine's own native country seem to have entertained some strange views. Believing sins committed after baptism to be doubly heinous, they were inclined to postpone the cleansing rite for their young people until after they had sown their wild oats; at the same time they worried lest a youth should die suddenly without being baptized. Monica, St. Augustine's mother, in planning her son's baptism, seems to have been torn between these two motives.

The idea of an evil worldly state brought about by man's wilful selfishness, and the consequent advocacy of the rejection of worldliness and the denial of self as essentials of godliness, characterize the medieval conception of life. From a multitude of available examples, I select three for brief consideration: the tractate *De Contemptu Mundi, sive De Miseria Conditionis Humanae* by Pope Innocent III, some illustrations from the philosophy of St. Thomas, and Thomas à Kempis' *Imitation of Christ:*—a prince of the Church, a master-theologian, a saintly mystic.

II

In January, 1198, a conclave of twenty-eight cardinals in the monastery of Septa Solis Clivisauri were electing a successor to Pope Celestine III. During the conclave three doves hovered above the forty-year-old Cardinal Lothario de' Conti and, so the story goes, the whitest of them descended sanctispiritually upon his head as he was elected Supreme Pontiff.[31] For the next eighteen years, as Pope

Innocent III, Lothario de' Conti was to prove himself a matchless champion of Papal authority and, as a chronicler has it, was to hold the lordship over the Roman Empire and over all the kings and princes of the whole world. Doubly significant it is, therefore, that in his younger days this future pontifical Bismarck piously expected of himself and secured and recorded the dismal reflections on life to which he gave definite form during his temporary eclipse while Celestine the Third was Pope.

This work, *De Contemptu Mundi, sive De Miseria Conditionis Humanae,*[32] is a most laborious essay in pious disdain and disgust of human life. Quoting Job and Ecclesiastes at every turn, and supplying them with copious footnotes, the future maker and unmaker of emperors undertakes to show compendiously and most minutely the pitiful vanity, worthlessness, and loathsomeness of man's existence. Some of this writing is piously filthy and is scarcely printable in an unanointed book like mine. My brief report of this treatise can do very scant justice to this nausea of malediction which medieval saintliness was so apt to approve in itself, but it should serve to call attention to it, which seems important. I shall simply quote and paraphrase, without comment or criticism and with at least partial apologies to modern taste. Consider the origin, the course, the conclusion of a man's life. "Man is made of dust, of mud, of ashes; worse yet, of the foulest seed; conceived in the itch of the flesh, in the heat of passion, in the stench of lust; and worse, in the depths of sin; born to labor, to dolor, to horror; more miserable still, to death. He acts wickedly, offending God, offending his neighbor, offending himself; he acts infamously, polluting fame, polluting conscience, polluting character; he acts vainly, neglecting the serious, neglecting the useful, neglecting the necessary. He is food for fire ever blazing and burning unquenched; food for worms, ever gnawing and eating without end; a mass of putrescence, ever noisome and horribly foul." [33]

"Planets and stars He made of fire; breeze and wind He made of air; fishes and worms He made of water; men and beasts He made of earth." Adam, at any rate, "was made of earth, but of pure earth; you, to be sure, were procreated by seed, but impure." And from his very conception man's nourishment is unspeakably vile. Besides, what a despicable sight infants are: "weeping, weaklings, imbecilic, not so very different from the brutes; indeed in many ways worse off than the brutes." And the mother's pitiful life: "she conceives with nastiness and stench, gives birth with gloominess and dolor, nurses with scantiness and labor, keeps watch with tirelessness and horror." (The worldly pleasure and pride which the writing of this and similar passages brought the rhetorician must have caused the pious Cardinal pangs of conscience; but he kept the rhetoric just the same.)[34]

"By their fruits you shall know them,"—and what is the fruit that man bears? "O base unworthiness of man's estate, O unworthy estate of man's baseness! Examine plants and trees. They bring forth flowers, foliage, and fruit; and you alas, bring forth nits and lice and worms. They exude oil, wine, balsam, and you, spittle, urine, and ordure; they diffuse the sweetness of fragrance and you give out abominable stench." Our life is brief; "few nowadays get to forty," and an old man's lot is deplorable throughout: "His heart is steadily afflicted, and his head impaired, the breathing grows heavy and the breath is fetid, the face is wrinkled and the stature curved, the eyes grow dim, and the members unsteady, the nose runs, and the hair falls out, the hands tremble and action slows down, the teeth decay and the ears are dulled. The old man is easily provoked, but slow to recover, quick to believe and slowly disillusioned, stubborn and greedy, sad and querulous, quick to speak, slow to listen, but not slow to anger, he praises the ancients, spurns the moderns, vituperates against the present, commends the past, sighs and worries, stupid and infirm." [35]

In whatever work one may engage, it is all strain, pettiness, and vexation. The vigils of learning are unavailing: "Indeed whoso understands more, doubts more: . . . Thus the rôle of knowledge is to know that one does not know." Expatiating on Ecclesiastes, Cardinal Lothario surveys the thousandfold ambitions and enterprises of men,—in pursuit of mastery over nature, over each other, in quest of wealth, power, honor,—and finds it all vain anxiety and a striving after wind: profitless care, fear, and solicitude, abhorrent throughout. Pair by pair he examines men in successive chapters: poor and rich, servants and masters, married and single, bad and good: the conclusion is ever dismal. Surveying the enemies which surround and infest us, a catalogue of ferocious beasts and noxious insects is cited. And man's own body is his enemy and prison: "Nowhere quiet and tranquillity, nowhere peace nor security, everywhere fear and tremor, everywhere labor and dolor." Not even sleep brings us solace, for then the terrors of dream-visions assail us. Brief and exceptional is happiness, and brief our life, and death is ever at the threshold. Tortured as we are by our own woes, we have also to share the miseries of those we love. And to the miseries of nature, man-made miseries and punishments must be added: "Men are beaten with clubs and slain with swords, burned in flames and buried under stones, they are torn to pieces with claws and forced into fork-shaped yokes, tortured by tigers, and scourged with scorpions, bound with chains and strangled with nooses, thrust into prisons and emaciated with hunger, thrown from cliffs and submerged in water, flayed, cut up, and stabbed." [36]

The Cardinal then surveys, in the second book of his tractate, the many vices and vanities of human character:

"greed and avarice, gluttony and lust, pride and ostentation." [37] Men worship riches and sell their souls for it; men cringe before wealth and power, and the poor are trampled and despised; men traffic in injustice, and their cupidity is insatiate. Gluttony and drunkenness and lust are minutely classified and described by Cardinal Lothario, and he abhors them the more explicitly as a result of his close survey. Arrogance, vanity, and ambition are shown to consume the lives of men, but the expected wine of attainment proves to be stale dust and ashes in the drinking, as the later Pope Innocent III doubtless experienced more than once.

The third book opens with a prelude of disgust: "How foul the father, how base the mother, how abominable the sister! Man is conceived indeed of blood putrefied by the heat of lust. . . . While alive he generated lice and worms, when dead he will generate worms and flies; alive, he gave forth ordure and vomit; dead, he will yield putridity and stench; alive, he fattened a single man; dead, he will fatten many worms. For what is more fetid than a human cadaver, what more horrible than a dead man?" The third book is devoted to the elaborate portrayal of the torments of the damned, and so requires no further notice, for we have Dante. Here again Cardinal Lothario, piously aghast though he is at the sinners' prospects, yet obviously enjoys the jingling rhetoric of his portrayal of hell: "Groaning and wailing, mourning and torture, hissing and crying, fear and tremor, dolor and labor, ardor and stench, obscurity and anxiety, acerbity and asperity, calamity and indigence, distress and grief, oblivion and confusion, griping and pricking pains, bitternesses and terrors, hunger and thirst, chills and fever, brimstone and flaming fire forever and ever." And then, his rhetorical essay in contempt and disgust finished, the Cardinal ends on the expected orthodox note: "From all of which may God deliver us, Who is blessed forever and ever. Amen." [38]

5

III

St. Augustine's theology impressed a Platonic cast on early medieval thought; the thirteenth century registered the ascendency of Dominican Aristotelianism; and the philosophy of the Church has sought to combine the two strains. These two traditions, the Augustinian and the Thomistic, just as their Hellenic prototypes, share common ground but differ in what they select for special cultivation and emphasis. Each one "endeavors to satisfy the legitimate demands which it is the proper function of the other to uphold." [39] The higher naturalism of Aristotle, as interpreted by St. Thomas, is not wholly untouched by that saintly wistfulness in this mortal world which so distinguished Augustinian Platonism. St. Thomas in the end likewise takes his refuge in God and in God's grace. But, while he does not deny man's ultimate insufficiency, his main concern is to realize and to make good the truth (which, as we have seen, is nowise foreign to St. Augustine) that vice is a perversion of human nature, that man's true being, capacity, and destiny are in the line of rationality and virtue. Without God, man is lost and of no avail whatever, but in reaching after God, man reaches after and attains unto the fulness of his own true and characteristic nature.

Thus while St. Thomas is no more sanguine than St. Augustine regarding man's arduous rise to perfection, he is more concerned to accentuate the naturalness of virtue to man, as involving his completion and fulfilment. We may in fair Aristotelian manner define *good* generally as the adequate performance of a being's characteristic function. Man's virtue then is nothing foreign grafted onto man, no appendage, but rather his unfoldment: our good concerns "that which we ought to be, because of what we are." [40] This teleological conception of moral value is central in Thomistic Aristotelianism. A man's *good* is in the attainment of his *end* signalizing the fulfilment of his *nature*. The perfect achievement of this end and nature is the Highest Good; each step in the direction of this Highest Good is a step in virtue; each halting or deviation or retrogression is vice.

With Aristotle, Aquinas regards reason as man's distinctive faculty. Directed by reason, our will follows the high road to perfection; lured by unregulated or unbalanced appetites and passions, we go astray. And here the thirteenth century theologian proceeds in a more distinctively Catholic manner. Man's perfect goal and complete happiness is in the vision of the Divine Essence.[41] Intelligent recognition and active espousal of the divine order characterizes the rational will of the saint; but when man turns away from this pious participation in God's order, turns *from* goods imperishable *to* goods that perish, a corruption and a destruction of the soul sets in, and a grievous betrayal and disloyalty. This is sin. The essence of evil is always the turning away from the divine imperishable good; the gravity of sin is measured in respect of this turning away, and the gravity of malice in sins depends upon the difference of objects that are thus pursued in preference to the divine vision. "From the very fact that man turns unduly to some mutable good, it follows that he turns away from the immutable Good, which aversion completes the nature of evil." [42]

Alone among all creatures man is not a passive instrument in the Creator's hands. He can turn aside from the path that leads to God, can reject and frustrate the divine fruition of his own nature; by refusing freely to identify himself with the divine order of reason, he can pervert and destroy his nature in sin. Hence his solemn responsibility, hence also his blessed opportunity in this life, to prove himself worthy of his high calling. This Aristotelian positive estimate of man's nature and this consistent emphasis on reason, human and divine, do not rely on mere authority and fiat, nor dismiss our finite scale of values as irrelevant to Deity. This position does not involve anthropomorphic naïveté in dealing with God. A universe necessarily involves a hierarchy of created being, from the less to the more adequate approach to divine perfection. This hierarchy is grounded in Reason, Reason which we express inadequately in our nature, but to which our own reason is not alien or indifferent. The evil in this world is one result of this gradation of created things; it makes alternative courses available for the will, to rise or to fall in the cosmic scale: thus we get realization through enhancement of being (good) or destruction through corruption, deformity, or privation (evil). The rise and the fall both exhibit the consistent rationality of the system in which we are active: a system of opportunity and a system of law and justice. "Evil is evil; but that there is evil, that is a good, not always in respect to the subject in whom the evil is, but in any case in respect of the whole: considering only the total order and its ultimate effects." [43] Compared with God's perfection, ours is naught, but our perfection is real and exalted compared with the depths of unattainment from which we emerge and the abysses of corruption to which we can sink. "The maximum and the minimum, the best and the worst, are the two aspects of the real; optimism and pessimism enfold each other:" created being ever falls infinitely short of God's infinite perfection, but in its limited way it ever does reflect and realize the divine.[44]

It would be interesting to speculate what the course of modern spiritual culture would have been had this Higher Naturalism and Humanism of St. Thomas' philosophy taken full possession of the European soul, and had that Renaissance of which M. Gilson finds the true beginnings in the thirteenth century [45] come to full self-realization unopposed. But this normal development was disturbed by the Scotist attack on Thomistic rationalism. St. Thomas had held this world the best possible *because* Divine Reason originated, sustained, and directed it, and he regarded our reason as reliable even though insufficient and only propaedeutic to faith. This pious rationalism Duns Scotus rejected and championed in its place God's perfectly free and unfathomable will. Good, evil, the whole range of values, in so far as they had ultimate status, had their source and ground in divine fiat. This Scotist invasion, although undertaken in the interests of unquestioning, pious faith, actually served to stimulate scepticism and impiety. The attempted banishment of reason from theology raised the number and the determination of those who, thus compelled to part company with theology, devoted themselves to the secular pursuit of truth.

Thus the elements for a new culture and a new type of evaluation were at hand. Uncertain that his truth, his beauty, his goodness, his justice availed ultimately or indeed meant anything to God, the Renaissance man was tortured with scepticism, or else, his spiritual vigor poisoned by sophistries, he easily disdained all principle and gave way to unrestrained impulse and passion; or yet again, though humiliated in his logic, and his values distrusted and discounted On High, the secular mind refused to surrender or submit, but undertook to build from the ground up and in this his world and life to attain and validate truth, recognize and vindicate supreme values. The Renaissance which started and might have continued under the aegis of the Church was increasingly forced to recognize itself as explicitly secular and to proceed on independent lines.

IV

Thomas à Kempis lived in an age of political, ecclesiastic, and intellectual turmoil and seething revolt. But monastic withdrawal claimed him entire: he lived in the light of his "highest wisdom; by contempt of the world to tend towards the kingdom of heaven." This wisdom is not to be attained by much learning; he would "rather feel compunction than understand the meaning thereof." It is gained only by intimate communion with God: "Let all doctors hold their peace; let all creatures be silent in Thy sight; speak Thou alone unto me." [46]

This world and this life he regards as of no worth; quite unlike the pious rhetoric of Cardinal Lothario de' Conti is the heart-gripping sincerity of the *Imitation of Christ:* "Here a man is defiled with many sins, ensnared with many passions, held fast by many fears, racked with many cares, distracted with many curiosities, entangled with many vanities, compassed about with many errors, worn away with many labours, burdened with temptations, enervated by pleasures, tormented with want. . . . Woe be to them that know not their own misery; and a greater woe to them that love this miserable and corruptible life! . . . Learn to despise outward things, and to give thyself to things inward, and thou shalt perceive the Kingdom of God to come in thee. . . ." [47] Sin and misery have the same source: in the inclination of the heart to turn from God and attach itself to inferior things.[48]

The miserable worldly life is a life of self and of the lusts of self. He who would find peace in God must first "forsake himself and go wholly from himself," see himself for what he is, a most vile worm, poor and contemptible, a wretched creature, imprisoned and loaded with fetters, nothing and less than nothing.[49] When the soul, thus scorning itself and its world, casts itself in utter self-surrendering humility before God, then, in familiar converse with Jesus, all becomes well, all wounds are healed, nothing is burdensome any more or difficult, and man welcomes all with a smile.

Thomas à Kempis has his moments of depression; he needs the sustaining thought of the life hereafter to steel his world-scorning and self-suppressing resolution: "Write, read, chant, mourn, keep silence, pray, endure crosses manfully; life everlasting is worth all these conflicts, and greater than these." But it is not likely that he constantly required this encouragement; the life of self-renunciation is for him one of intrinsic blessedness: "If I be left to myself, behold! I become nothing but mere weakness; but if Thou for an instant look upon me, I am forthwith made strong, and am filled with new joy." [50]

Against this gospel of utter effacement and contempt of self and complete self-sinking in God, is the view of life so characteristic of the Renaissance: a lyric, self-exploring, introspective attitude, exalting man and man's world, trusting man's thought and man's experience: a philosophy of humanism, naturalism, eager, reliant, but also infested with doubts and uncertainties. The early modern philosophy, discarding alike the negations of world-scorning piety and the naïve sanguine conceit of unregenerate man, raises the questions of the cosmic status of man and of man's values. It may be rhapsodically optimistic about the cosmos, as in the pantheism of Giordano Bruno, and heroically tragic about truth-loving man; or it may be placidly sceptical, as in Montaigne's *Essays;* or again, as in the *Thoughts* of Pascal, it may plumb tragic depths of despair born of devotion-in-uncertainty. Meanwhile a little-known little book reflects so vividly the Renaissance attitude towards life in its manifold aspects and the Renaissance estimate of human nature and its alleged perfections, that a brief mention of it may perhaps serve well to close this introductory survey of the problem of evil in ancient and medieval thought.

V

An ironical observer of man and his perfections is Giovan Batista Gelli (1498–1563), Florentine academician under Cosimo dei Medici and early master of Tuscan prose. His

Circe is cleverly conceived for his purpose. Restless in the company of the enchantress, Ulysses is anxious to leave her island and sail for Ithaca, but he also desires to restore to human shape the Greeks whom she had transformed into diverse animals and take them with him. Circe complies with his request on the condition that he ask this favor only for those who desire it. Thereupon follow ten dialogues in which Ulysses makes his offer to his former compatriots, now various beasts on the island. One after another they refuse him, without hesitation and not without reasons. Oyster and mole and serpent, hare and goat, hind and lion, horse, dog, and steer stoutly maintain that man is an arrogant wretch, of all creatures the most neglected by nature, afflicted with more wants and diseases, corrupted and evil beyond all others, spurred by more vain desires and more discontented than any of them. "After supper," the oyster tells Ulysses, "it is my method to shut up, and compose myself to rest, without leaving room for so much as one uneasy reflection, which is more than the wisest among you can often boast of." [51] Such oyster-bliss Ulysses clearly cannot match.

Man's alleged superiorities the beasts disdain as useless to themselves: the mole needs no eyes, nor the oyster ears or feet,—any more than man should want a pair of wings, so we are informed!—nor is reason required or desired by hind or goat. Their equipment is amply adequate for their station in life, which is more than man can say for himself. So they are contented and he is miserable: reason enough why they all bless their present lot and flatly refuse to be restored to human shape. The horse expresses his convictions on the subject concisely: "As I am, I find fewer things to hinder me from enjoying my ease, and from attaining that perfection and end which is agreeable to my kind and nature; whereas when I was a man, I came very short of doing the duties of a man." "The sole superiority Man could reasonably boast of," Ulysses is told, is "a preëminence in misery." [52] Precisely this animal contentment disgusts the ever-forward-reaching Ulysses. Tennyson's lines come to mind:

> And this gray spirit yearning in desire
> To follow knowledge like a sinking star,
> Beyond the utmost bound of human thought.

"Would you believe it!" he complains to Circe after his conference with the Hare, "he was naturally of so base a spirit, and so averse to any little trouble, that he rather chose to live in the most abject slavery, void of care, than to enjoy the most honourable post, . . . merely because men seemed to him to be subject to some trouble:" [53]

> One equal temper of heroic hearts,
> Made weak by time and fate, but strong in will
> To strive, to seek, to find, and not to yield.

Ulysses is about to sail away in disgust, when an elephant who had once been a philosopher, Aglaophemus, expresses himself as open to conviction, and asks Ulysses to state his arguments in favor of human superiority as clearly as he can. The former Aglaophemus has retained his philosophical openmindedness; the desired knowledge Ulysses readily undertakes to supply. In good Platonic manner he convinces the elephant that the intellect is a more certain and perfect source of truth than the senses, more reliable than imagination, nobler than sagacity, that as man is thus by virtue of his understanding alone capable of real universal knowledge, so likewise by his will he can choose or reject what his understanding judges to be right or wrong, proceeding not as appetite spurs but as reason directs him. Thus he alone in nature can aspire to virtue and eschew vice. Unique and noble is therefore man's destiny, quite unlike that of the beasts. "Man, by having his choice free, can attain an end more or less worthy as he thinks fit, by letting himself down to creatures much below him, or by emulating those as much above. He that elevates himself no higher than the earth on which he grows, will become a mere vegetable; and he that abandons himself to sensual pleasures will degenerate into a brute. Whilst he that looks with an eye of reason on the glories of the heavens, and contemplates the stupendous regularity of Nature, will change the earthly into a celestial creature; but he that dares soar above the gross impediments of flesh, to converse with divine objects, will become little less than a God. Who therefore can look without astonishment on man, not only the most noble, and the sovereign among animals, but who has this peculiar privilege indulged him by Nature, that he may make himself what he will?" [54]

The elephant, convinced, resumes joyously his former human shape and rôle of Aglaophemus and sails with Ulysses. The reasoning of Ulysses throughout is inspired by Florentine Platonism, but Gelli's beasts are keenly observant in their satirical accounts of man, and the book discloses both the exalted and the sardonic moods of the Renaissance mind.

CHAPTER III

PASCAL'S DESPAIR OF REASON

I

In the knowledge of truth is man's hope of freedom, and our whole dignity and worth are in our thought; yet thought is also the first source of our misery; it yokes us to plough in the marshes of doubt. He that increaseth knowledge increaseth sorrow, sighed Ecclesiastes, and the primitive wisdom of Israel had already passed judgment on intelligence in the old story of the Fall of Man. What banished Adam and Eve from Paradise? Eating of the tree of knowledge of good and evil. Profoundly significant is this Hebrew recognition that man's first woes were due to his inability to check his inquiring turn of mind. Dove, lamb, and sheep remained blissfully in Eden: they had not been moved to eat of the tree of knowledge.

Whether it be owing to our intelligence, or to our insufficiency of it, many of us pass from pious innocence in childhood to unsettled, unbelieving youth, and to half-believing or indifferent gray maturity, often wistfully recalling the green days of whole-hearted trust. It was not by this road that, in his brief span of thirty-nine years, Blaise Pascal reached the evening twilight of defiant faith and finality. His mind's history had proceeded on an entirely unconventional schedule. How amazingly unconventional, let Chateaubriand tell us in his *Génie du Christianisme:* [1] "There was a man who at the age of twelve, with *bars* and *rings*, created mathematics; who at sixteen wrote the most learned treatise on conic sections produced since antiquity; who at nineteen reduced to a machine a science existing wholly in the understanding; who at twenty-three demonstrated the phenomena of air-pressure and destroyed one of the great errors of ancient physics; who at this age when other men are barely born, having covered the round of human knowledge, perceived its nothingness and turned his thoughts to religion; who from that moment until his death, in his thirty-ninth year, sick and suffering all the time, fixed the language spoken by Bossuet and Racine, gave the model of the most perfect pleasantry and of the most vigorous reasoning; who finally, in the brief intervals between his ills, solved abstractly one of the highest problems of geometry and jotted on paper thoughts which partake as much of the Divine as of the human: this terrible genius was called *Blaise Pascal.*"

The early training of this amazing mind was calculated least of all to encourage sceptical tendencies, but rather to develop the self-assurance of the intellect. Étienne Pascal, himself a savant and mathematician of note, made the education of his son Blaise his main concern in life, and his deliberate aim was consistently to keep the youth above and ahead of his task. The boy should undertake no problem likely to overtax or baffle his abilities. This was to be no overfed infant prodigy: he was not to study Latin or Greek until he was twelve, nor mathematics before fifteen. His whole education was intended progressively to lead him, self-assured and confident in the powers of his mind, to more and more difficult problems. This complacent gait Blaise would not follow; learning that geometry had to do with lines and circles, bars and rings, he reinvented Euclid at the age of twelve, wrecked his father's pedagogy, and joined the elder Pascal's own scientific society.

In this very early and vigorous mental life, religion seems to have played no part. The father was no freethinker, nor the family as a whole in any way lax; but while altogether conformist and reverent, Étienne Pascal kept his faith and his science on genial neighborly terms. To the young mathematical genius, religion came incidentally and, as it were, in its place: it did not dominate his daily life as it did not disturb overmuch that of his father. It was later, at an age when vigilant minds begin to worry lest they lose their faith, that Pascal first really found faith as a dominant force in his own life. The Pascals were then living in Rouen, where the father was a high official. In January, 1646, while on his way to stop a duel, Étienne Pascal slipped on the ice and fractured a leg. The two medicos who attended him must have been versed in curing both soul and body, for by the time the broken leg was healed, the entire Pascal family was converted to the intense Augustinian Catholicism which Cornelius Jansenius, bishop of Ypres, had championed and of which the Abbey of Port Royal, under the guidance of St. Cyran, was the living heart.

If heretofore science and worldliness had marked the life of the Pascals, henceforth devotion to God and his grace were to claim them all: father, son, two daughters. From this time forth the débutante Jacqueline was bound for the cloister; her married sister Gilberte was to live a life of the most rigorous piety; the father's closing years were aglow with Jansenist enthusiasm. The intensity of Blaise Pascal's devotion fluctuated, but if he had lapses of worldliness, the return was to a piety doubly profound. One does Pascal an injustice in attributing his religiosity to his ill health. Ill health and the compulsory relaxation ordered by his physician sent him into the gay life of society, but he turned from it to experience a second conversion, soul-consuming and irrevocable. From that Monday night in November, 1654, until his death in 1662, Pascal was a warrior for the faith.

The citadel which he defended was a citadel besieged; Jansenism was under the cloud of heresy. The invalid genius whose youth had written new chapters in the history of science was now destined to write masterpieces of religious controversy, the *Provincial Letters* in which he champions St. Augustine and Port Royal against the Pelagianism, the casuistry, and the worldliness of the Jesuits.

The main issue between Jansenist and Jesuit is all important: it concerns the doctrine of grace and the salvation of man.[2] Does man's free will contribute to his own salvation; is salvation in any sense whatever earned by man or is it altogether a free gift of God? This problem is not exclusively Christian. The Hindu observes a little kitten in dire peril; the mother cat seizes it by the nape of the neck and carries it, limp and helpless, to safety. But see the baby monkey similarly snatched from danger: the old monkey does her best for it, but the little one also scrambles away for all it is worth. Which of these two is the better analogy of man's salvation by God? Hindu theologians argued ardently over the cat-hold and the monkey-hold theory.

The first essential of a religion of salvation is the recognition of the utter sinfulness of man; attenuate or explain away the actuality of evil, says the orthodox theologian, and you deny the religion of Christ, the Saviour of men. The whole scheme of salvation implies man's dire need of it. If man can save himself, what need of the Redeemer? So man cannot save himself because he is born in sin. Salvation then is a free gift of God to man, a gift which God does not owe to anyone. Shall we add: a gift which God does not grant to all? Unless we do, hell is likely to lose its salutary terrors; if we do add it, we open the door to a pack of vicious problems. Here, as we have observed already, the Church has traditionally leaned on St. Augustine's doctrine of grace against the dualistic heresy of the Manichean, which treats evil as coeval and coördinate with good, and likewise against the Pelagian heresy which is ambiguous and negligent of the fatal reality of evil and which regards man as actively contributing to his own salvation. St. Augustine's position is presumably orthodox, but what is the true Augustinian doctrine? Surely, we are told, it is not the Calvinist doctrine of predestination. According to Calvin, as Catholics understood him, man, tainted from birth with original sin, is bound for hell everlasting. But some men God predestines to salvation. A soul thus elected to grace is saved, justified, and sanctified by the free gift of God. God, then, predestines some men to heaven, others to hell, without any prevision of their sins and irrespective of repentance or merit on their part.

Against Calvinism uprise the followers of Molina, a Spanish Jesuit who in 1588 espoused a doctrine of salvation decidedly Pelagian. God has conditionally willed to save all, but upon man's actually availing himself of this sufficing grace freely bestowed by the Redeemer depends the effectiveness of the grace to save. And even when the saving grace is withdrawn, man still retains the power to reach after and regain it. This Jesuit view was abhorrent to Pascal: it rejected St. Augustine's truth along with Calvin's heresy. Whereas Calvin makes God's will the absolute author alike of man's salvation and of his damnation, the Jesuit doctrine makes both proceed essentially from the will of men.

A third position is that of the Dominicans, followers of St. Thomas. If all men are burdened with sin, all are accorded the gift of grace through Christ's death. This grace does not save and sanctify man, but it does open our eyes to see good and evil, it makes us capable of choosing the one or the other. But while our rejection of this gift of God will damn us, our acceptance of the gift is not sufficient for salvation. For saintliness and eternal bliss, God gives to the elect souls a second grace, free, irresistible, *grâce efficace.* So long as God thus sustains the soul of the elect, it is saintly. Should the hand of God be withdrawn, there remains to the soul a power strong enough to fulfill God's commandments, but not strong enough to save.

The fourth doctrine of grace is the doctrine of St. Augustine as interpreted by the Jansenists. This is the doctrine defended by Pascal. Adam's free choice of evil has tainted all mankind with original sin, and God with perfect justice could have damned us everyone. But in his all pure and free mercy God has elected some to grace. To some the grace of God has not been accorded at all; others God has willed to redeem and has given them grace which would have led them to heaven had they also been given the singular grace of perseverance, without which one cannot attain unto saintliness; to still others, blessed souls, God has accorded grace certain and infallible. Let each man believe, but believe with trembling, that he is among the elect; let him not judge that anyone, be he the most evil and impious, is among the damned so long as one breath of life remains. Man's free will brought evil into the world; God wills the damnation of the wicked conditionally and by prevision; the salvation of the elect souls God wills absolutely.

A dispute among theologians is apt to become arid and abstruse. Back of this trio of Catholic doctrines,—Molinist, Neo-Thomist, Jansenist,—we find two heresies in conflict: on the one hand, the heresy of pagan self-reliance, Pelagianism: man in a measure saves himself and receives grace as he deserves it; on the other, the heresy of fatalist predestination, which casts aside human will and responsibility as of no avail whatever, and regards Jesus Christ as having died not for all, but only for the elect. There is covert Pelagianism in the doctrine of Molina; the Dominicans had attacked it at Rome, and only a papal interdict of discussion prevented a cleavage. It is against this Neo-Pelagianism of the Jesuits that Bishop Jansenius of Ypres wrote his learned folio, *Augustinus;* and it was only natural that the Jesuits should reply by charging the Jansenists of Port Royal with Calvinist fatalism. The *Provinciales* exhibit with keen irony the dubious position of the Dominican followers of St. Thomas in this conflict. In more substantial agreement with Jansenius than with Molina, they were yet in verbal agreement with the latter, owing perhaps to the Jesuit dexterous manipulation of traditional formulas of orthodoxy. To open the eyes of the Thomists to the real beneath the verbal issue and to win them to the support of Jansenist Augustinianism and so prevent the threatened anathema, was Arnauld's hope; it was also Pascal's immediate object in writing the *Provinciales.*

From this immediate issue over the doctrine of grace, Pascal is led to attack the Jesuits on a larger front. The self-reliance of the Molinist view of salvation is typical of the laxity and worldliness of Jesuit morality. Resting on the learning of Arnauld and Nicole, and seasoning the intensity and severity of Port Royal with supreme controversial wit, Pascal lays bare, in a series of immortal letters, the unchristian compromise of the Jesuit with the powers of evil, Jesuit complacence, Jesuit pride and arrogance, Jesuit diplomacy and duplicity, Jesuit worldliness. Against Escobar's twenty-four new-fashioned church fathers, Pascal pleads for the old Augustinian faith, a faith from the world apart, a faith humble, vigilant, fearful, relying never on self but ever leaning on God and on Christ.

The *Provinciales* did not accomplish their immediate aim: the Dominicans did not turn from Molina to Jansenius, and Port Royal was condemned, for, as Pascal grimly observed, it was easier to bring more monks to vote against Port Royal than to bring arguments against it. But the brilliant attack on Jesuit unchristian laxity dealt the society of Loyola a blow from which it never recovered: as Sainte-Beuve observes,[3] Pascal destroyed forever Jesuit dominance in the government of the world.

I have not taken this time to discuss the Jansenist controversies of Pascal simply owing to the dialectic lure of the *Provinciales,* though that itself were reason enough. The *Provinciales* are in a sense propaedeutic to the *Pensées.* Against Molina's Pelagianism, Pascal was defending the Augustinian Christianity of Jansenius; but what real assurance did he have that any of these second- and third-hand alleged versions of the truth were themselves true? Was he right about Jansenius, or Jansenius about Augustine, or Augustine about Christianity, and what certainty availed of the truth of Christianity itself? The Jesuit could well lean back in his chair and quote his twenty-four doctors, himself being the twenty-fifth as occasion demanded. The Jesuit was not wedded to truth; he distinctly abdicated verity for probability. Would Pascal quote St. Augustine, St. Chrysostom, St. Ambrose, St. Jerome? The Jesuit father had Escobar's armory: Fernandez, Martinez, Suarez, Henriquez, Vasquez, Lopez, Gomez, Sanchez, and twice as many more. They didn't agree with each other, but what of it? If you would murder, here is Lessius to suit you; if not, there stands Vasquez on your side.[4] One needs many guides if one plans to travel many roads. But Pascal would travel the one single road of truth, truth absolute and incontrovertible. Probabilism and casuistry he found intellectually intolerable and morally detestable. It is not merely that Escobar's twenty-four doctors contradict each other; if he maintains against them all the cause of Augustine, Pascal is not simply pitting authority against authority, one lion against twenty-four asses. Pascal is not essentially a dogmatic theologian, and mere authority counts with him nothing at all. His orthodoxy is the orthodoxy of truth, not the orthodoxy of papal bulls. Nor is he overwhelmed by numbers nor by power. To the Jesuit fathers he declares nobly in the closing words of the *Twelfth Provinciale:* "You believe you have force and impunity on your side; but on my side I believe I have truth and innocence. . . . Truth lasts forever and triumphs over its enemies, for it is eternal and mighty like God himself."

On questions of fact he would not submit to Rome, and one cannot be sure that on questions of faith also he might not be ready to look beyond the Sorbonne and the Vatican. Pascal's early life had not been devoted in vain to scientific work: fact is fact for him, and truth, truth. He does not need Innocent the Tenth or the Seventh Alexander to tell him whether a certain doctrine is or is not to be found in the folio of Bishop Jansenius. He would repeat Galileo's words to the Inquisition, which had extracted a recantation from him regarding the movement of the earth: "It moves just the same!" Whether the earth moves or stands still is a question of fact, not of papal pronouncement. He would not turn from Arnauld to Escobar, or from Augustine to Molina simply because a Pope in Rome decreed that he do so. "If my letters are condemned in Rome, that which I condemn in them is condemned in heaven." Beyond the Sorbonne and the Vatican he looks to the eternal source and ground of all truth. "Lord Jesus, I appeal to your tribunal!" [5]

This then is the thorny problem which confronted the author of the *Pensées*. Unlike the Jesuit Sophists, he believes that knowledge is more than opinion, and truth than mere probability. A grab-bag of authorities would not do for him. Behind the authority he would go to test its sanction. He believes there is truth to be had; he has the test of it and would know if he had it; but he despairs of ever attaining it with his intellect. Here we perceive Pascal's scepticism, and also its limits. Behold this sick, suffering genius, racked by a thousand pains: what made him so discontented in his science, what made him so unsettlingly intense in his faith?

We have now come to a book of fragments, notes, jotted down or dictated by Pascal in the intervals between intense suffering; the whole forming a manuscript almost illegible and chaotic in its original state, a book nevertheless so soul-searching and soul-revealing that great minds do not know whether to be glad that it was never finished and polished off, or to wonder what amazing masterpiece it would have been had Pascal lived long enough to complete his work; a book beside which one puts the *Imitation of Christ* and St. Augustine's *Confessions,* and which French scholars would save and cherish above all other French books. This masterpiece is the *Pensées, Thoughts,* of Blaise Pascal.[6]

II

It is not for others only that Pascal planned his great Apology, of which only the random fragments are to be found in the book before us. He planned the Apology for himself first of all. The book was to contain letters, dialogues, eloquence, argument. Who can tell whether this sceptical passage or that infidel fragment expresses Pascal's own views or the views which, in a contemplated dialogue, he intended to combat? So Strowski warns us: imagine the *Provinciales* in the uncompleted state in which we find the *Pensées.* They would have been equally contradictory: a chaos of Jesuit tirades, Jansenist pleas, Pascalian dialectic.[7] But there, as here, the problems would have remained the same. In the *Pensées* Pascal has argued the case for faith, but he has also argued the case for doubt: we have them both side by side, and the contrast is eloquent.

For such knowledge as is vouchsafed to man Pascal relies on the method of geometry. It consists, according to him, in defining all our terms and proving all our propositions. Now, if we go from involved and complex terms back to plainer and simpler terms, we are led at last to primitive words that do not admit of definition. Similarly, if we trace a certain proposition to the propositions on which it rests for its proof, and these in turn to further and further prior propositions, we finally reach first principles and axioms which are undemonstrable. The geometrical method is thus perfectly certain so far as it goes, but inadequate and unconvincing in the end since it does not go far enough. Man, naturally helpless, sooner or later comes against a wall which he cannot surmount. This subtly precise game of science, in which the intellect manipulates its stock of concepts, affords Pascal no final satisfaction: what it proves, it proves well, but it does not prove what Pascal, what in fact all thinking men want proved and assured—the ultimates of life and of existence. So Pascal writes to Fermat, whom he calls the greatest geometer of Europe: "To speak frankly about geometry, I regard it as the highest exercise of the mind, but at the same time I know it to be so unavailing that I see little difference between a man who is merely a geometer and a skillful artisan." [8]

Let not the last phrase escape us. On the gates of his Academy Plato had inscribed the words: "Let no ungeometrical person enter here." Science demands the precise definition and demonstration of which geometry is the model. But for true wisdom, for an adequate philosophy of life, one has to be more than merely a geometer, content to begin with a first page of axioms and definitions. One must challenge the meaning of number, motion, space, time, yes, and also of Being, nature, world, life, thought, value, truth, beauty, good, God. The man who could perceive and express this truth as Pascal repeatedly perceived and expressed it may not give us the final philosophy of life, but he would die trying to attain it.

New troubles beset us now. If geometry is precise but not final, philosophy is neither final nor precise. Here is human thought overreaching itself in its effort to comprehend the universe, God and man, and falling far short of its goal, confused and inconclusive. How can you measure infinity with a yardstick? Suppose you climb to the top of Mt. Cenis, Montaigne wrote: are you really any nearer the sky than you would be at the bottom of the sea? Suppose, disdaining geometry, you attempt philosophy: are you any nearer final truth? Only your footing is less secure. "For what, after all, is man in nature? With regard to the infinite, he is nothing; with regard to nothing, he is all: a mean between nothing and all. Infinitely far from comprehending the ultimate, the end of things and their first principles are hidden from him in impenetrable mystery—equally incapable of seeing the nothing from which he issues and the infinite in which he is submerged."[9]

What are we to do then? Shall we go with the men of the world, such as Méré, whose wit exceeds their intellectual supply or demand, and who, as Leibniz tells us, set little value on what they do not understand? Or shall we more eloquently shrug our shoulders with Montaigne and, ignoring our duty to seek the truth, cheerily resign ourselves to our inability to find it? Pascal knew his Montaigne, every line and word, but he could not sink into the faint-hearted easy indolence of the *Essais*. The motto of Montaigne, "*Que scais-je?*" recalls Pilate's shrug: "What is truth?" Such disdain discloses the unheroic soul. As keenly as Montaigne Pascal recognized the pitiful limits of our knowledge, but to him this was no occasion for idle acquiescence. It is, in fact, the tragedy of his spirit. He feels as if he is ever on the brink of an abyss: the abyss of the all-important unknown.

Pascal considered another philosophical alternative: the Stoic wisdom of Epictetus. Behold a sage who knows nothing of man's essential ignorance, knowing only man's duty. But his severity, noble dignity and fortitude, are they not in the end merely pride, vain and futile?

There are Stoic moments in Pascal, and in him as in all of

us, so Sainte-Beuve reminds us, [10] there is not a little of Montaigne. But neither Montaigne's acquiescence nor the pathetic dignity of Epictetus can satisfy him. More intently and more unflinchingly he would face man's plight and seek a way out. We move on a narrow strip of knowledge between two oceans of ignorance. Not one law but has its counter-law, not one truth but turns out to be also false. Man treads no path that does not turn upon itself to bring him back to the uncertainty with which he began. Real truth must be eternal, the same in Toulouse and in Paris; but what of our truths and our justice? If you lived on this side of the river, it would be murder for me to kill you, my fellow. But you live on the other side of the river: in killing you I am no assassin but a brave son of my country. "A meridian settles the truth. . . . Truth this side of the Pyrenees, error on the other side." [11] Is our virtue an eternal value, or is it of this life only? We shrug our shoulders regarding the hereafter, yet how can we doubt that whether we be mortal or immortal makes all the difference in morals? Tragically halting and inconclusive is our thought on all ultimate questions. "Incomprehensible that God exists, and incomprehensible that he does not exist; that the soul is in the body, and that we have no soul; that the world is or is not created, that there is or isn't original sin." [12]

Is the field abandoned, then, in possession of the sceptic? Pascal cannot banish doubt, yet he cannot endure its withering effect. The notion of infinity overwhelms him. Kant was stirred to noble ardor by the sight of the celestial spaces; Pascal found their eternal silence harrowing: "When I consider the short span of my life, absorbed in the eternity before and after, the small space that I fill and even that I see, engulfed in the infinite immensity of spaces which I know not and which know me not, I am dismayed and amazed to find myself here rather than there; for there is no reason whatever why here rather than there, why now rather than some other time. Who has put me here? By whose order and direction has this place and time been allotted to me?" [13]

We are moving, faster than appears, to the climax of this drama of the spirit. Thought insists on scaling the infinite, and cannot scale it. Here is man's misery and here also man's grandeur, and here must we seek the way out. For consider: "Man cannot be incurably helpless, as Montaigne says, and at the same time have duties imposed upon him such as are pointed out by Epictetus." [14] Yet as far as thought goes they are both right. Reason cannot remove this contradiction: we must rise to a higher point of view if the fuller truth is to be revealed.

There is a hierarchy of orders, Pascal declares; from the lower to the higher is always an amazing leap. There is a material order, there is a mental order, there is an order of values—Pascal calls it *charité.* Just as all the length in the world will not give us breadth, nor all the length and breadth together give us depth, so no amount of matter, bodies, firmaments, stars and earths, can yield or are worth one little mind or thought. Mind, thought, is another, a higher order of reality. And so in turn the whole universe of matter and mind will not of itself yield one act of true charity, one moment of worth. Charity, value, again, is another, a still higher order of reality.[15]

Here is thought enmeshed in contrarieties. What will resolve the dilemmas of scepticism? A higher court than the court of reason: from the order of thought we must rise to the order of *charité,* of value. How is this ascent achieved? Shall we say that in Pascal's method the mind brings together approximations to truth, each by itself inconclusive, and that certain truth is attained by the deliberate fusion of a number of probabilities that cumulatively substantiate and stabilize each other? Certainty would then be a synthesis of a number of convergent probabilities, integrated by what Cardinal Newman was to call "the illative sense." Or shall we say that, confronted with radical antinomies, forced to choose between alternatives which reason cannot logically prove and alternatives which reason cannot sanely accept; forced between alternatives that challenge the powers of demonstration and alternatives that defy evident fact, we should not rest in agnostic suspense: our logic should yield to reality, we should bow before the incomprehensible certainty? The miracle of the Holy Thorn may be incomprehensible to the scientific intellect: only it is a fact to Pascal which he cannot ignore in his view of the universe. Or again shall we say that, while the intellect suffices for the establishment of scientific truth in detail, it is by itself incapable of attaining ultimate knowledge, that in order to know God all of man's being is required, total perception, the complete response of the soul? [16] The 'method' of the *Pensées* scarcely admits of being encased in a formula. Pascal's dialectic would escape agnosticism and also shamefaced contentment with faith; his tactics suggest the Hegelian, but his road and goal are more properly those of an aspiring saint, a mystic, self-critical in the possession of the truth to which he nevertheless explicitly submits.

On the night of November twenty-third, 1654, the night of his second conversion, Pascal did not reason, did not have to reason; he saw face to face, saw with a higher vision a higher light. Behold the truth of Montaigne and the truth of Epictetus: these two contrary truths are one in the truth of Christ. In Christ's Gospel the misery and the grandeur of man are made truly one: the child of sin is the child of God. To perceive this truth more than reason is required: this last wisdom, just as all ultimate truths and all first principles, can be known only by the heart. This indeed is the wisdom of all knowledge, to recognize its limits and to humble its vanity. We have been warned against the triple concupiscence: of sense, of science, of ambition,—and Pascal also writes: "I see my abyss of pride, of curiosity, of concupiscence." [17] Before we can rise to the higher perception, we must curb our pride, mortify the flesh, humble the barren vanity of the intellect, confront it with overpowering realities that transcend its comprehension, and compel it to acknowledge what it cannot demonstrate or understand. Some undertake to vaunt human nature; others decry it; still others find it amusing; but Pascal writes: "I esteem only those who search in groaning." [18] Nothing is more reasonable than this disavowal of reason, this submission to the heart. "The heart has its reasons, which reason does not know at all. . . . It is the heart which perceives God, and not reason. This is faith: God made evident to the heart, not to reason." [19] You may ask love to justify itself, to state its grounds. This it does: a catalogue of halting reasons, so many nothings, but the heart somehow transfuses these nothings into one ardent reality.

III

In order to possess the great truths of religion, how do we rise from the order of thought to the order of charity, from reason to the heart, from knowledge to faith? Inspiration is the perfect path; God in his grace must speak to man. There are humbler approaches, however: reason and custom may serve us here.[20] If they cannot establish our faith, they may yet help to remove obstacles to it, may prepare the way.

How are we to prove God's existence? "If there is a God, he is infinitely incomprehensible, since, having no parts nor limits, he is out of touch with us. We are thus incapable of knowing what he is or whether he exists. Accordingly, who would dare to undertake the solution of this question? Not we, we are out of touch with him altogether." [21] The Christian who believes without pretending to prove his faith is after all right, for how are any proofs possible here? "God exists, or he does not exist. Now, to which side shall we incline? Reason can settle nothing here: an infinite chaos is in our way. A throw is being cast, at the end of this infinite distance, which will come out heads or tails. What will you wager? By reason you can make neither the one nor the other; by reason you can support neither side." [22]

We have now come to the famous wager of Pascal, which has occasioned endless controversy. Is this a dialogue with an unbeliever, or is Pascal disputing God's existence with himself? Certain it seems that if knowledge about God is beyond the reach of our reason, then the recognition of its helplessness is the only reasonable course open to reason, and agnosticism the true wisdom. Does God exist or not? I do not know; I cannot say; how then can I wager? "The right thing is not to wager at all." [23]

But this agnostic withdrawal from the wager of eternity, is it not in effect itself a wager? To act so as to ignore the issue whether God exists or not is virtually to deny God's existence. This is indeed the most reckless of choices: to move blandly in the face of possible eternal ruin. Theoretically Pascal's reason counselled sceptical inaction, but he found the agnostic practice intolerable. If we were to wait upon certainty before acting, could we act at all? We must act today in preparation for tomorrow, although we may never see the morrow. Every step we take is a step in the dark. Whether we march or whether we stand still we are invariably gambling on the uncertain. It behooves us to use our poor reason in determining the nature of the hazards we run in this world of uncertainties.

God exists, or God does not exist,—and by God's existence Pascal understands here the whole of the Christian religion,—God exists or God does not exist. This is of all issues the most solemn and fatal; it imposes itself on you; you cannot shirk it; willy-nilly, Pascal says, you must wager, *il faut parier*. On which side will you stake your life, your soul? Since you must choose, let us see on which side your interest lies. Whether you choose the one or the other is, as far as reason goes, indifferent, for there is no reason either way. But what about your fortune, your beatitude or your irretrievable ruin? Either there is a God, perfect goodness and wisdom and power, and this world-course is a solemn drama of Divine Providence governing all destiny; or else there is no God, and this world is a vast machine of matter-in-motion, or else immense and irremediable chaos. Either there is a God, and your life and death are but the prelude to an eternal career of bliss or damnation; or there is no God, and your lot is as the lot of all other clods of moist earth. What have you to gain and what to lose if you choose one way or the other, heads or tails? Suppose you live your life as if God existed: you may, of course, miss the so-called pleasures of this brief life; but, again, you may gain an eternity of heaven. On the other hand, live your life as if there were no God: you may then have your sinful way here and now, and then death and nothing more; but, my soul, it is also possible that you may face eternal damnation. Staked against possible heaven and hell, what are the pleasures of this life worth? Nothing at all. The infinite is staked against the finite, today and tomorrow against eternity. How can you then hesitate about your choice? Choose for God: you thus insure yourself against the hazard of damnation, you stake your brief life on the chance of eternal bliss. Even if there were only one chance that God exists and ten thousand chances that there is no God, still the infinite disparity between the hazards involved would warrant your staking your life on God's existence.

Behold Pascal's immortal wager. But the soul of man replies: Be it as you say; all the same, you are forcing me to yield my life against my will. The fact is, I am so made that I cannot believe in God. Will you damn me for my inability? What am I to do? Even if my reason accedes, my heart resists the call of faith.

True, Pascal answers: if reason cannot help you here, habit and custom shall. Your heart is resistant because it is wedded to passion, to the lusts of this world. Break down the resistance to faith, curb your passions. You cannot believe? Enter anyhow upon the path of the believer, do as he does, act as if you were a believer, go to mass, take holy water. "This will make you believe and will stultify you, *cela vous abêtira*." [24] The word is terrible; we shudder as it comes from Pascal's lips and we dare not look at him lest we see on his face the ironic grin of the mocking unbeliever. Port Royal could not bear, or did not dare, to print this word. But there is no grin of mockery on Pascal's lips: terrible exhorter though he be, he never loses sight of the other side. To the unbeliever such artificial acquiescence seems debasing stultification. Mechanically to go through the motions of a ritual, to drug and stupefy myself into alien piety: "This is just what I fear, the soul protests." "And why?" Pascal replies: "What have you to lose?" [25] Eternity is at stake for you, and you are worrying over your sorry dignity and self-respect. Your supreme interest counsels the wager: close your eyes and plunge forward, blindly if need be; habit will sweep aside the obstacles in your way while you wait for the grace of God to illumine you with the higher light, to humble and transfigure and exalt you all at once.

IV

Pascal is one of the most defiant warriors for the Christian faith; but his wager has proved a precarious bulwark to orthodoxy. Orthodoxy demands a different sort of assurance.

Different is the assurance of St. Paul: "I know him whom I have believed, and I am persuaded that he is able to guard that which I have committed unto him against that day." [26] Here is straightforward, unquestioning trust. Now a certain type of believer demands for the voyage of his spirit, not only the full-blown sails of faith, but also the rudder and compass of understanding. Believe without understanding if you must, Clement of Alexandria would say, but if you believe with understanding, all the better. To the simple assent of faith the gnosis of Christian intelligence is as the man full grown is to the infant. This is the great confidence in the intellect which distinguishes the best of Scholastic thought, particularly the great succession of Dominican philosophers of the thirteenth century: philosophy is the handmaiden of theology, but it is a necessary introduction to it.

There has always been an opposite sort of believer who has felt that his faith is somehow compromised if it leans on intelligence. Defiantly he has scorned all proofs, as if to reassert the solidity of his faith by rejecting all rational basis for it. This is the view of Tertullian: Separate Jerusalem from Athens, the Church of Christ from the Academy of Plato. What are proofs and arguments to me? Do you say that what I believe is undemonstrable, that it is absurd? Well, I believe it just because it is absurd, *Credo quia absurdum est.* This type of mind is not exclusively Christian. You find it in Islam, in India. Here is Al-Ghazzali of Bagdad, scornful of all philosophy in his reaffirmation of Mohammedan orthodoxy; here are immemorial mystics of India deeming the surrender of intelligence a prerequisite of wisdom. Not far from here is also Duns Scotus of Oxford, *Doctor Subtilis,* uprising against St. Thomas for his reliance on the intellect. Will is superior to intelligence, according to him, and the only ground of faith is divine revelation. The arguments of reason are inconclusive in theology: you cannot prove God's omnipotence nor the immortality of the soul. In all his thinking Duns Scotus widens the breach between reason and religion, disclaiming any reliance on demonstration, firm and self-sufficient in his orthodox faith.

But there is danger in this defiant faith, danger of results wholly unintended by its champions. Do you disdain in your religion to rely on reason: would you separate theology from philosophy and science? Well enough: you remain then wholly devoted to your faith by fiat; your religion cannot be proved and does not have to be proved. But after you come others who take you at your word, that religion does not admit of proof, but who, unlike you, are mainly interested in what has to be and can be proved. They leave you to your undemonstrable faith and they go their own secular way. So it is that Duns Scotus, arch-believer himself, became a factor in the disintegration of belief which marked the collapse of Scholasticism and the beginnings of the scientific Renaissance.

Pascal likewise tells us that we know nothing and can prove nothing about the fundamentals of religion. We cannot know what God's nature is, nor even whether there is a God at all. Faith lacks rational ground; to the intellect of man the gospel of Christ is as St. Paul said it was to the Greek, folly. To all this the modern unbeliever nods approval: he has made his own anthology of passages from Pascal, and what Pascal has said on this score no one can say better. But when Pascal invites him to play heads or tails on God or Christ, the unbeliever declines. No gambler, he; he would stick to what admits of proof. Pascal may convince us that it is a far better bargain all around to wager on heads rather than on tails; he has not convinced us that heads have any advantage over tails, nor has he gained the man who is not impressed by the stakes, or who simply will not gamble.

For consider: the whole force of Pascal's wager as an argument for Christian faith is to be found in the immense disparity between the stakes for and against God. What decides Pascal's wager is the prospect of heaven or hell. But what warrants our judgment that, if there is a God, he has eternal bliss or else hell everlasting in store for us? Do we really know any more about this than we know whether God exists at all? True enough, you may either wager or not wager: there is here no third alternative, and Pascal insists that wager you must. But why is he so sure of the number of his alternatives and of the stakes involved? Do we have just two alternatives,—heads or tails? Pascal's geometrical bias has betrayed him where it should have served to sustain. The number of available alternatives may vary with each wager. Heads or tails if you are flipping a coin; but any one of six chances if you throw a die, or one in thirty-six if you throw a pair of dice. So a number may be either equal or not equal to another number, but whether you prefer the one to the other may depend on a different chance, whether it be equal or greater or less. If in the cases mentioned the number of alternatives is fixed,—2, 3, 6, 36,—the situation becomes increasingly more complex as we approach more serious issues. Logic should keep us vigilant here lest we stray through incomplete disjunction. Perhaps we may say: Newton is either correct or incorrect. But can we say: either Newton or Einstein? No more now than before Einstein: tomorrow a third alternative may be available for us. Who can say once for all in how many respects Newton may be wrong, or Einstein? Truth is one, but error is manifold. Can we say: either Plato or Aristotle, either St. Thomas or Duns Scotus, either Calvin or Molina? Still less can we split issues in morals: is every one of us either a saint or a sinner?

So here we must go back with Pascal to his wager and reexamine the throws and the stakes. Assuredly the man who denies God's existence is either right or wrong, and likewise the man who affirms God's existence is either right or wrong. We may grant to Pascal that whether either be right or wrong cannot be determined by reason: that is not the point now, but rather this: what *is* affirmed or denied when God's existence or non-existence is affirmed or denied? Am I to believe in God's grace with Augustine or with Molina? These are different views of God's grace, and in a measure different beliefs in God. Pascal has reduced his alternatives to two: heads or tails, either Jansenist Catholicism or atheism. If you could equate belief in God with Jansenist Catholicism, then you have your stakes, eternal bliss in heaven or hell everlasting, and then you may perhaps continue with Pascal's wager.

But surely other alternatives are available. You may believe in God and yet just because of your supreme confidence in his infinite love reject hell everlasting altogether; you may be a pantheist and long for reabsorption into the Infinite; you may be a Buddhist and look forward to the blessed selfless peace of Nirvana. Personal immortality may to you be a priceless boon and may decide you to stake your life on the side that would assure your soul of a hereafter; but you may have learned to look beyond the individual self and with the Positivist seek survival in Humanity; or, again, you may share the craving for personal extinction which characterizes a certain type of Oriental. If immortality is for you a nightmare and for me a cherished hope, your dread may lead you to gamble on materialistic atheism and my hope may lead me to gamble along with Pascal. With every shade of religious opinion a new set of stakes emerges and we have really a new wager.

To insist on the wager in Pascal's terms is to mix considerable bigotry with our scepticism. It is remarkable that a mind like Pascal, believing itself so hopelessly ignorant about God, should yet have felt so familiar with the operations of

Divine Providence in case any Divine Providence obtained. If it has come to flipping coins over God, if our reason is really incapable of knowing God's nature or even God's existence, then how can we say that, if God exists, he will deal thus and so with us? If you are dogmatic in your estimate of God's nature and sceptical about God's very existence, then you will have to flip a coin about it. But if you disclaim familiarity with the workings of a possibly existent Divine Providence, then you cannot list the stakes of your wager, then you do not know your alternatives, then you have no wager at all.

Do you then resign yourself utterly to withering scepticism? Let us see. The defiance of faith in Pascal's wager is dismal: face to face with possible irremediable ruin, yet altogether in the dark; forced to stake all blindly on a throw of destiny! If there be any such Divine Providence, ready to damn us forever for not believing in Him whom through no fault of ours we cannot know, then this idea would indeed be food for pessimists; here would be a real nursery of irreligion. Moreover, if we are condemned to incertitude, to wagers and possibilities, is not the casuistry of the Jesuit after all acceptable and sound? There is a disquieting similarity between the doctrine which Pascal combats in the *Provinciales*, and the advice which he gives to the unbeliever, to stultify himself if need be, by attending mass and taking holy water. Well does Saisset declare: "To replace certitude by probability, to appeal to interest instead of appealing to religion and to the heart, to make a machine of yourself, to stultify yourself, these are the detestable procedures which compromise the name of the Company of Jesus." [27]

There is a Pascal who, committed to eternal truth and finding this truth in Jansenism, attacked with heroic dogmatism the protean hosts of casuistry. There is another Pascal, the prey of general scepticism, who, doubting all yet unwilling to let go of his Jansenist faith, resorted to flipping coins to retain his hold on his God. These two Pascals are one, and reveal a most baffling genius. Pascal seems to counsel us thus: Proceed confidently with geometry in the realm of the finite, relying on the certainty of science; recognize however that all your finite certainties float in the ocean of infinite doubt; nevertheless yield yourself humbly to the call of faith, stake your life on the possible truth of Christianity.

Is this sensible? Surely it is blighting to reason. Deeper wisdom lies in Pascal's amazing treasury of thought. He is communing with the Saviour: "Be comforted," the Saviour says to him, "you would not seek me, had you not found me. I was thinking of you in my agony; I have shed such drops of blood for you. . . . Your conversion is my own concern; fear not and pray with confidence as if for me." [28] Here, we venture to think, is the most poignant as it is the most profound note in Pascal, poignant in the white-heat of the phrase: "I have shed such drops of blood for you!" profound and luminous in the initial, immortal words: "You would not seek me had you not found me." The soul groping in the dark marshes of doubt pushes on and refuses to sink back. In thus pushing on and refusing to sink back, in holding its course ever solidly ahead, it is itself proof eternal that there is solid ground ever ahead. Is God's truth done and finished and stored away on divine pantry-shelves beyond our reach; is it done and dead and laid out under divine seals which we may never break? Or is it not rather ever in the making? Is God himself the unreadable Preface of the book of creation, or is he not rather the living, careering heart of the book, ever to be sought and found, yet never encased in a formula: the infinite, eternal, ever-present Beyond?

A deal of religious perplexity is due to our trying to think of God as if he were a reality external to us and to our hunger and thirst after him. But, like the reality of all values, may not the reality of the divine be in the divine quest itself? The logical judgment expresses logical value; scientific thought, the search after knowledge and truth, is itself knowledge, insight, truth. Poetic activity, the pursuit of beauty, is itself the supreme manifestation of beauty. The indubitable evidence of the reality of moral value is our own endeavor after it. In science is Truth; in art is Beauty; in goodness is Good; in godliness is God. The ancient Hindu who conceived of the supreme Brahman as the divine worshipful urge which created all that there is, showed profound insight into the nature of spiritual reality. "You would not seek me, had you not found me. . . . Your conversion is my own concern; fear not and pray with confidence *as if for me.*"

How can man love God, how can he *know* God whom he has not seen except he love and know his brother whom he has seen? How can we reach the greater truth except through the lesser? Each truth that turns out to be also false, every good that we find to be also evil is, not a sign of our impotence and ignorance, but of our strength and wisdom. In the striving after truth, beauty, good, God, in the reach after eternal value, man attains unto the only real eternity there is, the eternity of the ideal. Only in the higher light is the lower light disclosed as dimness; only the larger good renders the lesser good evil. "When I was a child," St. Paul tells us, "I spake as a child, I felt as a child, I thought as a child,"—and quite rightly; but, he goes on, "now that I am a man, I have put away childish things." Only he might have said: "As I become a man, I am putting away childish things," for the full manhood of the spirit is ever *being* attained.

Here Pascal's own career, tragic as it is in its misery and in its grandeur, is a living symbol of this truth. What can be more crushing than this "tragedy of a powerful and energetic spirit in an imbecile body:" [29] prematurely burnt out and disintegrating in constant anguish? And the spirit of Pascal: what a tragic vortex of spiritual integrity and heroism, halting distrust, anguished contrariety, sophistry, stultifying bigotry, reckless hazard, and headlong surrender? But hear the high note that is sounded in this life of Pascal, a note the clearer and the more heroic because it rises from the dark depths of despond: from the abyss of benighted groping to the heights of aspiring intelligence. Read a page that has been called the noblest in French prose: [30]

"Man is but a reed, the weakest in Nature; but he is a thinking reed. It is not necessary that the whole universe should arm itself in order to crush him. A vapor, a drop of water, would be sufficient to kill him. But even though the universe should crush him, man would still be nobler than that which is killing him, for he knows that he is dying, and the advantage that the universe has over him. The universe does not know.

"All our dignity therefore lies in our thought. It is upon that that we must depend, not upon space and time which we cannot fill. Let us therefore strive to think well: such is the foundation of moral life."

CHAPTER IV

SCEPTICISM AND THEODICY

I

When a modern theologian reads "Whoso increaseth knowledge increaseth sorrow," he must know that Ecclesiastes was recording sad professional experience: the richer his store of life-wisdom, the more critical his conception of truth, the more perplexing his problem as a theologian. In the presence of the facts which Job's life provides, the office of God's advocate becomes very precarious. Pascal's tragedy, as we have seen, was the tragedy of a man who had sought geometric truth in the realm of piety. This is a peculiarly modern tragedy. The emancipation of secular thought from dogmatic authority imposed on the modern mind rigorous methods precluding the appeal to faith. The Cartesian reliance on rational demonstration and the empiricist's trust in sense-experience agreed in the abandonment of mystical or dogmatic fiat in the pursuit of real truth.

The Protestant recognition of the individual conscience, and the secularism that influenced the serious revision to which the Reformers subjected the medieval Catholic conception of Christian life and 'worldliness,' served only to emphasize the antithesis between faith and reason, an antithesis perhaps essential to Protestant theology.[1] The violent religious struggle roused in Catholic and Protestant alike the demand for assurance regarding the eternal truths to which they were committing their lives. But, if Calvinist or Lutheran could argue and hold his ground against Rome, doubts were sure to assail the inquiring mind: perhaps Arian,

Manichean, Paulician did not deserve their heretical infamy? Had their doctrines been better argued——?

But now, if we put the old problems once more on the carpet, what is to be our touchstone of verity? In dealing with an important theological issue, if several incompatible doctrines confront us, what is to be our choice when each doctrine may seem rationally indefensible or, worse yet, when the religiously absurd and monstrous hypothesis may turn out to be the least unreasonable or the most in accord with the facts of experience? [2] Can we piously abhor a heretic while freely acknowledging the superior logic of his position? Can we admit that a religious teaching is irrational, and still insist that it is God's very truth?

Despairing of winning an orthodox victory in the open field of argument, Bayle sought the gray alliance of scepticism and openly counselled the pious to take up the shield of faith and seek safety within the citadel of God's own Holy Word. Leibniz, convinced of the necessity of finding sufficient reason for the least item, would not admit that God's truth could be rationally untenable, and undertook its logical vindication. Strange reversed rehearsal of the Scotist-Thomist controversy! The shafts of Voltaire's satire sapped the bridge which Leibniz had erected to span the precipice of Bayle:—and then from Königsberg came a radically new type of engineer.

Being a heretic was a perennial experience to Pierre Bayle. His father and brother were devout Protestant clergymen; his own early training was non-conformist. Only once did he lend a willing ear to Rome, at the age of twenty-two: but all that he got from his seventeen months as a Catholic convert was to find himself, after the resumption of his Protestant confession, a fugitive and an exile from France and the object of persecution abroad. The king of France suppressed the

Protestant university of Sedan, where Bayle was professor of philosophy; but later in life Bayle was ousted from his professorship at Rotterdam because he was not orthodox enough to suit Jurieu's type of Protestant.

"Everything is in Bayle," Voltaire wrote, "but one must know how to find it." Only one design in this rich carpet of erudition and dialectic can be traced here. As it happens, it is the leading design in the texture. The problem of evil harassed his mind, and he vainly protests his resistance to dualism. We read the long articles in his *Dictionary,*—on Manicheans and Marcionites and Paulicians, and we cannot imagine him in the fifth century on the side of Augustine. It is of interest to note that it was in the land of the Albigenses, in Southern France, where Bogomile and Paulician heretics sowed perhaps the first hardy seeds of revolt against Rome, that Bayle's cradle was rocked.[3]

If God is the omnipotent, omniscient, infinitely good Creator of all that exists,—and what other conception of God is admissible?—then how is the presence of evil in the world to be accounted for? Lactantius before the days of Augustine had reported Epicurus' list of the available alternative answers, in a trenchant passage which Bayle quotes: "Either God is willing to remove Evils, and not able; or able and not willing, or neither able nor willing, or both able and willing. If he be willing and not able, he is impotent, which cannot be applied to the Deity. If he be able and not willing, he is envious, which is generally inconsistent with the nature of God. If he be neither willing nor able, he is both envious and impotent, and consequently no God. If he be both willing and able, which is the only thing that answers to the Notion of a God, from whence come Evils? Or why does he not remove them?"[4]

Bayle observes that no account is taken here of moral evil, which would have made the situation still more embarrassing.

The answer of Lactantius, according to Bayle, is weak and perhaps even heretical: it supposes that God "brings forth evil, for otherwise he could not make us know the wisdom, nor the virtue, nor the feeling of goodness." [5] What is this divine omnipotence which labors under such, for us, distressing limitations? Confronted with the problem of the compossibility of God's attributes (in view of the existence of evil), the Manicheans followed the Zoroastrian firm adherence to God's infinite goodness and made the best they could of God's omnipotence. St. Augustine, as we have seen, undertook to maintain God's attributes every one, and held man's (Adam's) free choice responsible for evil.

Christian orthodoxy recoils from the doctrine of a duality of world-principles and cannot tolerate a Creative Evil Power coördinate with God. But, apart from orthodoxy, what is offered to match the dualist explanation of evil? Man's choice brought evil into this world, we are told. The choice of evil by man God could not prevent without depriving man of freedom and moral dignity. He did not predetermine the evil choice but, being omniscient, he foresaw it; his perfect justice thus foreordained the inevitable consequences of man's choice: ruin irretrievable save by God's loving grace.

What would a Manichean or a Paulician reply to this doctrine? asks Bayle, and he is an ever-ready and patient reporter of heretical rejoinders.[6] In this doctrine of orthodoxy, the Manichean protests, all of God's attributes are compromised. What can we mean by saying that God could not prevent man's choice of evil without depriving him of moral dignity? Ask a surgeon: "If you could perform this operation without causing any pain whatever, would you not do it?" To be sure, but the surgeon does the best he can under the conditions which confront him. In order that a man may not be deprived of eyesight, he performs a painful operation. Shall we say of omnipotent God that he does the best he can? In order that man may not be deprived of moral freedom, he—allows him to choose evil? But what is this freedom and moral dignity to safeguard which God allows man to plunge into disaster? If this procedure exhibit God's perfect goodness, then what meaning do we attach to 'good'? Would not a good son, seeing his father about to jump out of the window, hold him back with chains if need be? If a queen were on the brink of an abyss or drowning in the water, would not the first lackey grab, embrace her, or even pull her by the hair out of danger, with little regard for the dignities of Her Majesty? What mother would let her daughter go to the ball knowing that she is to be lured away and seduced there? This is what Bayle's heretics understand by goodness and faithful and loving care. Yet here the son may well have insufficient certainty of his father's suicidal intent; Her Majesty may resent the lackey's undue or premature solicitude; the daughter may protest against her mother's lack of confidence in her. For the disastrous outcome in all these cases is in a measure uncertain. In God's case, however, omniscience precludes any possibility of doubt: it is as if the mother deliberately watched the seduction of her daughter without lending her a hand at the brink of the abyss. If insufficient prevision of the danger would alone excuse a spectator's passivity in the presence of impending disaster, then how is omniscient Deity to be justified in the circumstances?

Or shall we say that all these examples are inapplicable, that Adam's choice was a really free choice, without any influence of past experience, or any cue to indicate the course to be taken? But then did not even God know how Adam was going to use his freedom? Should we not, in that case question God's omniscience, and should we not further question his infinite goodness for giving man such a hazardous present without warning or safeguarding him in the use of it?[7] No, surely we cannot doubt God's perfect omniscience and prevision of man's choice. So the Augustinian puzzle is once more before us: how can a choice foreseen by God be a free choice for which Adam alone is responsible? If it was purely arbitrary, a free choice of indifference, how could we speak of responsibility at all in the circumstances? And if the choice was indeed representative, a characteristic expression of Adam's nature, then does Adam's responsibility for what he did preclude his Creator's responsibility for what he was? The more you speak of moral freedom and responsibility, so the heretic argues, the more embarrassing is your puzzle: how Infinite Goodness could create a chooser of evil? Or do you seek refuge in a subtle distinction: God simply *permitted* the introduction of evil into the world by man's free choice? But did not this concern God's own infinite perfection: was it quite indifferent to him whether evil came or did not come into the world, that thus, without causing, he should merely permit its introduction? Why did he permit evil, or even cause it? In order that his infinite justice and likewise loving grace might be revealed? So Jurieu writes: "God permitted sin in order to disclose his glory and his wonderful providence. . . . The creatures over against him are a *mere nothing; he loves his glory more than all his creatures,* for he has created all only for his glory." And Theodor Beza: "Man had to be created that he might be a vehicle for God's compassion." Had man not sinned, "God would have had no opportunity to show his compassion or his justice." But to say nothing specifically of God's infinite goodness, how could Infinite Perfection require or allow any such sentiments? How could *God* be acting *ad majorem Dei gloriam?*[8]

Still, we are told, had God foreordained man to choose only the good, the choice and the goodness would have been God's not man's. Such finite perfection would have been useless to God. So St. Basil points out: God would have us love him freely; constrained love is not acceptable to him. But now,—and this brings us back to the idea of freedom,—does perfection, either human or divine, necessarily involve the capacity to choose evil? Divine perfection presumably does not include this capacity. And, as Bayle's supposed heretic (this time a Marcionite) replies to St. Basil: Are the angels or the blessed saints in Paradise deficient in perfection because their choice is ever of the good, and is their love for God constrained on that account and unacceptable to him? [9]

The Manichean heretic insists: You cannot tone down evil, or regard it as the mere shadow in the lovely picture, or excogitate it out of existence, else you abandon the Christian doctrine of salvation. But the more seriously you take it, the greater your perplexities if you reject dualism and, holding God to be the omnipotent, omniscient, infinitely good Creator of all things, yet seek to foist upon man's will the sole responsibility for evil in this world. This fatal bias to evil in man's will itself requires explanation. Will you make God deliberately responsible for it? Then you have an Ahriman in your God? Or will you hold God nowise responsible for the evil bias in man? Then in strict logic you are virtually on our side and should openly come over. Your doctrine of the devil is a compromise which makes matters worse. Is the devil the father of evil, is his city more populous than the City of God, did he deceive Adam and Eve into making the fatal choice? But is not your devil created by God? "This is a thousandfold more damaging to God than to say that he is not the only necessary and independent being." Just consider with what monstrous burdens you load God in order to escape this alleged heresy of dualism: "The unique principle which you admit has, according to you, willed from all eternity that man should sin and that the first sin should prove a contagious affair; that it should produce ceaselessly and without end all imaginable crimes on the face of the earth; and has thereupon prepared for the human race all conceivable woes in this life: pestilence, war, famine, pain, vexation, and after this life a hell where almost all mankind will be eternally tormented." [10] Thus we are involved in additional difficulties regarding God's justice and goodness: whatever may be said of Adam's supposed free choice, the countless millions born with the taint of original sin lack this freedom: how do they deserve an eternity of hell-torments?

In this brief exposition it has been possible to give only samples of Bayle's tireless dialectic. The last-quoted passages will give a fair foretaste of the soul-perplexing diet which was served to the pious and the inquiring in the endless columns of the *Dictionnaire historique et critique.* On page after page the heretics advance their arguments, with three or four lines of non-committal historical recital at the top, and below, two long, closely-printed folio columns of commentary, audaciously critical and flanked by dozens of references and choice asides on the margins. And if a more systematic treatment of the perplexities of theodicy is demanded, it is abundantly supplied, with controversial zest, in the *Réponse aux questions d'un provincial.*

Voltaire's words return to one's mind: Everything is in Bayle. What is really to be found here? Was this man another dismayed Pascal, or a sneering Voltaire before his time? How Bayle personally estimated the plight in which he found himself is of great interest to others besides his biographers, and may lead to serious difference of opinion. But even more significant was the plight into which Bayle involved his more intelligent readers: here we see him in more than one sense a precursor of the *Encyclopédie.*

We have considered Bayle's diagnosis: what is his printed prescription for counteracting the insidious heresy in dealing with the problem of evil? By no means undertake to disprove the heretics' doctrines, he tells us. Their position is, in strict logic, more formidable today than it was in St. Augustine's time. Do not try to prove the orthodox doctrine or you may find God's sublime attributes slipping out one by one. Above all, do not seek refuge in the notion that our ideas of goodness, justice, wisdom, power, perfection are altogether inapplicable to God. This path leads to disaster, for in that case what can we know or mean by goodness or justice, and what reason can we have for preferring God to the devil, or anything to anything else? [11]

So Bayle advises us,—from sad experience,—do not argue at all, but stand your ground firmly on God's own Holy Word. Go to the Bible for your facts. The Bible records how man brought evil and the disaster consequent upon evil. This Bayle declares, is my fact, which I may not be able to explain but which you dare not ignore. *Ab actu ad potentiam valet consequentia.* I have thought this matter over and here, in a second edition of my *Dictionary*, I give you my second thought: "Why did God permit men to sin?" you ask me, and I answer you: "I can't say at all, I only believe that he had reasons for doing it, reasons worthy of his infinite wisdom, but past my understanding." [12]

To this conclusion Bayle invites us time and again, both in the *Dictionary* and in the *Réponse aux questions d'un provincial.* Before you begin arguing with a Manichean heretic or with any of his cousins ask them first this question: "Do you accept the Scriptural account as a fact?" If they do not explicitly accept it, refuse to argue with them. Do not match reason with reason for you will come out of it the loser. St. Basil disputes poorly; he should simply quote his Bible. Fight heresy not with logic but with God's Word, and with unquestioning submissive faith in it and with determined abasement of reason. Tertullian's "It is certain just because it is impossible; I believe it just because it is absurd," is the surest refuge. The less reasonable your belief, the greater the triumph of your faith. "No reason!" he quotes St. Evremont. "Just this is the true religion: no reason!" "Blessed are they that have not seen, and yet have believed." [13]

But then what of rational knowledge? Do we renounce it and resign ourselves to scepticism? And why do you fear scepticism, Bayle replies, if it alone best assures you the retention of your choicest treasures of religion? Scepticism, he read in La Mothe le Vayer, is of all philosophies the one "least contrary to Christianity, and the one that can most submissively receive the mysteries of our religion." [14] But if reliance on faith and the Bible alone justifies the Christian's acceptance of the orthodox doctrine of evil, what in turn justifies this reliance in preference to the heathen's reliance on his own Scriptures? How is one to justify his preference for one religion over another? Shall we judge them by their fruits? But if by fruits we mean superior virtues, the manifest nobility of many pagans and atheists will embarrass us seriously. Indeed during the religious wars in France the unusual mánifestations of virtue and the strict morality of a man roused suspicions regarding his orthodoxy.[15] The truths of religion are not to be proved by appeal to the virtue of the believer any more than by sound arguments.

This tenacity of faith is nowise to be confused with aggressive dogmatism. Such faith is not to be constrained, and Bayle's championship of tolerance is one of the noblest features of his work. But what are we to think of this surrender of reason on the field of battle and this retirement within the citadel of unreasoning faith? Is it whole-hearted mysticism, or reluctant scepticism, or irony tragic or malicious? Was Bayle's faith only assumed, or self-imposed, a pious act of self-resignation? We who inherit the spirit of criticism which Bayle himself helped to vindicate in modern thought, we who follow him marshalling his heretics' arguments against orthodox doctrine, find it hard to conceive how he could, on top of all his arguments, have sincerely "taken up the shield of faith." So accustomed we are to seeing Voltaire's tongue in his cheek that we seem to notice a sarcastic tongue in Bayle's cheek also. And when we think of Bayle's long controversies with unlovely advocates for God, we may well understand his occasional deliberate satire. One example must suffice: Bayle is 'explaining' at the end of his *Dictionary* his frequent reference to the virtues of pagans and atheists. He argues that many motives lead men to virtue, of which belief in God is not the strongest or the most usual. After thirteen paragraphs of stimulating discussion, Bayle points out in the fourteenth that, on good theological ground, one could say "that if there are people whom God does not abandon to the point of letting them sink down to Epicureanism or atheism, it is principally those fierce souls whose cruelty, audacity, avarice, fury, or ambition might well ruin a great country. Can we not say on the other hand that if God abandons certain people so as to permit them to doubt his existence or his providence, it is mainly persons whose temperament, education, lively ideas of virtue, love of fine glory, and keen sense of dishonor serve to curb them and keep them in the path of duty." [16]

But there is deeper irony in Bayle. Lacking as it is in that Pascalian intensity which cuts right through the heart, Bayle's thought is yet involved in irony, tragic and without sneer, a self-humiliation of the inquiring mind and the last arrow of debased reason. It is the irony of Pascal's "*Cela vous abêtira.*" So Feuerbach writes: "The contradiction of faith and reason in Bayle has a *tragic significance*. . . . He really believed, but he believed in contradiction with himself, with his nature, and with his mind." [17] Piously disdaining to accept what reason seemed to warrant, and rationally humiliated in cherishing what ran counter to good logic, Bayle's spirit was racked by an antinomy which was spread through all his writings. Was his tragedy perhaps the tragedy of Protestantism, which would go a way, but not the whole way, with reason? The last word which Bayle's dying hand wrote was "*Vérité*—Truth."

Bayle advocated scepticism as an inducement to unquestioning faith, but the effect of his writings was greatly to increase scepticism *about* religion. The eighteenth century was a century of reason and proof and evidence, and Bayle proved a disintegrator of belief. How strong a factor for infidelity this professed champion of faith was, may be judged from the reaction and rebound that he aroused quite as much as by the undoubted influence of Bayle on the avowed freethinkers of the next generation. It was an age committed to proven truth and, if the determined unbelievers flaunted Bayle's "Not proven," those within the besieged citadel of faith discounted his counsel and insisted on making a sortie on the battleground of reasoned argument. Chief of these champions of pious reason was Gottfried Leibniz.

II

Bayle's dilemmas shook orthodox assurance; even those who did not perceive the blighting irony of his proffered consolation in faith were disconcerted by his sceptical dialectic. Queen Sophie Charlotte of Prussia, sore perplexed, sought the wise counsel of Leibniz, and it was to the gentle solicitations of this *Princesse Divine* and to Leibniz's daily conversations with her, particularly during the summer of 1708, that we owe the *Theodicée*. Against Bayle, Leibniz undertakes "to demonstrate the agreement of faith with reason." [18] Against Bayle he champions God's goodness and man's freedom and would justify the presence of evil in this best of all possible worlds.

Leibniz treats Bayle's refuge-in-faith as the refuge of desperation. He refuses to allow the instability of reason in theology, and his *Theodicée*, as Cassirer observes, is really a *Logodicée:* [19] no anti-rational faith is valid. But, if theology is to be established on a rational basis, the logical consistency of its fundamental ideas must be vindicated. How is human freedom compatible with God's prevision of our acts and with God's infinite wisdom? How is the idea of all-perfect creative Omnipotence to be reconciled with a mechanistic cosmology and with the idea of a created world which includes evil? How are we to evade the perils of Manichean dualism? Can good and evil have the same ultimate source and ground? Leibniz's entire enterprise is one of reconciliation, and his work is a controversial writing designed to overcome, explain away, or tone down Bayle's supposedly insuperable difficulties.[20]

God's foreknowledge, the decrees of Divine Providence, the causal determination of every event, "the very nature of truth, which is determined in the statements that can be made about future events:" [21] all seem to militate against human freedom. To meet these objections, Leibniz insists on the distinction between his two fundamental principles: the law of contradiction and the law of sufficient reason. The former involves geometrical, the latter hypothetical necessity. The former precludes, the latter allows of contingency, and it is the latter, not the former sort of necessity which is implied in divine prevision of our acts.

We err if we confuse causal with geometrical necessity: the connection of two events as cause and effect with the relation of a theorem to the definitions and axioms from which it proceeds and to the corollaries which it involves. "There is, in the chain of facts in nature, something malleable, which the chain of mathematical truths does not afford: the former may always have been other than it is, which is wholly inadmissible in the case of the latter." [22] Not necessity but contingency is the law of nature, and causality is grounded and completed in finality. This serious teleological revision to which Leibniz subjects the Cartesian mechanistic cosmology recalls the Platonic Socrates' experience with the philosophy of Anaxagoras recorded in the *Phaedo*, which Leibniz translated. Just as the continued presence of Socrates in his prison-cell was due not only to his bones and muscles and to the rest of his mechanical equipment, but above all and fundamentally to his resolution not to defy the verdict of the Athenian court by running away, so the whole world-process is to be explained mainly by the operation of final causes: the law of the best is supreme in nature; the nisus towards perfection is the *raison d'être* of things in the cosmos.

In this teleologically conceived contingent world, freedom seems to be a function of individuality and intelligence. "Every soul is a world by itself, independent of everything except God." This presumably means that the unique self-expression of each monad is conditioned only by its own characteristic relation to the universe: "That is to say," Leibniz goes on, "each substance expresses the whole sequence of the universe according to the view or relation that is appropriate to it." This spontaneity is intelligent in human souls, thus constituting us free beings. The more clearly and perfectly we understand ourselves and our actions, the freer we are. Perfect freedom would characterize an act determined by infinite wisdom to the best possible end, and accordingly the freest of beings is God.[23]

There can be no question here of our freedom of indifference: each soul-monad expresses its own unique character. I am thus, to be sure, 'responsible' for my acts, since I alone could be their unique author, but praise or blame could attach to anyone for acting as he does only if we take Leibniz's monadism more consistently than he takes it, and pushing its pluralistic implications to their logical conclusion, land in atheism.[24] In that case what meaning could 'praise' and 'blame' have? If, however, we adhere with Leibniz to the universal harmony of the individual monads, which constitutes them a cosmos, and think of God as the monad of monads,[25] or as the supreme reality of which the monads are all unique individual expressions or foci, then, if there is aught blameworthy in the world, whose can the blame be but God's?

This challenge Leibniz can meet with the obvious retort that, since God is infinite perfection, all that is blameworthy or evil must necessarily be contrary to his nature. Grant that evil is not contrary but rather appropriate to your nature or mine, are we *to blame* for thus differing from God? Leibniz, like St. Augustine, seems to have designed his idea of human freedom so as to transfer the guilt of evil from God to man. But ultimately "only that can have guilt and responsibility which creatively brings forth something new; that is to say, in this system only God." [26] So God, were he evil, would be blamable for it, but being perfect good, is only to be lauded; we, however, can only be characterized as thus and so, good or evil, but, strictly speaking, deserve neither praise nor blame. Perfect good is in God and our good is in our small sharing in the divine perfection. Our 'evil' then is in our falling short of being divine, but since not-being-God is essential to our being what we are, or to our free self-understanding expression of our unique individuality, what room can there be for blame or indeed what positive meaning could we attach to evil? We are thus confronted with the whole problem of the nature of evil. Leibniz follows a difficult course: he must not excogitate evil out of existence and he must by all means hold omnipotent God blameless for it. This is an enterprise which taxed St. Augustine's genius, and it taxes the genius of Leibniz.

"If God exists, whence evil? If he does not exist, whence good? The ancients attributed the cause of evil to matter, which they believed to be uncreated and independent of God; but we who derive all being from God, where shall we find the source of evil? The answer is, that it should be sought in the ideal Nature of the creature, in so far as this Nature is comprehended in the eternal truths which are in the understanding of God, independently of his will."[27] The last clause is the important one: as in the entire *Theodicée*, so here Leibniz's main endeavor is to reconcile the various attributes of divinity in conformity with those of nature and human nature. Evil cannot be wholly independent of God, but God's infinite goodness would remain untarnished provided the evil in creation did not proceed from God's will, even though it was comprehended by his understanding. Perfect Deity must will the creation of the best of all possible worlds, but perfect understanding must comprehend that this best of all possible worlds is bound to include evil.

The truth of the foregoing Leibniz would exhibit by examining the nature of evil. This, according to him is threefold: metaphysical evil is the imperfection characteristic of all finite being; physical evil is suffering; moral evil is sin. Leibniz is inclined to tone down suffering and to treat it as the outward result of sin. Both suffering and sin are ultimately referred by him to finite imperfection, and so evil in the last paragraph turns out to be but finitude. This settlement of the problem seeks escape from pessimism by explaining away the moral aspect of evil. This is apparent also in Leibniz's reluctance to recognize moral evil as ultimately positive. Condemnation of God's will is thus precluded, but we could scarcely call this view optimistic, for condemnation is here precluded by a viewpoint that precludes the recognition of all moral value. The wretch tormented by the fear that his business has gone bankrupt is here consoled by the reassurance that in fact he has had no business whatever.

This summary statement of Leibniz's procedure we should now make somewhat clearer. Keenly aware though he is of the difficulty of the problem of evil, Leibniz yet warns us against the tendency to exaggerate the evils in life. Vice and suffering are in the world, yet assuredly the pleasures in life exceed the pains, and with regard to virtue and vice the rule is rather mediocrity than iniquity. "There is incomparably more good than evil in mankind, just as there are incomparably more homes than prisons." If, resisting the melancholic tendency to distort the facts of life, we see them in their proper perspective, then evil is disclosed as the striking and deplorable exception. "I am not astonished that men are sometimes sick, but . . . I am astonished that they are sick so occasionally, and that they are not always ill." [28]

Such as it is, physical suffering is mainly a natural consequence of moral evil or sin: "Sins must bear their penalty with them through the order of nature." [29] Indeed pain is conceived by Leibniz as a feeling of a checked or unattained perfection: "I believe," he writes in the *Nouveaux Essais*, "that at bottom *pleasure* is a feeling of perfection and *pain* a feeling of imperfection, provided it be marked enough to make us capable of perceiving it." [30] Physical evil, immediately resulting for the most part from moral evil, is ultimately disclosed as a sense of imperfection or metaphysical evil.

Leibniz's treatment of moral evil or sin is very perplexing. Considering the pronounced Christian motivation of his writing, he seems bound not to reason sin out of existence; on the other hand how can he, in a Christian theodicy, reduce moral evil to metaphysical evil, treat sin as merely negative, as the imperfection of finitude? This is perhaps Leibniz's hardest dilemma: either sin is merely negative, imperfection, or it is positive, anti-perfection. If the former, no condemnation can arise at all; if the latter, then how are heaven and hell admissible, for who can be ultimately to blame for sin but God, the author of the agents of sinful acts?

Confronted with a similar perplexity, Bayle had been inclined to seek refuge in dualism, much as he professed his horror of the monstrous doctrine. The Zoroastrian-Manichean solution of the problem of evil repelled Leibniz as much as it had repelled St. Augustine, but there is a duality of principle in the divine nature even for Leibniz: God is all-creative, "his power tends to Being. . . . His will tends to good," but "his wisdom tends to the true." [31] Being perfect, his will necessarily wills the good, the characteristic good under all circumstances. The characteristic good under the circumstances of finite existence is imperfect good. God's will is here coöperant with his understanding, which comprehends and is in accord with the eternal truths of all nature, which are "more inviolable than the Styx." God can no more have made finite existence without imperfection than he could have made a four-angled triangle. Finitude and unmixed perfection are incompatible; a finite world without evil is thus inconceivable: to God's perfect understanding it is self-contradictory and thus inadmissible. "There are truly two principles, but they are both in God, to wit his *Understanding* and his *Will.* The Understanding furnishes the principle of evil, without being sullied or evil thereby; it represents natures as they are in the eternal verities; it comprehends the reason for permitting evil; but the will only tends to good. Let us add a third principle, that is God's Power: it precedes even the Understanding and the Will; but it acts as the former indicates and as the latter demands." [32]

Physical evil and moral evil are thus instances of metaphysical evil, the essential imperfection of all finite existence. "The ultimate origin of evil must not be sought in the divine will, but in the original imperfection of creatures, which is contained ideally in the eternal truths constituting the internal object of the divine intellect, so that evil could not be excluded from the best possible system of things." [33] God does not will sin and suffering directly; they are involved as inevitable features of any created world, and of all possible worlds the one created by God, Leibniz informs us, is necessarily the best. To reconcile here God's will with his understanding, Leibniz makes use of the distinction between God's antecedent and his consequent will. "God wills antecedently the good, and consequently the best." [34]

But there is grave danger here that, in his optimism, the theologian is betraying the moralist. If all 'evil' is in the end explained as really imperfection, finitude, what distinct meaning can then attach to the term 'good'? Does it not also need quotation marks? Is not 'goodness' then simply metaphysical perfection? To characterize Perfect Deity as *good* would then be a tautology rather than a necessary or axiomatic truth. If goodness means metaphysical perfection, infinitude of attributes, it is only a superfluous and indeed a confusing term. But if we use it in a moral sense, then metaphysical perfection, boundless maximum of reality, need not be exclusively good. As Bertrand Russell points out, "perfection understood in this sense, though it does appear to involve God's infinite goodness, involves equally, except on a purely privative view of evil, his infinite badness." [35] This is perhaps the reason why Leibniz is apt to treat evil as negative, the *privatio boni* of finitude. "God is infinite, and the devil is limited." [36] But this is another way of abandoning the moral meaning of evil by reducing it to imperfection, the limitation of finitude. Thus God's vindication has been accomplished, but the resulting laudation has lost the distinctively moral note, and the 'best' of all possible worlds is not really either good or evil: it is simply finite. To be sure, even Leibniz did not resist the tendency which we observe in some of his followers, to exploit his optimism as if he had established it in a moral sense. In stricter logic, however, Leibniz's teleology and theology in the end preclude the real recognition of genuine moral values. The advantage of Leibniz's placid rationalism over the sceptical mazes of Bayle or over the tragedy of Pascal's defiant faith is a decidedly dubious advantage, for the placidity has been purchased too dearly. Leibniz has paid for his theodicy with his ethics.

III

Archbishop William King's *Essay on the Origin of Evil* may move the author of the *Theodicée* to write Critical Remarks, but the main purpose of both is the same: Assuming "the Government of an infinitely powerful and benevolent Author of Nature," to answer the question, Whence come Evils? in conformity with the assumption.[37] Ever since the days of Epicurus and Lucretius, men's observation of defects in nature has been apt to lead them to atheism. The Dublin archbishop undertakes to reëstablish the bulwarks of orthodoxy, if possible without appealing to revelation. King is archiepiscopally prevented from toning down the veils in this world in the manner of Leibniz; ecclesiastic theodicy must always lag behind the secular in its whitewashing of the cosmos. Though the archbishop may observe that there is "much more Good than Evil in Nature," [38] yet we know that this cannot be so as far as human life is concerned; the Christian agent of salvation is bound in the end to emphasize man's sinful state and to give us a subsection "Concerning the Scarcity of Happy Persons, and the General Corruption of Mankind." But he is comforted in the end by the consideration that our earth is so small a part of the whole system of the universe (How next to nothing!) that even if it were all stained with corruption, clouded and benighted with darkness and vice, yet it would be but as a very small spot in a beautiful body, not lessening but increasing the comeliness of the whole. We do not know that this is not the case, and so the learned Archbishop counsels us not to be depressed by the only evidence which we have. "The whole Work of God may be bright and beautiful, tho' that Point which constitutes our World seem by itself rude and unadorn'd." [39] It may be bright and beautiful; the Archbishop, unable to show that it is, undertakes to demonstrate that it must be.

The demonstration proceeds along fairly familiar lines. King's 'Seventhly' in his analysis of the First Cause establishes God's infinite power and goodness, and thus, since no doubt is admissible of God's attaining his ends, "the World is as well as it could be made." Is this best of all possible worlds good without qualification? King notices that God's goodness is limited by his wisdom and by his power, all three being infinite, and would be nowise jeopardized if the world contained only the least evil possible in a created world. Does King prove this last, or does he only variously assert it? The concluding paragraph of his second chapter exhibits the predestined character of his reasoning. He certainly knows what he wants: "If we can point out a method of reconciling these Things with the Government of an absolutely perfect Agent, and make them not only consistent with Infinite Wisdom, Goodness, and Power, but necessarily resulting from them . . . then we may be supposed to have at last discover'd the true Origin of Evils, and answer'd all the Difficulties and Objections that are brought on this Head, against the Goodness, Wisdom, Power, and Unity of God. Let us try therefore what can be done in each kind of Evil. . . ." [40]

He tries well. Of evils, like Leibniz, he recognizes three kinds: imperfection, natural evil, and moral evil. All three kinds are explained, and their presence justified without discredit to God, first by appealing to the observation that absolute perfection can characterize only a self-existent Being and is thus peculiar to God, and that therefore all that is created contains necessarily imperfection; secondly, by insisting that this world contains the minimum possible of imperfection or evil, since God's infinite goodness, wisdom, and power could only create the best possible world or rather the least imperfect. King meets his objectors with the refrain: "If that had been best God would undoubtedly have done it." [41]

The basis of King's optimistic assurance, aside from his *a priori* reliance on God, as exhibited above, is in the appeal to the Whole, to the Entire System. Natural evils are not necessarily punishments for sin: rather should we say that sins are evil because we disapprove of them as leading to natural evils. Some natural evils are consequences of and punishments for sins, but others are inherent in the very character of created, that is, of imperfect existence; yet, while in relation to particular human purposes or taken by themselves, they may appear as evil, in relation to the whole they must be admitted, since without them a greater evil would arise. We should remember that everything in nature has its place, nor is it meant merely for man's pleasure. A viper is a viper and could not be a viper without its venom any more than a knife could be a knife without its cutting edge; yet nature is harmonious withal, and we should consider that vipers "gather the poison out of the earth." Thus King, while not relying on an anthropocentric teleology, yet would not quite dismiss it.[42]

With regard to moral evils, or sins, King seeks refuge in free will, in a theory which is decidedly, but not consistently

Scotist. God's will is determined by nothing outside of him and it is the ultimate cause of good: things are not chosen because they are good, but good because chosen. God's choice of anything constitutes it thereby good, and makes goods agreeable to one another. This last, which is King's real criterion of goodness, is made the consequence of the divine election. In this principle, of constituting acts and things good by willing them, we men share with God, as is evidenced by our moral conscience.[43] But, if this be so, how are sins, or undue elections, to be explained, and how are they consistent with God's infinite power and goodness? King vindicates God by informing us that had God omitted to create free agents, or intervened to compel their choices, or else translated man to a medium in which he would not be tempted to choose amiss, in any of these three cases graver imperfections would have resulted than now obtain. So in every case God has chosen the lesser of evils.

Thus convinced that this world *must be* the best possible, or the least imperfect, Archbishop King yet feels, in a lay moment, the difficulties of his problem; at least there are required in its investigation "some things which are too subtle for all to comprehend."[44] Towards the close of his book, we find the thought that evils necessarily arise "from a competition or . . . a *Conflict of two Infinites, i.e.*, Omnipotence and Goodness. . . . These Attributes amicably conspire together, and yet restrain and limit each other. There is a kind of Struggle and Opposition between them, whereof the Evils in Nature bear the Shadow and Resemblance. Here, then, and no where else, may we find the Primary and most certain Rise and origin of Evils."[45] This is scarcely a surrender to Manicheanism, but it suggests an idea, better thought of by Leibniz, of a duality of character in God to which even ostensibly orthodox theology was inclined to appeal in explaining and justifying the presence of evil.

CHAPTER V

EIGHTEENTH CENTURY OPTIMISM

I

In 1709, one year before the publication of the *Theodicée*, the main principles of Leibniz's optimism had been anticipated by Shaftesbury's work, *The Moralists: A Philosophical Rhapsody*. To treat Leibniz as a plagiarist would mean to ignore essential differences in treatment and execution of the two plans and to overemphasize the general agreement in teleology and in optimistic attitude as well as in the appeal to the idea of harmony. Leibniz, to be sure, avows that, had he seen Shaftesbury's work before writing his own, he would have quoted at length from it, as it contained almost his entire *Theodicy*, but more agreeably turned.[1]

Thomas Hobbes, setting out from naturalistic premises and pursuing a rigorous logic, had portrayed human life in terms of the mechanics of insatiate desire. Man originally and in the state of nature is an anarchic individual of unlimited greed, and therefore of negligible security because of universal conflict with his rivals. Good, evil, justice have no meaning for him, since he has no standards or laws, nor can have them until, led by selfish regard for security, he curbs himself by entering into the social pact which makes Leviathan his absolute lord and legislator. This doctrine shocked Britain, made it the first business of every philosopher to square himself with Hobbes, and thus served to initiate systematic British ethics. It is against Hobbes' portrayal of human nature that Shaftesbury aims in his *Inquiry concerning Virtue or Merit*.

9

Human conduct is not adequately described in terms of selfishness and anarchic individualism. Gregariousness, emulation, a lively regard for the good will of others, active benevolence are as natural to man as insatiate greed. Benevolence is as normal as egoism, and moral progress consists in the advance from 'the private self-affections' to 'the natural, kindly, or generous affections.' It is precisely by the cultivation of benevolence that one gains increasingly the chief and the most certain means of happiness in life; while undue selfishness breeds unhappiness, and unnatural affections, running counter both to public and to private interest, lead to extreme misery. Happiness as well as virtue lies in the perfection of man's normal benevolence. Of the sanctions of morality, Shaftesbury emphasizes first the moral sense and next the loving and reverent regard for God's will.

This vindication of human nature from the calumnies of Hobbes reflects a complacent and rhapsodic view of life, keen to perceive light and color, but rather insensitive to the dull and dark areas. Shaftesbury's theodicy is an appeal from the particular evils besetting our life in detail to the system and harmony of the whole. We cannot understand the individual or the particular situations unless we see their relation to the whole of which they are parts. If we follow the right path we shall be led from system to system, in ever-expanding comprehension, until we come to see everything in relation to the All, the Universe, and thus perceived, it is perceived as good.[2] This enjoyable pursuit of the ever-larger harmony seems to have just suited Shaftesbury's temperament, and his philosophy is intended as the expression of that genteel good-breeding and refined taste which is manifest in the active perception of the Universal Harmony and the rhapsodic response to it.

The fuller our understanding of anything in its relation to its appropriate system, the more adequate our perception that it is as it should be. So strongly is Shaftesbury impressed by the positive instances supporting this contention that where the facts seem to point otherwise, he readily takes refuge in finite ignorance. "In an infinity of things, mutually relative, a mind which sees not infinitely can see nothing fully, and must therefore frequently see that as imperfect which in itself is really perfect." [3] "Seeing fully" means to Shaftesbury seeing optimistically: to know the world perfectly is presumably to know it perfect; to his ears, discord is but incompletely perceived harmony. It does not occur to him that the harmonies we value may therefore, be, for all we know, only conventional or deceptive incidents in a vaster discord and ultimate perversity.

Shaftesbury does not deduce the perfection of the world from the perfection of the Creator, but would establish his optimism on a direct report of the facts of existence and on inferences from the actually observable order and harmony of the cosmos. His 'theodicy' is thus not necessarily theistic; the idea of God is for Shaftesbury a focus of religious devotion and aesthetic exaltation rather than a principle of cosmological explanation. Shaftesbury does not argue that God, being perfect, necessarily created a world with the least imperfection that finitude allows. In his view the world is not the best possible, but is simply perfect. Things are as they ought to be conformably to the system of the whole of which in the last analysis they are all parts. "When (nature) seems most ignorant or perverse in her productions, I assert her even then as wise and provident as in her goodliest works. . . . 'Tis good which is predominant; and every corruptible and mortal nature by its mortality and corruption yields only to some better, and all in common to that best and highest nature, which is incorruptible and immortal." To doubt this smooth-working teleology in the Whole, in view of the "constant and unerring" order and harmony we observe in the part, seems irrational to Shaftesbury. All is therefore ultimately as it is for the good of all: "And what is for the good of all in general, is just and good."[4] If our present life's experience does not assure us completely of this truth, the appeal to the life hereafter is bound to dispel the last doubt.[5] Therefore we "ought to rest satisfied, . . . and not only so, but be pleased and rejoice at what happens, knowing whence it comes, and to what perfection it contributes."[6] Indeed from the assumption that all things are as they are because of their relation to the whole, and the admission that the whole can conceivably exclude all evil whatever, Shaftesbury concludes that it actually does exclude it. Thus the universe itself contains no real or ultimate evil.[7]

The insistent optimism of this benevolent invalid was perhaps not quite convincing, but as a reaction against Hobbism and cynicism, his optimism proved widely influential. Leslie Stephen notes Shaftesbury's warm reception "in Germany, where sentimentalism is more congenial to the national temperament";[8] but Montesquieu's praise of Shaftesbury is no less extravagant than Herder's. In Britain his influence, direct through Hutcheson to Adam Smith, spreads out in other directions also, cultivating cosmic affability and assurance.

The placid optimism of Francis Hutcheson, while confident that God is the author of a universe perfect and harmonious throughout, rests more explicitly on the benignant Providence directing the course of human life. Our Heavenly Father orders all things for our greatest good, blessing and rewarding or kindly admonishing or exhorting us as we may need it. Notwithstanding all misfortune or suffering which may beset us, experience, in the view of this disciple of Shaftesbury, warrants a firm persuasion that God permits "no further evil than what the most perfect constitution requires or necessarily brings along with it."[9]

This general docility is characteristic also of Adam Smith,

who succeeded Hutcheson as Professor of Moral Philosophy at Glasgow. God being perfect in power, goodness, and wisdom, there is always bound to obtain in the world "the greatest possible quantity of happiness." [10] And he counsels moderation of practical demands in keeping with his inexacting logic and easy-going observation of life's actualities. "What can be added to the happiness of the man who is in health, who is out of debt, and has a clear conscience?" [11] So Pope lisped:

> Reason's whole pleasure, all the joys of sense
> Lie in three words: health, peace, and competence.

II

To the Christian mind of Bishop Butler, the actuality of sin and suffering in the best of all possible worlds did not admit of doubt. If however sin and suffering could be related as cause and effect, our confidence in the rule of Divine Providence would remain unimpaired. The more ultimate problem raised by the presence of the cause in this proposed relation does not seem to have disturbed Butler unduly. The sufferings in this world would not shake his confidence in the divine government of the world provided only that they are not undeserved. However lax in his metaphysical demands, Butler is strict and clear enough on the ethical-juridical requirements of the situation. "Moral government consists, not barely in rewarding and punishing men for their actions, . . . but in rewarding the righteous and punishing the wicked . . . in an exact proportion to their personal merits and demerits." [12] Butler has no illusions on this score: no such complete concurrence of fortune and merit can be held to obtain in the world of our experience. But he maintains that there is sufficient indication of a tendency towards such concurrence to justify a presumption in favor of Divine Providence, and then proceeds to extract strength from weakness: the indication is insufficient and therefore points necessarily to a future life for its completion.

Regarding all this, absolute certainty neither obtains nor is demanded; in theology as in science we live on probabilities, and Butler is content if his approximations to truth are no more remote than those of the scientist. Indubitable knowledge is out of the question, but in our groping we are not entirely without guidance. Butler's teleology, conceiving of human life as under divine government and of happiness and misery as normally consequent on virtue and vice, is "a moderately optimistic view of the distribution of happiness and misery in human life: optimistic enough to justify the venture of faith in the morality of the world-order, and yet sufficiently moderate to recognize the incomplete attainment of tendencies and consequences of which it observes the beginnings in this life, and so to demand, for the full fruition and perfection of the moral order, a future life for man." [13]

III

David Hartley's reluctance to subscribe to all the Thirty-Nine Articles necessitated a change in his choice of a career. But, if the vicar's son turned to medicine as a life-calling, his interests and his writings ever revealed a scientist doubled with a moral philosopher. John Locke and Gay suggested to him his association theory; from Newton he learned to think of motion as the basis of sensation. Combining the two lines of thought, Hartley advanced a doctrine of bodily and mental process which is clearly materialistic in implication notwithstanding his own professed ardor for the immateriality of the soul.[14] Sensations have their occasion in cerebro-neural vibrations; persisting simple ideas, in 'vibratiuncles' or diminutive vibrations, the repeated association of two sensations resulting in the excitation of the simple idea of one in the presence of the other. The mechanistic basis of this theory is resisted in the interests of morals and piety, and it is in his estimate of man and God that Hartley invites our attention. His loyalty to the idea of God's infinite benevolence leads him, in his account of human weal and woe, to an amazingly reckless optimism.

The doctrine of vibrations, according to Hartley, seems to require that we regard pain, not as the opposite of pleasure, but as "pleasure itself carried beyond a due limit." Contrariwise, "some painful sensations, as they decrease by time, or the removal of the cause, pass into positive local pleasure." Pleasure and pain, are thus closely allied. Is the mixture of the two which we experience a pleasant or an unpleasant one? Hartley defends the sanguine view. The very mixture of pain in our normally pleasurable experience serves to enhance the pleasure. The "nascent ideas of fear and horror" which the view of a precipice or a cataract rouses in us heighten our pleasure in the spectacle. Discords in music give a relish and keep the sweet harmonies from cloying; a certain degree of obscurity in poetry has a similar effect; children's first laugh is a nascent cry from fear, "stopped of a sudden"; all our worries and perplexities redound to our subsequent contentment.[15]

Hartley regards man's happiness as assured by the very constitution of nature. Of the seven primary colors, he observes, green is the middle one and the most agreeable to the eye, and (or should we say, and *therefore*) the general color of plants, of external nature is green. Hartley's arguments for the infinite benevolence of God do not suggest the impression of having been required to convince their author. Between two alternatives he does not recognize a third: God is either infinitely benevolent or infinitely malevolent. The latter alternative could scarcely be entertained by a man who regards the idea of a balance of misery over happiness in human life as inconceivable. Never doubting that human life is on the whole a happy one, Hartley is rather concerned to banish pain altogether in the last paragraph, so zealous is he for the defense of God's exalted benevolence. In his 'thirteenthly' on this high topic, he reduces the optimist's alternatives to a list of five, making

1. Each individual infinitely happy always. Or
2. Each individual always finitely happy, without any mixture of misery, and infinitely so in its progress through infinite time. Or
3. Each individual infinitely happy, upon the balance, in its progress through infinite time, but with a mixture of misery. Or
4. Each individual finitely happy in the course of its existence, whatever that be, but with a mixture of misery as before; and the universe infinitely happy upon the balance. Or
5. Some individuals happy and some miserable upon the balance, finitely or infinitely, and yet so that there shall be an infinite overplus of happiness in the universe.[16]

The fifth alternative, many of us fear, is the best we can expect, with serious doubt regarding the last clause; and most of us should thank our lucky stars if the fourth were assured to us; but nothing less than the third would satisfy David Hartley. Happiness in man's life, he observes, is mixed with misery, but the mixture is not permanent; pain is reclaimed by pleasure, and the ultimate state is joy unalloyed. For the accomplishment of this happy transmutation, Hartley proposes a law which he derives from his principle of association. The tendency of this law, he thinks, "is to convert a composite state of pleasure and pain, in which one of the ingredients is inferior to the other, into a pure state consisting of the predominating element, and equal in intensity to the difference between the two original factors." Here is hedonistic alchemy: the philosopher's stone being a bar of pleasure-gold greater than the iron-woe which is to be transmuted. While our pains in general seem to be more intense than our pleasures, there are not, on Hartley's reckoning, as many of them, so, "after the destruction of the pains by the opposite and equal pleasures," the remainder will be pure pleasure. Thus we are told "association . . . has a tendency to reduce the state of those who have eaten of the tree of knowledge of good and evil, back again to a paradisiacal one." Because of this "infinite prepollence of happiness over misery," we may advance from the third alternative variety of optimism in Hartley's list to the second. Nor need we stop short of the very first. In the eyes of God, seeing past, present, and future in one glance, the first three propositions are equivalent. Thus, Hartley would conclude, though in our imperfect range of vision happiness seems mixed with misery, yet "all difficulties relating to the divine attributes will be taken away; God will be infinitely powerful, knowing, and good, in the most absolute sense, if we consider things as they appear to him." The truth of the matter would then be that "all individuals are actually and always infinitely happy." [17]

Leslie Stephen calls this "optimism run mad." [18] However, Hartley warns us, while our wish for the third supposition, and its convertibility into the second and the first seem to be some presumption in its favor, yet we cannot determine absolutely for it as against the fourth and fifth. The chapter on God's infinite benevolence is the work of a physician who was also engaged in the composition of prayers.

In the edition of the *Observations on Man* (1791) prepared by Hartley's son, the third volume contains notes and additions by Hermann Pistorius, Rector of Poseritz in the Island of Rügen. The good pastor regards pure happiness as inconceivable, for to find pleasure in enjoyment man requires desire, and "in desiring and needing, he must find pain and disquietude:" a circumstance which Schopenhauer was to observe and exploit in an altogether different manner. Pleasure, we are here told, demands comparison with pain. A state of incessantly increasing pleasure (with correspondingly decreasing pain) is thus more truly happy than "a pure, unalterable, and on that account limited happiness." While, therefore, Pistorius does not consider man's state to be one of "absolutely metaphysically infinite happiness," this being the prerogative of God, he regards it as perpetually increasing, and ever capable of further enhancement. It is comfort enough.[19]

IV

A country gentleman with abundant leisure and convinced that an independent fortune is simply a God-given opportunity freely to select one's own work, Abraham Tucker assumes in his reader a patience as unlimited as his own leisure. *The Light of Nature Pursued*—through seven long volumes—is a work of unparalleled wordiness and distention, but for all that exhibits critical power, a felicity for apt illustration, an occasional directness of attack, and an indefatigable zeal. It should not be forgotten that the last volumes of the work were written after Tucker had lost his sight, with a writing device contrived by himself.

This inquiring man of leisure perceives evils enough in the world, but is assured none the less that the net balance is on the side of good, although he finds "the art of bookkeeping in the commerce of pleasure" very hard to attain. But that evil should exist at all, his Christian mind regards as a difficult problem. The Divine Creator of all, whatever else he is, must be infinitely good. "Infinite power and wisdom avail us nothing of themselves. . . . The contemplation of omnipotence, omnipresence, and omniscience, without goodness, has most of anything else driven men into atheism. . . ." Now if the evils in this world could not be prevented, "where was the almighty power of God? if he knew how not to prevent them, where was his wisdom? if he could, and might have prevented them, but would not, where was his goodness?" Tucker rejects several of the traditional solutions. To refer the evil in the world to the material element in it indicates perhaps the channel of evil but not its fountain-head. To ascribe evil to free will only shifts the problem one step. To reduce evil to the inevitable imperfection of the finite requires that we consider whether it "cost omnipotence more trouble to make an angel than an oyster." To take refuge in rhetoric and ask: Can't God do as he pleases, and do we deserve a better world than we do get, is to miss the point entirely, which is "not what the clay has a right to expect, but what we conceive it likely that a beneficient potter would do." Nor may we seek an escape in dualism, for even on a Zoroastrian basis "the good principle must have furnished his antagonist with fitting subjects to wreak his malice upon, and concurred in the production of evil, by giving his creatures a capacity of suffering by it." [20]

Tucker would solve his problem by saying that infinite goodness, according to our comprehension (*the prospect* of satisfaction in the welfare of others) is incompatible with the infinite (inexhaustible) power of God who is completely happy in himself. So our problem itself is due to our lack of comprehension. That God is good Tucker cannot doubt and assures us that "were our vision a little enlarged we might perceive every dark place surrounded with a splendor of light." Assume God's perfect goodness and equity (and God to Tucker can be either infinitely good or infinitely malicious), then "since . . . none of us have anything besides what we received from the divine bounty, and that bounty flows alike upon all, it follows unavoidably that there must be an exact equality of fortune among us, and the value of each person's existence, computed throughout the whole extent of his Being, precisely the same." Long catalogues and eloquent accounts of the ills with which our lives are beset only serve to show Abraham Tucker "how great a weight and variety of evils are consistent with infinite goodness: and . . . how strong must be that necessity which could introduce them into a plan contrived in mercy and loving kindness." [21]

Perhaps all our troubles and tribulations serve to complete the happiness of certain invisible beings! This is a fancy in which Tucker seeks refuge and peace, a fancy in speculation which he matches with one in calculation: though the evils in this world seem dire and many, yet "our whole amount of suffering may be equivalent to 'a minute of pain once in every twenty-two years:'" [22] whatever that may mean,—a gem of confirmed optimism, which may serve to temper our harsh judgment of pessimistic statistics.

V

Bolingbroke brought to philosophical discussion the intemperate partisanship and the haranguing style of a political pamphleteer. He declaims instead of reasoning and replaces refutation by the most scurrilous railing in which he consigns the world's greatest minds to Bedlam. His is not the cold light of reason, but rather the politician's fire with abundance of heat and volumes (five of them) of smoke. Even after discounting his violent manner, the matter and substance of his philosophical essays are disappointingly confused and flimsy. One cannot help recalling Burke's question, "Who now reads Bolingbroke? Who ever read him through?" If he is read at all, it is as a vigorous, though blustering, assailant of rationalistic orthodoxy and a curiously sceptical champion of deistic optimism, and is read largely for the sake of others, as a preface to Pope and a footnote to Voltaire.

Bolingbroke professes to combat, in the name of 'theism,' both atheism and orthodoxy, but his chief object of attack is the theologian. Against the atheist he maintains God's existence on teleological grounds, but he denounces the orthodox divine's account of God and of the world. If God is almighty and infinitely perfect, how dare you decry God's creation? If God is perfect, so is his work: "Everything, which God has done, is for that very reason right." [23] This is to be the thesis of Pope's poetic theodicy. The perfection of God, which is the conclusion of a teleological argument, is for Bolingbroke the premise of an optimistic conclusion: the heavens declare the glory of God, and God's heavens are bound to be bright and clear. But actually they seem to be cloudy. This need not disturb our theodicy if we are only careful to avoid anthropomorphism. Bolingbroke carries on tireless polemic against Clarke and other theologians who maintain that God is perfectly good and just in our meaning of these words. We can prove God's wisdom and power conformably to our ideas of wisdom and power, but not so his justice and goodness. This does not warrant the theologian's seeking refuge in the idea of appropriate readjustments after death, nor the atheist's denying the operation of divine goodness and justice altogether. Not your happiness and mine, but the design and harmony of the whole is the determining aim of creation; and if we consistently see our own happiness and misery in the light of the whole, anthropomorphic complaint is replaced by the most devout adoration of supreme and incomprehensible Deity. The latter idea is Shaftesbury's and dictates the optimism of Bolingbroke, but its conjunction with the former virtually undermines the moral basis of theodicy. Bolingbroke's sophistry and his implied ethical scepticism should have led him consistently to pessimism: "If once the concept of God's goodness was abandoned, then the cold mechanistic view of the world offered no more a protection from pessimism." [24]

That Bolingbroke actually seems unaware of this duality of motive in his thought is due to his excess of polemical zeal and deficiency in logic.[25] So he flays the orthodox divine for blaspheming God by calling his creation corrupt and evil, and also for regarding God in the image of man by calling him just and good in our human sense of the term. The sceptical and pessimistic implications of the latter form of harangue become explicit in the thought of Voltaire, but neither these implications nor the fundamental inconsistency of Bolingbroke seem to have been apparent to his English pupil. While, as Lessing put it, Alexander Pope "merely borrowed the finest and most sensuous expressions from each system, without worrying about their truth," [26] the *Essay on Man* is in the main a rhymed version of that optimistic acceptance of God's perfectly harmonious world which Bolingbroke shared with Shaftesbury. God is the author of all: therefore, whatever is, is right.

However we may judge of the merits of the *Essay on Man* as a work of poetic art, we are bound to recognize its immense and far-reaching influence on eighteenth century thought. In Germany, as we shall see, it initiated a whole school of versified theodicy. This great vogue of Pope's work was partly due to his "almost unique felicity of expression," [27] which fixed favorite articles of the eighteenth century creed in striking epigram and proverb. That Pope's contemporaries so readily accepted proverbs in place of proofs, and, even while suspecting Pope's orthodoxy, joined in his optimistic refrains, is itself characteristic of the more popular thinking of the Enlightenment.

One keynote of Pope's theodicy is the declaration of the essential harmony of the cosmos. There is a Universal Order, divinely directed, in which all creatures have their proper rôle and place. They are in and for the system, not the system for them:

> The Universal Cause
> Acts not by partial but by gen'ral laws;
> And makes what happiness we justly call,
> Subsist, not in the good of one, but all.

Man errs in thinking that his pleasure and contentment are God's chief concern:

> Has God, thou fool! worked solely for thy good,
> Thy joy, thy pastime, thy attire, thy food?

If we see our own life in its cosmic setting, our discontent will be swallowed up in adoration of the stupendous harmonious Whole. In this Whole that stretches

> From infinite to thee,
> From thee to nothing

the least is as much in God's sight as the alleged crown of creation:

> To him no high, no low, no great, no small;
> He fills, he bounds, connects and equals all.

There is a hierarchy of being, but it does not involve a gradation of happiness:

> Order is heav'n's first law; and this confessed,
> Some are, and must be, greater than the rest,
> More rich, more wise; but who infers from hence
> That such are happier, shocks all common sense.[28]

Unprotestingly man should recognize his place in nature, nor chide Providence if it crush him when its laws demand it:

> Shall burning Aetna, if a sage requires,
> Forget to thunder, and recall her fires? . . .
> When the loose mountain trembles from on high,
> Shall gravitation cease if you go by?

If it seems irrational and unworthy of Providence thus to make brute nature triumph over human purposes, we should trustfully keep in mind that the whole design is not known to us:

> So man who here seems principal alone,
> Perhaps acts second to some sphere unknown,
> Touches some wheel, or verges to some goal;
> 'Tis but a part we see, and not a whole.

Perhaps; but surely this is slight logical basis for the confident optimistic rhetoric that rests upon it: the more so as according to Pope himself, God's plans are forever beyond our complete grasp. The first Epistle was all about the Universal Whole; now Pope bluntly tells us to try to understand what we can, our own nature:

> Know then thyself, presume not God to scan;
> The proper study of mankind is man.

Pope's estimate of human nature scarcely warrants complacent optimism. Man is a creature of self-love and contending passions, and reason, though a guard, is no sure guide; the best that we can hope for is "the virtue nearest to our vice allied." But reason, as it teaches the interrelation, reveals our own social destiny: the whole universe is one system of society, and the pursuit of our own highest good involves the promotion of the good of others. So in the lives of men the law of the general harmony is seen to operate, and

> Thus God and nature linked the gen'ral frame,
> And bade self-love and social be the same.

This resolute confidence does not waver even when confronted with the iniquity of tyrants and traitors. Who knows, perhaps even the anti-social lives of wicked men are part of some divine purpose, which we may not fathom but should not doubt. Indeed this would be no more mysterious than the thousand calamities in nature, calamities to us, not to God:

> If plagues or earthquakes break not heaven's design,
> Why then a Borgia or a Catiline?
> Who know but He, whose hand the lightning forms,
> Who heaves old ocean, or who wings the storms,
> Pours fierce ambition in a Caesar's mind,
> Or turns young Ammon loose to scourge mankind?
> From pride, from pride our very reas'ning springs;
> Account for moral as for nat'ral things:
> Why charge we heav'n in those, in these acquit?
> In both to reason right is to submit.

Who knows indeed? And since we do not know, Alexander Pope harangues at us to believe:

> All nature is but art unknown to thee,
> All chance, direction which thou canst not see;
> All discord, harmony not understood;
> All partial evil, universal good;
> And spite of pride, in erring reason's spite,
> One truth is clear, Whatever is, is right.[29]

Now, as Pope's editor points out, "the logic of assertion, and often of vituperative assertion, in which Pope abounded, is available for every system, and his admission that God is the instigator of evil, was a fit foundation for a pessimist philosophy:" [30] or, rather, for axiological anarchy. If what to us is clearly cruelty, injustice, and discord may, indeed must, be the reverse in the divine view and harmony, then justice and injustice, harmony and discord may well be interchanged in our view as we grow in wisdom; and radically more than this, they may well be interchangeable at any time if theodicy requires it. This ready surrender, not only of our available standards of value, but of any standards of value that involve ultimate antithesis of good and evil or any disvalue, is cavalier complacency which is sinister in its moral implications. If justice and injustice are both in the end somehow good, then of course there is no ultimate evil. But what then is good and right? Whatever is. Thus in Pope's eulogy of God's world, value-categories are in effect abandoned in favor of existential,—and then the eulogy itself loses meaning. Here, as in the case of Leibniz, theodicy exacts too high a price. Job's censure to his orthodox friends comes to mind:

> Will ye speak unrighteously for God?
> And talk deceitfully for him?
> Will ye show partiality to him?
> Will ye contend for God?
> Is it good that he should search you out?
> Or as one deceiveth a man, will ye deceive him? [31]

VI

Optimism dominates and dictates the tone of the popular philosophy of the Enlightenment in Germany.[32] Reimarus finds in the inanimate world no intrinsic perfection but only means to perfection which animate beings alone can possess. The final goal and purpose of creation, in his view, is man's greatest happiness. That in this world, created by God thus explicitly for man's sake, pain abounds, is a problem which Reimarus would meet with the old arguments. Less than twenty years after the death of Reimarus, Kant is to indicate the true uniqueness of man in nature: his moral-spiritual character; but this radical turn in the discussion is too early for the Hamburg professor.

So Mendelssohn (1729–1786) firm in his assurance that the world-course is directed by an infinitely wise and benevolent Creator for the good of his rational creatures, regards the evils in the world as necessary to set off the greater resultant good and as becoming less and less as the goal of perfection is attained: this life exhibiting in part what is to be fully disclosed in the hereafter,—God's justice and loving-kindness and infinite wisdom.

An interesting record of German philosophical thinking before Kant is Johann Georg Walch's *Philosophisches Lexicon.* Walch's treatment of the problem of evil manifests the strong influence of Leibniz and Wolff, even in his criticism of their ideas. Walch holds that good and evil are in general relative, except moral evils or sins, which according to him "are and remain evil." Evil he defines as "that which negates and opposes the capacities of man which God as his maker has bestowed upon him, and from the nature of which we can judge that God thereby designed us through the exercise of them to attain blessedness." Just as the highest good is in love of God, so the utmost evil (höchste Uebel) is to be sought in our willing, in perverse inclination and emotion in general, and especially in perverse self-love. [33]

But how is this corruption and misdirection of the will to be accounted for? Regarding the origin of evil, Walch's final conclusion manifests the influence of Bayle's *Dictionary.* While he reacts against any tendency towards dualism, and leans on Augustinian and Leibnizian ideas, his conclusion suggests pious scepticism: "If we turn to the origin of evil, how it comes to be in the world and why God permits it, this is something on which man with his reason should not speculate." On one point, however, Walch is firm: God's blamelessness in the circumstances. The crux of the problem of evil concerns sin, and sin cannot be explained as due to God-implanted bias to evil in man. Man is responsible, not God. "Man as man must be a rational being. Were it not for his freedom, he would not have needed reason. As a man he was a creature, and a finite substance, in that he could err and sin. In these circumstances God found it conformable to his reason to permit the fall of man." [34]

But we ask: "If God chose to create such a world in which evil and sin were to be chosen by man, is he wholly blameless for the consequences?" Walch, after seeking refuge in the distinction between the possibility and the actuality of sin, gives us an answer which shows that in his treatment of this problem he has not been engaged in a real inquiry: "God, considering the possible worlds and finding the best among them, determined to create it, hence this best of all possible worlds could not have been omitted. Had God passed it over, it would not have been the best world; had it not been the best world, God would not have created it." [35] Q. E. D.

In sharp distinction from the Leibniz-Wolffian rationalistic optimism, the mathematician Maupertuis undertakes to show by empirical calculation that life actually yields a decided balance of pain. This president of Frederick the Great's Academy is an eighteenth century Hegesias who audits the hedonistic books of life, pronounces it mostly a bankrupt concern, and, far from condemning suicide unreservedly, is kept from Hegesian advocacy of it only by his Christian hope of restitution in the hereafter. His *Essai de philosophie morale,* he assures us, is not the result of personal disappointment: on the contrary, he argues, if with all his successes he still finds tedium in life, how can any man's lot be regarded as better?

In good mathematical manner he begins with definitions. Pleasure is "all perception which we would rather experience than not experience." [36] Pain is the reverse: any experience which we should prefer to terminate or to replace by another or by sleep and insensibility is an unpleasant experience. In calculating and comparing pleasures and pains Maupertuis takes into account the two factors of intensity and duration; their product determines the pleasure or displeasure of a certain experience; the sum of happy moments constitutes the good of life, and the sum of unhappy moments its evil; and if a comparison of these two sums shows a balance of pleasure, our life is to be accounted happy; if the contrary, it is a life of unhappiness.

Examining life from this angle, happiness on earth, according to Maupertuis, is seen to be decidedly exceptional. Were it possible to blot out all but the really cherished moments of our experience, "perhaps the entire duration of the longest life would be reduced to a few hours." All efforts to reason pain out of existence are futile: "The philosopher who would say that gout is not an evil, would be talking nonsense; or, if he merely meant to say that gout does not render the soul vicious, then he would be uttering a triviality." [37] The organization of the human body is such as to disappoint optimistic expectations. Pleasure is experienced only by certain parts of our body, but we can feel pain anywhere. Continued intense pleasure leads to satiety and disgust, but the more intense and the longer a pain is, the more painful it is. To be sure this is not true of the higher satisfactions and dissatisfactions of the mind; but the sages who can find lasting felicity in justice and in truth are so decidedly in the minority that, despite Aristides and Newton, life on the whole remains an unhappy affair.

If our career ended irrevocably at death, neither the Epicurean pursuit of pleasure nor the Stoic apathetic deliverance from pain would avail us aught substantial, and we might well lend an ear to the Stoic apologist for suicide, and, we may add, hearken even to Hegesias. It is the unsatisfactory character of all these solutions, however, which turns Maupertuis for comfort to Christianity. The hope of life after death, of which the Christian religion assures us, and the light which it throws in the darkness of human life with its teaching of whole-hearted love of God and man, these transfigure our present life and can make it blessedly happy. Maupertuis does not pretend to certainty in the matter, but his mind is pragmatically settled on the venture: "If I meet the system which alone can fulfil the desire which I have to be happy, should I not then recognize it as the true system? Am I not bound to believe that he who leads me to happiness is one that would not deceive me?" [38]

The Leibniz-Wolffian theodicy did not remain caviare to the general in Germany. Under its influence, and also under the influence of English deism, a decided optimism invaded German thought, and brought together the strict conformist and the liberal in theology to join in praise of the essential and ultimate 'bestness' of things as they are.

This movement of thought affected literature; a whole school of philosophical poets sought to do Alexander Pope's work in German; and they surely deserved the description which has been applied to their British colleagues: "a generation of philosophical organ-grinders." The pioneer and the champion praiser was the Hamburg senator Barthold Heinrich Brockes (1680–1747). In nine volumes of verse published in the course of twenty-seven years, he compiled an elaborate rhymed inventory of nature in all her departments, finding her in every detail a precious gift of God to man. "Brockes' entire nature-poetry is a rhymed physico-theological argument." [39] In this pious undertaking Brockes reveals himself as liberal in his theology, inexhaustibly benevolent, and insufferably patient. In this patience the reader cannot follow him, for his verse is dull beyond compare. Were it not for his influence on the thought and literary taste of his day, only the ludicrous absurdities into which his poetic theodicy often led him would serve to keep his memory alive; even so his dullness is atoned for, and in his praises of Providence he adds to the gaiety of nations. It were a penance to read his five hundred sixty-eight lines on "The Sun," or his long catalogues of natural wonders, *Die Wundergaben unsers Körpers*, some of which are as it were pious parodies anticipating Whitman at his very worst. But who can resist Brockes when he gets primer-like and soft:

> God calls to us in each forget-me-not:
> "Forget me not!" [40]

Or when he lists the good points of the wolf:

> In how many ways the wolf is of decided use to us!
> His skin keeps us well protected from the bitter winter chills;
> From his organs are extracted remedies to cure our ills. [41]

Or when he cites a real jewel of theodicy, as in his eulogy of the goose:

> Goose-grease doth relieve consumption; goose-gall lotion, too, is good;
> Goose is good to eat; for dizzy spells we often use its blood;
> Skin and feathers likewise useful: doth not this bird radiate
> God's omnipotence, God's wisdom, and God's love for man's estate? [42]

Respectable alike as a thinker and as a poet is Albrecht von Haller (1707–1777), some of whose philosophical verses, particularly those *Ueber den Ursprung des Uebels*, are readable alongside Pope's. Optimism and theodicy are not with Haller, as with Senator Brockes, the hobbies of dull comfortable complacency. Here we have a mind of marvelous precocity and as marvelous scope and command of intellectual treasures, for whom writing poetry was a duty as well as a joy, who undertakes deliberately to instruct his fellowmen in rhyme. Important, he thinks, is first of all the right attitude towards life:

> A spirit well-disposed can sweeten even gall,
> But a perverted sense turns everything to wormwood.[43]

We cannot shut our eyes to existing evils, and Haller castigates or bewails them in rhyme: superstition, humbug, oppression, vanity, bereavement. But if we see particular things in relation to the whole, the picture changes. A scale from God to nothing is the universe, and in this scale man is

> Ambiguously kin to angel and to brute.

This scale of existence is the best possible; of all available worlds the infinitely wise and good Creator has chosen the least imperfect. To be the best, it had to be more than a machine, it had to include free moral agents, and their possibly evil choices, and the necessary consequences of these:—the poetic syllogisms are not unfamiliar. God's ways are hidden from us: how can we blame our Maker for what we in our blindness cannot perceive?

> Perhaps is this our world, which like a grain of sand
> Swims in celestial seas, the evil's fatherland!
> Perhaps this petty speck of error and of dole
> Swells the perfection of the universal whole.

Perhaps; at any rate Haller is ever confident that in the end all will be made blessedly clear:

> When Thou reveal'st to us the secret of Thy ways,
> Then all creation, Lord, shall bow to Thee in praise! [44]

This sort of poetic theodicy comes to be a recognized duty. Friedrich Hagedorn (1708–1754) and Johann Peter Uz (1720–1796) lay aside their anacreontic lyre and their martial patriotic trumpet to chant the praises of the Almighty. As Uz informs us in his rhymed *Theodicée:*

> Thus Leibniz has unlocked the shrine of destiny,
> And clear illumined is his path.[45]

But on this path neither he nor Hagedorn seem to have tarried long. A far more richly gifted soul is moved in early youth by tender love and by wooden preaching to praise God and his creation more ecstatically, and in a poem of six cantos, *Die Natur der Dinge, oder die vollkommenste Welt,* C. M. Wieland (1733–1813) discusses in rhyme existing philosophies and theologies. The last lines might well have been anticipated from the start:

> So evil step by step does vanish, and our life
> No more embittered is by discord and by strife.
> The future age at last God's love will truly praise,
> And all shall be revealed. . . .
> Those groping now in gloom will swim in seas of light,
> Will join the harmony celestial, infinite.[46]

Thus Wieland at the age of eighteen. When the poet was almost eighty, he was to hear another youth singing another song. "Life is a precarious matter," Arthur Schopenhauer told Wieland; "I have resolved to spend my life meditating upon it."

VII

Leibniz's theodicy became on the Continent the rallying-ground of theological and moral optimism, and a bulwark against the sceptical invasion of Bayle; and similarly Shaftesbury's philosophy of harmony stimulated resistance to Hobbist moral infidelity. But both Hobbes and Bayle found a vigorous, if also a decidedly scandalous, protagonist in the Dutch-born physician Bernard Mandeville, with his *Fable of the Bees, or Private Vices, Publick Benefits.* Mandeville shares Bayle's distrust in reason, whether theoretical or practical, and also Hobbes' account of human nature as naturally selfish; but his professed moral demands are radically different from those of Hobbes, while the conviction that his demands are unrealizable rouses only ribald scorn in him, and no tragic irony as in the case of Bayle.

Mandeville's avowed 'rigoristic' conception of virtue admits no moral value in any act unless it be wholly free from selfishness and passion in its motivation.[47] But while such ascetic and purely rational conduct is alone virtuous, human life does not provide instances of it. Life does not afford what alone would render it morally worthy. All our acts do in fact proceed from selfishness and passion; and not only is this true, but were it not for selfishness and the passions, society could not prosper. Precisely that which man, morally speaking, ought not to do, contributes to the greatness and the prosperity of the state. So honesty is made to appear the worst policy:

> Fools only strive
> To make a Great an Honest Hive.[48]

Luxury, wastefulness, pride, envy, lust, and a score of similar passions which we rightly condemn as moralists yet serve to yield the springs of redoubled effort, the occasion for wide employment of labor, the source of conflict and through conflict achievement and greatness. Society thrives on vice: on this foundation social pessimism may well rest while theodicy collapses.

Confronted with such a moral-social paradox, a utilitarian would seek refuge in a redefinition of virtue and vice, holding only that to be virtue which leads to the increased happiness of all; while a Kantian, unimpressed by Mandeville's social-political exhibition, would stoutly reaffirm that rigorous devotion to duty alone constitutes an act virtuous. Mandeville himself seems delighted to find all socially sensible conduct vicious; he is the *Advocatus Diaboli* of the eighteenth century; in his laughing down of alleged human nobility and in his obscenity, he is one with Goethe's Mephistopheles. It is of Mandeville versus Kant that one is bound to think when one reads the Prologue of *Faust*.

Mandeville's laughter of scorn is ribald; the sneer of Swift is a sneer of tragic bitterness. In an age of intellectual self-assurance and of all too general profession of complacent universal harmony, of "shams and windy sentimentalities," as Carlyle put it, Swift's brutally keen eyes saw stupidity, bigotry, hypocrisy, servility, arrogance, cruelty; the world abounded in worms, serpents, jackals, and magpies. Condemned to wait in obscurity and inaction while dolts thrived and prospered; growing up in circumstances in which even kindly patronage was galling to his indomitable pride; conscious of his unrecognized genius and as bitterly sensible of the dread cloud that was lowering over him, to envelope his mind in darkness; unwilling to silence those who maligned his relations with "Stella" by an admission of his impending fate, which would have earned him their insulting pity and only confirmed them in ascribing to incipient lunacy his judgments of life which he was convinced were only too sane, Swift's cup of bitterness was ever running over. "He resembles a victim tied to the stake and slowly tortured to madness and death; while from his proudly compressed lips there issue no weak lamentations, but the deep curses of which one syllable is more effective than a volume of shrieks." [49]

It is not particular individuals that rouse his hatred and disgust, but rather the collective medley of nations, professions, and communities. Is he angry at mankind for being so irremediably worthless? So he writes to Pope: "I tell you after all, that I do not hate mankind: it is *vous autres* who hate them, because you would have them reasonable animals, and are angry for being disappointed."[50] Is this the explanation of that grim kindliness which has made the most devastating satire of human pettiness and futile vanity a children's classic? And is it not also an irony justifying Swift's estimate of human insight, that his masterpiece has been removed from the library to the nursery?

"Where heroes are scarce, Krali-Marko is a hero," so runs a Balkan proverb. So man is a giant—among Lilliputs; but in the society of real giants, he earns the verdict of Brobdignag as being "the most pernicious race of vermin that nature ever suffered to crawl upon the surface of the earth." If *Gulliver's Travels* is a satire on mankind in general, *The Tale of a Tub* selects the avowed ministers of the Lord for special attention. Swift's coarseness in dealing with them, and with other professed spiritual guides, is deliberate: in righteous indignation he rolls his scavenger's cart right through the alleged sanctuaries, to dump its contents on the sham altars, the while Jove pronounces judgment on humanity:

> Offending race of human kind,
> By nature, learning, reason blind;
> You who through frailty stept aside,
> And you who never fell—from pride;
> You who in different sects were shammed,
> And come to see each other damned
> (So some folks told you, but they knew
> No more of Jove's designs than you)—
> The world's mad business now is o'er,
> And I resent these pranks no more—
> I to such blockheads set my wit;
> I damn such fools! Go, go, you're bit.[51]

In the same year (1759) which saw the publication of Voltaire's *Candide* Samuel Johnson worked overtime for a week on *Rasselas,* to earn the money needed to bury his mother decently and to pay her debts. The story of the Abyssinian prince reflects no illusions of individual or social stable welfare, nor hopes of real progress; it depicts human life torn between the heartaches of frustration and futile struggle, and the tedium of "tasteless tranquillity." Rasselas and his companions, having escaped from the "happy valley" of cloying enjoyment, seek life-ennobling outlet for their energies, and finding it nowhere within the assured reach of man, decide in the end to return to the cushioned ease of Abyssinia. This is the last chapter, "The Conclusion in Which Nothing is Concluded." In the face of rising discontent on the one hand, and still stubborn placidity on the other, Johnson refuses to blink at the facts, but he also refuses to gamble on possibilities and takes refuge in conservative reaction. Things are bad enough; but don't make them worse by following idle dreams of making them better. Leave bad enough alone! Do your part, such as it is, in this world, without unseemly whining or cowardly hope. Avoid speculation, keep your feet on the ground. But know once for all that man has to have religion and that it had best be the established one; resting on it, curb hasty impiety in your curse of this wretched life by remembering that the story is only half told here and now: God's justice has the last word after all in the life after death. So Alfred de Vigny was to say: Christianity is a religion of despair, since, turning away from this life, it looks forward to the hereafter.

VIII

Eighteenth century theodicy rested on the rationalist assumption that knowledge of the ultimate nature of the cosmos was within the mind's reach, to be derived from fundamental axioms in the mind's possession. Regarding the validity of proposed deductions reason may clash with reason without losing self-confidence; but the humiliation of reason, by the dismissal not only of its proffered eternal verities but of its claim to reach eternal verity undermined the very basis on which any theodicy could rest. In this attack on the citadel of reason David Hume was the most consistent and most effective aggressor.

British empiricism, setting out more systematically with John Locke, had repudiated the doctrine of innate ideas and had undertaken to trace the origin of all alleged knowledge to experience and ultimately to sensation. Locke's thought, reluctantly metaphysical but in its intention resolutely pious, retained ideas of a divinely directed cosmos which he had scarcely derived from his empiricism. Unsatisfied with this mere hospitality to Divine Providence, Berkeley's more definitely metaphysical mind undertakes to reinterpret Locke's empiricism in an idealistic sense: he reduces the world to minds and their ideas, finite minds participating in the infinite experience of God's mind: the necessary connection of ideas in the finite mind, and the agreement of mind with mind, proving the cosmic system of ideas in the Infinite Mind's experience. On this basis trust in Divine Providence could rest, and materialism and infidelity were to be confuted.

David Hume's still more rigorous application of Locke's method led him to challenge just this necessary connection of ideas, the alleged objectivity of cosmic order and harmony. Holding that Locke's proof of the subjective character of the secondary qualities of objects (colors, sounds, tastes, smells, etc.), applied with equal force to his so-called primary qualities, and refusing to admit anything for which experience did not supply a warrant, Berkeley had reduced all alleged material existence to mental contents: existence is perceived existence; a body is its qualities, and these are ideas. Hume carried this procedure further. Experience does not disclose to us minds over and apart from mental contents any more than it discloses to us bodies over and apart from their qualities. Just as a 'body' is a sum of perceived qualities, so 'mind' is to be equated with ideas. This turn in empiricist theory cut the ground from under Berkeley's pious idealism. Berkeley's metaphysics could translate the mechanistic formulas of physical science and treat natural laws as uniform ways in which God connects ideas in our minds; but if now minds were to be reduced to clusters of impressions and ideas, what assurance or what possible proof remained for the Infinite Mind's synthesis, of divine harmony or Divine Providence? From the order, coherence, necessary connection of our ideas, Berkeley had inferred God's existence. This alleged necessary connection Hume now undertook to test in strict empiricist manner, and found it wanting in objectivity.

Hume's classical analysis of the idea of causal relation brought this course of thought to a focus. Causal relation is reducible to spatial contiguity and temporal succession, with priority of the 'cause.' As to the alleged 'necessary connection' to cause and effect, it amounts to constant conjunction of the two in past experience, habituating us to their being experienced together and leading us in the presence of the former to expect the latter. This excess of empiricism, exhibiting "the insuperable difficulties, which attend first principles in all systems; the contradictions, which adhere to the very ideas of matter, cause and effect, extension, space, time, motion; and in a word, quantity of all kinds," [52] roused Kant from his dogmatic slumber and stimulated him, in the vindication of science which he undertook, to revise and reconcile the empiricist and rationalist theories of knowledge. But to theodicy or to any speculation about ultimate cosmic origins or direction, Hume's conclusions proved devastating and unrelieved.

The *Dialogues concerning Natural Religion* are Hume's

contribution to the disintegration of rational theology and theodicy. Incapable of proving the objectivity of necessary connection between two simple events, and always dealing with particular bits of experience, what could justify our venture to pronounce upon the eternally necessary plan and direction of the alleged cosmic whole or trace the origins of the world from eternity to eternity? [53] Analogy, our refuge in the absence of demonstration, could scarcely yield the idea of an Infinite Being, or of unlimited perfection, or harmony, or wisdom, or goodness, or power: experience discloses only limitation and particularity. Limping as we do from one item of experience to another, how are we to make the giant leap to All-Comprehending Deity? The venture is past our reach, and unreasonable.

If Hume thus saps the foundations of rational theology, he is no less destructive to theodicy or optimism. Even if our own terrestrial environment proved on the whole satisfactory to us, it would not justify assured estimate regarding the world as a whole, for how can we be sure of our competence to pronounce what is ultimately good: "Could a peasant, if the *Aeneid* were read to him, pronounce that poem to be absolutely faultless, or even assign it to its proper rank among the productions of human wit; he, who had never seen any other production?" For all we know, "many worlds might have been botched and bungled, throughout an eternity ere this system was struck out." This world may be "very faulty and imperfect, . . . only the first rude essay of some infant deity, . . . the object of derision to his superiors, . . . the production of old age and dotage in some superannuated deity. . . ." [54] We have no conclusive evidence, no real data, only analogies and conjectures. And moreover within the range of our experience, human life scarcely warrants sanguine reassurance about the Whole. "Weakness, impotence, distress, attend each stage of that life: and 'tis at last finished in agony and horror. . . . Observe . . . the curious artifices of Nature, in order to imbitter the life of every living being. . . . Besides, . . . man is the greatest enemy of man. Oppression, injustice, contempt, contumely, violence, sedition, war, calumny, treachery, fraud; by these they mutually torment each other: and they would soon dissolve that society which they had formed, were it not for the dread of still greater ills, which must attend their separation. . . . Were a stranger to drop, on a sudden, into the world, I would show him, as a specimen of its ills, an hospital full of diseases, a prison crowded with malefactors and debtors, a field of battle strewed with carcases, a fleet floundering in the ocean, a nation languishing under tyranny, famine, or pestilence. . . ." [55] This is an eighteenth century foretaste of Schopenhauer.

In the presence of these ills, who can argue reasonably that we are in the care of a benevolent or indulgent Father? Are we not rather in the hands of a rigid master, exacting much for the little that he gives us; or, more reasonable still, is not our origin and direction of existence a grievous perplexity? To recognize it and try to bear it is all that we can intelligently do, without making ourselves dupes of miserable illusions. Think straightforwardly, as far as you can, and should it get past endurance,—why, play a game of backgammon. It is the gray cheer of scepticism.

IX

Edward Young's entire life was an alternation of gratitude and manifold lively sense of favors yet to come. Having lavished seemly and unseemly praise in recognition and in anticipation of presents, pensions, and preferments, his copiously solemn muse, raising its glance ever higher, undertakes the most sublime of themes, and perchance the most rewarding, in pious prospect: to vindicate the cosmos or to flatter Divine Providence. How Young's *Night Thoughts* were received by the Dispenser of Eternity, it were indiscreet to judge here; but they did earn him great fame in England and all over the Continent: a fame as great as the oblivion which followed it: the former still possessing historical interest, and the latter quite deserved.

The *Night Thoughts* are intended to turn the soul from the vanities, evils, and disappointments of this life to the stable and assured blessedness of life hereafter. In his younger days Young had courted the muse at high noon in his heavily curtained rooms by the light of a candle set in a skull. "By night an atheist half-believes a God." So through nine *Nights* he pours forth pious declamation for the edification of his imaginary Lorenzo, and is like the rest of us who "pay themselves the compliment to think they one day shall not drivel." He is not afraid of argument in rhyme:

> Where'er I turn, how new proofs pour upon me!
> How happily this wondrous view supports
> My former argument!

Nor does he resist tears; he would "trace these briny rivulets to their springs." Nor is there anything new either in his arguments or in his tears. Suffering, he informs us, is man's desert; indeed it is his blessing: if not one, then the other; both leave God blameless. Let us receive, be chastened, and praise the Lord:

> Amid my list of blessings infinite
> Stand this the foremost: "That my heart has bled."

But all in due season and measure—and not forever:

> Since virtue's recompense is doubtful here,
> If man dies wholly, well may we demand,
> Why is man suffered to be good in vain? [56]

There is occasional wit, and a happy turn of thought or epigram, and very occasionally even good verse in the *Night*

Thoughts. But neither is Young's light clear and steady enough, nor his flame sufficiently pure and bright to justify devoted or critical loyalty. His misty and many-worded melancholy satisfied the pre-romantic world that did not quite know what was troubling or stirring it, only to be forgotten as it did come to know and feel itself better. From Edward Young one turns away as from the Cardinal Lothario that was to be Pope Innocent the Third. In the life beyond of which they were both so assured, may these two rhetorical but unconvincing contemners of this world keep each other company.

CHAPTER VI

THE DESPAIR OF CIVILIZATION

I

The eighteenth century registered a shift from reasoned theodicy and complacent optimism towards manifold disdain, revulsion, and rebellion: a shift gradual at first which gained momentum. A movement which found its two leaders in Voltaire and Rousseau is not to be defined in a simple formula; the transition of the European mind from the placid Enlightenment to the Romantic revolt involved a revision in logic which not only elicited new conclusions from old premises, but likewise imposed radically new propositions for new syllogisms.

The theodicies in prose and in verse had agreed that "Whatever is, is right"; the new spirit could have found its motto in the words of Marcellus in *Hamlet:* "Something is rotten in the state of Denmark"; but there was grave disagreement in diagnosis as to what was rotten. Voltaire, embittered by the stupidity, intolerance, and cruelty of men, dismayed by the brutal indifference of nature to human weal or woe, defiantly scorned the idea of benevolent Divine Providence as a superstition, but, holding fast to his trust in the intellect and in civilization, never lost faith in progress through enlightenment and tolerance. Rousseau's diagnosis was both simpler and more radical: God is good, and so is man as God made him; evil is not in nature but unnatural, due to the corruption of man by civilization, with its pride of intellect, its depravity, injustice, and oppression of man by man.

This is no mere pundit controversy: both as allies and as opponents these two men loom large, not only in the history of ideas, but in the pages of Europe's political and social life during the last century and a half. The seething multitudes which greeted Voltaire on his triumphal return to Paris in 1778, after an absence of thirty years, stormed the Bastille eleven years later. Marat read Rousseau's *Contrat social* to enthusiastic audiences in the public squares of Paris, and Robespierre undertook to make revolutionary France worship at the shrine of the Savoyard Vicar. Empress Catherine of Russia, aghast at perceiving the real drift of the new ideas, ordered Voltaire's bust to be removed from her desk to the lumber-room, but her caution was tardy and futile.

The earliest revolutionaries of Russia were avowed Voltaireans and endeavored to reënact in Petersburg and in Moscow the Paris drama of emancipation. Young Tolstoy carried around his neck a medallion with Rousseau's portrait, and it was on the centenary of Rousseau's death that Tolstoy began in earnest his social and religious apostolate. While a good deal besides Voltaire and Rousseau has entered into the Russian Revolution, whose tenth anniversary was celebrated but yesterday, is it quite beside the point to indicate the clash of motives, both social-political and cultural-religious, which divide Russian liberal and radical opinion today: and is it altogether misleading to compare this clash of motives with the clash in the French Revolution of the Voltairean and the Rousseauistic strains?

II

Voltaire's earlier attitude towards the problem of evil was similar to that of Bolingbroke and Pope. Convinced of God's existence and of God's infinite perfection, he regarded criticism of God's world as inadmissible. The strongest argument for God he found in the admirable order of nature:

"The Heavens declare the glory of God."[1] In the hands of Voltaire this teleological argument was a double-edged sword: what the heavens declared to him regarding God or what meaning he attached to his glory would depend on what his inquiring eyes saw in heaven and especially on earth. So long as his view of life was in the main contented, the evils in life would present no insuperable difficulties to his belief in God. Man of course has his defects and vices, imperfections of his finite nature.[2]

Voltaire is not overwhelmed either by our vices or by our woes; they are part of the universal order, and in that order man is the happiest and the most perfect of beings. Indeed in his critique of Pascal, Voltaire expressed grateful acquiescence in things as they are, grateful surprise that they are no worse. "You are surprised that God has made man so limited, so ignorant, and so little happy; why are you not surprised that God has not made him more limited, more ignorant, more unhappy?"[3] He was pleased to note Pope's agreement with him in this sentiment; before them both Leibniz had recorded the same complacent astonishment. Toning down evil as he did, Voltaire in any case found it no grave embarrassment in his theodicy. Sometimes he agrees with Bolingbroke (or Bolingbroke with him): we may not and we need not think of the eternal, infinite Almighty God as good and just in our human sense of these terms. Goodness and justice are purely human in connotation and inapplicable to Deity: "It is quite as absurd to speak of God as just or unjust in this sense, as to speak of God as blue or square."[4] The anthropocentric view of nature and the anthropomorphic view of God are equally naïve: in the cosmic machinery each part has its place, but no part is unique, hub and center. A mind like Voltaire's could not permanently neglect a moral estimate of God, but his reasoning on the subject is halting: even we imperfect men pursue goodness and justice, then surely perfect Deity is bound to be good and just despite the apparent injustice and evils in this world.

This view of God and nature was insecure: a radical change in Voltaire's estimate of man's lot in nature was certain to change Voltaire's attitude towards God. Actually, in Voltaire's experience, man, God, and nature seemed to conspire to wreck his optimism. The age of which Voltaire was the outstanding spokesman was an age committed to the Universal Harmony, an age of trust in human character and human intelligence, yet Voltaire's own life was a long struggle with injustice, stupidity, bigotry, and cruelty. He did get the best of it in the clash of wits with the Lords of the Earth, but when the Rohans sent their lackeys to beat him up and had him locked in the Bastille, had him banished from Paris, he had no recourse. The Great Frederick might call him to Berlin and profess to treat him as a friend and equal, but after all to the royal cynic, Voltaire was just an orange to suck.

The cruelties of ecclesiastic bigotry embittered him against all organized religion, and he undertook to crush the infamous sanctity which in the name of God shackled the human mind and turned man against man in bloody wars. "So many frauds, so many errors, so many disgusting absurdities. . . . Our religion . . . is unquestionably divine, since seventeen centuries of imposture and imbecility have not destroyed it." [5] Pouring contempt and ridicule on God's prelates did not deepen Voltaire's piety. The manifold reaction against his earlier optimism came to a head in 1755, and in his poem on the disastrous Lisbon earthquake he shocked Europe with his violent disdain of theodicies and ideas of Divine Providence. The bitter irony of the novel *Candide ou l'optimisme* reveals a scepticism of a decidedly pessimistic cast, which is familiar also to the readers of the *Dictionnaire philoso-*

phique. The best of all possible worlds had been subjected to a sneering scrutiny and docile optimism pierced all the way through.

The whole discussion is now put on a humanistic plane. The vast harmony of the universe, which in ways thinkable or unthinkable transfigures our evils into elements of perfection, does not meet Voltaire's demands; nor the view that goodness and justice as we understand them are not to be ascribed to God and that God's perfection is untarnished by any evil or injustice with which our life may be beset. It is precisely the question of God's alleged goodness which concerns Voltaire, and in insisting on it, he distinguishes himself sharply from the complacent rationalists of the Enlightenment. Do the facts of life justify belief in a benevolent Divine Providence, and if they do not, what standing ground is left for despairing but unyielding humanity?

How is placid theodicy to dispose of a Lisbon disaster? Is Lisbon engulfed because of its sins? But then why not Paris and London as well? Or, if the earthquake is a mere event in the order of nature, is it beyond the reach of Divine Goodness to prevent, or has it been preferred by Eternal Wisdom as the least evil of all possible alternatives? Would the universe have been worse for sparing Lisbon this disaster? Is God testing Lisbon's virtue in his fiery furnace? Or is He the impassive spectator of his anguished creation? Or is matter, crude and resistant to Divine Perfection, the source and medium of our woes? These are all blind alleys and lead us to shuddering confusion. Voltaire exclaims: "Alas, I am like a doctor; I know nothing." [6]

Thus we are left groping in the twilight of despair; the book of destiny is closed to us. We are atoms tormented but thinking, measuring the heavens and piercing the infinite, but ignorant of our own station and of our own lot. To pretend to wisdom is tragic folly; we can neither affirm nor deny the presence of the blessed Providence which we do not perceive. Voltaire abandons Plato and rejects Epicurus; Bayle is wiser in his doubt than they with their professed knowledge; Bayle, "the advocate-general of the philosophers," [7] is great enough and wise enough not to have a system.

This dark scepticism is not of the tragically pious variety as Pascal's; it is deliberately and sneeringly aggressive. In this wretched world one of Voltaire's undoubted joys, during the latter part of his life, was flaying optimists to disclose their unsound substance. His irony is blighting. What do you mean by your formula that "all is well in this world?" Ordered it is in accordance with moving forces and necessary laws; but can you mean that it is a happy world, that all is well with you, with me, that no one suffers? "Here is an odd general good, composed of gallstones, gout, and all sorts of crimes, sufferings, death, and damnation." So Shaftesbury, Bolingbroke, and Pope speak of the universal order, and universal it is: "flies are born to be devoured by spiders, who are in turn devoured by swallows, and swallows by shrikes, and shrikes by eagles, and eagles are born to be killed by men, who in turn live to kill each other and to be consumed by worms or by devils, at least in thousand cases to one." [8] The novel *Candide* is an elaborate satire on this best of all possible worlds. Far be it from poor Candide to doubt the 'metaphysico-theologo-cosmolo-nigology' of the great Pangloss, but his own experiences leave him sorely perplexed again and again. "If this is the best of possible worlds, what must the others be like!" But he never gives up hope; fleeing from Portugal and bound for Paraguay, he remarks: "Now we are going to another world, . . . it is in that one, no doubt, that all is well." And all *is* well: in Eldorado! But, outside of Eldorado, even Candide in the course of time becomes weary of Pangloss' philosophizing: "That is well said,—but we should cultivate our garden." [9]

This in fact was Voltaire's solution, in so far as he had any solution. Renouncing theodicy and entangled in the gray webs of doubt, he never lost his faith in civilization: this at least was at hand and reliable,—cultivating our garden. "Let us work without reasoning; . . . this is the only way of making life endurable." [10] One can live through Monday by this gospel alone; whether intelligent man can thus live through the week of life is an open question, which we cannot quite ignore. But it was not with this question that Rousseau confronted Voltaire; rather with the bold assertion that Voltaire had made a cosmic tragedy of evils which for the most part man had brought on himself, and that precisely by becoming civilized. So the issue was sharply drawn.

III

To appreciate the violence and the immediate effectiveness of Rousseau's attack on civilization, we should keep in mind the fundamental contrast which this vagabond genius presented to the culture of his time. Here was a man hypersensitive, violently lyrical, irresponsible, nomadic, with a longing for the ideal and a leaning for the degenerate. Sentimental like his father who gave him his early maudlin training, and like his father unstable; a coward before duty yet reckless in adventure; chafing under the hardships of one trade after another, and running away from his native Geneva in order to escape a beating from his master; induced to change his Calvinist faith by Father Pontverre's excellent Frangi wine, Mme. De Warens' fine blue eyes, and the dazzling prospect of a trip over the Alps; disgusted with the priests that made him Catholic; tasting the bitterness of the lackey's life in Turin and at the same time glowing in his sense of inner superiority to his outward status, yet with dastardly cruelty ruining a young servant girl's future by falsely accusing her of theft merely to avoid a slight personal embarrassment; sighing impatiently for his great chance but incapable of steady pursuit of the real opportunity presented to him by Count Gouvon; running away from his slow good fortune in order to follow another young vagabond who had caught his fancy; living on the bounty of Mme. De Warens, trying study, music, going off with his music master only to abandon him in Lyons when the old man falls down on a street corner in an epileptic fit; advancing slowly from a charlatan to something of an expert in music; living on terms of irresponsible intimacy with Mme. De Warens; dreaming of the brilliant future that is to atone for his undistinguished present and disreputable past; and then going off to Paris at the age of twenty-nine to conquer the world with a new system of musical notation. The Academy of Inscriptions damns him with faint praise; he languishes hoping for the smiles of great ladies, and gets some; goes off to Venice as able secretary to an incompetent and unjust ambassador; in spite of efficient personal record, is dismissed without pay, and finds officialdom as slow to recognize a plebeian's just claims against an aristocrat as academies of learning to welcome a new idea. And so, chafing and rebellious, he sees his years pass and leave him behind, unrecognized and misunderstood, his life one of ardent longing, inarticulate, unrealized. "Deep down within him," Gerhard Gran writes, "there constantly muttered a still inarticulate protest; the Genevan in him revolted against the worldly splendour he saw about him; the vagabond was sometimes seized by an inexpressible longing to get away from the golden cage of the artificial world in which he felt imprisoned; the democrat was offended in his innermost depths at the sight of the social chasms that separated human beings; the mystic shivered in the cold atmosphere of intellect in which he moved." [11]

Almost two thirds of his life are gone, when suddenly like a flash of lightning he sees the wisdom that is to be his wisdom, and like a peal of thunder he makes it reverberate all over the world. Rousseau's own account of his conversion is justly famous: it reveals him so vividly that after reading it we need not be surprised at his gospel. Walking one hot afternoon on the road from Paris to Vincennes bound on a visit to Diderot, he read in a newspaper the announcement of a prize-essay set by the Dijon Academy on the subject: "Has the restoration of the sciences and the arts contributed to purify or to corrupt manners?" (1749). "If ever anything resembled a sudden inspiration," he writes, "it was the movement which began in me as I read this. All at once I felt myself dazzled by a thousand sparkling lights; crowds of vivid ideas thronged into my mind with a force and confusion that threw me into unspeakable agitation; I felt my head whirling in a giddiness like that of intoxication. A violent palpitation oppressed me; unable to walk for difficulty of breathing, I sank under one of the trees of the avenue, and passed half an hour there in such a condition of excitement that when I arose I saw that the front of my waistcoat was all wet with my tears, though I was wholly unconscious of shedding them. Ah, if I could ever have written the quarter of what I saw or felt under that tree, with what clearness should I have brought out all the contradictions of our social system; with what simplicity I should have demonstrated that man is good naturally, and that by institutions only is he made bad." [12]

Some of this is probably maudlin romancing, but that all of it was pure invention, that Rousseau's first plan was to write the usual hackneyed essay in praise of culture and that Diderot suggested to him the less conventional idea, does not rest on sufficient evidence. What was revolutionary was not Rousseau's thesis itself, that arts and sciences have served to corrupt society; the Dijon Academy was of course prepared for an essay on the negative side of the question proposed, and the thing had been done before. What was original in Rousseau's thesis was "the fervour, sincerity and conviction of a most unacademic sort with which it was presented and enforced." [13] Rousseau's whole life had been a preparation for this essay: this harangue which shocked and impressed all France was in fact an apology for his own life. The intensity was lyrically motivated.

Rousseau's first complaint of civilization is the complaint of a Diogenes. In plain noonday he searches Paris over with a lantern looking vainly for a real man, and finding only varnished masks. He finds, in place of genuine ardor, stereotyped, elegant passion; artificial and deceptive politeness instead of candor, the same conventional veneer on all sides hiding the real individual, cowardice and hypocrisy, arrogance or servility according to the code that imposes itself on each man, to keep him in his place. And in this soil of cultured artificiality vices and depravity flourish like weeds: no more sincere friendship, genuine respect, firm confidence; instead of these, suspicion, slander, fear, arrogance, treachery, all hiding beneath a uniform and perfidious veil of etiquette.

This corruption of human nature, Rousseau declares, not only follows the spread of the arts and sciences, but it is in proportion to that spread, and is indeed the effect of the spread. Egypt, Greece, Rome, the Empires of the Orient, one and all went down in decay and degradation due to their becoming civilized. But the rude races of history, the earlier Romans, the Scythians, the Germans abide in history as models of pure, simple human nature. Science and art cannot help corrupting morals: they themselves originate in corruption. "Astronomy is born of superstition; oratory springs from ambition, hatred, flattery, and deceit; geometry, from avarice; physics, from vain curiosity. . . ." Were it not for injustice, what need would there be of jurisprudence; were it not for tyrants, wars and conspiracies, what history would there be to write? Vain in their aims, dangerous in their results, bred in idleness, pride, and luxury, and nourishing them, art and science are the more pernicious the more they are respected and pursued; and there results a civilization artificial and treacherous, worshipping fine words and elegant manners rather than heroic deeds and a true heart. From this view Rousseau turns with disdain, and would appeal to the Almighty for redeeming ignorance and genuine virtue: "Almighty God, thou who holdest in thy hands all souls, deliver us from the enlightenment and the baneful arts of our fathers, and give us back our ignorance, innocence and poverty, the only goods that can render us happy and that are precious in thy sight." [14]

Rousseau's chief protest against civilization, then, is that it has robbed man of his primitive genuineness and freedom, and that it has corrupted a life of rude equality into one of tyranny and enslavement. To the defenders of the arts and sciences Rousseau sought to make his point clear; so he writes to King Stanislas: "It is not from science, I am told, but from riches that, in all ages, sprang nobility and luxury. I never said that luxury was the child of science, but that they were born together and that one could not go without the other. This is how I arranged this genealogy. *The first source of all evil is inequality:* from inequality sprang riches . . . from riches, luxury and idleness. From luxury came the fine arts, and from idleness, science." [15]

And what is the origin of inequality, the fountain-source of all evil? Rousseau gave his answer in his second essay, a necessary corollary to the first. In this revolutionary work, Rousseau painted the life of the savage as a life of uncorrupted virtue and freedom, a life in which there obtained physical inequalities of strength and skill, but no artificial enslavement of man by man: instead of this, simple coöperation in a rudimentary society, utilizing the abilities of each for the good of all, and elementary comfort of life without luxury, but also without squalor. In learning how to work metals and to cultivate the soil, man saw opportunities to grow above the heads of his fellows; this chance he took, and the institution of private property, raising the rich over the poor, demanded a social and political order that would safely and permanently keep the poor under the heel of the rich: and this is indeed the clear though not always frankly avowed purpose of governments, enslavers of mankind. Private property and the inequality which it breeds and signalizes is the root of the tree civilization, of which arts and sciences are the blossoms, and moral corruption and misery the fruits. "The first man who, having enclosed a piece of ground, could think of saying, *This is mine*, and found people simple enough to believe him, was the real founder of civil society. How many crimes, wars, murders, miseries, and horrors would not have been spared to the human race by one who, plucking up the stakes, or filling in the trench, should have called out to his fellows: Beware of listening to this impostor; you are undone if you forget that the earth belongs to no one, and that its fruits are for all." [16]

These writings were not intentionally incendiary, but their revolutionary implications are evident. When Rousseau stated that, were he a chief in Nigritia he would hang the first European who entered his lands or the first native who left them, he was in effect telling the rude masses of Europe how they might deal with their own elegant, civilized oppressors. Rousseau's passionate style was "like the fateful writing on the wall during Belshazzar's orgy:" [17] "The money that passes from the hands of the rich to those of those artisans who furnish their superfluities, is lost for the subsistence of the laborer, and he has no coat, because others need ribbons. . . . We must have sauces in our kitchens, and that is why so many sick people lack broth. We must have liquors on our tables, and that is why peasants drink water. We must have powder for our wigs, and that is why so many poor have no bread." [18]

To participate actively in a civilization of oppression and exploitation which he was denouncing proved more than even Rousseau's inconsistency could bear. He would simplify his own life, would go as far back to nature as he could. He had been the avid pursuer of aristocratic favors, ambitious for economic competence and social preferment, theatrical and musical fame, yet, dalliant and sensitive vagabond that he was, he had always chafed under the daily routine of gainful, civilized occupation, and under the constant risk of humiliating slights confronting him in the aristocratic society in which he furtively moved, and his romantic soul in the garish elegance of the salon dreamt of the green foliage of untamed nature. So he gave up the chance of a career of some profit to support himself by copying music at so much a page. He discarded his sword and gold buttons and courtly apparel, sold his watch, and when a thief stole the forty-two fine linen shirts of his Venetian days, contented himself with plainer apparel. He had set out on his return to the primitive.

To some of his contemporaries this seemed an elaborate pretence, obstinate pose, maniacal oddity. Of course all the fine ladies of Paris wanted their music copied by Jean Jacques' hands, and Grimm sarcastically remarked: "Why don't you rather start a lemonade stand: all Paris will come to you and you'll get rich." [19]

To Voltaire, Rousseau's thought and practice seemed alike misguided. "I have received, sir," he wrote him, "your new book against mankind. . . . Never before has so much wit been devoted to render us all stupid brutes; on reading your work, one is moved to walk on all fours." [20] Rousseau did not miss the opportunity of returning the compliment when the poem on the Lisbon earthquake appeared. Excepting death, which is scarcely in itself an evil, he wrote Voltaire, most of our physical ills are due to our own perverted form of life. Who is to blame if twenty thousand houses, six and seven stories high, were huddled together in an earthquake area? Had the inhabitants of Lisbon lived as nature intended man to live, as primitive men live in the plains or forests, the few who first felt the tremor would have speedily fled across the fields, and in any case would have been in no imminent danger. Besides, who knows, perhaps those who died in Lisbon escaped thereby worse and more prolonged sufferings. Rousseau repeats familiar arguments from Pope and Leibniz: if God exists, He is perfect, He is wise, puissant, and just; then all is well, and our souls are immortal, and it makes little difference whether we do or do not live thirty years longer; and perhaps these thirty years which I miss are necessary to the order of the universe. These two beliefs, in the immortality of the soul and in a beneficent Providence, he feels, desires, hopes, and will defend to his dying breath. And he wonders at the contrast between Voltaire and himself: "Sated with glory and disillusioned about vain greatness, you live free in the lap of plenty. . . . Yet you find only evil on earth. And I, unknown, poor, and tortured by an incurable malady, I meditate joyously in my retreat and find that all is good." [21]

Rousseau concludes that it must be his hope, which Voltaire lacks, which saves him from pessimism. But is it to be admitted that one who is personally comfortable should praise the Lord regardless of the evils he sees in the world about him, simply because they do not hurt him? As John Morley writes: "It is hard to imagine a more execrable emotion than the complacent religiosity of the prosperous." [22] Voltaire's indignation and despair in the circumstances are nowise to his personal discredit, nor does he lose here by comparison with Rousseau. In the years when he championed indefatigably the cause of the poor widow and orphans of Calas, Voltaire wrote: "During that time not a smile escaped me without my reproaching myself for it, as for a crime." [23] We should look in vain for anything like this in the *Confessions* of Rousseau.

The important difference between Voltaire and Rousseau is not in their views of Divine Providence: here the two are only rehearsing Bayle, Leibniz, and Pope. What is significant is their estimate of civilization in relation to their estimate of nature and God. Voltaire, as we have seen, while despairing of finding evidence of a providential plan or meaning in this sorry world, yet never loses his confidence in the upward climb of man or his faith in enlightenment. But Voltaire despised the stupid masses: oxen that need yoke, whip, and hay.[24] Life is a sorry jest, which intelligence may enable us to understand and endure. Now Rousseau took just the opposite view: praising the Lord, clinging to the faith which Voltaire unsettled, glorifying nature and the free ignorant savage, and tracing all our evils to the very civilization in which Voltaire found man's one glimmer of comfort. So in the significant contrast which we are here observing, it is Rousseau who appears as the pessimist: disdainer of civilization and of the cultural values, as perversions of the primitive soundheart nature.

What is this nature which Rousseau worships as perfect and the corruption of which by society and civilization he constantly bewails? The concept of nature has not been defined clearly by Rousseau, nor has he used it consistently in a manner to allow of precise definition by others. Höffding [25] has distinguished three views of nature which may be found in Rousseau's works. "Nature," in a theological sense is for Rousseau the simplicity and harmony of God's original creation, contrasted with its artificial perversion by civilized man. Man has distorted God's work: salvation thus involves the restoration of the majestic simplicity of God's work. In a naturalistic sense, "nature" is purely instinctive existence, without reflection or imagination, a life of action in response to purely physical needs and stimuli. The transformation of this life into that of civilization is unwholesome and unnatural: "If nature destined us to a healthy life I dare almost affirm that the state of reflection is a state contrary to nature, and that thinking man is a depraved animal." [26] So the primitive man's senses and bodily powers are keener than those of civilized man: he can see with the eagle, he can follow a scent, he can track his victim, he is fleet-footed like the deer, he pursues, he is agile, vigorous, resilient. But he devises tools, he loses his own bodily strength and skill, and the more reflective he becomes, the more helpless is his naked self face to face with nature. If in his theological conception of nature Rousseau depreciates man's work to glorify God's, here he strangely exalts our animal inheritance over our human achievement.

Rousseau's third use of the term "Nature" is in a psychological sense. In affirming the essential and natural goodness of man, Rousseau means that man's fundamental, primitive impulses are good: *men* are evil, but *man* is good. This is the appeal to the heart, to those inner feelings and longings in which man, despite untoward circumstances and unfortunate or even disreputable careers in society, may yet claim for himself the virtue and the precious worth for which his heart thirsts. Here is perhaps the most significant strain in Rousseau's thinking: this flood of feeling in which all literature was soon to be submerged, this protesting and craving and likewise complacent individualism of the misunderstood, of the insulted and injured, the eulogy of the vagabond and his inner alleged purity, the cult of the criminal and of the prostitute, victims of social inequity and iniquity. Rousseau in Venice weeps at the feet of Zulietta, and with better right in cold Petersburg, Raskolnikov is to weep at the feet of Sonia. This third view of nature is manifest in the nostalgic, wistful, and only half-expressible emotionalism, sentiment that could degenerate into sentimentality, a heart-breaking sense of alienation in the actual and the hunger of the heart after vanished or unrealized perfection: an orgy of meditation and melancholy and advertised solitude; the individualism of sensitive suffering souls for whom this world was too much, yet who, like Rousseau, felt "stifled in the universe." [27] It is the quintessence of romanticism.

So we find these central ideas of Rousseau in his three major works which in a sense form a trilogy: "Man is born free, and everywhere he is in chains." Taking man as he is, what should be done to save or recover for him as much of the freedom of his primitive state of nature as possible in civil society? This is the theme of the *Contrat social.* In *La nouvelle Héloïse* Rousseau exalts unconstrained, straightforward love, in contrast to the elegant conventionalized passions of the salon. This is the emotional, romantic return to nature, to genuine and unashamed and consuming devotion. And in the *Émile* he would safeguard through education man's natural gifts, and thus allow them free range to develop and come to fruition so that the human nature of the child, created perfect by God, may not be corrupted by wrong social training. And the same redemption of human nature from the corruptions of civilization he proposes in man's religious life, in the *Profession de foi du vicaire savoyard:* not a Christianity of theological rigid orthodoxy, elaborate ritual, ecclesiastic pomp and circumstance, but rather an intimate mystical-emotional faith, individual spontaneous outpouring of the human soul, a religion of tenderness, charity, trust, and soul-soothing quietism. Thus we see Rousseau chafing in the strait-jacket of civilization, wriggling uncomfortably, and trying to win for himself and for others as large a measure as might be of that blessed lost freedom and spontaneity which he imagined that uncorrupted primitive man had.

"His eventide moods he scorns in the morning," Boileau had written in his Eighth Satire, and Rousseau found his own portraiture in the words. There is little logic or consistency in his works, and less of it in his life. The man who advocated education of children according to nature sent his own children one after the other to the Foundlings' Asylum. The man who glorified the simple life of freedom in the bosom of nature lived that life as the protégé of one aristocrat after another. The man who exalted intimate and utter personal devotion was morbidly suspicious of his own friends and forgot or lost them in a manner that is apt to invite mingled contempt and pity. And yet the ideas which so passionately possessed him, and the new passions to which he gave so thrilling an utterance, became mighty forces in the thought and in the life of mankind.

Shall we dispose of the matter easily by styling Rousseauism the vagabond tradition in our modern life, the impetuous outpouring of the uncontrolled, the defiant protest of the submerged, the sentimental pathos of the morbid, the neglected intimate, and the misunderstood? Is distrust of Rousseauism and resistance to its romantic nonsense an acid test of sanity in a modern man? So large and so real elements of truth are implied in the very asking of these questions that one is only too apt to lapse into error by mistaking the partial for the more complete truth. The verdict which Rousseau passed on civilization and on our cultural values can be estimated in more adequate and more contemporary terms if we consider in this connection the gospel preached in our own day by the man whom we may regard as Rousseau's greatest pupil, for he was more than a mere pupil: a volcano of passions but also a granite-wall of resolute will, an iconoclast less sentimental and more candid and heroic than Rousseau. A century after the death of Voltaire and Rousseau, in 1878, Count Lyof Tolstoy, fifty years old, was definitely turning from a life of cultured ease, elegance, literary fame, and complacent religious unbelief and indifference to an agonized soul-searching contest with the problem of the eternal values of human life. At the middle of life and at the turn of the road, the Voltairean smooth scepticism on which his youth had been nourished proved unavailing. Did he then once more turn to Rousseau whom he had earlier in life cherished and partly forgotten? It were quite inadequate to interpret Tolstoy's modern apostolate as a simple conversion from Voltaire to Rousseau; but the career of the evangelist of Yasnaya Polyana does illustrate in contemporary terms the clash which in the eighteenth century ranged Voltaire and Rousseau in opposite camps. And the Russian's way of meeting and solving his problem serves to accentuate the main issues, and thus enables us to reach a truer estimate of this modern disdain of civilization and cultural values.

IV

There is a mistaken notion that at the age of fifty, after he had written *War and Peace* and *Anna Karenina*, Tolstoy suddenly turned right about face and changed his entire course and view of life. On more careful scrutiny, however, we find in the later Tolstoy only the explicit recognition of a truth which must have been lurking in his inner being all his life. His favorite game as a child was to search for the green stick on which was carved the secret of universal happiness. This green stick was supposedly buried somewhere on the family estate, but the children never found it, for an essential condition of success while looking for it was *not* to think of a white bear. Tolstoy's whole life may be called the hunt for the green stick of blessedness.[28] He sought it in the transports of passion and in the thrill of the gambling table, in the vast calm and untamed grandeur of elemental nature, in the dare-devil intoxication of ever-present death and in the hardening of the soul through war, in the serene joys of a happy family life, in the glowing sense of ever-growing literary fame, social prestige, power of wealth: ever insatiate and never satisfied. When he had seemingly scaled the heights of human ambition, he recoiled from life: the height on which he stood was the brink of an abyss.

It is quite clear to any intelligent reader of the novel *Anna Karenina*,—I am referring here particularly to the account of Levin's tragic character,—that we have there, not merely the portrayal of struggle and anguish, but the portrayal of them by a man who is himself anguished and struggling. When the book *My Confessions* appeared, the world perceived the conflict in Tolstoy's inner life, a conflict between the artist and the man, the struggle of a man whose work the world admired and approved, but who could not admire his own work because he was not sure that God approved it; indeed doubted whether there was any God to approve it, and found his life poisoned by the doubt.[29]

The more he saw of life, the more he thought, the less satisfied he became. "What is the meaning of it all?" he kept asking himself. He had six thousand *desyatines* of land in the government of Samara, and three hundred horses. Suppose he had sixty thousand *desyatines*, and as many horses: what then? He was a famous writer. But suppose he became still more famous, more famous than Gogol, than Pushkin, Shakespeare, Molière, than any writer in the world: what then? What was it all about? Why should he, Count Tolstoy, author of *War and Peace* and *Anna Karenina*, with his thousands of acres, horses, healthy, rich, respected, admired, loved, possessing all that men desire: why should he be living at all? "Is there any meaning in my life," he asked, "which will not be destroyed by the inevitable death awaiting me? . . . I felt that the ground on which I stood was crumbling, that there was nothing for me to stand on, that what I had been living for was nothing, that I had no reason for living."

The problem is radical enough, and Tolstoy's solution of it was as bold and radical. The enlightened men of his own class seemed to be in the dark as far as the question of ultimate values and lasting satisfaction was concerned, so he turned to the peasants, amazed for the first time in his life by the idea that, despite their poverty and ignorance, they lived contentedly on their bread and onions. Life must have a real meaning, he thought, and in their humble way they must know this meaning. The peasants told him to live according to Christ's law, and in all sincerity Tolstoy tried to find this law in the Gospels. His discoveries were revolutionary. He found in the Sermon on the Mount five commandments, like five signposts pointing him to solid ground out of his spiritual quagmires.

Jesus condemned murderous anger and contumely, and preached considerate and generous respect of man for man. Jesus branded sensuality, veiled or unveiled, the flagrant or the contemplated degradation of woman to serve as a mere instrument of lust. Jesus denounced the willing surrender of a man's free conscience to his official superiors implied in the taking of military or bureaucratic oaths of unquestioning obedience. Jesus tore down the barriers separating one nation from another, and applied the moral law to international relations: not merely love your neighbor, but love your enemy, the alien; love all mankind. And fifthly, in a commandment which Tolstoy regarded as the keystone of his moral edifice, Jesus condemned unreservedly the use of force and the law of retribution, and preached the law of love, non-resistance.

Tolstoy observed that these commandments of Jesus ran, not only counter to the general practice of society, but in some cases also counter to the avowed principles on which the social order rested. The search for spiritual peace had sent him to the Gospel, and what he learned there involved him in a radical critique of the life and the fundamental ideas of modern civilization.

The root of evil, Tolstoy declared, is selfish exploitation of man by man. This lust for self-assertion and self-gratification, sexual, economic, political, social, intellectual, taints the entire system of so-called civilized life. We imprison or exile or kill those whom we haven't reformed or who haven't reformed us. We employ the best years of a nation's young manhood in the training of men to kill other men similarly trained. We hold sacrosanct an economic system in which one man luxuriates while and often just because a hundred starve. We condone lust, glorify it in literature and provide for it in practice, whether in the form of regulated or unregulated prostitution or in the less candid form of unstable, pretended marriages. At the basis of our systems of law and public security is hatred masked as righteous indignation and the spirit of revenge parading as retributive justice. And we declare that philanthropy is well enough in its place, but that we must have force and violent compulsion, if civilization and the social order are to be maintained.[30]

What are we to do then? Shall we withdraw from this wicked world to live the romantic hermit life à la Rousseau in the bosom of uncorrupted nature? Or shall we resign ourselves to the inevitable, considering that the whole system of society involves exploitation, that we cannot change the system, that our drop in the bucket doesn't make any difference one way or the other, and we should not make ourselves miserable over it? Tolstoy took a different stand, and here his integrity puts Rousseau to shame. Rousseau's attack on civilization is largely an apology for his own life: society is to blame, not he; even in his *Confessions* Rousseau challenges mankind to show a better man than himself. He saw himself as a victim, never as a villain; even his remorse over his vices only illustrates the wretchedness of the environment that had perverted him or hampered his true self-expression.

Tolstoy is of a different temper; the intensity of his convictions is Pascalian, and the consequent radical reform of his everyday life calls to mind pages from Pascal's biography.[31] He begins with himself. What is to be done? means to him: what am I, Lyof Tolstoy, to do? Here I have been writing world-famous novels, and have been portraying the tree of human life, its decayed and leafless branches; but what am I really? One of the caterpillars on the tree of human life. I criticize exploitation, and myself exploit people and live comfortably on their daily toil. I, Lyof Tolstoy, am like a horseman who observes that the horse he rides is exhausted. What is to be done? Write fine books about tired horses, remain seated on the horse's back and philanthropically hold up the beast's head? No, but first of all get off the horse's back. Before I can honestly engage in philanthropy and undertake to relieve the sufferings of the poor, I must stop living a form of life that necessarily causes poverty in the social order. This problem, Tolstoy says, is quite simple, and is made complicated only by those who do not wish to solve it in their own lives. The Chinese say: If there is one man idle, there is another dying of hunger. If I consume what I have not myself produced, I am simply eating the dinner which someone else has earned and doesn't get, and no amount of argument can change the ugly fact.

Here, then, I must start. I must make other men work

for me as little as possible, and must myself work as much as possible. I can take care of my own room, I can look after my own garden, I can clean my boots, indeed, I can make my boots, I can go into the fields and by honest labor produce the equivalent of the food which I eat. And only when I have done this, my own share of the daily labor upon which the sustaining of human life depends, only then can I presume to talk of philanthropy or teaching my fellowmen or the higher life.[32] I cannot write novels, or philosophize, or make a catalogue of a million beetles, or calculate the distances of the stars, or paint sunsets and compose symphonies, and count myself superior to the ignorant and ill-smelling peasant who in the meantime has been feeding me,—or worse yet, who has been producing the bread that I eat today while I, captain of trade or finance, manipulate the market so that his bread and that of thousands of others may be gathered into my storerooms. This supposed division of labor, Tolstoy says, is a subtle fallacy with which we seek to cover a plain and ugly fact. It is a fact that in one day or even in one hour a skillful commercial transaction may make me the legal possessor of what thousands have labored for days or months to produce. It is a fact, but it is none the less iniquitous, and the civilization that sanctions it has not been touched with the true spirit of Christ.

The alleged superiority and dignity of mental work is subject to a similar criticism. Why am I the choice beneficiary of the social order? Because of my supposed high order of intelligence, because of my genius? But in that case I should be able to see more clearly than others this real truth of human life, and seeing it should mend my life accordingly. The maximum time that I can spend in really profitable mental work, that is, work vigorous and not detrimental to mind or body, is five hours daily. I sleep eight hours. What do I do with the eleven hours that remain? Let me spend part of that time in relieving the peasant in his manual labor, so that he may have chance to think at least half an hour.

But you say that modern civilized life is too complicated to allow of such transformation? So much the worse for civilized life then: this gaudy edifice of culture does not atone for the misery of millions on which it rests, nor is it worth the human price which its elegant beneficiaries pay for it. "The greater part of my life and yours is taken up with satisfying, not our natural wants, but wants invented by us, or artificially inoculated by our education, and that have become habitual to us; and nine tenths of the work which we devote to satisfying these demands is idle work." [33] So Tolstoy condemned the powers of darkness within us: violence, arrogance, lust, desire to oppress, exploitation. He saw these as it were inextricably bound up with modern civilization. To rid human life of them he was prepared to sacrifice civilization. And he conceived of another social order in which men labored in the spirit of brotherhood, each doing his share, each freely bringing to mankind his peculiar gift of intelligence or intense exquisite feeling or spiritual genius. In this social order of Tolstoy's vision, agriculture, industry and trade involved no exploitation, science and philosophy truly enlightened human life, art was not aristocratic and exclusive, but rather perfected the universal communion of men in the direct language of feeling, and religion, instead of chaining men to stony creeds and wooden ritual, knit men together in living brotherhood, entered the human soul and opened its windows to admit the sunlight of God.

We need not waste time criticizing the details of Tolstoy's own practice as a reformer, if we remember his words written to Engelhardt in August, 1882, words which he could have written with even stronger conviction twenty-five years later: "People say to me, 'Well, Lyof Nikolaevitch, as far as preaching goes, you preach; but how about your practice?'

The question is a perfectly natural one; it is always put to me, and it always shuts my mouth. . . . Condemn me, if you choose,—but condemn *me,* and not the path which I am following. . . . If I know the road home, and if I go along it drunk, and staggering from side to side, does that prove that the road is not the right one? . . . Do not yourselves confuse and mislead me, and then rejoice over it and cry, 'Look at him! He says he is going home, and he is floundering in the swamp!' . . . My heart is breaking with despair because we have all lost the road; and while I struggle with all my strength to find it, and keep in it, you, instead of pitying me when I go astray, cry triumphantly, 'See! He is in the swamp with us!'" [34]

If we are candid, we are bound to admit the evils in our modern civilized society which Tolstoy so vividly exposes to view. But before we can pass judgment on his remedies, the conclusions of his diagnosis must be estimated. Because the evils which Tolstoy combats are so largely evils of civilized life, does it follow that civilization as such is an evil, and that moral progress and cultural progress conflict essentially and all along the line?

V

Our age burns incense on the altars of progress, but is getting decidedly dubious regarding its idolatry. The rapidity with which so much of our boasted humane culture collapsed at the first impact of savage, elemental forces during the Great War: the surrender of organized labor, the ready acquiescence of academic and literary leadership, the prostitution of organized religion in the service of international slaughter, the diabolical application of the latest science and the most expert technology to the perfecting of engines of war, particularly in the use of poison gases, the extension of hostilities to the submarine and air-regions, increasingly dangerous to numberless non-combatants, and the cynical humiliation to which the noblest purposes of man were subjected by the turn of international politics after the conclusion of the proclaimed War to End War: all these have made many men draw back with dismay, distrusting the goddess Civilization, and doubting the stability and the essential soundness of the whole structure of Western Culture.

This confirmed or incipient social pessimism is not without ground; these last years have served only to exhibit more obviously the seamy underside of the outwardly resplendent cloak of modern civilization. In our modern age we have perfected technical skill beyond the wildest dreams of the past, have harnessed nature to do our bidding, have almost abolished time and space; but have we become spiritually cosmopolitan, citizens of the cosmos? Have we, in transcending the provincial boundaries of our material environment, transcended and overcome likewise spiritual provincialism? In the amazing perfection of our means of communication, have we perfected correspondingly our sense of ultimate direction? We move much faster: do we know any more clearly whither we are going, the nature of our journey or our destination? We can share our ideas so much more readily and universally: that is, share them with eye and ear; but what is the final meaning of what we have to say to each other? Is it not one of the deplorable aspects of our modern civilization that spiritual culture has lagged behind material progress, that we see all about us veriest apes of the spirit manipulating the latest devices of applied science, as if the jungle itself were equipped with wireless and radio for the broadcasting of simian wisdom?

Let us ask then: Does the disdain of civilization rest on a sound diagnosis, and are Rousseau's or Tolstoy's proposed remedies really appropriate? Civilization does involve perversion and corruption of human life, but is it only or essentially corruption and perversion that it involves? Is civilization adequately defined as perversion and corruption? Rousseau, Tolstoy, and other social pessimists condemn the cultural process because of the evils in which it is entangled. This condemnatory verdict is a wholesome shock to rouse man from the slumber of cultural complacency, but it is nonetheless one-sided. A more careful look into the relation of civilization to morality and perfection generally discloses the deeper truth as lying between the two shallower extremes of complacency and despair.

This deeper truth we may formulate as follows: The advance of civilization does not involve the perfection nor yet the perversion of human nature,—that is to say, neither one of these two to the exclusion of the other. What we call the advance of civilization is rather the spread of the field on which human aims are pursued, realized, or frustrated: a spread and an intensification of all available values, positive and negative. Civilization is a great opportunity, but it is also a grave hazard: in its advance man learns how high he can rise, but also how low he can fall.

This essential truth may be examined and exhibited in detail in every field of human endeavor. The more complex our civilization, the more varied, the subtler, the more momentous become both attainment and frustration, whether moral, intellectual, aesthetic, or religious. Read and interpret the decalogue in terms of modern civilized experience. "Thou shalt not kill—shalt not steal—shalt not covet:" observe the almost measureless expanse of range alike in vice and in opposite virtue here. These commandments have mellowed; enriched in meaning, they are much more difficult to fulfil than in primitive life, but the virtues they inculcate are also loftier and richer. Consider justice, or brotherhood, and see the sweep in range of meaning in them as a result of civilization. In the realm of science the same results obtain. A little knowledge is a dangerous thing, and still more dangerous is much knowledge: dangerous in its disturbing of traditional stolidity, dangerous in its being misapprehended and misapplied, a sword double-edged in possibly foolish hands. Shall we say then: Blessed are the ignorant, or repeat the words of Dostoyevsky, "In Germany everyone can read and write, but everyone is stupid," implying presumably the rare wisdom of the illiterate Russian peasant? Intellectual progress is an opportunity *and* a hazard, even in purely intellectual terms: every solution only serves to give rise to still vaster problems, in which the chance of greater truth is confronted with the chance of more serious error, truth and error alike increasingly fundamental. So in art, success and failure alike are in the beginner elementary, but in the work of the master both are complex and grave: a child's house of blocks compared with a Gothic cathedral, a primitive woman's crooning against a Beethoven symphony. So even more truly is it also in religion. Man's idea of God gains in significance, but also in complexity. Piety in civilized life may be more profound, but it is likewise immeasurably more difficult than in primitive religion.

This view of human life cannot be described either as optimistic or as pessimistic. Dispiriting to the laggard, it is a challenge inspiring to the heroic in human nature. The parable of the servant who hid the single talent entrusted to him may here be adapted to our purpose. Spiritual life is a venture in values. To him that hath shall be given: this is the promise to the aspiring; but from him that hath not even that which he hath shall be taken away: this is the censure of the slothful and stagnating. And the old stories of Prometheus and of the Garden of Eden may now be seen in a somewhat new light. The uprising of man from the so-called state of nature to the level of civilization is both tragic and sublime. The tree of knowledge is the tree of the knowledge of good *and* of evil: eating of it cost man his primitive, paradisiacal innocence, and it was his first sin and guilt and made man's life a tragic enterprise. But it also made him a traveler on the road of real moral attainment and moral dignity: deliberate, aspiring, heroic. Not in the unruffled innocence of Paradise, but in the storm and stress of spiritual endeavor is man's real, living perfection to be sought. "The best world for a moral agent," Royce told us, "is one that needs him to make it better." [35]

Man's true path upward is not in negating civilization, not in utopian simplification of modern life, though Tolstoy is to be honored for having pointed out how much larger share of homely self-reliance is possible for man even in the present highly specialized social order. Tolstoy himself recognized that evil is not to be remedied simply by a change of environment or reorganization of the social structure, but through a personal reformation of one's own life in the social system in which one lives, a system, however, which must never be allowed to overawe the individual's conscience.[36] The problem which modern society presents to the alert individual conscience is this: How may I participate in this complex life of civilization, yet in and through it contribute to the attainment of ever more adequate fair play, economic and social and international and inter-racial justice? Tolstoy even in his ploughing and cobbling was still Tolstoy,—but how are those millions for whom ploughing or cobbling, those for whom factory, shop, or store is the day's work, how are they to find in the vast complex social enterprise of modern civilization in which they *must* participate, meaning and satisfaction and stimulus, sweetness and light? This is a fundamental problem of modern civilization, but this problem is not solved by the utopian proposal to reject culture and seek perfection in peasant or in primitive conditions of life. In saying this I do not for one moment seek to dismiss the truth, so forcibly uttered by Tolstoy, that the callous exploitation of man by man is essentially vicious, and that morality demands respect for the spiritual dignity of one's fellowmen and wholehearted participation in the work and in the larger life of mankind. But the attainment of this goal demands, not the cultural impoverishment of humanity, but rather the spiritual and moral enrichment of our cultural inheritance.

CHAPTER VII

THE DEVIL IN MODERN POETRY

"Nothing is less poetical than optimism," Leslie Stephen wrote; "for the essence of a poet's function is to harmonize the sadness of the universe." [1] More rhapsodically the Scandinavian sage Sören Kierkegaard has expressed the same idea: a poet is "an unhappy creature tormented by deep anguish, with lips so formed that his sighs sound like beautiful music." [2] We may share the ancient Orphic view that Zeus made the gods from his smiles, and men from his tears, and thus regard grief as the essential theme of the poetic utterance of human life; or less gloomily we may observe that grief is an experience more intense and less common than joy, and thus on both counts more stimulating poetically. But in either case the dominance of the tragic note in great poetry will not escape us, the note of dolor, dismay, and divine discontent, and Shelley's lines in the poem *To a Skylark* will come to mind:

> We look before and after,
> And pine for what is not:
> Our sincerest laughter
> With some pain is fraught;
> Our sweetest songs are those that tell of saddest thought.

The next three chapters are devoted to the pessimistic strains in modern poetry. This field is large, and compression is imposed by the natural bounds of our present undertaking. A study of the despondent, wistful, utopian strains in modern romantic poetry, and the romantic disdain of the actual, would throw light on our general inquiry, but is apt to lead us far afield. On the other hand, the major poets of pessimism demand a more intimate individual study of life, character, and work than can be accorded to them in a general discussion of a 'movement.' An effort has been made here to combine the merits of the two methods, by dealing more intimately and in greater and more various detail in the next two chapters with Giacomo Leopardi and Alfred de Vigny, while in this chapter, instead of a general comparison of pessimistic strains and tendencies, the conception of supreme evil has been selected as a window through which we may look into the inner life and into the view of life of several modern poets. If a man's idea of God is sure index of his spiritual temper and outlook, then doubtless a poet's idea of the devil should reflect his sense of the source and ground of evil and his poetic reaction towards it. Naturally enough, and also fortunately for our purpose, this theme brings together a number of poets of disdain and despair who would have interested us in any case, but it also brings, for comparison and contrast, poets whom we can scarcely call pessimistic, and who should serve to make the final impression more balanced. We shall turn first to the Devil of the Genesis story, as portrayed in Milton's *Paradise Lost* and in Byron's *Cain*, and in the latter part of this chapter shall consider the conception of Mephistopheles in several of the more significant versions of the Faust-saga.

I

Milton found the setting of his epic in the Book of Genesis, and Biblical tradition imposed on him certain elements in his theme which he perhaps would not have freely chosen, and some which he deliberately revised or rejected. While *Paradise Lost* has supplied thousands of men with what they have believed to be Biblical impressions, so that Milton's poem has actually played the rôle of Scripture, particularly in Protestant experience, Milton's readers have as a rule come to the poem with the demonology of tradition, have carried away rich memories of Satanic stratagem, strife, and seduction, but have often missed the deeper ideas of his ethics and theodicy. Even Dante, for whom the medieval world-view was surely no poetic fiction, appealed to the keener perception that distinguishes poetic from prosaic truth:

> O ye who have sound intellects, observe
> The doctrine that is here, hiding itself
> Beneath the veil of the unwonted verses! [3]

Milton, heir to the wisdom of antiquity, was also a live participant in the thought of the seventeenth century, critical and non-conformist in theology, cosmology, morals, and politics alike. It is clear to the more careful reader that in *Paradise Lost* Milton undertakes to portray a world in which evil is rampant, and ruinous to man, but casting no discredit on God, nor yet prevailing in the end over good. If we keep in mind the years during which the blind poet created his masterpiece, we can well perceive how much of himself he was bound to utter and how completely he was to enter into the world of his epic, himself a protagonist. Thus we shall not be surprised to find Satan no mere vehicle of an abstraction, but vitalized by ardent imagination and intense feeling into a living figure, the most living in the whole poem. We shall not forget that Milton would

> delineate so,
> By likening spiritual to corporal forms,
> As may express them best; [4]

but we shall also remember that *Paradise Lost* is not a mere allegory. We may surmise that even for Milton's cold reason Satan possessed a reality which, by way of comparison, Mephistopheles could scarcely have had for Goethe's intellect. But in dealing with Goethe and Milton alike, the more important question concerns, not the seriousness of their demonology, but the moral scale of values and the sort of theodicy disclosed in their delineation of Evil Powers and Principalities, whatever assortment of them they may have selected for the purposes of their poems.

The dominant trait of Milton's Satan is proud, rebellious, resentful self-will. His uprising against the Almighty is conceived as having been provoked by God's exaltation of his newly begotten Son as cosmic king anointed, to whom all knees in heaven should bow. That Milton was willing thus to revise theology, to regard the angelic host as more ancient than the Son of God, and the latter as a more lately chosen sole favorite of the Almighty, was clearly dictated by poetic considerations as greatly enhancing the dramatic qualities of the revolt in heaven. But the headlong violence of Satan's resistance and the readiness with which his cohorts joined in the rebellion manifest only too clearly the indomitable haughtiness of these "thrones, dominations, princedoms, virtues, powers," [5] that must have been chafing and smouldering under the sway of the Eternal all along and needed only a spur and a spark to flame up in open defiance. One single counter-note of loyalty to God is sounded by the seraph Abdiel, but his pious zeal is seconded by none, and the Satanic apostasy overwhelmingly prevails in the dread council; one full third of the angelic host join the revolt.

Here is confirmed, hardened sin: deliberate and passionate rejection of that loyalty to the higher and the better wherein all good consists. Satan and his followers have not merely stumbled; unlike Adam and Eve whose lapse, due to deception, while demanding expiation, yet does not shut out the prospect of redemption, the Satanic hosts and Satan most of all are the very embodiments of irreconcilable disdain and malice, demanding final overthrow but altogether precluding salvation.[6]

This essential wickedness is not unreservedly repulsive. In his devotion to his chosen aims, Satan exhibits ardor and heroism; he abundantly deserves the brave loyalty of his lieutenants. Milton had too keen moral perception and too fine poetic taste to paint Satan all muddy black, after the fashion of the ugly devils of popular fancy. His Satan is no ignoble leader and his calls to arms do not remain unanswered. There is no scene in hell like the one in heaven when God asks his angels:

> Which of you will be mortal to redeem
> Man's mortal crime; and just the unjust to save?
> Dwells in all heaven charity so dear? [7]

and the heavenly choir stands mute, and no patron or intercessor appears on man's behalf until finally the Son of God offers himself as the redeemer of man. There is compelling majesty in Satan's character and career: sublime pride, courage, flaming independence, untrammeled spirit of criticism. Milton not only gave the devil his due, but in many ways put himself in Satan's place: the Prince of Darkness is drawn with so much understanding because Milton himself was a free spirit, indomitable, proud. But all the more impressive is the clarity of Milton's perception that ardent devotion does not by itself avail if its object is unworthy. It is the cosmic pity of it that such high virtues here are so perverted; courage in such a godless cause is doubly ruinous because so heroic. Satan's fanatical egotism is rendered the more deplorable by the majestic proportions which it assumes. The end does not always justify the means, but often damns them.

The determination to pervert and undo God's work, while dominating Satan's mind, does not exhaust it to the exclusion of other ideas. He is no mere text or formula or moving abstraction, but a living and complex individuality. He has a noble solicitude for his warriors, and on occasion shows fine disinterestedness in his devotion to the common cause. He is not unresponsive to beauty nor even to the call of pity, nor is he lacking in chivalry. But the master passion of his being, while admitting coëxistent emotions, does not tolerate any rivalry; it prevails and subjugates the rest.

This domination of Satan by his great passion, the rebelliousness of his self-will against the sway of the Higher, is what constitutes him the personification of evil. His whole career represents the defiance of passion to reason. The dramatic version of the first conclave of incipient revolt in heaven anticipates Spinoza's ethical analysis: upstart outlaw passion demagogically inciting and drawing to itself all the other feelings, disdainfully rejecting the loyal counsel of sanity, and plunging headlong, nor drawing back, but stubborn and resolute unto perdition. Reason is not extinguished here, but it is humiliated. While organizing his plans of battle, Satan is not really unaware of his ultimate defeat.

> He from heaven's height
> All these our motions vain sees, and derides.

Nor is he insensible to the glorious state from which he has fallen. But defeat is not defeat to him so long as he remains resistant, nor is a state really glorious to him if it demands submission:

> What though the field be lost?
> All is not lost; the unconquerable will
> And study of revenge, immortal hate,
> And courage never to submit or yield,
> And what is else not to be overcome. . . .
> The mind is its own place, and in itself
> Can make a heaven of hell, a hell of heaven.
> What matter where, if I be still the same,
> And what I should be?

So again, when about to tempt Eve:

> Revenge, at first though sweet,
> Bitter ere long, back on itself recoils:
> Let it: I reck not. . . .

So again in *Paradise Regained:*

> I would be at the worst: worst is my port,
> My harbour, and my ultimate repose:
> The end I would attain, my final good.

Thus triumphant in Satan's being, rebellious resentful self-will pours out all the treasures of an archangelic nature into the determined and ardent pursuit of perverted aims:

> To do aught good never will be our task,
> But ever to do ill our sole delight;
> As being the contrary to his high will,
> Whom we resist. If then his providence
> Out of our evil seeks to bring forth good,
> Our labour must be to pervert that end,
> And out of good still to find means of evil.

So directed and devoted, Satan's will renders its own virtues vile and is its own final punishment. This he perceives: misery devours him, but still to him no misery is like submission:

> Which way I fly is hell; myself am hell;
> And in the lowest deep a lower deep
> Still threatening to devour me opens wide. . . .
> The lower still I fall; only supreme
> In misery; such joy ambition finds.[8]

Such resolution, if supporting devotion to high aims, loyalty to the Ever-Highest, would have made Satan worthy of his archangelic post; as it is, his very virtues, in being perverted, have made his wickedness the blacker. Even so man, created in God's own image, may yet choose beastliness for his aim and sink lower than the beasts. To Milton's mind good and evil characterize opposite directions of the will, as led by reason to the pursuit and the humble worship of the higher aims that elevate and exalt man to God, or as driven by upstart passion to degrading lusts and ambitions. This latter is the illusory freedom of the fool, real inward enslavement, for

> This is servitude,
> To serve the unwise, or him who hath rebell'd
> Against his worthier. . . .

But where the lower is directed by and loyal to the higher, the lower is itself elevated and ennobled. So-called sensuality may be mere nature, animal instinct; or it may be sinful beastliness, as in Adam and Eve immediately after the fall; but it can also be pure innocence, as in Paradise before the fall; directed and concurred in by reason, it becomes a supreme instance of body working up to spirit. Man's evil and ruin is in his being deluded into self-degradation by changing the direction and aim of his pursuit, with consequent bedeviling of his zeal and loyalties. Milton speaks in *Lycidas* of "blind mouths:" unintelligent avidity. This is evil, when the soul thus turns away from God; this is moral idolatry:

> Their Maker's image . . . then
> Forsook them, when themselves they vilified
> To serve ungovern'd appetite.[9]

Man is created in God's own image, and his true destiny is increasingly to grow like unto God: "Ye shall be holy, for I am holy." The negating of man's true career, when passion triumphs over reason and ignoble lusts replace high loyalties, is therefore a negation of man's humanity. So Christ, in *Paradise Regained*, speaks of those who are

> Scarce men,
> Rolling in brutish vices, and deformed.

But when man, resisting the lure and drag of passion, upreaches with redoubled vigor towards the divine, repentant but never despairing, he rises the stronger because of his downfall and possesses a paradise within him, *happier far*, as the Archangel Michael promises Adam. With Christ's grace evil is turned to greater good. So the angelic host sings glory to Christ, to the divine plan of redemption of man and confutation of the Evil One:

> Who seeks
> To lessen thee, against his purpose serves
> To manifest the more thy might: his evil
> Thou usest, and from thence createst more good.[10]

We may agree in calling this "the main idea of the poem:" [11] evil is self-destructive, and good is ever-living. Satan works only by divine sufferance, and in the end his work is to be undone by divine grace, and thus Satan will see

> How all his malice served but to bring forth
> Infinite goodness, grace, and mercy shown
> On man by him seduced: but on himself
> Treble confusion, wrath, and vengeance pour'd.[12]

That *Paradise Lost*, composed as it was by blind, defeated Milton under the Restoration, portrays evil so grimly, yet breathes such unshakable confidence in God's justice and love and in the final triumph of righteousness, is, despite aspersions old and more recent, assurance enough both of the stern manliness and of the sound buoyancy of Milton's character.

II

In his *Cain: A Mystery*, Byron represents Adam and Eve repentant and subdued worshippers of God, with their children timid and unquestioning: all but one. In this first family the sacrificial chant of awed acquiescence is disturbed by the resistant silence of Cain. He refuses to bow in prayer to a God who forbade man knowledge and allotted him death for his fruition. Grave doubts torment him:

And this is
Life?—Toil! and wherefore should I toil?—because
My father could not keep his place in Eden?
What had *I* done in this?—I was unborn:
I sought not to be born; nor love the state
To which that birth has brought me. Why did he
Yield to the serpent and the woman? or
Yielding—why suffer? What was there in this?
The tree was planted, and why not for him?
If not, why place him near it, where it grew
The fairest in the center? They have but
One answer to all questions, "'Twas *his* will,
And *he* is good." How know I that? Because
He is all-powerful, must all-good, too, follow?
I judge but by the fruits—and they are bitter—
Which I must feed on for a fault not mine. . . .[13]

It is his first soliloquy and it sets the tone of the drama. Byron had read his Bayle, and those acquainted with that formidable armory can recognize many an old weapon here. But, whereas in Bayle's folios affirming faith is battling with scepticism, Byron's drama is the contest of doubt and denial, with denial in the ascendant. Lucifer is but the steady undertow of Cain's wavering uncertainty, sweeping him on to unsounded depths of negation. Cain is not sure that the Creator is good: Lucifer is certain that he is not good:

Lucifer. He is great—
But, in his greatness, is no happier than
We in our conflict! Goodness would not make
Evil; and what else hath he made? But let him
Sit on his vast and solitary throne—
Creating worlds, to make eternity
Less burthensome to his immense existence—
And unparticipated solitude;
Let him crowd orb on orb: he is alone
Indefinite, Indissoluble Tyrant;
Could he but crush himself, 'twere the best boon
He ever granted: but let him reign on!
And multiply himself in misery!

> Spirits and Men, at least we sympathise—
> And, suffering in concert, make our pangs
> Innumerable, more endurable,
> By the unbounded sympathy of all
> With all! But *He!* so wretched in his height,
> So restless in his wretchedness, must still
> Create, and re-create. . . .[14]

Nichol has well called Byron's drama "mainly a dialogue between two halves of his mind." [15] Upon the dread doubt of Cain, Lucifer would imprint his seal of denial without doubt or dread; in Cain he recognizes his unwitting worshipper, unwitting but not unresponsive: "Thou speak'st to me of things which long have swum in visions through my thought," Cain tells him:

> I feel the weight
> Of daily toil, and constant thought: I look
> Around a world where I seem nothing, with
> Thoughts which arise within me, as if they
> Could master all things—but I thought alone
> This misery was *mine*. . . .
> Never till
> Now met I aught to sympathise with me.
> 'Tis well. . . .[16]

Will this troubled doubt be clarified and precipitated into unqualified defiance, and Cain join the rebel group of Lucifer? Lucifer relies on strength and unhumbled pride and professed passion for truth as substitutes for happiness, and he imparts his scorn of submissive ease to Cain:

> I will have naught to do with happiness
> Which humbles me and mine.

But Adah, Cain's wife, distrusts, dreads, and pities Lucifer by turns:

> Thou seem'st unhappy: do not make us so,
> And I will weep for thee.

"Alas!" Lucifer answers, "those tears!"

Couldst thou but know what oceans will be shed—
. . . The myriad myriads—the all-peopled earth—
The unpeopled earth—and the o'erpeopled Hell—
Of which thy bosom is the germ.

Adah is beyond his reach, but on Cain he urges open rebellion, refusal to submit:

Nothing can
Quench the mind, if the mind will be itself
And centre of surrounding things—'tis made
To sway.[17]

What is it that still binds Cain to the Creator's tether on this mortal earth? His inability to disdain utterly what he loves as well as what he hates: both due to his lingering attachment to his petty sphere and to his inadequate perception of its pettiness. So Lucifer undertakes Cain's education in disdain; but it is precisely this enlightenment which brings the midnight to his soul: the promised immortality proves ruinous. As Lucifer and his neophyte pierce the infinite spaces like sunbeams, Eden vanishes from sight and the earth becomes an invisible speck, new worlds come into view,—with Edens in them, and men, and serpents,—come into view, and vanish, and leave Cain with an increasing sense of the Vast Incomprehensible:

Lucifer. And now I will convey thee to thy world
Where thou shalt multiply the race of Adam,
Eat, drink, toil, tremble, laugh, weep, sleep—and die!
Cain. And to what end have I beheld these things
Which thou hast shown me?
Lucifer. Didst thou not require
Knowledge? And have I not, in what I showed,
Taught thee to know thyself?
Cain. Alas! I seem
Nothing.[18]

It is not in this seeming nothingness, however, that the heart of Cain's tragedy is to be sought, but rather in the boundless reach of his unrealized thought when contrasted with this seeming nothingness:

> Thou show'st me things beyond *my* power,
> Beyond all power of my born faculties,
> Although inferior still to my desires
> And my conceptions.[19]

Thus actuality humiliates his ideals: his world petty, his problems provincial, his aeons but moments of unreckoned eternity, his joys and his sorrows alike of no avail, his truths delusions and his virtues naïve, and his beauty a phantom that fades on closer view. Cain's one undimmed beauty, Adah's face, has now become a torture: their love for each other and for their children are agonies, for they are but the begetters of future untold sorrows.

Thus the inner tragedy must out, and we move inevitably to the ruinous climax. It is not simply jealousy of Abel which leads Cain to murder, nor yet, as in Vigny's conception, just indignation that the offerings of the indolent herdsman should have been preferred to those of the hard-working tiller of the soil. It is the reek of sanctified blood which maddens Byron's Cain. That his own perplexed but straightforward offering of herbs and fruits is rejected, while Abel's submissive sacrifice of bloody lambs ascends in brightest flames to heaven, seems to Cain like a horrid substantiation of Lucifer's charges: God does delight in torture, torture to man's soul, torture to innocent lambs and their bleating mothers:

> Give way! this bloody record
> Shall not stand in the sun, to shame creation!

Abel resists the sacrilegious attack on God's altar, and the first murder stains the earth. Zillah's shriek of terror follows, and Cain's chaos of horror, and Eve's unspeakable curse upon him. Adah's unfailing loyalty like one bright star deepens the enveloping midnight, but it makes good Cain's words of her in this dread hour: most beautiful when nearest:

> *Cain.* Leave me! . . .
> *Adah.* I fear
> Nothing except to leave thee. . . .
> My office is
> Henceforth to dry up tears, and not to shed them. . . .[20]

The beauty of *Cain*, Goethe said, "is such as we shall not see a second time in the world," and Shelley called the play "a revelation never before communicated to man." [21] Wherein is it thus tragically unique? Byron's Lucifer is not altogether unfamiliar; his indomitable pride recalls *Paradise Lost*, and his cynicism *Faust;* Ackermann calls him "Milton's Satan and Goethe's Mephisto in *one* person.[22] Unique is not his own character but his relation to Cain. Byron records neither a losing nor a winning struggle between man and the Great Deceiver. Strictly speaking, Cain is not tempted at all. In Lucifer he finds only the full measure of his protest, the completed sentence of his own verdict, the resolution, in negation, of his own halting doubts. The tragedy of Cain is not, as Byron exhibits it, a moral tragedy; it is a tragedy of cosmic circumstance. The real hero of the drama is the *spirit* of Lucifer: Cain seems destined to attain to Lucifer's stature, and, in his undertaking to realize this destiny, Cain rises to the heroic. But to play the rôle of Lucifer transcends Cain's powers, and therein lies his tragic ruin. In rushing towards Abel's blood-dripping altar to destroy it, Cain would join Lucifer and his troop of

> Souls who dare look the Omnipotent tyrant in
> His everlasting face, and tell him that
> His evil is not good!

But the protestor against the shedding of the blood of lambs sheds his own brother's blood, and becomes more odious in his own sight than the God whom he had defied. Therein is the tragic pity of it, for Cain's sustaining confidence is shattered; his confidence that evil is *not* inevitable (that is why he had resented God's admitting it into his world). He resists the docile submission of his parents, brother, and sisters; he will not call evil good, and he seconds Lucifer's rebellion. But on one point he had been adamant, that evil is not "a part of all things:"

> Not of all things. No—
> I'll not believe it—for I thirst for good.

That this thirst for good should lead him, even while protesting against murder, to murder, is an irony so ruthless, so in the spirit of utter negation, that it leaves him reeling and aghast:

> And who hath brought him there?—I—who abhor
> The name of Death so deeply, that the thought
> Empoisoned all my life, before I knew
> His aspect—I have led him here, and given
> My brother to his cold and still embrace,
> As if he could not have asserted his
> Inexorable claim without my aid.
> I am awake at last—a dreary dream
> Had maddened me;—but *he* shall ne'er awake!

That there should be evil at all had tortured him before; but now he is brought low by this doubt settling into conviction: there is no real good,—a thought more crushing than his mother's curse, more than the brand of God upon his brow:

> It burns
> My brow, but nought to that which is within it!

In this sense we can understand the tragic intensity of the three last words of the drama: "Peace be with Abel!—But with *me!*" [23]

Thus we perceive the depth and the source of the Byronic despair. Byron is indeed of the Satanic school, pursuing single truth but doubting, indeed scorning, alleged real good.

His despair springs from his cynicism, but the fact that it is *despair* which springs from his cynicism shows him to be something decidedly more than a cynic. So Cain envies Abel even as he pities him; he wishes himself dead, but he does not repent: his tragic estimate of things is only confirmed, not altered. If the depth of Byron is cynical despair, his exaltation is vigorous and fearless integrity of spirit. Abel's bloody corpse at Cain's feet shows him his own ruin, but that fact too he will face squarely, along with the forbidden tree of knowledge, and the serpent, and the flaming swords of the cherubim at the gates of paradise, and his own unwanted life of toil and tragedy. He will not content him with what he *is*.[24] This "rage and fury against the inadequacy of his state to his conceptions" [25] is tragic, but it is also sublime. In Lucifer's parting words to Cain we may read Byron's own wisdom:

> *One good* gift has the fatal apple given,—
> Your *reason:*—let it not be overswayed
> By tyrannous threats to force you into faith
> 'Gainst all external sense and inward feeling:
> Think and endure,—and form an inner world
> In your own bosom—where the outward fails;
> So shall you nearer be the spiritual
> Nature, and war triumphant with your own.[26]

Of this intrepid resistance Byron's works provide a series of monologues: his virtues and his vices alike are those of unsubmission. So in *Childe Harold:*

> But quiet to quick bosoms is a Hell,
> And *there* hath been thy bane; there is a fire
> And motion in the Soul which will not dwell
> In its narrow being, but aspire
> Beyond the fitting medium of desire;
> And, but once kindled, quenchless evermore,
> Preys upon high adventure, nor can tire
> Of aught but rest; a fever at the core,
> Fatal to him who bears, to all who ever bore.[27]

Furthermore "the *Manfred*-idea . . . that knowledge brings trouble and unhappiness" [28] has as its obverse that in the pursuit of knowledge and truth we attain our tragic human dignity. So in the Hall of Arimanes, Manfred is not humiliated but stands his ground:

> His sufferings
> Have been of an immortal nature—

So even on his death bed he refuses to yield:

> The Mind which is immortal makes itself
> Requital for its good or evil thoughts,—
> Is its own origin of ill and end. . . .

This is the sublimity of the Byronic mood, but in the heart of the sublimity is ever the canker and the venom of the cynical idea:

> Beautiful!
> How beautiful is all this visible world!
> How glorious in its action and itself!
> But we, who name ourselves its sovereigns, we,
> Half dust, half deity, alike unfit
> To sink or soar, with our mixed essence make
> A conflict of its elements, and breathe
> The breath of degradation and of pride,
> Contending with low wants and lofty will,
> Till our Mortality predominates,
> And men are—what they name not to themselves,
> And trust not to each other.[29]

The cup of truth is bitter: this is Byron's philosophy in a word. Bitterness mixes with his ribaldry, and tears with his laughter as he regards the cup, but also bitter and fierce joy with the despair, as he proceeds to drain it to the last drop. His perception of the truth may be half-blind, and sometimes blind altogether; his own conduct and feelings are frequently false, theatrical, at times even disgusting. But beneath the ashes, there still glow his fierce integrity and devotion to truth, and to these flaming brands he will owe his lasting ardor in the hearts and minds of men.

Leconte de Lisle, in his *Qaïn*, portrays a Cain irrevocably converted to anti-theism. Ten centuries of sleep have made the first human rebel only the more adamant as he awakes. He challenges divine implacable injustice:

> Unto the inert clay did I say: "Suffer, weep!"
> Aroused I longings, and enchained them with a ban?
> Stirred ardent love for good beyond the reach of man;
> And dreams immortal in time's hour-engulfing sweep?
> Urged man to scheme, and crushed the executed plan?
>
> Oh misery! Said I to the dread Lord of earth,
> The jealous God, tormentor of the human host,
> Who rides the winds, and roars his orders thunder-tossed:
> "Life is indubitably good: do give me birth!"
> What care I for this life at such a frightful cost? [30]

To be sure this resistance is impotent, but at any rate it saves man's moral dignity. Yet is man so utterly impotent before Yahveh? Behold the Creator, repenting him of his unworthy work, plans the submergence of man by the Deluge. But Cain undertakes man's cause; the Ark is built, and spite of the Deluge, man will live, will bear future witnesses of Yahveh's evil work, and these witnesses in days to come will rise to cast him out of his creation. Cain hurls a grim shaft of prophecy: From hour to hour the mutinied might of man shall loosen the clutch of Thy dread arms, shall break the sacred yoke, shall refuse to hearken to Thy Voice. Let blood of priestly oppression flow, and lurid smoke rise to heaven from human holocausts: the children of men will one day rise in their cradles, will rise to laugh, no longer knowing Thee. Mellowing knowledge and virtue will lift man up; he will defy Thee, will spurn Thee, will ignore and forget Thee. Thy silly starry dome will be pierced by the eye of man and, in the sweep of worlds on worlds past reckoning, Thou and Thy alleged majesty will be engulfed and lost. Man's honor will reject Thee, and man's intelligence will rule Thee out.

This hope of final sane awakening from the theological nightmare does not sustain Leconte de Lisle. The rest of his work is usually, though not invariably, lacking in the benignity and respect for man which inspire the revolt of *Qaïn.* There is lofty disdain and aristocratic despair, and supreme artistry in the utterance of both, but on these icy perfections gleam scarcely any rays of compassion or whole-hearted brotherhood in woe. Leconte de Lisle can portray the evil chaos of existence, but he evokes no tragic pity. "Imagination, passion, learning, unrivalled skill were his, yet something stiffens all his gifts and repels our sympathy: whether coldness of heart or narrowness of soul we cannot tell." [31]

Byron's favorite type of hero (he had a gallery of them) was wrapped in the dark mantle of evil memories and black forebodings. These gentlemen of the melancholy brow parade gloomily through the pages of a dozen literatures, their past rising up to blight their future, doomed lovers emanating despondency, particularly in the hearts of romantic maidens. Russian literature, adolescent in Byron's day, was deeply touched with his wistful-sardonic rebelliousness: Pushkin's Eugeny Onyegin is only the chief of a not inconsiderable company.

It was a bold stroke to make the Fallen Angel himself stir pity and almost hope as well as dread, and that is what Michael Lermontov (1814–1841) did in his "eastern tale," *The Demon.* The exile from heaven, swimming in the infinite seas of space, finds peace nowhere; the mastery which he has over the earth, and the evil which he sows in it, give him no joy in the harvest, and his cosmic scorn only embitters him the more. Flying over the Caucasus, he sees unmoved the panorama of majestic beauty, and he sniffs at the more intimate charms of the Georgian landscape. But when he sets eyes on Gudal's daughter, a flood of forgotten memories warmly sweep over his icy being, and anguish of new longing possesses him. Thamara is both terror-chilled and consumed by the mysterious spirit's ardor. To escape him, she flees to the convent-cell,—but he is here also. In his new love for her he sees, if not salvation for his demon-soul, yet bliss despite his damnation: if she but answer his entreaties, he would cease tormenting and misleading mankind; indeed he would make his peace with heaven, would let creation bloom again in blissful ignorance of evil. All his infinite passion of hell he would melt into love for her, and she would be worshipped goddess and queen of creation. For one moment Thamara wavers, and it is her doom and her death. But the Angel of Heaven bears her aloft in the uplands of infinite space. The Demon contests his precious charge, but is overborne and is plunged once more into his past: a pathetic, eternal 'it might have been':

> The conquered Demon cursed his longing,
> His maddening dreams where love had shone;
> And once again he stood relentless,
> In scornful arrogance, and dauntless,
> Amidst the Universe—alone.[32]

III

The "Prologue in Heaven" with which *Faust* opens is clearly reminiscent of Job, not only in the setting but also in the fundamental conception of the Devil, revealed by the Hebrew poet in one telling phrase. To God's unqualified praise of Job's integrity, Satan answers with a sneer: "Doth Job fear God for nought?" This cynical dismissal of genuine piety, sophisticated disdain alike of innocence and of heroism, moral scepticism, and the vulgar laughing-down of nobility of whatever sort: this blighting spirit of derision is the spirit of Goethe's Mephistopheles.

His first words are anticlimax to archangelic laudation. He cannot follow their lofty speech, but of low insinuations he has an abundant store. The sublime is to him an object of ridicule; man's heavenly gleam, reason, Mephistopheles declares, only makes him beastlier than any beast. With all his lofty aspirations, man is like a grasshopper,

> That springing flies, and flying springs,
> And in the grass the same old ditty sings.[33]

The exalted and the tragic alike are rejected by Mephistopheles; a cheerful cynicism carries him through, with a lackey's wink behind the back of Divine Majesty. Neither fierce Miltonic pride nor Byronic rebellious pathos characterize him, but vulgar disdain of worth.[34] He openly avows it:

> I am the Spirit that Denies!
> And justly so: for all things, from the Void
> Called forth, deserve to be destroyed.[35]

He recognizes higher powers (even in the diabolic world he is no Lucifer or Satan but a Prince of the Realm), but no high worth; negating all 'good' and deriding the pursuit of it, he is at home with 'evil':

> Thus, all which you as Sin have rated,—
> Destruction,—all with Evil blent,—
> That is my proper element.[36]

The heavenly choir is distasteful to his ear, "a harsh, disgusting strumming," [37] but the ribald songs of the drunken students suit his taste, and the unspeakable orgies of the Witches' Kitchen and the Walpurgis-Night. It is devilish magic that thus upsets and transposes all values. "Fair is foul, and foul is fair," screech the Witches in *Macbeth;* so Mephistopheles urges Faust to drink the witch's potion, to warm his heart with new desire, to be introduced to the beauty of the world: topsy-turvy beauty, Mephistopheles observes:

> Thou'lt find, this drink thy blood compelling,
> Each woman beautiful as Helen.[38]

After Gretchen has been lured to her ruin, Faust's wild remorse evokes only a heartless laugh from Mephistopheles: "She is not the first." [39] This contempt for despoiled virtue is in keeping with his scorn for all that is pure and noble. Here is malicious sophistry, mocking alike exultation and despair, the unflecked bloom of innocence, lush fruition, withered and decayed undoing. Up and down is all one; there is no real direction:

> Descend, then! I could also say: Ascend!
> 'Twere all the same.[40]

Of this philosophy of sneering negation, the conclusion is ashen nihilism: so Mephistopheles at the death of Faust:

> Past and Pure Naught, complete monotony!
> What good for us, this endlessly creating?—
> What is created then annihilating?
> "And now it's past!" Why read a page so twisted?
> 'Tis just the same as if it ne'er existed,
> Yet goes in circles round as if it had, however:
> I'd rather choose, instead, the Void forever.[41]

Regarding Faust, Mephistopheles' plans are clearly formulated from the start: " Dust shall he eat, and with a zest." [42] Insatiate hunger for final and permanent achievement has left the poor scholar disenchanted: his intellect has but revealed its own limitations, and the pursuit of truth has proved its futility. If the higher life thus fails to attain its goal, where is lasting satisfaction to be found? Mephistopheles promises it with assurance, exacting as payment, however, ultimate delivery of Faust's soul. For this bargain Faust is quite ready, provided he formulate the terms of the contract:

When thus I hail the Moment flying:
"Ah, still delay—thou art so fair!"
Then bind me in thy bonds undying,
My final ruin then declare! [43]

But in this compact the poor Devil is bound to lose. A supreme moment of sterile satisfaction, a moment without future, would indeed be the spiritual end of Faust, and he needs no blood-bond to seal his commitment. But all that Mephistopheles can bring to him either arouses a bitter aftertaste or stimulates still further his ever-outreaching desire. What Faust demands, an experience that would justify complacence-in-fruition, would, if it were attained, be indeed his evil and ruin, for it would negate his active and aspiring self. But if it were not for Faust's pursuit of this ever-receding goal, he would not put forth the strength that is in him, and his active self would not even be affirmed. Thus in pressing after an aim which, if attained, would prove his stagnation and ruin, Faust is actually working out his salvation, and Mephistopheles is in fact undoing his own bargain. In Faust's relations with Gretchen, more than the Witch's potion is active; genuine love enters to agonize the conscience-smitten and then the bitterly contrite Faust. And manifold venture, instead of sating him, only leads him to understand better what he really demands.

Goethe's devil has *esprit*, sophisticated wit, as Paulsen points out, but not *Seele*, positive, believing, productive, upbuilding, upward-tending, loving spirit.[44] An enemy of the light, as his name signifies, Mephistopheles opposes serious inquiry and is out of patience with 'problems.' He is an expert in make-believe and pretense. He would deceitfully build up credit and morale; he would relax vigilance over principles, and lull criticism or conscience by luring ease and lust. So we cannot believe him to be aware of the holy work in which he is unwittingly taking a part. It is not his own cunning, but higher wisdom of which he becomes the vehicle and the expression, when he characterizes himself to Faust as

> Part of that Power, not understood,
> Which always wills the Bad, and always works the Good.[45]

The truth behind these words is an enigma eluding the spirit of denial. Persistent devotion, even in the form of insatiate desire, alone in the end can teach it:

> A good man, through obscurest aspiration,
> Has still an instinct of the one true way.[46]

This obscure sense is clarified by experience, and Faust becomes aware of what constitutes real worth: significant and aspiring activity, not mere possession or enjoyment. This wisdom is taught to Faust; the teaching of it is the main theme of the Second Part of the drama. The possession of innocent Gretchen,—possession exacting without offering whole-hearted self-surrender, nor dignified by something higher and nobler than itself,—had brought only ruin and remorse, but through ruin and remorse, real though incomplete enlightenment. The possession of Helen proves an unsubstantial and transitory phantom, save in the refinement and spiritual mellowing of Faust's nature through devotion to ideal beauty. Political, military, social achievement expand his range of ambition rather than affording final contentment.

So long as Faust believes that blessedness is to be found in the placid moment of conclusive attainment, his failure to reach this desired placidity is to him a source of despair. The tragedy is thus one of inevitable frustration. Frustration, however, is not the last word; the devil himself is unwittingly helping Faust to a higher enlightenment; we have God's word for it in the Prologue:

> Man's active nature, flagging, seeks too soon the level;
> Unqualified repose he learns to crave;
> Whence, willingly, the comrade him I gave,
> Who works, excites, and must create, as Devil.[47]

So frustration itself teaches Faust what it cannot teach cynical Mephistopheles: respect for the aspiring present. True, he is led to a clearer perception of over-individual values; but that is not all, nor the main thing. Faust's solution of the problem of life is not merely in terms of social uplift and lofty practicality, not in the mere draining of marshes and building of dikes, to make habitable ground for millions of men. The important lines should not escape us:

> Though not secure, yet free to active toil. . . .
> A land like Paradise here, round about:
> Up to the brink the tide may roar without,
> And though it gnaw, to burst with force the limit,
> By common impulse all unite to hem it.
> Yes! to this thought I hold with firm persistence;
> The last result of wisdom stamps it true:
> He only earns his freedom and existence,
> Who daily conquers them anew.[48]

The last line, in the original, is decisive: "Who daily *must* reconquer them":

> Nur der verdient sich Freiheit wie das Leben
> Der täglich sie erobern muss.

The worth of human life, as Faust comes to know it, is not in fervid enjoyment nor yet in thrilled or placid contemplation of past attainment, but in noble endeavor and high hazard: in place of the marsh of stagnation, a paradise of active toil ever challenged by floods, and a paradise because thus ever challenged. Only this perception of the eternal worth of high endeavor can exalt the fleeting moment and seal it with eternal worth: it is eternal as a link in an unending chain of achieving, ever forging ahead. Faust had bound himself to be damned as soon as he found any finite satisfaction self-sufficing. But mellowing experience brought him to cherish the moment of noble striving for himself and others: and he was thus forever beyond the reach of Mephistopheles.

> While man's desires and aspirations stir,
> He cannot choose but err.[49]

So God declares in the Prologue, and so the hazard of evil is ever with us,—but also the resistance to it, and rejection of dull placidity, and divine discontent, for in them is our salvation. In our reaching up towards the ideal, Divine Love draws us upward and on: ever upward-leading and ever-receding: an ideal forever real because never completely attained, and a grace ever blessing because never quite deserved. So sing the angels as they bear aloft the immortal soul of Faust, away from the clutch of 'Old Iniquity':

> Who, ever aspiring, exerts himself,
> Him can we redeem.[50]

"In these lines," Goethe said to Eckermann, "the key to Faust's rescue may be found. In Faust, himself, an ever higher and purer form of activity to the end, and the eternal Love coming down to his aid from above." [51]

IV

Goethe's masterpiece was the outstanding result of a great and natural revival of interest in the Faust-idea on the part of German poets, and Goethe has remained in full possession of the field over a score of actual and aspiring contestants.[52] But, though some of these rival *Fausts* have at least earned their oblivion and should not be disturbed under their dust, others are significant examples of philosophical poetry, revealing as they do a variety of temperaments and outlooks: buoyant-heroic, gloomily resolute, hopelessly sullen, defiant, wailing, sneering, cynical. Even where they are only outline sketches, they are as it were windows through which we may look into the inner world of the poets. My choice of the *Fausts* I shall consider is determined by my interest in the philosophy of life of their authors.

The original warp on which the various Faust-textures are

woven is to be found in the sixteenth century *Histories* of the dread magician. *The Tragicall History of Doctor Faustus*, by Christopher Marlowe (1564–1593), the earliest *Faust* of real literary merit,[53] was based on an English version of the German *Faustbuch*, and reproduces through the medium of a fervid imagination the sixteenth century atmosphere. Marlowe's Faust, craving

> A world of profit and delight,
> Of power, of honor, of omnipotence, [54]

would "try his brains to gain a deity." Marlowe introduces a good and an evil angel who strive with opposing counsels for his will's dominion; the devil's prospectus proves irresistible, and Faustus signs his soul away. The Elizabethan Mephostophilis is obedient servant to his master Lucifer, but for all his cunning, arch cynicism, and horseplay, wistful gloom pervades him as he remembers his lost heaven:

> Thinkst thou that I who saw the face of God,
> And tasted the eternal ioyes of Heauen,
> Am not tormented with ten thousand hels
> In being depriv'd of euerlasting blisse?

So at first Faustus has to lend, not borrow, consolation; but later on he pays in full for his intrepidity. His will is almost turned to repentance by the Good Angel's pleading, and Lucifer himself has to appear, to reseal the pact of Faustus' doom. The poet holds redemption possible until the end, if Faustus would only repent: Marlowe's magician proceeds to ruin because of his deepening conviction that he cannot repent. Aside from the comical horseplay, some of it supposedly irreverent, which Marlowe appears to supply on demand, the real tragic action evidences nothing outstandingly damnable except a corruption of the moral will through magical arts: yet repeatedly he comes forth better than expected. He had dreamt of glutted lust and wealth and empire.

Actually his first demands of Mephostophilis after the signing of the soul-contract is for more knowledge about his newly chosen destination: "First will I question with thee about hell." The Emperor is and remains his "gratious Soveraigne." Five pages before his final damnation, the apparition of Helen of Troy fans the sputtering and largely fancied lust into a white heat of consuming imagination:

> Was this the face that Launcht a thousand shippes?
> And burnt the toplesse Towres of Ilium? [55]

One suspects the Marlowe's Faustus would not have been damned had he not believed his damnation inevitable. The final monologue, a masterpiece of hopeless remorse, is the more tragic because one pities rather than understands Faustus' hopelessness. Here the contrast with Goethe is significant: Goethe's serene refusal to admit ultimate ruin for his hero, compared with the unfathomed gloom of Marlowe's doomed magician.

Fifteen years before Goethe's earliest version of *Faust*, Gotthold Ephraim Lessing (1729–1781) was projecting a drama on the subject; the completed play is supposed to have been lost, but the Fragment and outline sketch that we have are in Lessing's characteristic spirit of virile intellectual self-reliance. In Lessing's *Prologue,* sundry devils bring the reports of their achievements to Satan's court. An ambitious princeling of darkness proposes the plan of corrupting God's favorite, Faust: but how? Faust has no vices nor frailties; his whole soul is devoted to the pursuit of knowledge. Satan replies jubilantly: This craving for knowledge is the surest hold we have on him! So Faust's ruin is plotted in the diabolical conclave. But the Heavenly Host is vigilant. The Angel of the Lord causes Faust to fall into profound sleep, and in his place creates a phantom double of the famous scholar. On this phantom Faust the devil tries his guile, only to be disabused in the end of his error. It is the devil's delusion that man's search for truth may prove his undoing. All that the devil does with the phantom Faust is seen as in a dream by the real, sleeping Faust, who on waking thanks Providence for the vision and applies himself to the pursuit of truth and virtue with more zeal than ever.[56] This is the sort of *Faust* we should have expected from that Lessing who wrote: "Did the Almighty, holding in his right hand *Truth*, and in his left *Search after Truth*, deign to tender me the one I might prefer,—in all humility, but without hesitation, I should request—*Search after Truth*." [57]

Radically different is the treatment of the Faust-theme by the pessimists. The Viennese dramatist Franz Grillparzer (1791–1872) projected a continuation of the first part of Goethe's drama. In it Faust was to seek salvation and blessedness "where it is really to be found: in self-limitation and contentment of soul." [58] He would break with Mephistopheles and seek only humble peace. Becoming the tutor and friend of a youth, the friend of a worthy family, the friend and later the trusted and accepted lover of a maiden as pure and simple as Gretchen,—is blessedness really in sight for him? Mephistopheles watches him, slyly encouraging, cat-like in his own assurance of finally pouncing upon his poor victim. For Faust is unfitted for innocent joys: the very love and trust of men, and particularly of his beloved, only sharpen the cruel sense of his own past ignominy. Rather than drag his innocent maiden with him, to save her from being sullied by his attachment to her, he calls the devil and demands immediate settlement of the dreadful contract, the one saving grace of his damnation being that he is damned alone.

Heinrich Heine (1799–1850) had too keen a sense of humor to write a Faust-tragedy after Goethe, but humor sufficiently keen and characteristic to match Goethe's sixty-years' work by four weeks spent on a Faust-ballet. *Der Doktor Faust* is a *Tanzpoem* in five acts, with Mephistophela as prima ballerina! The richness of choreographic imagination which Heine lavishes on his work does not concern us, but rather his conception of the Faust-problem and his solution of it.

In Heine's view "the revolt of the realistic, sensualistic love of life against the spiritualistically old-catholic asceticism" is "the essential idea of the Faust-saga." [59] But this revolt was also one of naturalism and humanism, against otherworldliness, a revolt of Hellenic stimulus and inspiration. This explains the classical cult of beauty alongside the coarser voluptuousness of the rejuvenated Faust. It is the double fire of the Renaissance which is coursing through his veins. In the old Histories, Faust is represented as causing Helen of Troy to reappear in all her beauty before his students: an experience which thousands of Homer's readers in the Renaissance must have shared.

The zeal for worldly wisdom, the worship of classic beauty, and rank sensuality thus mixed and clashed in the early modern soul. The contrast and the conflict of the last two are portrayed by Heine in his third and fourth acts. In the third, Faust's orgy of lust at the dance of the witches (on the *Hexen-Sabbat*) end in unspeakable revulsion and disgust: unrefined sensuality has outraged his intelligence and his imagination, and mere beastliness has refuted itself in his life. Against this lurid and nauseating riot is the serene heavenly beauty and harmony of the classic island of Helen: "Real plastic felicity without dismal memories, without foreboding empty longing." [60] The invasion of this island's rhythmic peace by the discordant fury of the Witch-Duchess whom Faust had rejected at the Witches' Sabbath, and the riot of destruction which ensues, symbolize the deadly clash between the two types of Renaissance sensuousness. This early modern dream could not last; a disenchantment came, but with it also new resolution; the island of blessed beauty is a ruin, but Faust's sword is plunged to the hilt in the breast of the Witch-Duchess.

Heine would seek Faust's redemption where Grillparzer had looked for it; but, like Grillparzer, he expects only disaster in the end. The Faust of Heine's ballet decides to find his bliss in the quiet joys of home life, but this salvation comes too late for the cosmic nomad. Mephistophela is a ravishing and a sinister princess of evil: seductive grace and scoffing abandon, but also dark cunning, and ruthless disdain in the end. She exacts, with scornful laughter, the full terms of her hell-contract with the Doctor. Thus Heine's ballet ends tragically, in contrast to Goethe's tragedy which, as Heine almost tells us, concludes with a heavenly ballet. Heinrich Heine wept; he could also laugh at his own tears; but he grudged them too: so beneath the lightmindedness of this ballet is the asperity of the wretched invalid and world-contemner, who in the end wept that life was not even worth his tears. Bahnsen called him a "humorous pessimist." [61]

> I have seen through you, Nay; I have seen through
> The world's vast plan—and I have looked too long,
> And much too deep; for all my joy has vanished,
> And deathless troubles rankle in my heart.
> I see right through the hard and stony cover
> Of all men's houses and of all men's hearts,
> And see in both lies and deceit and torture.
> I read men's thoughts by looking at their faces,
> Most of them evil. In the blush of maidens
> I see the trembling wish beneath the shame;
> Upon Youth's proud and visionary head
> I see the cap-and-bells of stupid folly;
> And twisted phantom-pictures, crazy shadows
> Are all I see,—until I scarcely know
> If Earth's a madhouse or a hospital.[62]

This bitterness is contested by acid self-irony:

Alone by my midnight lamp
I rhymed my groans and my sighs:
They're published by Hoffman and Campe
In small octavo size.[63]

V

Tears without laughter, and unrelieved melancholy pervade the work of Austria's chief lyric poet, Nikolaus Lenau (1802–1850). He found a word in Homer which, he said, fitly described his soul: "black all around," [64] but it was black all around because of the inky blackness within. Lenau was ever wrapped up in his own midnight, and when it really extinguished the last flicker of intelligence, in 1844, even then the poor madman retained a protesting conviction of his subjectivity: "I am not a *delirious*, but a *lyric* poet." [65]

Lenau's Faust is Lenau himself, vainly thirsting for absolute certainty and complete self-possession. What passes for knowledge is occasional obscure glimpsing of an alien world; but he would not be satisfied were it even lasting and clear, unless he encompassed, literally comprehended the world that he knew, unless he made it his own exclusive content and possession. This is solipsistic fury:

Thus I myself stand face to face with God:
That knowledge only brings me happiness
Which is my own, from him alienate;
Myself I must forever feel as mine! [66]

Despairing of getting his questions answered by Heaven, Faust turns to Hell, and Mephistopheles is ready enough to help. He has already saved Faust from the brink of death, so as to have him for his own in life and in eternity. He will show Truth's own face to Faust, but he promises him even more: sensual raptures, the joy of triumphant love and of triumphant hate, fame, honor, power, wealth. He plots to draw Faust away from Christ, then to alienate him from Nature, to isolate and throw him upon his bare self, without refuge or solace:

> Then let my hell-fires circle him around:
> This way and that he'll wince and creep and bound,
> And, like a scorpion, will sting himself.[67]

In thus plotting Faust's ruin, the devil is looking beyond: by undoing God's fair creation he hopes to experience the joys of counter-creation:

> Corrupting his, I'll be creating mine.[68]

Faust has demanded in his bargain truth itself. Mephistopheles proceeds to teach him the truth about himself, and first, that he is capable of gross sensuality. The man who in one scene pronounces himself beyond the saving touch of woman's love, and that the love of his dearest friend's own sister, in the next scene seduces a village girl intoxicated by the strains of Mephistopheles' violin and by the wild dance that whirls her to dishonor. Lenau's account of the devil's fiddling is almost uncanny: one hears the gay, luring abandon of the Magyar dance, but through it and beneath it is another, sinister lure, the veriest vortex of sensuality. The village girl will meet Faust again, a-begging with her unwanted child; he will see her yet once more, a nun in the cloister by the sea, but beneath the waves that splash against the convent's walls the bones of Faust's child are whitening, and his remorse and self-contempt will henceforth poison even low pleasure. Mephistopheles is hateful to him; but, Mephistopheles says, right now you need me most, to harden your weakness and make your sick soul more callous and resistant.

Faust is brought under the spell of Princess Marie's beauty and inner perfection. Here at last is real love which consumes him and could, he is convinced, heal and bless. But the Princess is unresponsive; her thought and heart are Duke Hubert's. Mephistopheles directs the Duke to the royal villa and induces a clash between him and Faust in which the latter comes out a murderer. This act seals Faust's doom: for not only love but nature also have now been alienated from him. Every leaf and blossom in the forest calls him a murderer. He curses Mephistopheles for robbing him of his innocence, but the devil simply hands him a jug of strong wine.

Faust's wail at the grave of his mother is in fact a farewell to life. The man who had sought wisdom and joy in his unattached individuality now finds himself indeed left to his own desolation. But Mephistopheles promises to exalt him through self-worship:

> My Faust, I'll build to thee a holy shrine,
> In it thy thought thou'lt worship as divine,
> Beneath a rocky dome thou'lt bend thy brow,
> And to thyself thy supplications vow.[69]

This counsel is accepted by Faust as a resolve of desperation:

> Inclined to no one, under no one's sway,
> I follow, inwards destined, mine own way.[70]

This seems to have been Lenau's rational perception of the essence of evil: rebellious alienation of the part from the Whole. So he writes in 1836 to Hans Martensen: "Perhaps all evil may well be conceived as a malorganization of life, as a revolt of individual life-organs which, oblivious of their relation to the holy life of the whole, and their submissive duty, would set themselves up as central, and, subjecting other allied organs to their demands, in the end upset these organs and themselves, and hasten death, since all life is nothing else but a joyous subordination and coöperation of the particular organs in the larger activity of the soul." [71]

And now Faust craves storm, danger; the threat of destruction thrills him fiercely; he would sail in the teeth of the wind and forget in the struggle of the present the disaster of the past. But all is vain. He is unfit for either storm or quiet; he cannot take life as it comes, in the sanguine manner of a Görg. Engulfed in his self-centered midnight, he is tortured by the conviction of his own insufficiency and nullity:

> My self, all empty, meager, dark,
> Now hems me round, a coffin stark;
> While blows for wilful self I hit,
> The devil cast me in the pit.
> Entombed alive in murky depths defiled,
> I shook myself awake, eyes bulging wild,
> And set myself, with boundless wail and groan,
> To gnaw my flesh and bone.
> But now my heavy bonds I strain, I sever!
> But now more ardently than ever
> I stretch my arms—out there, above,
> From this my house of death—to God, to love!
> To, God!—Not God, but woe: the same old thought:
> *"I'm but a creature!" crushes me to nought.*[72]

Thus hopelessly humiliated in the very ground of his pride and self-reliance, Faust is finally wrecked. His parting shot is one of despair and defiance at alleged reality:

> I am a dream, with joy, and guilt, and smart,
> So—dream this dagger plunged into my heart!
> *(He stabs himself)*.[73]

VI

To tragic sense and melancholy, Christian Dietrich Grabbe (1801–1836) added coarse-grained cynicism. He could scarcely have felt an alien in the world which he depicts in his dramas: his own life provides but footnotes to the drunken fury of his verse. Lifelong gloom only deepened the impressions of his childhood in the prison-overseer's lodgings, and alcoholism wrecked whatever he had of self-reliance and self-respect. His dramas are apt to go to wrack and ruin even as his own life; their germ-ideas are sometimes titanic, but they belie their promise in not maturing. The blood-dripping sword gleaming above smoky ruin fascinated Grabbe's imagination,—witness the list of his protagonists, giants of world-wrecking might: Sulla, Hannibal, Hermann, the Hohenstaufen, Theodor von Gothland, Napoleon. These were to be tragedies exhibiting the self-undoing of self-propelled and self-seeking power; but Grabbe lacked the serenity and the nobility needed to realize concretely over-individual values.

Faust is a cousin-german of Don Juan, and the differences between the two illustrate significantly characteristic qualities of Teutonic and Latin ways of life and thought. The Spaniard fascinated Romantic imagination; Byron's own characteristic version of the theme had set the tone, and stimulated imitators and rivals: Pushkin's dramatic sketch, *The Marble Guest*, and Lenau's unfinished *Don Juan*, pursuer of ever-new raptures in defiance of the law that

> The God of rapture is a God of bounds.[74]

The influence of Byron's *Cain* and *Manfred* on Grabbe's work is evident, both in fundamental conceptions and in execution of detail. But it was certainly a flash of genius in Grabbe to put the German Doctor and the Spanish libertine in one drama. *Don Juan und Faust*, with the Devil to complete the sinister triad, was the theme for a world-master; as it is, even in Grabbe's hands, the play is gripping and attains occasionally to grand horror in its conceptions. Goethe's Faust recognized the two souls in his breast:

> One with tenacious organs holds in love
> And clinging lust the world in its embraces;
> The other strongly sweeps, this dust above,
> Into the high ancestral spaces.[75]

These two souls of Goethe's hero Grabbe would separate and

embody in two rival heroes: a dramatic strategy doing more violence to Faust's character than to Don Juan's.[76]

The contrast between Faust and Don Juan in their rivalry for the love of Donna Anna provides the action of the drama: Faust, a will for dominion and possession ever frustrated because never content; Don Juan, as insatiate as Faust, but ever drunk with the present moment, reckless of the future and oblivious of the past. In vain his lackey Leporello reminds him of his past amours: he knows only *the one:* she of the instant. Killing Donna Anna's bridegroom and her father disturbs his conscience not at all; he is a man of one idea at a time, and his mind is filled with Donna Anna's love. And, knowing him for what he is, she hates him, but loves him too despite herself. Faust she dreads and abhors; the devil has put her in Faust's power, in his prison-palace on the top of Montblanc, but Faust craves her beyond mere sensual possession; he will have her free and complete love or nothing. Rejected love turns into fiendish hate, and Donna Anna dies.

The antithesis between the two men is perfect except for their common disastrous destiny. Don Juan asks sneeringly:

> Why strive for superhuman heights,
> When you are just a man?

Faust retorts:

> Why be a man,
> If I strive not to rise beyond the human? [77]

When Faust, his hatred turned to bitter remorse over the death of Donna Anna, seeks atonement by planning to kill the slayer of her father and bridegroom, Don Juan meets him with the same nonchalance with which he is awaiting his 'marble guest,' the slain governor's ghost. Is Donna Anna dead? His ship will not sink under that blow:

> I spread
> My sails again, by new winds onwards blown.[78]

On this prince of the burning moment Faust would impress the verdict of eternity; but the devil will have none of it. He will have them both: first Faust and then Don Juan. Faust is damned by his inability to attain joyous peace and to rise above remorse; Don Juan, by his stubborn nonchalance and distaste for repentance: he is what he is and would rather be Don Juan damned than a saint in Paradise.

So the devil has them both, the insatiate and ever-wistful seeker and the ever-reckless and insatiate possessor. The world is the devil's and the fullness thereof; in it those of alleged virtue do not prevail, for God is too far to hear them in the hour of their great need; the devil's own have power and principality, but they too either fall short of attainment, or find its wine wormwood, or else have their reckless laughter laughed back at them in final damnation. Life is a fraud in any case; even true love cheats itself. So also Lenau's Don Juan consoles the wailing Donna Isabella after she has yielded herself to him believing him to be her beloved Antonio: love is ever an affair of mistaken identity:

> The one that in your arms you hold
> Is never he that charms your heart.[79]

Dante ended his *Divine Comedy* with praise of "The Love which moves the Sun and the other stars." Grabbe is at the opposite pole; he sees Hate at the helm of the cosmos, and worse, not simple Hate, but Hate the fiercer because burning with the memory of hopeless love. It is as if Lermontov's Demon had returned to earth. Myriads of ages ago the devil had loved titanically, and that is why his hatred now is so unspeakable.[80] Therefore he lures and drives men to seek blessedness in consuming devotion, so as to grind them the more utterly to dust. Travel we Faust's way of Don Juan's, Grabbe tells us, it is all one in the end: both ways lead to the devil's abyss.

In such a world of nightmare, where is the hand of Providence to be seen? Were God omnipotent, how could he ever expiate the guilt of having created this tragic chaos? Atheism is after all a consolation. Did not Stendhal write: "God's only excuse is that he really doesn't exist?"
So Grabbe:

> No, no!
> There is no God! This to his honor
> Alone will I believe! [81]

Or perhaps there *was* a God, Faust speculates before the corpse of Donna Anna:

> There was a God once, but he went
> To pieces, and his smithereens are we.[82]

This desolate thought Philipp Mainländer is to erect into a philosophical system, as pretender to the gray crown of Schopenhauer's dynasty.

CHAPTER VIII

LEOPARDI'S LYRICAL PESSIMISM

I

An Italian youth in his teens had roused scholars and academies of scholars to admiration for his philological talents; the dispenser of literary reputations in his epoch had called him "the perfect Italian writer." [1] To this lavish dispenser, Pietro Giordani, the youth, Giacomo Leopardi, wrote letters which are masterpieces of passionate style. They reveal him as engulfed in black melancholy and are all-important to the understanding of his pessimistic poetry. His happiness is wrecked, he writes, by ill health, which robs him of his one joy, study; wrecked also by his own thought: he must think, yet thinking tortures and consumes him. [2] Condemned to solitude, denied the relief of escaping from himself, spent, shattered, and almost blind, without diversion or hope, he is crawling towards his premature grave.

A tragic life it was, thus to reach its conclusion of despair at nineteen. Yet the early years had been happy with a scholar's joy and pride and dreams. The boy Giacomo—he was born in 1798—had been not too obviously frail, and amazingly precocious alike in ability and in ambition. His brother Carlo and sister Paolina readily yielded him the palm of leadership in all the children's games and pageants: he was the sweet-voiced Filzero, he the Achilles, the Pompey; when the children played at mass, it was Giacomo who officiated as priest.

Up to the age of ten the boy was instructed privately; after that began one of the most marvelous careers of premature self-directed study on record. The Palazzo Leopardi in Recanati housed a library of sixteen thousand volumes. It became the nursery of Giacomo's childhood and the graveyard of his adolescence. A devouring zeal for learning possessed the lad; in four months he learned Greek by himself, and then, in addition to his Latin and French, English, Spanish and Hebrew so that he could argue with the Hebraists of Ancona.[3] His brother Carlo, waking at midnight, would see him on his knees before his little table, poring over folios as big as himself.[4] He read, he translated, wrote commentaries, collations, sermons and orations, verses in the classical manner, a poem on the Earthly Paradise, an epic in three cantos on the Three Wise Men, translations from Horace, a tragedy of his own, *Pompey in Egypt*. He required a catalogue of his works, beginning with 1809, when he was eleven! Three years later he began a History of Astronomy, to contain all doctrines philosophical and mathematical. He wrote Latin commentaries on Greek authors, collected fragments of second century Church Fathers, wrote an essay *On the Popular Errors of the Ancients*, translated Homer's *Batracomiomachia*, attempted the *Odyssey*.

These are not all juvenilia; some are readable even today. Creuzer had spent a lifetime on Plotinus, but in his third volume he could quote to advantage from the boy's work.[5] Still in his teens, Leopardi played a learned prank on Italian Hellenists with his "Hymn to Neptune, of Uncertain Greek Authorship," alleged to have been discovered by a still less certain Signor Three Dots.[6] Young Leopardi leaped from achievement to achievement, and he dreamed great dreams: already in correspondence with the learned, what a future awaited him! In his clerical habit he walked about town, climbed his favorite hill, watched the clouds, the Adriatic in the far distance:

> With thoughts
> How vast, with what entrancing dreams the sight
> Of that far sea inspired me, those blue hills,
> Which yonder I discerned and which some day
> I hoped to cross, and to my future feigned
> Worlds unexplored and unexplored delights! [7]

But nature is not so easily cheated, and it exacted a terrible price of the precocious, ambitious genius, exacted it slowly but ruthlessly, and left him at the threshold of young manhood a complete physical wreck. The Leopardis suffered from a hereditary tendency towards rickets and nervous infirmities. To check the onset of these ills, Giacomo needed sound nourishment and a vigorous gay outdoor life. Six years of unremitting mental exertion, precisely during adolescence, ruined whatever chance his physique might have had. While the boy was learnedly mastering obscure folios, his bones were degenerating, his spine was being curved beyond redemption, his eyesight ruined. There emerged from the Leopardi library a hunchback with an emaciated face, protruding cheek-bones, a dilated mouth, complexion earthy and ugly: [8] a rude jest of matter at the expense of mind.

Of his parents, the one who would have averted the disaster could not see it coming, and the other did not have eyes for anything of so slight importance. Count Monaldo Leopardi was a hopelessly orthodox and reactionary small-town savant, a thriftless nobleman and a passionate book-collector. He confessed he had searched for his betters without success; all the same, when confronted with bankruptcy, he surrendered the entire management of his estate to his wife, and when the pittance she allowed him proved insufficient for his personal expenses, he would try to wheedle money out of her by pretending to be buying books, or else, in collusion with the servants, would resell wine and wheat which she had bought for the household. Very naturally he retired to that part of the house where he was allowed to reign undisturbed and innocuous. In his library Count Monaldo watched his first-born's mental progress with excusable pride: had he not collected the books which his son was reading, was he not Giacomo's literary guide? Perhaps an archbishop, a cardinal was maturing before his eyes (he was set on an ecclesiastic career for his son): how was this father to notice the impending bodily ruin? When Giacomo was a hopeless hunchback, Count Monaldo saw only another reason for his making his career in the Church: the ecclesiastic habit would make the hump less apparent.

Leopardi was of course born of a woman; in truth, however, he had no mother. One does not have the heart to write objectively of the Countess Adelaide: adamantine, avaricious, arrogantly pious. She was determined to restore the Leopardi fortune: but to restore it for whom? She did not care for her children, regarding them as liabilities. When her Pierfrancesco was born, she censured her husband's incontinence. She gave no sign of maternal love; her children's kisses were rebuffed: "Give them to Jesus!" she would say; no affectionate word was tolerated in their letters; they dared not inquire after her health. Coldest pious disdain of the earthly and the human mixed in her with the crassest greed. Her children were to her simply souls which she piously prepared for heaven, yet her whole life was absorbed in piling coin on coin. Giacomo was inexpensively and safely out of the way in the library. Not only did she neglect him in his boyhood; again and again she refused him assistance when he manfully spent his mite of strength in trying to earn his way. The Leopardi fortune was restored, but the least of it was grudged to the one great Leopardi. If the memory of one's mother is a man's last support in a wretched world, Leopardi's mother would alone be sufficient to explain his midnight gloom. It is an unbelievable story, but husband, daughter, and son bear witness to it. "I wish you could spend a single day in our house," Paolina wrote a friend, "to see how one can live without life, without soul, without body." [9] Has ever man written of his mother what Leopardi wrote in his *Zibaldone?* I cannot bring myself to quote—one sentence must suffice: "She considered beauty a veritable misfortune, and seeing her sons ugly or deformed, she thanked God for it, not in a spirit of heroism, but with all her heart." [10]

Doubly touching, by contrast, is the passionate devotion which bound Giacomo to his brother Carlo and sister Paolina. Other friends and attachments Recanati did not afford. The townsfolk had felt him superior and had thought him proud; now they saw him humped and emaciate; they had their chance at him, and they took it. They mocked him for his deformity which they could see, and sneered at his genius which they could not understand. The town urchins made a vile round of doggerel to ridicule the hunchback when he appeared on the street. In vain the uncle Carlo Antici wrote from Rome, as early as 1813, urging the need of rest and change of environment, and inviting Giacomo to his home. In vain the youth himself, already wrecked and finding life in Recanati intolerable, begged for permission to leave. Paternal vanity and affection would not permit the young candle to burn anywhere but in the Leopardi library. To Countess Adelaide, Giacomo's scholarship and genius were no source of additional income. Even in her safe and sane Recanati she allowed her children no diversions and no freedom whatever: was she now to let Giacomo wander into the wicked and wasteful world? She was far too pious and penurious for that. Bitter and pathetic are the lines in *Le ricordanze*, that masterpiece of Italian blank verse, of which, as of all Leopardi's poems, Mr. Bickersteth has given us such fine English versions, which I quote:

Here I drag on, forsaken, all obscure,
Without love, without life; and growing harsh,
As needs I must mid this malignant crew.
Here, self-despoiled of virtue and charity,
I make myself a scorner of mankind
By reason of the herd which hems me round.
Away, the while, flies cherished youth, more prized
Than fame and laurels, more than the pure light
Of day and breath of being: without one joy,
Vainly, in this inhuman dwelling-place
Mid trouble piled on trouble, I lose thee
My barren life's one solitary bloom.[11]

II

Like a ray of light in his prison, his correspondence with Pietro Giordani flooded his soul with the life of the great world of letters. Giordani's praises sustained and exalted the wretched youth; his letters also helped to perfect Leopardi's spiritual transformation. The change had been going on for some time. The young pedant, engrossed in philological erudition, became a lover of true poetry, became a lover and himself a poet. Translating the poetry of others no longer satisfied him. The love of poetry served to rouse the lyrical mood; the complacent though miserable little scholar saw himself with the clear eyes of the poet:

I feel life's flame within me almost dead;
And, gazing round me, in the world there's nought
That I can now behold save my death-bed.
I feel o'erwhelmed by the vast weighty thought,
So that, with speechless lips and visage blanched,
I hide my pain no longer: it will out.[12]

Love itself was to him no longer mere literary material; Geltrude Cassi made him feel its bittersweet empire, made him a young Petrarch. Partly in rebellion against his father's bigotry, partly under the influence of Giordani's liberalism, his entire political outlook on life altered. His religious orthodoxy followed the same road as his political conservatism. Black despair engulfed him. "What do you say of diversion?" he writes Giordani. "My single diversion in Recanati is study; my single amusement is that which is killing me; all else is weariness, *noia*." [13]

The publication of Leopardi's two patriotic poems, which followed Giordani's five days' visit to Recanati, brought his life to a crisis. The *canzoni* marked the poet's full revolt against his father's reactionary politics; with one leap Leopardi found himself in the front rank of Italian writers,[14] but not in the estimate of his father. Doubly distrustful now, Monaldo flatly refused his son's petition to leave Recanati. Leopardi determined to run away from home, and sought to secure a passport, but his father discovered the plot, and Carlo did not have an opportunity to deliver the letter in which Giacomo was to bid his father farewell: "I would rather be unhappy than undistinguished: I would rather suffer than be bored: so much more injurious do I find boredom (*noia*), in my case the mother of deadly melancholy, than any bodily disease." [15] The son had to submit to his father, but the incident cost Count Monaldo the last scrap of his trust and devotion. His mother had never had them.

Giordani and other friends tried to secure for him a paying position in Lombardy, at Bologna—in vain. A period of melancholy stupor was followed by a strange readjustment and a grim resignation. His imagination came as his ally against suicidal reason. In view of his physical and mental state, is it a wonder that he did not kill himself? A greater wonder, in the face of it all, is the vigor of his intellect and his creative imagination. During these killing years in Recanati he was writing poetry, prose, literature, philology, philosophy, and all the while he was almost blind. Towards the end of 1820 his health improved, and he plunged into work again, studying in particular philosophy. Of the seven volumes of his *Zibaldone*, of thoughts on literature, life, and philosophy, the year 1820 had contributed less than three hundred pages, but during the following year he wrote over eleven hundred pages! Naturally, in the course of the summer, he wrote Giordani: "My eyes have turned me into an owl, hating and shunning the daylight." [16]

In the fall of 1822 Leopardi was at last permitted to go to Rome, as a guest of his uncle Carlo Antici. But Rome was not Rome to the young poet. To his brother Carlo he recounted his heart-breaking disappointment. Modern Rome was not the Eternal City for which the young poet and classical scholar had longed; it was simply a big bulky town. The women were ugly, the men stupid; they shrank from ideas and did not care for real literature. Some of this may be mere tactics, not to appear unsafely jubilant over his escape from Recanati. But one cannot doubt the meaning of his report that only at the grave of Tasso did he find real relief and joy, in tears. "For God's sake, love me," he exclaims in a letter to Carlo, "I need love, love, love, fire, enthusiasm, life." [17] He failed in his effort to secure satisfactory employment. Angelo Mai, now Librarian at the Vatican, did not assist him, and Niebuhr, the classicist and Prussian ambassador, most faithful in his efforts, obtained nothing Leopardi could accept. Later Niebuhr tried to get him to go to Berlin, to Bonn, as professor; but the Italian feared the rigors of the German winter. A career in the Church he would not consent to, now or at any time.

The spring of 1823 saw him back in Recanati. He began the writing of his *Operette morali*, contributed to the *Antologia*. At last a position came his way: the publisher Stella asked him to come to Milan to direct a new edition of the works of Cicero and do other literary work for him. Leopardi left Recanati for the second time, stopping on his way at Bologna. He was now twenty-seven, yet two-thirds of his life had already been spent. Ten days in Bologna with Giordani and his friends had pleased him so much that he returned there from Milan to work for Stella; to increase his salary he gave language lessons to the Counts Pepoli and Pappadopoli. During the cold winter he had to keep to his room wrapped up in a sack of feathers. Bologna, taking Giordani's lead, welcomed him as a great scholar and poet, and for the first time since childhood Leopardi had a taste of happiness. The work he had to do, however, was beyond his strength, and, to cap it all, he had to convince his father, who was doing nothing to help him financially, that it was not below the dignity of a Leopardi to work for a publisher and to give language lessons! [18] The winter of 1826 he spent in Recanati, compiling an Italian prose anthology for Stella, returned the following spring to Bologna, proceeded in June to Florence, where he was welcomed in the liberal Vieusseux-Capponi circle of the *Antologia*. Here he met Alessandro Manzoni, his peer in genius and his contrast in experience and in philosophy of life. Physically he was very miserable in Florence, suffered from bad teeth and eye-troubles (he had to stay indoors until sundown); add to this stomach ailments. The initial welcome of the optimist liberals cooled perceptibly after they had time to digest his *Operette morali*. Somewhat later he removed to Pisa, where climate and environment suited him, and where he resumed creative poetry which had lagged for several years. At the University the students applauded him; he was in tolerably good health. But the respite was short. His brother Luigi's death was a severe shock to his extremely nervous state, and he found himself increasingly unable to work for Stella, after the completion of the anthology of poetry, and felt he could not honorably accept the publisher's money. The terrible night, *orrenda notte*, of Recanati confronted him again. There he had to return from Florence, in November, 1828, with an apology to his father for bringing with him overnight his young friend Vincenzo Gioberti.[19]

Now there seemed to be no release from his black prison-house; but once more his poetic imagination came to his rescue: to this dismal year and a half we owe some of his finest lyrics, including *Le ricordanze* and *Canto notturno.* Unbelievable spectacle: the man is almost a corpse, yet he creates masterpieces of the most painstaking and perfect artistry, and to Pietro Colletta he sends a list of his projected works: literary, political, moral, metaphysical, psychological, philosophical, philological, including an elaborate comparative study of the five languages, Greek, Latin, Italian, French, Spanish![20] His despair beat down his pride, and he finally accepted Colletta's offer of anonymous subscriptions for his support. Relying on this aid, he left Recanati on April 29, 1830, never to return. Pathetic in its deep gratitude is the letter in which he dedicates the 1830 edition of his poems to his Tuscan friends: "I have lost all: I am a log which feels and suffers," but "your love will remain with me all my life, and will perhaps stay by me even after my body, which is already dead, has turned to ashes."[21] He entrusted the manuscripts of his philological works to Professor De Sinner of the Sorbonne, who was to edit and publish them, but who disappointed Leopardi's hopes. The winter of 1831–32 he spent in Rome together with the young Neapolitan Antonio Ranieri, whose devotion to the poet was to be the last refuge of his dolorous days. Before returning to Florence in the spring he had been elected member of the Accademia della Crusca.

What bound him to Florence now was a passion, the most violent of his whole life and the last, for Signora Fanny Targioni-Tozzetti, wife of a Florentine professor. Friends he had; friends who admired, pitied, helped; but in no woman had he evoked genuine love.[22] The Recanati girls whom he watched out of his window died at the dawn of youth, leaving only memories which he later wove into lyrics. Signora Geltrude Cassi, who spent a few days at the Palazzo Leopardi with her daughter, did not even know that she had roused the first real passion in the heart of the nineteen-year old library eremite. Some years later he loved Contessa Teresa Carniani Malvezzi, a brilliant blue-stocking who tried to keep to literature and friendship and, becoming frightened, terminated the relation. And here in Florence he was to lose his heart yet a third time, to a frivolous coquette who found pleasure in having the first poet of Italy hanging on the least flutter of her eyelashes and collecting for her autographs of famous men all over Europe. Herself pursuing Antonio Ranieri, she used Leopardi as a handle to hold his friend. Cruelly she humiliated the proud poetic soul, but when once Leopardi shook off the baneful enchantment he emerged finally disillusioned, passion-proof. *Consalvo, Aspasia, A se stesso* are the poetic chronicles of this great passion and of the revulsion from it.

His father's publication of the ultra-reactionary *Dialoghetti*, which the public had mistakenly attributed to Giacomo, caused the poet publicly to repudiate the book, and this fact made it doubly hard to do the necessary thing now that all his sources of income, including the Florentine, were exhausted: apply to his father for a regular allowance. He did so, and was told that he should have to apply to his mother. And he had to do it, for the twenty scudi a month that were finally granted him. Ranieri's insistence finally took him to Naples where the two arrived in October, 1833, and where, until his death on June 14, 1837, the great poet of the dolorous life found, if not love, yet devoted friendship and tireless nursing at the hands of Ranieri and Ranieri's sister Paolina. A bright page, but the end of it is flecked: forty years later Ranieri could write a book of self-righteous abuse of Leopardi's memory.[23]

In Naples the dying Leopardi wrote the satirical epic, *Paralipomeni della Batracomiomachia*, and also his greatest poem *La Ginestra*, the Broom Flower, blooming on the desert slopes of Vesuvius, where his own last days were spent, in view of the volcano, reminder of the ashen nothingness of all things living and the futility of all effort. Here friends visited him, notably the German poet Platen. Shall we again recount his maladies old and new: a swollen knee and leg, digestive ills, violent nosebleed, asthma, neurasthenia, inflamation of the lungs, dropsy, general bodily disintegration? In this already decayed body the spirit was alive and creative until the last breath. The closing lines of his poem *Il tramonto della luna* Leopardi dictated two hours before he expired.

III

Writing to Sinner in 1832, Leopardi protested against those who attributed his pessimistic philosophy to his ill health (thus Niccolini: "I am a hunchback and ill, therefore there is no God"): "Before dying I shall protest against this weak and vulgar notion, and beg my readers, instead of blaming my illnesses, to turn to the disposal of my observations and reasonings." [24] Leopardi's protest is warranted against those who would treat his ideas as purely pathological phenomena only of clinical interest. But the adequate interpretation of Leopardi's pessimism requires also an insight into his own dolorous life. His judgment of life was not the result simply of impassive external observation but also of intensely tragic personal experience. The truth is well expressed by Mestica: Leopardi's pessimism is essentially lyrical.[25] The poet and the philosopher were not two men but one.

Turning from his erudition to consider his own life, in a lyrical, introspective mood, young Giacomo is overwhelmed with melancholy. Bewailing his lot in his letters to Giordani, he enlarges on the idea in his *Zibaldone!* "I was terrified to find myself in the midst of nothingness, and myself nothing. I felt as if suffocated with the thought and feeling that all is nothing, just nothing." [26] Recoiling in horror from his present, he seeks refuge in the past. Life is bad; it is getting worse; but it has not always been bad. This is the consolation of the classical scholar: consolation and double bitterness in the contemplation of the Golden Age. In the life of the race, as in his own life, the age of childhood, the Age of Fable, is the happy one. Ancient thought was constructive, creative; modern thought is mainly negative, destructive, critical.[27] Against the straightforward nobility and happiness of the ancients, Leopardi sees modern society petty, disillusioned, irresolute, and unheroic: this is the sting of the early patriotic odes:

> Oh turn, my native country, and look back
> On those bright multitudinous companies,
> And weep, and cry out on thyself with scorn.[28]

Rebelling against the miserable pretenses of civilization, Leopardi joins Rousseau in sighing after the spontaneity and naturalness of primitive man, with his unquestioning trust in truth, beauty, virtue, love. Not only has civilization corrupted man and blighted his life with ills of body and soul; it has also enslaved him; it has robbed him of the very conditions of happiness. So Leopardi writes in his *Zibaldone*, on his first sally into the great civilized world, in Rome: Man would be happy could he always retain the blessed illusions of his youth; by himself man would have held fast to these illusions; it is social life which has served to disillusion the individual; society is therefore the original and continuous cause of human unhappiness; the natural life of man, the happy life, is thus a life of solitude. Thus the youth who had been eating out his heart in lonely Recanati.[29]

Contrary to general opinion, from Aristotle down, Leopardi regards man as the least social of all beings. Having more vitality than other animals, man has more self-love, and is thus more anti-social. Back of all human motives is this basic instinct of self-preservation and self-assertion; it is vigor, energy, drive. Developed as it is usually into the deliberate pursuit of selfish ends to the disadvantage of others, it becomes explicit egoism; the desire for our own happiness makes us haters of our fellows; the fountain-head of our weal becomes the source of wickedness and woe. The desire for pleasure is limitless; satisfaction is decidedly limited; we are thus doomed to disappointment; and the stronger a man's desires the more unhappiness is in store for him and the more unhappiness is he likely to cause.[30] There is no hope in prospect: civilization and so-called progress only multiply our desires and accentuate the selfishness of men. Jesus himself recognized this natural and miserable proclivity to evil, and by calling it "the World" emphasized the antithesis of nature and virtue: "My Kingdom is not of this world." [31]

So here is man as reason reveals him to us: naturally engrossed in futile selfishness: miserable and wicked. Not easily do we face this truth; the lure of happiness is too strong:

> The boy, like a raw lover, hotly woos
> His life, though it will cheat him.[32]

A youth rises from his books sanguine in his hopes that, whatever life may bring to others, his own life will be a happy one, virtuous and ardent. But life in due time teaches us all its own grim lesson: we see that ruthless cold selfishness, hatred and envy, slander and deceit, are not exceptional; we are disillusioned, and lose the sole comfort and happiness of our being. Justice, patriotism, glory, faith, love: these are disclosed to us as illusions, phantoms; but without them our life is of no avail and our world is naught.[33] We find ourselves in pursuit of a felicity which is forever beyond us: "always desirous, although incapable, of infinity," [34] we are forced to realize that our house of bliss is founded on sand.

Is it any wonder that men cleave to the phantoms of blessedness? Like the lover in Leopardi's dialogue on Tasso, who, whenever he dreamt of his lady, avoided her the next day, knowing that the actual sight of her would only spoil the greater beauty of his own vision of her, even so we all shrink from the unlovely actualities of life, and "praise and exalt those opinions, though untrue, which generate acts and thoughts noble, energetic, magnanimous, virtuous, and useful to the common or the private weal; those fancies beautiful and joyous, though vain, that give worth to life; the natural illusions of the mind." [35] If increased knowledge thus robs man of his source of happiness by dispelling his illusions, is not Rousseau right in calling a thinking man a corrupted being? A destroyer of phantoms, philosophy leaves man with nothing to sustain him, and is thus a bane not a blessing.[36]

All the same, though illusions be precious, disillusionment is inevitable:

> Phantom-shapes, nought else
> Are glory and honour; prosperity and joy
> A mere desire; life is without use,
> Unprofitable woe.[37]

The truth, if truth there be, is that there is no real and absolute truth, nor any other stable value. This is Leopardi's principle of relativity. British and French empiricism influenced his view of the impermanence of value, but more particularly was he brought to this conviction by his aesthetic studies which revealed to him the instability of the beautiful. Beauty is a matter of shifting taste and opinion. There is no proving beauty to him who does not see or feel it; it is undemonstrable because purely conventional; it reflects custom, the prestige of popular renown; or else it expresses illogical caprice: in either case it is altogether relative.[38]

The other values are no better off. Good and evil are nothing absolute. A horse may disapprove of a wolf devouring a sheep, but the carnivorous soul of the lion would not condemn the wolf, would only envy him. Good is good and evil evil simply with regard to this or that particular being. Morality is a matter of *mores*. Protagoras did not go altogether astray. Of truth and knowledge, the more we attain the more we perceive their sinuous unreality. This melancholy conclusion the young scholar of Recanati had reached early: in the very first volume of his *Zibaldone* is a weary exclamation: "Oh infinite vanity of truth!" Thought and knowledge are not only unattainable; they are unnatural and baneful to man. Hebrew allegory here agrees with the Greek: eating of the Tree of Knowledge cost man his Eden; the myth of Psyche teaches the same moral. "He who does not reason does not err. . . . He who does not think is wisest of all." There is no absolute stable infinite value. There is nothing infinite; all is finite, relative and impermanent. The infinite is a mere idea; it is simply the horizon, the ocean of the unattained which always stretches just beyond our vision. We know and we can know no infinite.[39]

Leopardi would save, if possible, the fundamentals of religion. God's infinite perfection, negated in an absolute sense, may be accepted as relative: perfection as we understand perfection, relatively. But it will not do: the notion of Divine Providence must go with the other illusions. Is it not an instance of our uncritical view of things? Man has imagined himself the crown and goal of creation, has conceived the entire course of things as explicitly designed to serve human ends. Time had been when Leopardi, despairing of life about him, had bewailed its unnaturalness, still confident of the all-wise benignity of Mother Nature. But the gloom deepens in his soul with the growing conviction that nature is no mother to us: stepmother, rather, to whom all our woes and agonies of soul and body are naught. The materialistic strain in Leopardi, connected with the French origins of his metaphysics, discloses itself in his developing view of nature. The world-course is not a divine pageant of Providence, but of brute, blind, unresponsive matter. We are lumps of thinking matter, drifting along in the stream of nothingness. Spirit is a mere word: matter is all-in-all.[40] Yet even of this we cannot be ultimately certain, for metaphysics in the last chapter is a blank.

> Inscrutable
> Is all, save pain.[41]

But, you say, is it not absurd to think that, with infinite pains, nature should produce so fine creatures as ourselves, only to cast them aside? Is it absurd? Here is a boy that most painstakingly has made a toy, a house of blocks, and—with one wave of the hand or one kick wrecks it all and turns to something else. So Nature tells the poor Icelander: "Do you imagine that the world was created solely for you? . . . If I injure you in any way, or by any means, I am not aware of it, or very seldom; nor if I delight or benefit you, am I conscious of it. . . . And finally, if by some accident I happened to destroy all your race, I should not be aware of the fact." [42] A little classic on the geocentric predicament of man's vanity is the dialogue *Il Copernico*. The more we realize the immensity of the universe, the more clearly is our own petty insignificance exhibited.[43] A stanza of sombre grandeur and majestic melancholy from *La ginestra* haunts the mind: Leopardi on the slopes of Vesuvius ponders on the vanity of human life:

> Oft times upon these slopes,
> Desolate, sombre-clad
> In the now hardened flood which still seems surging,

I sit by night; and o'er the landscape sad
Watch in pure azure skies
The constellations star by star emerging,
To which yon ocean lies
A distant mirror, till in calm profound
The world with sparks is glittering all around.
And when I gaze on those far bodies bright,
To me mere specks of light,
And yet in truth so vast
That land and sea, therewith in contrast brought,
Are but a speck; to which
Not only Man, but even
This globe, where Man is nought,
Is quite unknown; and when my eyes I cast
On star-groups, poised in heavens beyond our heaven,
Which distance so enshrouds
They seem to us like clouds, to which not Man
And not earth only, but these stars of ours
In magnitude and number infinite
With the sun's golden light, all blent in one,
Either are unknown or, remote as they
To earth, appear a speck
Of nebulous radiance; what then in my sight
Appearest thou, O son
Of Man? When I remember
Thy state on earth, of which the soil I tread
Bears witness, then in contrast call to mind
That of this mighty Whole
Thyself thou deem'st as lord and end designed,
And how it oft hath pleased thee to fable
That to this obscure grain of sand, called Earth,
The authors of this universe descended
For thy sake, and not seldom would with thee
Converse familiarly, and that this age
Insults good sense by giving vogue once more
To long-derided myths, although of all
It seems instructed best,
And most enlightened; what, then, shall I call
The feeling, what the thought, that in my breast
I entertain of thee, poor mortal seed?
Is laughter or is pity thy due meed? [44]

So the starry dome of heaven, which had turned Kant's mind to the thought of the moral law, stirs Leopardi's thought to the desolate conclusion of the indifference of ruthless nature.

More than Giacomo Leopardi's woe is involved here, more than the hopeless state of Italy, of mankind. A stone hurled from a cliff into an Alpine lake stirs the quiet depths in increasingly spreading circles and shivers the still reflections of tree and mountain and shoreline. Thus, Carducci observes, in Leopardi's poetry personal human happiness sinks in the confused depths of cosmic infelicity, *doglia mondiale.*[45] This is not the world-woe, *Weltschmerz,* of the romanticists; Leopardi's doctrine of *infelicità* expresses the grim conviction that the misery of mankind is inevitable, essential and unaccountable. Infelicity and mystery: behold our life and world.[46] We may think our unhappiness the result of unlucky or malign accident, and remediable: if this or that had not been, all had been well with us—and would be yet, if only this or that were to transpire. Miserable by necessity, we insist on believing ourselves miserable by accident. So a man lying on a hard and uncomfortable bed turns from side to side and thus spends the whole night, always hoping that the next turn will make him comfortable. But the truth is that the bed itself is wrong, and impossible it is in any position to find comfort on it.[47]

> Nought is worthy
> Thine agonies, earth merits not thy sighing.
> Mere bitterness and tedium
> Is life, nought else; the world is dust and ashes.
> Now rest thee. For the last time
> Abandon hope. Fate to our kind hath given
> No boon but death. Now scorn thyself, scorn Nature,
> Scorn the brute Power whose reign
> We know but by our woes, which are its pastime;
> Scorn all that is, for all is vain, vain, vain.[48]

This inevitable evil of our mortal state Leopardi's intellect explains in materialistic terms of blind necessity, unresponsive indifferent nature. But his imagination projects the shape of a woeful, malign Power, whose vast outlines are only suggested in the fragment of his uncompleted *Hymn to Ahriman:*

> Lord and Creator of all things, unfathomed
> Iniquity, consummate power and consummate
> Intelligence, eternal
> Fountain of woes, director of all motion. . . .[49]

In the last volume of the *Zibaldone* there is a black entry: "All is evil. That is, all which exists, is evil; that all things exist, is an evil. . . ." [50] This wholesale damnation is retailed in a hundred maledictions throughout Leopardi's works. Man is ferocious, destructive, odious; hatred and envy devour him. Women have a taste for each other's misfortunes. "Man is always as wicked as his needs require," we read on the last page of his published Works, and the last page of the *Zibaldone* is a pessimist's rosary: "Men regard life as Italian husbands do their wives: they must needs believe them faithful, although they know them to be otherwise. . . . The rarest thing in society, a really endurable person. . . ." Turks, Leopardi says, are inferior to their horses; [51] and on the score of happiness he repeatedly prefers the lot of animals to that of men; the lines from the *Night-Song of a Nomadic Shepherd of Asia* are the first that come to mind:

> O flock of mine reposing, happy flock,
> Of your own woe, methinks, quite unaware!
> How do I envy you! . . .[52]

And more boldly even, Leopardi prefers the utterly unconscious life of the *ginestra* blooming on the slopes of the volcano:

> And thou beneath
> The deadly weight shalt unresisting bow
> Thine innocent head full low:

But not bowed up till then in fruitless prayer
Or mien that cowards show to supplicate
The future tyrant: neither head erect,
With frantic pride aspiring to the stars,
Scorning the desert, where
Thou hadst both birth and home,
Not of thy choice but such as chance allowed:
But wiser, but so far
Less weak in this than Man, that thou didst never
Deem thy frail stock endowed
By fate or thee with power to live forever.[53]

The logic of these preferences is clear, and Leopardi draws it: non-existence were better than this our life. The greatest blessing Juno could bestow on Biton and Cleobis, beloved sons of her priestess, was to make them die gently in the same hour. For even the unconscious existence of plants and flowers is a spectacle of woe. "Enter a garden of plants, herbs, flowers. Be it as flourishing as you please. Be it in the best season of the year. You can't turn your eyes in any direction without finding suffering. . . . This rose is hurt by the sun which has given it life; it shrivels, languishes, withers. . . . Ants have infested this tree, grubs the other, flies, slugs. . . . The gardener goes wisely breaking, cutting live branches. . . ." [54] This passage should not be mistaken for maudlin: it is characteristic, not of the sentimentality, but of the morbid sensitivity of Leopardi.

IV

In a world thus revealed to his reason as vain, wicked, worthless, what is man to do? Obstinately hope for a better life after death, or turn a misanthrope, or seek refuge in disdainful apathy, or in suicide? Leopardi glanced down some of these paths, but he did not follow any one of them.

Of relief and peace in the hereafter, Leopardi's thought registers a gradual extinction. With the abandonment of his religious beliefs and his trust in Providence, his belief in immortality is also eclipsed. To be sure there is his letter of farewell to Sinner, written six months before his death, in which he expresses the fear that he will not see him again "unless it be 'on the fields of asphodel.'" Is this simply one Hellenist quoting Homer to another, or shall we conclude with Sainte-Beuve and Carducci that to his last breath Leopardi cherished a lingering *perhaps* about a life after death? [55] Be that as it may, certain it is that the entire course of Leopardi's thought discourages hopes of immortality. The world will not alter after my death; it will continue to be the same callous nature: what grounds do I have for any hopes? Proving the soul a simple entity, in good scholastic manner, avails nothing: if you are so uncertain and mysterious about the origin of this unique simple entity, what can you really know about its destiny? Why may it not perish, despite its simple substantiality, in ways as unknown to us as those in which it is alleged to originate and to exist alongside perishable compound flesh and blood? Not along the path of hope lay Leopardi's course: "Hopes of glory or immortality are things concerning which even the time to laugh at is gone by." [56]

A misanthrope and a hater of his kind Leopardi never was. While his ills and deformities robbed him of woman's love, the devoted friendship which he commanded in so many men and women was certainly an index of his character: ardor with patience, kindliness with heroism, candor without insolence: here was one who pitied, who smiled with grim irony, but to whom malice was alien. Giulio Levi calls him "an angelic nature fallen in a lower world." [57]

He had his stoical moments, of course, but his was an apathy of utter indifference, not the Stoic's serene acquiescence in the ways of Providence. By actual experience he found that resignation diminished pain, and remembered how, when little Luigi had thrown Pierfrancesco's fishing-rod out of the window, the lad's weeping had subsided upon his mother's saying that *she* would have thrown it out any-how! Leopardi knew the hedonistic paradox and showed an occasional streak of Taoistic wisdom: indifference to happiness is more likely to lead to happiness than the pursuit of it. But, while man can suffer passively, he will not work in vain; resignation breeds torpidity, and Leopardi was consumed with a zeal for achievement. Indifference to pain, to evil perhaps; but apathy with regard to his activity and creativeness was impossible to him. Here is a man who to the Stoic list of *adiaphora*, things that do not matter, had added reason also, the Stoic stock of reliance. Yet, holding life nothing worth, he yet held to the last scrap of life and was creatively active to the end.[58]

Why did he not commit suicide? Was it because "life is a thing of so little moment, that a man, as regards himself, should not be very anxious either to retain it or to leave it?" [59] He was not always so indifferent. The idea of suicide haunted Leopardi from the days of his disenchanted youth. The lines from the *Ricordanze* come at once to mind:

> Already in my youth's first turbulence
> Of ecstasy, of anguish and desire,
> Ofttimes I called on death, and hours by hours
> Would lean o'er yonder fountain, pondering
> The thought that 'neath its water I might quench
> All hope and grief forever. . . .[60]

He argued the matter with himself: is suicide contrary to nature? But is it more unnatural than continuing this our unnatural life? [61] To the subject of suicide Leopardi devoted his *Dialogue between Plotinus and Porphyry*, and *The Younger Brutus* and *Sappho's Last Song* lead plainly to the suicide's conclusions:

When a brave man is bold
And death to live prefers,
Shall nature blame his weapon as not hers? [62]

So Brutus; and Sappho:

Death be our choice. Casting to earth the veil
It scorns, the naked soul shall fly to Dis
And mend the brutal blunder of the blind
Distributor of luck.[63]

Leopardi sang of Brutus and Sappho, but his own choice was the choice of Plotinus. Plotinus' own final consent, however, scarcely expresses the whole thought of Leopardi: "Let us live, my Porphyry, and together comfort each other; let us not refuse to bear that part which destiny has assigned to us of the evils of our race." A fundamental conflict in Leopardi's soul makes him cleave to the life his reason has disdained, and out of this conflict springs his subtly lyrical poetry. It is the clash between Leopardi's reason and its peer, his imagination, and it brings us to one of the most significant aspects of his spiritual life.

V

Leopardi's reason has convinced him of the illusoriness of all that might make life worth living, has convinced him of the actuality of stupid, wicked woe as the sum and substance of the world. But his imagination lays hold on this sorry texture of life and irradiates it with its own glow of noble passion. In the very expression of his conviction that life is of no worth, worth most precious is experienced. This is the salvation of the philosopher by the poet. "The philosopher is not perfect if he is merely a philosopher. . . . Reason needs the imagination and the illusions which reason destroys." [64] Precisely in this intense dualism and conflict are we to seek the dynamic force of Leopardi's poetry. Leopardi himself, early in his poetic career, recognized the character of his lyrical activity: "Works of genius have this peculiarity that, even when they represent the nothingness of things, even when they clearly demonstrate and make us feel the inevitable unhappiness of life, when they express the most terrible moods of despair, yet to a great mind, even though it may be in a state of extreme depression, disillusionment, blankness, *ennui*, and weariness of life, or in the bitterest and most paralyzing misfortunes (whether with reference to deep and strong feelings or to anything else), they always serve as a consolation, rekindle enthusiasm; and though they treat of and represent no other subject than death, they restore to such a mind, at least momentarily, that life which it had lost. . . . And the very knowledge of the irreparable vanity and falseness of everything beautiful and great is in itself a certain beauty and greatness which fills the soul, when this knowledge is found in works of genius. The very contemplation of nothingness is a thing in these works which seems to enlarge the soul of the reader, to exalt it and satisfy it with itself and its own despair. . . ."[65]

It is no ordinary inconsistency we have here, no mere refusal to face the logic of one's argument. Leopardi's reason faces it: that life is worthless; but this further has to be taken into account, which reason cannot readily conceive: can a life be utterly worthless whose vanity has been so nobly and beautifully uttered; can love and beauty, virtue and justice and glory and truth be all illusory, if in imagination they have been so perfectly expressed? We shall fail to comprehend Leopardi's work if we treat him only as a pessimistic intellect. Confronting the intellect and sublimating its conclusions is the imagination of the poet. In lyric contemplation thought itself is swallowed up and despair yields sweet negation. This poetic alchemy is disclosed in the little masterpiece *L'Infinito*:

Always dear to me was this lonely hill,
Ay, and this hedge that from so broad a sweep
Of the ultimate horizon screens the view.
But, as I sit and gaze, my fancy feigns
Space beyond space upon the further side,
And silence within silence past all thought,
Immeasurable calm; whereat well nigh
Groweth the heart afraid. And as I hear
The wind sough through these thickets, then between
That everlasting silence and this voice
I make comparison; and call to mind
The Eternal, and the ages dead, and this
The living present, and its clamor. So
In this immensity my thought is drowned:
And sweet to me is shipwreck in this sea.[66]

So we read *Canto notturno*, in which man, face to face with nature, is revealed as less than nothing, and yet as sublime notwithstanding his nothingness; and *Aspasia*, bitter contrast of love's vision with the actuality of the beloved, humiliation not ignoble: and *Alla sua donna*, pure vision of the ideal lady:

Despite the countless woes
By fate predestined unto Man from birth,
If in thy essence, as my thought depicts thee,
Thou wert belov'd, existence to thy lover
Would be a heaven on earth.[67]

This is not escape from woe, but sublimation of it. Even though the beast may be happier than man, since he desires less and thinks not at all; even though genius may be called a capacity for unhappiness; yet thought, which shatters man's happiness and discloses his nothingness, likewise exalts him. Pascal's reflection on man as a thinking reed has not escaped Leopardi: "Nothing proves the greatness and the power of the human intellect, or the loftiness or nobility of man, quite so much as man's ability to know and thoroughly to understand and to feel deeply his own littleness." [68] But is one to marvel or to rail at a Power which has given man the poetic reach for the sublime and has denied its attainment in actuality and reason? "*Bella provvidenza!*—Fine Providence!" Leopardi exclaims,[69] perplexed by man's duality of character:

> Humanity, if wholly
> Worthless and frail thou art,
> Mere dust and shade, how can thy feelings show
> Such loftiness? If part
> Divine, how can thy noblest impulses
> And thoughts with so much ease
> Be roused and quenched alike by things so low? [70]

Perplexed he is, but not crestfallen, nor will he settle back in stagnant desolation. Be the world and life as it may, aspire and create he will, for it is the wine of his being. He perceives clearly that "all the value of human life is in the creation of the inner man." [71] In the hazardous leap of the spirit towards the phantoms that ennoble life, Leopardi finds the only true dignity and the salvation of our souls. This is no easy-going or calculating hedonist, but a grimly heroic soul:

> At all times I have viewed
> Craven and abject souls
> Disdainfully. . . .[72]

"Man, who gets used to anything, cannot get used to inaction," Leopardi writes, and, again in the *Zibaldone*, combing his languages to find a word that will best express the forward reach of the heroic: "One should live εἰκῆ, *temere, à l'hazard, alla ventura.*" [73]

But reason proclaims all aspiration futile and heroism ridiculous. Leopardi himself repeatedly ridicules the modern cult of progress, particularly in the satirical *Palinodia.* Despondent pages about progress abound also in the *Zibaldone.* Isn't self-perfection futile? In trying to rise out of the morass of life we only sink more deeply. Blessed be those of little soul and little thought: they are spared the great anguish. The poet's own life, however, was dominated by the heroic motive, notwithstanding the misgivings of his intellect. In an empirical world of mechanical necessity, Kant urged us to live *as if* God, freedom, and immortality were real. In a world vain, wicked, and woeful, Leopardi lived and created *as if* beauty, virtue, truth were realities and not the phantoms that his reason proclaimed them to be. A call to high endeavor is the poem *To a Victor in the Ball-Game*, and the spirit of noble hazard inspires the *Dialogue of Christopher Columbus and Peter Gutierrez.* "What is understood by a state free from uncertainty and peril? If content and happy, it is to be preferred to any other whatever; if tedious and miserable, I do not see what other is not to be preferred to it."

This longing for unrealized worlds, and the sense of desolation and weariness in the midst of the actual, are modern, romantic emotions. They would have scandalized the ancients; but, as Graf observes,[74] Petrarch could have understood them, and Pascal, and Chateaubriand. Leopardi's experience and estimate of this weariness, *noia*, were various, and his fragmentary writings about it are likely to confuse us. Sometimes *noia* is the utmost of insufferable monotony and stagnation, emptiness and desolation and disgust with life, a killing sense of the nothingness of all, "the most sterile of human passions, daughter and mother of nullity," weariness everlasting, *noia immortale.*[75] Carducci has traced its genealogy to the *athymia* of St. John Chrysostom, the *acedia* of Christian cenobites, the *accidia* of Dante.[76] To Jacopssen, Leopardi writes in June, 1823: "For some time I have felt the emptiness of existence as if it were something real which weighed heavily on my soul. The nothingness of things was to me the only real thing. It was always with me, like a frightful phantom; I saw about me only a desert; I did not see how

I could subject myself to the daily cares and exigencies of life, being quite sure that these cares would never lead to anything. This thought so obsessed me that I thought I should lose my reason." [77]

Leopardi's *noia* is not mere negation, however; it is the sense of checked activity, frustrated attainment, yes; but it is not inactivity, it is not mere failure. Man is condemned to *noia* because he finds the world hemming him in, because, in his desire, thought, imagination he is beyond and above the actual world that encases him. And a man will be the more surely destined to experience *noia* the more intense and the more expansive his desire or his spiritual activity. So *noia*, exquisite dolor of weariness, has also the element of sublimity. It is not any particular dolor or weariness, but "life itself fully felt, experienced, known, fully present to the individual and engrossing him." [78] And this sense of the utter emptiness of life is not itself mere negation: itself is positive, and the intensity of imagination in works of genius makes the experience of *noia* sublimely beautiful. Thus weariness overcomes itself, *noia si disannoia*, "by the same lively feeling of universal and necessary weariness." [79] The sublimity of *noia* is well expressed in *Pensieri* lxvii and lxviii; I quote the latter: "Life-weariness is in some respects the most sublime of human sentiments. Not that I believe that from the investigation of this sentiment those conclusions result which many philosophers have thought to gather from it; but nevertheless, to be unable to find satisfaction in any earthly thing, or, so to say, in the whole earth; to consider the inestimable amplitude of space, the number and astonishing mass of the worlds, and find that all is little and petty to the capacity of our soul; to imagine the number of the worlds infinite, and the universe infinite, and feel that our soul and our desire would be still greater than such an universe; always to accuse things of insufficiency and nullity, and endure that want and emptiness which we call life-weariness; this seems to me the greatest sign of grandeur and nobleness which human nature presents. Let it also be noted that life-weariness is scarcely known to insignificant persons, and very little or not at all to the lower animals." [80]

Imagination saves us in a worthless world: we take refuge in our cherished illusions. Heroic aspiration saves us: we refuse to bow our head to the actual, and press forward to worlds unrealized. And sublime contemplation also saves us: in the noble perception of the emptiness which is life, life itself is transfigured by our very condemnation of it: the sublimity of the ideal judgment is thus revealed. These heroic emotions have in them nothing of arrogance or cruelty, nor hatred of one's fellows. Leopardi openly protests, and it is in the last volume of the *Zibaldone:* "My philosophy not only does not conduce to misanthropy, as some superficially observe, and as many accuse me; it essentially precludes misanthropy." [81] *La ginestra* has rightly been called, as for instance by Carducci,[82] Leopardi's capital work. Here is the pitiful nothingness of man, against callous, omnipotent nature, and here man's sublimity also, in refusing to submit and stagnate. Leopardi's poem is a call to mankind, to band in holy alliance of solidarity and brotherly love against the unfeeling brutality of nature:

> Noble of nature he
> Who fearlessly can raise
> His mortal eyes and gaze
> Upon our common doom, and frankly owns,
> Subtracting nought from truth,
> The evil apportioned us, and that our state
> Is humble and very weak;
> Who proves himself a great
> And gallant sufferer, and doth not seek
> To add fraternal strife,
> Worst of all ills in life,

Unto his sorrows by accusing Man
Of causing his distress, but lays the blame
On the true culprit—her, who though of mortals
Mother by birth, by choice is their stepdame.[83]

Is virtue an illusion? "But, if this illusion were shared by all," Leopardi writes Jacopssen, "if all men believed, and wished to be virtuous, if they were compassionate, bountiful, generous, magnanimous, full of enthusiasm; in a word, if all the world were kindhearted (for I see no difference between kindliness and what is called virtue), would not all be happier?" [84]

There is a paradox in Leopardi, which Francesco de Sanctis has expressed finely: "Leopardi produces the contrary effect of that which he intends. Not believing in progress, he makes you desire it; not believing in liberty, he makes you love it. He calls love and glory and virtue illusions, and kindles in your breast an endless desire for them. You cannot leave him without feeling yourself the better, and you cannot come near him without first wishing to pull yourself together and be purified, in order not to have to blush in his presence. He is a sceptic and makes you a believer; and while he sees no possibility of a less dismal future for our native land, he rouses in your breast an ardent love for it and fires your heart for noble deeds. He has so low an estimate of human nature, and his own soul lofty, gentle and pure, honors and ennobles it. . ." [85] The ardor of the ideal lover and the true hero animate him ever; one day he copied in large letters in his *Zibaldone* these words in which Barthélemy eulogizes Aeschylus: "His heroes would rather be struck by lightning than be guilty of any baseness, *and their courage is more inflexible than the fatal law of necessity.*" [86]

CHAPTER IX

ARISTOCRACY WITHOUT ILLUSIONS: ALFRED DE VIGNY

In the presence of the Almighty Voice out of the Whirlwind agonized Job does not "set his cause," but, awed into submission, "abhors himself and repents in dust and ashes." Pascal, despairing of knowing God with his reason, would gamble on possible assurance through faith, even though the price were the surrender of our thought wherein, he perceives, lies all our dignity. Alfred de Vigny's body and soul were not racked with all of Job's torments, neither did he survey or sound with Pascal all the marshes of doubt in which our mind gropes. But though unable to move forward with assurance, Vigny does not yield; he stands his ground; man's sorry estate rouses in him pity and never scorn; he honors man's moral integrity above the unreckoned majesty of the Divine, for man can die for a principle, and is thus greater than God.[1] Here is a grim aristocrat's pride, Stoic dignity and fortitude without the compliant Stoic trust in Divine Providence, and never a sign of misanthropy. In poetry, in politics, in religion, he inhabits the ivory tower of his own ideals, unassured but unyielding, an aristocrat despite disillusion.

I

The epidemic of dolor and general despondency which characterized romanticism manifested itself even in some non-romanticists during the early nineteenth century. Byron, Lamartine, and Musset, Chateaubriand and Senancour

(*Obermann*), Goethe's *Werther*, Heine and Lenau, Ugo Foscolo and Leopardi express the various strains of this universal threnody: Christian-mystical, antitheistic, sentimental, metaphysical, passionate, stoical, misanthropic, humanitarian. As the nineteenth century gets beyond its romantic adolescence, positivism, materialism, realism take possession of it; the microscope replaces meditation in literature. Alfred de Vigny was a pioneer among the romanticists, and from his ivory tower he saw the hosts of naturalism invade the land. We should not, however, regard *Les destinées* as merely belated romantic wails. Vigny, who prided himself on having marched first, was not a mere follower even of himself. The development in his thought is real and consistent. Byron's influence on his ideas is undeniable; that of Schiller has been pointed out;[2] that of Frederick the Great is not unlikely;[3] to understand Vigny adequately, however, we should see in him more than someone's disciple or the member of a school.

Those who are bound to reduce a philosophy of despair to personal disappointment, and pessimism to pique, find the case of Alfred de Vigny more puzzling than Pascal's or Leopardi's or Schopenhauer's. Pascal's or Leopardi's lifelong ill health, Leopardi's mother, and also Schopenhauer's, Leopardi's loveless life, and Schopenhauer's long vain struggle for recognition would have driven unphilosophic men to despair and suicide. Vigny lived to see in his own life reasons enough for his gloom, but he was a poet of pessimism at a time when, strong, handsome, and brilliant, he met the smiling eyes of love and fame. To be sure, we may call him a pessimist born; or we may thumb our psychiatries in search of Greek terms to describe this odd despond: melancholia dysthymia;[4] or we may simply quote Shakespeare's Salarino to Antonio, in the *Merchant of Venice:* "You are sad because you are not merry."[5] But Brunetière has rightly perceived in Vigny's pessimism a metaphysical suffering: "the dull anguish that the enigma of destiny stirs at the bottom of the heart." [6] If this woe, which to the 'once-born' man appears so unaccountable, is recognized, we may better appreciate the significance of Vigny's own life-experiences as contributing to intensify his pessimism, to motivate it in detail, and later in life also to alleviate it and to turn his eyes from darkness towards light.

He was an aristocrat from the cradle to the grave: an aristocrat first of all in the traditional sense: proud of his name and race. Somewhat past midway in his life he recorded his inability to imagine finer characters than those in the chronicles of his family. His every thought of his father was a joy; of his mother, a blessing. What if we learn that some of the ancestral dignities which the poet treasured were mythical? Perhaps 'Admiral' Barraudin was no admiral, and perhaps no Vigny blood was really shed in the Crusades. We need not go so far back. Alfred's father did fight Frederick the Great, did enter the king's tent to ask permission to seek his brother's body on the field of battle. And Alfred's mother did rear her son in the spirit of aristocratic dignity; she did teach him that nobility was a trust and a duty. He felt himself the last of a great house; the Revolution had wrecked its fortunes, and Vigny wrote in his book the long list of lost family estates. He faced his own life, noble, and poor as a noble is poor, a respectable poverty, rich in honor and self-respect.

The essential nobility of his character it is difficult to assail. Did he marry Lydia Bunbury for the sake of her expected millions, and couldn't Sir Somebody Bunbury remember his son-in-law's identity beyond the fact that he was a French poet, so that kind Frenchmen had to go down the list of poets until he exclaimed: "Vigny? Yes, I believe that's my man!" But Vigny writes that he never asked his father-in-law for a penny, and in any case, when the Bunbury millions failed to materialize, when he found himself mated to a disinherited invalid to whom his inner life was a closed book and who could not even read his poems, he gave her, if not love, at least all the devoted care which pity and his sense of honor dictated. We cannot ignore the Dorval affair; even if Vigny tried to raise Marie Dorval to his own level, the fact is that he descended to hers. He did live to write: "I feel in me a secret shame for the first time in my life." [7] But dignity is not lacking in the betrayed lover's withdrawal; *Samson's Wrath* is not an ignoble revenge.

The heart of his youth had gone to Napoleon; in the *compagnies rouges* under Bourbon royalty, the young officer dreamt in vain of combat and promotion, he "stifled, imprisoned, within this wooden horse which would never be opened in any Troy." [8] The Bourbons did not give him any recognition, yet during the revolution of 1830, had the Duke D'Enghien or the Duke De Berry made a stand in Paris, he would have risked his life for a house he disdained. Louis Philippe did notice him, but Vigny, never insolent, was never servile. For eighteen years he "resisted all the seductions of the house of Orleans." [9] Disillusioned with Napoleon, repelled by Bourbon lack of integrity and courage, disdainful of the bourgeois nobility of Louis Philippe's shops, ever distrustful of democracy, especially after 1848, Vigny took refuge in the dignity of his own inner being and remained to the end "incorrigibly aristocratic." [10]

He craved fame: what poet doesn't? But he craved perfection above popularity; he would himself have uttered the words which he puts in the mouth of Milton in *Cinq-Mars:* "Were my verses to remain unread for a hundred years after my death, I should still ever write them." Six times the French Academy spurned him in favor of other candidates, some of them scarcely remembered today; [11] and when he was finally elected a member, the clash with Molé over his speech of reception poisoned Vigny's great day of honor. He had his great days, of course: the days of the fame of *Cinq-Mars*, the night of *Othello*, the wonderful first night of *Chatterton*. But where was lasting satisfaction to be found? When, in his youth, he had put on the new uniform of the Red Company, he had not experienced the expected thrill to the full: "So that is all!" And he lived to find glory disappointing more than once, for what is one to think of glory, he said, when the sculptor of the Laokoön is unknown?

Pride inhabited his ivory tower, the sad pride of disillusion. But steps of devoted pity led downstairs to the beds of pain where day and night for years he nursed first his beloved mother and then his wife until they both very gradually sank into the unknown. His father's last words to him had been, "Make your mother happy." That charge he fulfilled to the last. "Blessed be then the former misfortunes which deprived my father and grandfather of their great chateaux in the Beauce, since they have made me know this joy of a workman's wage brought to one's mother in secret, without her knowing it." [12] When, after twelve years of torture, the 'vulture of Prometheus' (cancer of the stomach), which his doctors neither recognized nor subdued, finally consumed him in 1863, was his cry of distress unto God a coward's cry? Twenty-nine years earlier he had written: The man of honor at his death "looks at the cross with respect, fulfils all his Christian duties as a formality, and dies in silence." [13]

II

Job atop the ash-heap suffers torments, but his real agony is that he cannot, as a loyal servant of God, make sense of his torments. His torture is really religious. Vigny's despair of life is also due, not so much to his direct experience of evil or to his observation of specific evils in life, as to the half-felt, half-reasoned conviction that in this world inner worth neither prevails nor avails. We live in a world which is callous or even hostile to virtue and high endeavor, a world which includes pure evil but not unmixed good. In this world nobility is humiliated, the innocent suffer, and even generous love may work the ruin of the soul. This essential callousness and injustice of God, Nature,—call it what you will,—Vigny could not understand and refused to accept with submission. The ever-present sense of it poisoned his joys:

> My heart, with joy infatuate,
> My drunken heart, has launched its fate
> In torrent floods of laughter proud;
> But Sorrow's Self before my face
> I see, my laughter I efface,
> My brow in mourning I enshroud.[14]

Our very virtues serve to wreck us, so alien to worth is life. Vigny's works are cantos of an epic of disillusion. *Cinq-Mars* chronicles the earlier chapters of the bankruptcy of the aristocrat; the last chapters were written before Vigny's own eyes. Excellence and nobility of character make men inevitably failures in an ignoble world. The multitude may tremble in awe before the Great Man, but condemn his life of power to solitude; so Moses prays to God to let him sleep the sleep of oblivion:

> O Lord, I've lived my life in lonely majesty:
> The sleep of Mother Earth now vouchsafe to me![15]

But more often the genius is crushed; society is too frivolous for Gilbert, too materialistic for Chatterton, too cruel for André Chenier. The world in which a Robespierre disposes of human destinies does not tolerate "the aristocrats of intelligence":[16] it would level all down to the nothingness in which it abides.

Samson's consuming love for Delilah should exalt both, but it destroys him. The woman he loves betrays him to the

Philistines. Is Samson ruined because his love is sensual and self-seeking? But self-forgetting devotion may also prove our undoing. A masterpiece of poetic despair is Vigny's *Eloa.* At the grave of Lazarus, moved by pity for the grief of Mary and Martha, Jesus shed a divine tear. Of this tear of Christ's love is born the angel Eloa. What fatality leads this celestial maiden of pure love to meet the Fallen One? Eloa is moved to pity, to love; she would redeem Lucifer, yet is herself swept into the abyss. This spectacle of human life in which high worth and virtue are frustrated need not make us misanthropic; man deserves pity, not hatred. But if Vigny is never a hater of men, he is not a lover of God; his thought and mood are antitheistic. Behold Jephthah's daughter, virgin innocence sacrificed to a malign Deity. Behold Sarah in *The Deluge:* had she married Japhet, son of Noah, she would have been saved with his household; but she loved Emmanuel, and neither her love nor his innocence avail to deliver them from the rising flood of God's wrath.

Is this view of the Almighty too harshly Hebraic? Then turn to the Gospels, Vigny says; come with me to Gethsemane. Here is, not human, Divine Innocence, on bended knee crying out: "Father!"

> But dark the sky remains, and God does not reply.[17]

In place of doubt and evil, Christ would bring to man blessed certainty and confident hope. But the night is callous, and in the woods the Son of God hears the tramp of the mob and sees the blazing torch of Judas Iscariot. Moreover why does Christ die? To atone once for all for man's sins? The death on Calvary should then be expiation enough. Did not Christ cry out on the Cross: "It is finished!" "Was there not enough divine blood for the salvation of the human race?"[18] There is a Pascalian overtone in this note. Vigny is scarcely a Jansenist, Léon Séché to the contrary,[19] but there is in his thought not a little of Pascal's grim struggle with the enigmas of truth and faith. "His Diary often reads like a continuation of Pascal's *Thoughts.*" [20] Faguet's words about Vigny may well be read in a reverse order: "He does not believe in the ideal, but he adores it." [21]

But, we are told, God's ways are not man's ways, and his plans for man are past finding out:

> Your glance forever fix beyond this mortal span:
> That guiltless men should die, seems fathomless to man;
> Be not thou overwhelmed with this, nor seek reply;
> Unlike our pity is the pity from on High;
> God makes no covenant with man; his hand of fate,
> Creating without love, destroys us without hate.[22]

And we are asked to look beyond this life. Note the irony in the closing lines of *The Deluge:*

> "Your father does not come: shall we be punished, then?"
> "Though death should separate, no doubt we'll meet again." [23]

No doubt, but what reason do we have for hope of anything better? The prisoner in the Iron Mask has seen nothing in this life to justify his trust in any hereafter:

> " I do not want it: chains await me there." [24]

What is this look beyond the grave but a look of despair? "The truth about life is despair. The religion of Christ is a religion of despair, since he despairs of life and only trusts in eternity." [25]

If we turn away from God to contemplate Nature, we turn from injustice or possible malignity to stone-blind impassivity.

> I'm deaf to all your moans and sighs, and scarcely sense
> The progress of the human comedy immense
> Which vainly seeks a silent audience in heaven. . . .
> A mother I am called, but I'm in truth a tomb;
> My winter sweeps your dead as in a hecatomb;
> My spring is dull to all your adorations. . . .[26]

Turn from God to nature, and back to God; the conclusion is the same:

> In this chaotic world, I see nothing assured
> But *Suffering and Death*, in which our life is moored.[27]

What is man to do, then? Prayers and supplications are vain; vain all violent imprecation, and vainest of all is hope. Understand clearly the firm foundation of despair, and then consider man's estate: tragic and pitiful it is, but despicable never! Do not resist dark contemplation: "It is bad and cowardly to seek distraction from a noble woe so as to diminish suffering. One should reflect upon it, plunge the sword courageously to the hilt." [28] Face God, face nature grimly without murmur and without appeal. Stoic fortitude is alone noble, not the Stoic trust in a somehow-good universe, but rather the fortitude of utter silence without hope or plea: the silence of utter despair in which all is lost save man's tragic dignity, "this half-silence . . . the true Stoicism of an anguished soul and an averted spirit, . . . the religion of honor and valor." [29] A Stoic portrait is that of the dying wolf teaching the hunter who has killed him

> How one should leave this life and all its ills and grime:
> You know it well indeed, you animals sublime!
> What meaning and what gain from this earth do we wrest?—
> Noble alone is silence: weakness, all the rest.
>
> To groan or weep or pray, is all a coward's moil:
> So do with might and main your long and heavy toil,
> Where'er the path assigned to you by Fate may lie,
> And then, like me, without a whimper, suffer, die.[30]

The stanza "Le silence" concluding (or appended to) *Le Mont des Oliviers* is a poetic document of the dignity of despair:

> If in the Holy Garden of Gethsemane
> The Son of Man did pray to God, and prayed in vain;
> Deaf, blind, and unresponsive to our misery,
> If Heav'n did spurn our misbegotten world of pain,
> This scorn divine my mortal honor will defy
> With scorn, and silence cold will be my one reply
> To God's eternal silence and to God's disdain.[31]

So this is the only respectable way out: not wailing, not hopeful, but grimly resistant. Do not seek comfort; steel your soul in 'saintly solitude': the hyenas never attack the traveler so long as he stands up and keeps marching on. This somber fortitude exalts man; and it also stimulates generous compassion with his fellows: against the malign majesty of God or the blind majesty of nature, man's is the tragic majesty of woe:

> Live thou, cold Nature, and in waves of life be borne
> Triumphant over us, since this is fate's decree;
> Live ever thou and, goddess-like, presume to scorn
> Us humble passengers that should rule over thee:
> Far more than all your power or all your splendors vain,
> I love the majesty of man's unyielding pain:
> A single word of love you will not get from me! [32]

The penultimate verse, in Vigny's words, contains the sense of all his philosophical poems: "the spirit of humanity, the utter devotion to mankind and to the betterment of its lot." [33]

"Were I a painter," Vigny wrote, "I should like to be a black Raphael: angelic form, somber color." [34] This spirit of aristocratic standards and generous fortitude serves in Vigny's life the purposes of a religion. It is the Religion of Honor. The stories in *Servitude et grandeur militaires* are cantos of an epic on Duty. Here is a Kantian exaltation of Duty: routine devotion to one's army vow even when it involves heart-breaking, hateful obedience (*Laurette ou le cachet rouge*); grim devotion to a disillusion which has nullified all but man's own self-respect (Captain Renaud); noble self-effacing devotion to duty (Admiral Collingwood). "The sentiment of Duty ends by so dominating the mind as to permeate one's character and become second nature, just as constant use of wholesome nourishment can change the quality of one's blood and become a factor in one's constitution." [35] Thus arises honor: "Honor is conscience, but conscience exalted . . . . It is the poesy of duty." [36] Here is the purest and the bravest of religions, an intense and elevated sense of self-respect, "a manly religion, without symbols or imagery, without dogmas and without ceremonies." [37] "Conscience should be divinized," Vigny wrote in his *Diary*,[38] planning his novel *Daphné,* with Julian the Apostate as its hero. Julian's character fascinated Vigny: "If there is metempsychosis I have been this man. His rôle, life, character would have suited me best of any in history." [39] It is the character of a man who, disillusioned and unable to believe, yet sees clearly man's utter need of belief and devotion; an intensely religious man without a religion, an essentially contemplative soul plunging deliberately and entirely into action, into the battle of ideals and devotions.

Is Julian's life, is Vigny's utter failure? But how are we to reckon failure and success? Here the words of Captain Renaud come to mind: "I saw clearly that events are nothing, that the inner man is everything." [40] And this inner integrity and worth, candor and fortitude and generosity preserve and ennoble man in the very pit of disaster. Here Vigny recalls Leopardi: "The contemplation of misfortune itself gives the soul inner joy that comes from attending to the idea of misfortune." [41] This is a treasure of truth which is always ours: "Let us be consoled for all by the thought that we enjoy our thought itself, and that nothing can rob us of this joy." [42] A somber treasure! All the same, adversity has not crushed us so long as this devotion to truth still remains. "The day when man has lost all enthusiasm and love and adoration and devotion, let us bore to the center of the earth, put in five hundred billion barrels of powder, and let it blaze to pieces in the firmament!" [43]

From this resigned devotion and despairing generosity there gradually arises a defiant optimism. "Vigny traverses despair, but does not rest in it." [44] Among the last songs of the poet of the ivory tower are songs of light and trust, grimly jubilant songs of an aristocrat despite disillusion. The poet of despair ends on a note of hope. It is a hope in man, in woman, in work, and in civilization. Already in 1843 Vigny's poem *La sauvage* showed how far he had travelled beyond Rousseau's idolatry of the primitive. Fleeing with her children from the cruelty of the Hurons, the Indian savage woman seeks refuge for herself and her orphans in the home of an English settler. Here man has made himself master of nature, has wrestled with nature's wild domain, has vanquished and humanized it. In the midst of the trackless woodland waste is a garden and a home, a library, the Bible, Shakespeare. To this refuge the savage woman is admitted. There is irony in the hospitality. Time was when the Almighty rejected the sacrifice of the hard-working tiller of the soil, to accept the blood-smelling smoke of the idle herdsman. But here Cain has his revenge: nomad savagery, disdainful of work and of womankind, is here abased before law-abiding, home-building thrift.[45] This is the voice of civilization as it penetrates the jungle:

> She says, in building each new city: "See!—
> You call me Law, but I am Liberty!" [46]

This eulogy of civilized man expresses a faith in the progress of ideals, a faith even in the midst of disaster, of shipwreck. So in the poem *The Bottle in the Sea*, as the storm rages and the waves beat the dismayed ship to pulp against the unsuspected and uncharted rocks, as the waters sweep over the decks, the sailors do all in their power to save their boat and their lives. But when all effort proves futile, the captain does the one thing left to him: he records latitude and longitude of the unmarked reef which the wrecking of his ship has served to discover; he issues the warning, seals the precious knowledge in a strong bottle, and trusts it to the waves that sweep him and his crew to death. The bottle floats long and alone on endless seas, but at last it comes within the reach of human eyes and human hands. The captain's hope is not frustrated, nor is his death and the death of his men in vain. One more step has been marked in man's mastery over brute nature. This poem is a song of courage and hope and glory to explorer, sailor, craftsman, scientist, warriors all in man's great combat with nature:

> The true God, God Almighty, is the God of thought.
> The seed that Fate on our deep furrowed brows has cast,
> Neglect it not, to harvest be it ever brought;
> Reap, gather in the grain, the soul's own treasure vast;
> All redolent it is of saintly solitudes:
> Then toss it to the sea, the sea of multitudes!
> God's finger will conduct it safe to port at last.[47]

A chant of hope, of trust in man is also the poem *La flute:* if efforts prove unavailing, and your cause seems to falter and fail, and the harmony you are endeavoring to create turns to discord, do not despair. The flute, not the flutist, is at fault:

> Blame not the soul of man, the beggar-body blame;
> What wretched organs here our mind's endeavors shame!
>
> . . . .
>
> Like crude translators of some bright celestial bard
> They stammer. . . .[48]

The poem *L'Esprit pur*, Vigny's last, written six months before his death, is impressive in its noble assurance. One should have Vigny's *Diary* and his *Correspondence* well in hand to appreciate fully the noble pathos of this swan-song.

Vigny contemplates the past glories of his house, and then considers his own lot:

> Dead, all of them, their names forgot without renown;
> But read the writing in the Golden Book Divine:
> "Two families of France the road of life passed down;
> Their last descendant now ascends the holy shrine
> And writes his name, but not upon the rolls obscure
> Of proud knaves, useless rich, but on the tablet pure
> That Destiny unto Pure Spirit doth assign." [49]

The influence of Comte on Vigny's thought is evident here, although the poet had too keen a sense of individuality to find unqualified peace in the Cult of Humanity, and his problems were too metaphysical in character to be resolved altogether by anthropocentric or geocentric positivism; his altruism, moreover, had the note of grim pity that scarcely accords with the bright cheer of Comte's humanitarianism. Vigny is brimful of fertile ideas, and his mind is never encased in a formula. Faguet observes the great concentration of his style: "In his *Diary,* which is the key to all his thought, he sometimes sketches in half-a-dozen lines a whole philosophical system that would have done credit to a great thinker." [50] So we should not be too assured in recording Vigny's final diagnosis and remedy: utopianism in the face of adversity, grim optimism. For what avails the prospect, be it never so certain, that the shipwrecked captain's bottle will some day reach port, that the youth of France will some day read Vigny and with him honorably face this world's despair? In the total economy of the vast chaos which we call the universe, what avail the progress or the stagnation, the prosperity or the ruin of France, human profit or loss, terrestrial book-keeping? Climb Montmartre, look at the immense city of Paris: "a little higher, what would this city be, what would be this earth? What are we in God's sight?" [51]—a thought that had disturbed Montaigne also, and harrowed Pascal.

We may perhaps regard Vigny's resolve to trust his destiny to man's spirit and to enlightened posterity as a Pascalian hazard and plunge of faith. Or we may, and I think with more justice, perceive in these last poems the wisdom of Leopardi's capital work, *La ginestra*. Has God put us in this sorry world, face to face with brute unresponsive nature? Our only hope and reliance then is to be sought in our inner sense of generous honor. Fortitude, self-respect, pity bind mankind in resistance to Stepmother Nature. Slowly but surely scientist and poet and artisan and seer are writing in the Book of Pure Spirit the mastery of man's soul over its callous medium. Slowly but surely, as duty and pity become our master passions, human life is redeemed from the brute and human society becomes a true republic. This deepening of cosmic confidence disdains the supernatural and the ritualistic-liturgical aspects of Christianity, but it is permeated with the Christian spirit of benevolence, and with respect for weak but aspiring human nature. Vigny's benevolence was not merely a poetic gesture, nor was it limited to the tender care for his mother and for his wife. The poet of *Stello*, of *Chatterton* championed actively the cause of individual needy authors, and made their lives more bearable.[52] At New Years' Eve he would review the twelvemonth past and thank Heaven that he had done no evil to any human soul, nor written against his conscience nor against his fellow men.

There are in Vigny gleams of a Zoroastrian hope in the extinction, and more, even in the reclaiming of evil. In his Diary is the outline of a projected poem, *Satan Saved*. In another passage he contemplates that at the Last Judgment, "God will come to *justify* himself before all souls and all life. He will appear and will speak; he will tell clearly the why and wherefore of creation, of the suffering and the death of innocence." Is this a sentence from Vigny's Theodicy? The next sentence reads: "On that day it will be mankind, brought to life, that will be the judge, and the Eternal, the Creator will be judged by the generations of men." [53] It is like a double-edged commentary on a verse from the Book of Job.

Do we really know enough to hope? The map is never finished, and the beast of prey is never quite banished from our souls. And, who knows, perhaps God regards man's enterprise as a boy watches the building of a bird's nest: almost finished, and a brush of the hand destroys it all. Are our terrestrial prospects any more secure? Vigny has no answer; he only knows that any other course but that of duty, honor, pity would be cowardly and would tarnish the one grain of gold in this world of dross: man's moral endeavor. "I am an epic moralist," he writes.[54] In all his dismay and despair he never doubts the inherent and unshakable worth of noble effort: "What matters it," we read in *Daphné*, "if the good is only done, whether one is or is not trampled under foot?" [55] The ship is being submerged; what am I to do? Epictetus the Stoic tells me: "Drown like a man." Vigny:

> "Toss your work to the sea, the sea of multitudes."

CHAPTER X

THE WARP OF SCHOPENHAUER

A philosopher's view of life is a fabric of the spirit in which thread-patterns of reasoned truth or error are woven into the warp of his personal character or bias, the temper of the man. In some cases the woof may be so thick or the warp so thin that the texture produced is of a scientific or otherwise colorless impersonality. In other cases the thinnest and most threadbare woof strings together the strong cords of sentimental or fanatical bias. In still other cases warp and woof color and reflect and modify each other in reconciled or unreconciled rivalry. These are humanly the most interesting textures of the spirit, and, who knows, perhaps the most precious. "The sort of philosophy a man has," Fichte told us, "depends on the sort of man one is."

I

Towards the middle of the fourteenth century a priest and warden of the House of the Teutonic Order on the bank of the Main, in Frankfurt, wrote a book which Martin Luther declared had taught him more of God and Christ and all things than any other next to the Bible and St. Augustine. The kernel of this *Theologia Germanica* is a gospel of self-denial. Sin is infatuate self-will, blindness to good and to God; in the true life of Christ the self must be forsaken and lost, must die altogether. "Be simply and wholly bereft of self. . . . Put off thine own will, and there will be no hell." [1]

Five centuries later, on the right bank of the Main, opposite the Frankfurt House of the Teutonic Order, the deepening twilight of old age was bringing peace to another evangelist of denial. Arthur Schopenhauer felt himself at home in the *Theologia Germanica.* Breaking its intellectual theistic shell and casting it aside as nothing worth, he found in its kernel-doctrine of salvation the same truth which had been uttered in dark sayings of ancient Eastern seers and which he had sought his life long to express and to establish in reasoned terms. "Buddha, the Frankfurter, and I," Schopenhauer used to say: one in their pessimistic insight into life. For the essential difference between religions consists in this, he thought, whether they are optimistic or pessimistic. Despite the superficial bond of monotheism, the essentially optimistic tone of Judaism makes it really alien to the deeper spirit of Christianity. It is the perception of evil in the Old Testament which Christianity has seized upon and emphasized: the sense of sin, the doctrine of the Fall, which Schopenhauer calls the redeeming feature of Judaism.[2]

True Christianity, Schopenhauer insisted on every occasion, is a gospel of deliverance *from* life. The world is to it a synonym for evil; St. Augustine identifies salvation with the end of the world. Here is no complacent gospel of happiness: "The swiftest animal that bears thee to perfection is suffering," Meister Eckhart wrote, and the very symbol of Christianity is the cross. What Meister Eckhart teaches "in the fetters of his Christian mythology," [3] the Buddha urges more simply and clearly, unencumbered by theism. Woe is universal and woe is begotten of selfishness, and deliverance from woe is deliverance from self. This deliverance from the bonds of self, this crucifixion of the flesh, this peace of stilled desire Schopenhauer did not attain; only old age in the course of nature brought him a measure of it. But he read the wretched riddle of life and recorded its solution: that which saints lived out and mystics saw in blessed vision, he undertook to analyze and to prove.

It is easy and it is futile to taunt Schopenhauer with not having practised what he preached. His very failure to do so may serve the more clearly to illustrate his text. Life he compared to a tragedy, in which the hero may leave the stage and even step into the audience to watch the play, biding his time and cue, all the while keenly aware of the tragic dénouement in which he is to play his part. It is a sorry play Schopenhauer witnessed on the stage of life, and a sorry actor he was in many ways, yet with all his frailties not altogether unheroic. A more intimate glance into his life and heart may not lead us to admire, but it will enable us to understand, and to pity without scorn.

II

The average man accepts the world without question. He is apt to ascribe suicide to a fit of madness, and the unqualified rejection of life impresses him as the utterance of a diseased mind. Those who would explain Schopenhauer's pessimism pathologically find no lack of material in his family's history. The Schopenhauers, of Dutch ancestry, had long been settled prosperously as merchants and landowners in Danzig. The philosopher's great-grandfather, Johann Schopenhauer, had been, in 1716, host to Peter the Great, and had warmed his stoveless guest-chamber by burning gallons of brandy on the stone floor. The grandfather, Andreas Schopenhauer, married Anna Renata Soermans, to whom the troubled strain in the Schopenhauer family may be traced. She was adjudged insane and placed under a guardian's care during the last years of her life. Her two younger sons were clearly tainted: Michael Andreas was from his youth an idiot; Karl Gottfried, who studied in Göttingen, dissipated mind and body in riotous living and died of consumption. The two elder sons had apparently exhausted the family's stock of intelligence. Steady and enterprising, they pushed the Schopenhauer house to the front rank in Danzig. Johann Friedrich, however, died young. Heinrich Floris, the eldest, was a powerful, intelligent, hard, proud, defiantly independent and choleric patrician, a man of inflexible honor, ruthless candor, volcanic wrath, impenetrable depths of gloom—and epically ugly.[4]

When he sought the hand of the beautiful light-hearted Johanna Henriette Trosiener, almost twenty years younger than himself, she accepted him readily, without any illusions of romantic love, but with great respect for him and for his preëminent position in the life of the city. His patrician pride impressed her, and for his storms of wrath she had had abundant training in the house of her own violent father Trosiener. So she married him, and retired to his country villa, with its art treasures, horses and spaniels and octave of lamb-bells, its garden and little lake, and the sea in the distance. Here Johanna would read French and English novels all week, and on Saturday Heinrich Floris would return from the city, sometimes bringing guests along. Only once did he ride over in the middle of the week, to announce the fall of the Bastille.

The Danzig oligarch, travelling with his wife, was expecting a son and heir, and wanted him to be born on English soil. But Johanna's homesickness cut their tour short, and the child was born a Danziger after all, on February 22, 1788. He was baptized Arthur, because his father wanted the future head of his house to have a cosmopolitan name, the same in English, French, and German. The son was to be a free European patrician, like his father. But the oligarchy of Danzig was in danger. Heinrich Floris, who refrained from making use of a Polish title of nobility or from accepting Friedrich's invitation to settle in Prussia, was not the one to submit to Prussia's encroachment on his native free city. When, in 1793, the Prussian troops entered Danzig, the Schopenhauers were on their way to the free city of Hamburg.

To prepare him for a commercial career, young Arthur was sent at the age of nine to Havre. There he spent two years with the family of a M. Grégoire, for whose son Anthime he conceived great friendship. He returned to Hamburg knowing French better than German, and all his life remembered his Havre years as his happiest: a sinister reflection on his life at home. There seems to have been little capacity for happiness in Schopenhauer's being, and much in his youth to develop his genius for gloom. His parents, especially his mother, cultivated the society of literary and learned men, but he was definitely intended for a merchant's career. Arthur's heart loathed banker's books and craved poetry, art, learning. His honored father was inflexibly bent on ruining his life; his light-hearted mother was impatient with his moods. Between the two, the boy was lone and depressed; his sister Adele, who was to cherish him with such sad devotion in after-years, was yet too young to understand.

"My son shall read the great book of the world," Heinrich Floris said, and met Arthur's insistent pleas for a classical education by offering him as an alternative an extended tour to France and England, on the express condition that he definitely accept his own commercial plans. The lure succeeded, but the long journey did not realize the expected pleasures. The youth had already shown uncanny insight into the dark recesses of life. In England, where he spent some time in a boarding-school at Wimbledon, he had an eye only for the restrictions and the bigotries of English life. In Toulon the hopeless lot of the galley-convicts depressed him, and in Lyons he saw men and women merrily promenading in streets and in the square where but ten years before their parents had been mowed down by grapeshot. Through Switzerland, Bavaria, and Austria the Schopenhauers proceeded to Berlin, where they separated, the father returning to Hamburg, the mother and son to the old Danzig home, where Arthur was confirmed. His gloomy moods the parents perceived but did not understand. His mother urged him to overcome his remote bearing with people and grow more affable; his father wrote him to improve his epistolary style and penmanship and writing-posture, as behooved a future solid banker. Arthur returned to Hamburg to eat his heart out in the commercial office of Senator Jenisch.

The Schopenhauer's change of residence had proved very costly, and the Danziger's commercial preëminence remained only a memory to him in Hamburg. Heinrich Floris did not become a naturalized citizen of his adopted city. Sullen and broken pride, financial worries, growing deafness and lapses of memory and recognition embittered his last years, and when one day in April, 1805, he fell into the Hamburg canal, the accident was judged by many, and later by his son also, as a case of suicide.

III

His father's death made Arthur's life doubly hard, as now a sense of honor and pious loyalty to his paternal will bound him to a hateful occupation, the while his mind and heart perversely courted literary and scientific interests. His mother had a gift for suiting her cheerful self, and resolved to make the most of her young widowhood. Leaving her son to his ledgers, she moved with Adele to Weimar, arriving there just before the battle of Jena, and was very soon at home to all the Olympians. It was the second spring of her spirit. Twice a week her salon welcomed men like Goethe, Wieland, Grimm, the two Schlegels, and especially Fernow, to whom she was particularly devoted and the writing of whose biography was her first literary venture. The Duke Karl August smiled on her at court. She wrote Arthur of her many suitors: a Frankfurt merchant, a noble *Kammerherr*, a Councillor Conta who ordered his every minute to suit her wishes; all this she rehearsed to her son in frank delight, breathing the divine air of the German Olympus and thrilled with the new powers and talents which Weimar was bringing out. And meanwhile from his counter Arthur wrote her wailing letters: "All is disintegrated in the stream of time. The minutes, the countless atoms of pettiness into which each action crumbles are worms which gnaw and destroy all that is great and resolute. The dreadful commonplaceness crushes all aspiration. There is naught to be serious with in human life; dust is not worth it. What are eternal passions for this petty wretchedness?

> Life is a jest; and all things show it:
> I thought so once; but now I know it." [5]

And not only the merchant's ledgers kept him from soaring to perfection: a poem written during these months reveals only too clearly the tortures of his soul, torn between the tug of flesh and the flight of the spirit:

> Oh lust, oh hell,
> Oh senses, oh love,
> Not to let go,
> Nor yet to vanquish!
> From Heaven's summits
> You've dragged me down
> And cast me here
> In this earth's mire. . . .

Even more clearly is the voice of the later pessimist heard in these verses:

> What more desirable indeed
> Than utterly to vanquish
> This empty miserable life,
> What no desire could ever consummate,
> Though heart should break with longing on the spot.
> How fine 'twould be, with light and gentle step
> The desert of this life on earth to roam,
> The footstep never sticking in the mire,
> The eye-glance never turned away from Heaven.[6]

Was it desire to be rid of epistolary nightmares, was it a rare flash of maternal pity, was it plain good sense on Johanna's part which led her at last to consult with Fernow whether Arthur was too late to begin preparing for the university, and on his advice to release her son from the bonds of commerce? In 1807, at the age of nineteen, he plunged into Greek and Latin, first at Gotha and then at Weimar, with such intensity that in the short span of two years he leaped into the University of Göttingen.

If his mother had thought of curing his pessimism by putting Homer in his hands, she was sorely mistaken. In her Weimar salon the sun, moon, and stars of Germany shone in turn around Arthur but did not penetrate his midnight. Johanna found his wailing presence in Weimar far more intolerable than his wailing letters had been. She could administer bitter pills to others, and told her son in so many words to condemn the world elsewhere, if he must, but to leave her in peace. Keep to your own lodgings, she told him: in my home, of course, you are a welcome guest, when I am at home to guests, "if you would only refrain from all your disagreeable disputing which makes me also cross, and from all your lamenting over the stupid world and the misery of mankind, for all this always gives me a horrid night, and I do like sound sleep." [7]

The philosophical bent of Schopenhauer's mind asserted itself early. "Aenesidemus" Schulze in Göttingen started him with the advice to avoid all philosophers, and especially Aristotle and Spinoza, until he had first mastered the divine Plato and the marvelous Kant. From Göttingen he proceeded to Berlin, hoping to learn from Fichte, but found his *Wissenschaftslehre* (*Science of Knowledge*) to be only *Wissenschafts-leere* (*Empty Knowledge*). Physical science, literature, history, art, classical learning, all were to him soil in which his own philosophy was germinating. Here was no young pedant being initiated into technique, but one who felt himself a young titan and was already preparing to provide the materials for the next chapter in the history of philosophy. At Weimar, in April, 1811, he confided his plan of life to the seventy-eight-year-old poet Wieland. "Life is a precarious matter: I have resolved to spend mine meditating upon it." [8] The death-earnest manner which commended itself to Wieland and to Goethe amused the Jena flappers who tittered at the young man sullenly gazing by himself out of the window. "Little ones," Goethe advised them, "leave him over there in peace; one of these days he will grow above the heads of us all." [9]

His mother tittered with the flappers, when she was not out of patience with her son. On receiving her copy of his doctor's dissertation, *On the Fourfold Root of the Principle of Sufficient Reason*, she remarked that the root smelled of the apothecary. The son replied that men would be reading him when not one copy of her works was to be had. She retorted that the entire edition of his works would then still be unsold. A grim fate was to fulfill both prophecies, the mother's before the son's. Back of these sour family pleasantries there was serious tension between the two. Johanna's manner of life was taxing the Schopenhauer estate; but doubly irritating to the son were his mother's intimate relations with the courtier Müller von Gerstenbergk whom she had living in her own house and with whom Schopenhauer refused to come to any terms. Johanna would not sacrifice Müller to Arthur, and the son broke forever with his mother.

Meanwhile an interest in Goethe's theory of colors, which led to Schopenhauer's writing a special treatise on the subject, brought him into intimate contact with the old poet, for whose genius Schopenhauer retained a reverence which no other German besides Kant commanded. The theory of vision and colors, however, was only a special interest. Schopenhauer's main attention was already being devoted to a philosophical system that was to mark the step beyond Kant. In Dresden, to which he had been drawn by its music and art-treasures and by the fine library, his aggressive assurance earned him, in a literary circle, the epithet *Jupiter tonans.* But, along with the Jovian thunders, quietly the philosophy of his life was germinating within him. We can now trace, in the eleventh volume of Paul Deussen's definitive edition of the *Works*, the genesis of Schopenhauer's system, in the original notes and rough drafts from the years 1812–18. The reading of these early sketches deepens the impression that his philosophy was in the main fixed as early as 1814, and adds force to his words written in 1813 in Berlin: "Under my hands and still more in my mind grows a work, a philosophy which will be an ethics and a metaphysics in one:—two branches which hitherto have been separated as falsely as man had been divided into soul and body. The work grows, slowly and gradually aggregating its parts like the child in the womb. I become aware of one member, one vessel, one part after another. In other words, I set each sentence down, without anxiety as to how it will fit into the whole; for I know it has all sprung from a single foundation. It is thus that an organic whole originates, and that alone will live. . . . Chance, thou ruler of this sense-world! Let me live and find peace for yet a few years, for I love my work as the mother her child. When it is matured and has come to the birth, then exact from me my dues, taking interest for the postponement." [10]

IV

When the work was done, in 1818, Schopenhauer was convinced, and remained convinced throughout his life, that he had solved the riddle of existence and pointed out the path of salvation through insight. He planned accordingly to have his signet-ring engraved, with the Sphinx falling headlong into the abyss. To Brockhaus in Leipzig he offered his work as "a new philosophical system, new in the full meaning of the term, not a new exposition of old ideas, but a most coherent course of thoughts, which have never before come into any human head. The book . . . will, I am firmly convinced, be in the future the source and the occasion for a hundred other books." [11]

Brockhaus accepted the work of the thirty-year-old sage sight unseen, as the clean copy of the manuscript was not yet completed. Unavoidable delay in the printing of the book threatened to delay Schopenhauer's projected trip to Italy and also filled him with quite ungrounded suspicions of his publisher's honesty. A disgracefully bitter correspondence with Brockhaus ensued, which the latter with perfect right definitely terminated.

At the end of September, 1818, Schopenhauer left for Italy by way of Vienna, and was already in Rome before his own copies of *The World as Will and Idea* reached him. Time brought together in Italy four great contemners of this world, who, as Gwinner puts it, could well have held a Congress of Pessimists: Chateaubriand was in Italy, and of course Giacomo Leopardi, ten years Schopenhauer's junior, and Byron was in Venice. Schopenhauer did not come to know Leopardi until late in life, when Adam von Doss helped to introduce him more intimately to the Italian poet's works. For his failure to meet Lord Byron, which grievously disappointed his sister Adele, he had his own jealousy to blame. Goethe had given him a letter of introduction to the author of *Childe Harold*, but he spent three months in Venice without making use of his opportunity. Italian beauties claimed his heart no less than the beauty of Italy. As he was walking one day on the Lido with his Dulcinea, a rider galloped past them. "Look at the English poet!" the Venetian girl cried out ecstatically, and remained as in a revery the rest of the day. Schopenhauer put his letter of introduction away, but lived to regret his pique of jealousy in after years.

His Italian trip was brought to a sharp conclusion by disastrous news of the failure involving the Muhl house in Danzig, in which part of his share and all of his mother's and sister's shares of the family estate were invested. He fought hard to win his mother and sister to his side against the proposed thirty per cent. settlement and, failing this, held out alone. It was his patrimony that assured him of freedom, of learned leisure, and he was determined on teaching Herr Muhl in Danzig that one could be a philosopher without being a simpleton. In the end he recovered his money from Muhl intact—only to lose it later in Mexican bonds.

His wrangles over the thirty per cent. settlement served to estrange him still further from his mother, and this time, alas, also from his sister. To her, who had idolized him and shared his many glooms, this estrangement was a bitter sorrow which poisoned her increasingly lonely life.

The Muhl trouble, which for a time had endangered his economic independence, helped to confirm him in his decision to enter the academic career, and after some preliminary inquiries, he applied for and was admitted to a docentship at the University of Berlin: a crusader for philosophic truth in the very citadel of Hegelian charlatanry, no less! His expectations may be judged from the *Vita* which he submitted to the Berlin Philosophical Faculty, and also from his letter to Dean Böckh, to the effect that no time for his lectures would suit him quite so well as the hour in which Herr Professor Hegel held his *Hauptkollegium.*[12] The anticipated reduction of the Hegelian fortress did not take place, nor did Beelzebub have to make a sortie. Apart from a brief encounter with Schopenhauer at the first trial lecture, in which Hegel seems to have got the worst of it, the latter was apparently unaware of his young colleague's existence. Schopenhauer's lectures proved a complete fiasco. He retained the announcement of his course in the Berlin catalogue until 1832, and later planned a second attempt in a South-German University, but his first course of lectures was really his last.

The reader of the lectures, in the ninth and tenth volumes of Deussen's edition, will find Schopenhauer's academic failure hard to explain. The few who listened to them must have found the delivery attractive, if the reports of Schopenhauer's gifts of oral discourse are to be at all credited. Clarity, keen logic, driving power, brilliant style, ready and most varied allusion, irony, grim humor, all were his. But philosophy in Berlin was under Hegel's sway. What chances had this avowed enemy to attract many students when he had put his lecture-hour to compete with Hegel's main course?

The book into which he had poured his life was fulfilling his mother's cruel prophecy. Herbart reviewed it with appreciation, notwithstanding his radical disagreement with the philosophy of *The World as Will and Idea.* Jean Paul Richter described it as a philosophical work of genius, bold, many-sided, keen and profound, and compared it to a desolate bottomless Norwegian lake, sunk in a dark wall of steep cliffs, where the sun never penetrates, and only the stars of the day's sky are seen, and over which no bird flies, and no wave stirs.[13] The book, for all that, fell stillborn from the press, though its very title should have kept it alive. "The Kantian antithesis of the thing-in-itself and the phenomenon, the phenomenalistic doctrine that the world of our experience and knowledge through understanding is only a world of ideas, the turn in metaphysical standpoint from the theoretical to the practical reason, the observation that the true essence of things consists in Will," writes Windelband, "all these fundamental doctrines of Kant, Fichte, and Schelling were comprehended in Schopenhauer's catch-word." [14]

Assured that he had solved the world-enigma, Schopenhauer had to feed his pessimism on that bitterest of diets, the apathy of mankind. He was convinced that the professional guild was in conspiracy against him, to undermine him if necessary, to condemn him to eternal silence if possible. For his part he reacted with savage vigor: poor young Beneke's review he denounced as a liar's patchwork; if he had called Fichte a windbag, he now turned on Hegel, the Beelzebub and Caliban of philosophic Germany, with vitriolic diatribe and abuse. Even so loyal a disciple as Frauenstädt could not stomach them, but Schopenhauer insisted on retaining and underscoring them in his works. One doubts whether his own 'arrival' in the fifties gratified him any more than the simultaneous collapse of Hegelianism.

Life bristled also with petty annoyances. One of them cost him a pretty penny. In the private entry which he shared with another lodger in Berlin he found one day three strange women gossiping. He complained to his landlady and was assured that the disturbance would not be repeated. But it was, and as the landlady was absent at the time, he himself asked the three women to leave. Two of them complied, but the third, a seamstress, refused, whereupon Schopenhauer, coming out of his room a little later with his walking-stick and finding her again in his entry, again asked her to leave. Upon her second refusal, he shoved her out, and when she once more returned, pushed her more violently down the stairs. The result was a lawsuit for bodily injuries, which passed through many courts; in the end Schopenhauer was condemned to pay the sewing-woman fifteen thalers a quarter as long as she lived. When she finally died he recorded the event epigrammatically: *Obit anus abit onus.*

V

The cholera which swept off Hegel in 1831, frightened Schopenhauer out of Berlin, and after some thought he settled on Frankfurt as permanent residence, and there, with a brief intermission in Mannheim, he spent the rest of his life. Seventeen years of almost complete silence followed the publication of his masterwork, but when *The Will in Nature* appeared, in 1836, it stirred not a leaf in philosophical Germany. The acceptance by Rosenkranz and Schubert of Schopenhauer's insistent suggestion that the text of the first edition of the *Critique of Pure Reason* be used in their edition of Kant's Works was a flash of recognition of a man whom everybody had apparently agreed to ignore. To be sure, the Norwegian Royal Society of Sciences in Drontheim crowned his prize-essay on the *Freedom of the Will* in 1839; but the very next year the Danish Royal Academy rejected his prize-essay on the *Basis of Morality*, although it was the only one that had been submitted for the competition. The Danish disapproval of his disrespectful treatment of the Post-Kantian *summi philosophi* had been responsible for their rejection of his work, and it roused his fury. He published both essays together, marking them on the title pages "crowned" and "*not* crowned" respectively. But crown and no crown were all one to the unresponsive public. For over twenty years he had been assembling supplements to his main work, manifold illustrations and elaborations as well as further discussions of special topics. But Brockhaus refused to undertake a second edition of *The World as Will and Idea* with its Supplements, and only Schopenhauer's pathetic insistence and his offer of his manuscript gratis finally induced the publisher to risk the venture, in 1844,—and thus for the second time to lose his money.

Was it Charles Lamb who resolved, if his contemporaries would have none of him, to write for antiquity? Thirty years of unrecognition had not sapped Schopenhauer's own confidence in the eternal truth of his philosophy, but they had countersigned and sealed his disdain of the *Zweifüsser*, bipeds, among whom he had to live his life. The image of the Sphinx plunging into the abyss was to have been his signet; now he chose for the top-cover of his snuff-box the picture of two horse-chestnuts, to remind him of the deceptive values and false appearances of existence. To apathy he replied with disdainful assurance, proud and pathetic: "If at times I have felt unhappy, that has been due, after all, only to a blunder, to a personal confusion; I have mistaken myself for someone else and complained of his woes: for instance, a *Privatdozent* who has not obtained his professorship and who gets no students; or for one maligned by a certain Philistine or gossiped about by a certain scandal-monger; or for the defendant in a lawsuit for assault; or for a lover disdained by his precious maiden; or for a patient kept at home by his illness; or for such other persons afflicted with such miseries. But I myself have been none of all these; that was all alien fabric of which, let us say, my coat was made, which I wore for a while and then discarded for another. Who am I, then? The author of *The World as Will and Idea,* who has given the solution of the great problem of existence, a solution which perhaps displaces all previous ones, and which at any rate will keep busy the thinkers of ages to come. I am that man, and what can trouble him during the years that he still has to breathe?" [15]

"Where thy treasure is, there will thy heart be also." In judging Schopenhauer's personal pessimism, as in passing judgment on his private life, we should not lose sight of the passage just quoted. Nietzsche could ask ironically what sort of a pessimist was this that played the flute; and Kuno Fischer and others might doubt if Schopenhauer's pessimism was really fast color, or even if it was genuine.[16] Here is a man who has managed to retain his share of his patrimony and has lived comfortably as a gentleman all his life. He has watched the tragedy of World-Woe on the stage of life, more rapt than anyone else, but seated all the same in a most comfortable seat. Here is a man who preaches asceticism to others, but confesses with ready resignation that he is too sensual to practice his own gospel. But does Schopenhauer's own sensuality prove him insincere, and does his sturdy good health and his outwardly comfortable life prove him merely petulant in his pessimism? Surely *Video meliora proboque, deteriora sequor* was written before his time; and surely it is a plebeian's analysis and conclusion that a man cannot be a genuine pessimist, and should not be one at all, if he dines every night at the *Englischer Hof.* Back of all this discord between Schopenhauer's philosophy and his personality, there are, as Volkelt points out against Kuno Fischer, the discords in Schopenhauer's personality itself. If we are so well acquainted with these discords, and in general with the dark sides of Schopenhauer's character, we owe it to Schopenhauer's own candor. No one is a hero to his valet, and while in some respects Schopenhauer was always on parade, he was "no hypocrite, but the sincerest character that ever was." [17] Much of his cynical frankness regarding himself reflects his contempt for the bipeds, *Zweifüsser*, on the same principle that leads Dostoyevsky's character Prince Valkovsky, in *The Insulted and Injured*, to show his contempt for the 'hero' by reciting the most shameless stories in his presence.

There are unlovely, amusing, pathetic, revolting traits in Schopenhauer's character. He was sensual; he was in many ways shameless. Something of a coward he was, and afflicted from his childhood with fright that bordered on mania. When he was six years old, his parents returning from a walk found him in perfect despair, imagining that they had abandoned him. During his adolescence and while a student in Berlin he worried over his imagined and unimagined diseases. In 1813 he feared conscription; the fear of the small-pox sent him out of Naples, and the fear of the cholera led him to move from Berlin to Frankfurt. In Verona he was obsessed with the worry that he had taken poisoned snuff. Although he found street-noises intolerable, and consequently reckoned man's intelligence in inverse ratio to his capacity to endure noise, his fear of a fire caused him always to live on the ground floor. He was morbidly suspicious; a noise at night would make him jump and reach for the sword and loaded pistols that he always had by his bedside. Suspicion was particularly strong where his chief treasures were concerned. All his life he was afraid of plagiarists; he distrusted his publishers, even Brockhaus; and, after the manuscript of his *Parerga* had been repeatedly rejected by the publishers, and Frauenstädt had finally found one willing to print it in Berlin, Schopenhauer wrote his own arch-evangelist not to let any man have a look at his essays, lest they steal his thoughts before publication![18]

Even if his pride is to be counted a virtue, still how shall we condone his consuming vanity and his importunate love of flattery? When, after the publication of the *Parerga und Paralipomena,* his philosophy began to bring him fame in the fifties, he classified his main followers under the rubrics of apostles and evangelists: Adam von Doss was his *Apostel Johannes,* Dorguth his *Urevangelist,* and Frauenstädt his *Erzevangelist.* His disciples could not quench his thirst for adulation; no worship was too excessive. The man who had disdained the popular philosophers, and, in his utter obscurity, had found comfort in the Arabian proverb, "Among quartzes, adamant is outlawed," now devoured every line written about himself. The first business of his evangelists was to write about him; the second, to scour the journals and newspapers for scraps of Schopenhaueriana. Send everything that mentioned his name: he would pay the postage! There is really no quoting of samples here; a liturgy of self-glorification is in his letters of the fifties until disgust mingles with pity in the reading. Was there ever so great a man, whose old age correspondence was as petty?

Behold all these things are fact, but what use is to be made of them? Paint Schopenhauer as black as you please: sensual, selfish, surly, sullen, stubborn, self-conceited: have you disproved his pessimism, or only ballasted his text with footnotes? Is the beggar insincere in his appreciation of riches? No more is Schopenhauer in his gospel of world-contempt and asceticism. But actually the case against Schopenhauer is not as strong as it is sometimes made out to be. Did he fight tooth and nail with Muhl for his patrimony? Did he worry lest his mother should try to deprive him of part of his share? Did he keep his valuable papers hidden in falsely labelled envelopes, to mislead possible thieves? Schopenhauer's main defense may be gathered from his dedication of the second edition of *The World as Will and Idea* to the memory of his father. Convinced of his inability to make a professional success and earn his own livelihood, Schopenhauer regarded his economic independence as an indispensable condition of his doing the work on which his life had been staked. Therefore his veneration for his father who had made him economically independent, therefore his constant readiness to battle for his funds with anyone, therefore his almost morbid fears of thieves and swindlers, which led him to suspect even the friend of his childhood, Anthime Grégoire. Vain he was all his life, defiantly vain throughout the long years of his obscurity, gloatingly vain and arrogant when fame at last arrived, and, as he put it, the Nile reached Cairo. But if his old-age letters are so petty and pitifully naïve in their insatiate eagerness for praise, they admit perhaps of another interpretation. Schopenhauer had served his long sentence of apathy; when at last the doors of his cell of unrecognition crashed through and the light of sunshine gleamed on his white head, the man who had defiantly written in his obscurity, "I am the author of *The World as Will and Idea!*" displayed no false modesty in his hour of fame. His masterpiece was his own child; we can charge his vanity to paternal pride. Besides, Maria Groener urges, was he so conceited after all, considering who he was? Did not Goethe write: "Only ragamuffins are humble!" [19]

Hard-hearted he was, but simple kindliness was not altogether extinct in him. Of decided interest is the story of his devotion to his dog Atma, and particularly the intimate account of his daily life as observed by Lucia Franz, in whose father's apartment Schopenhauer lived as a lodger for over a year, until his death in 1860. We have had the Schopenhauer portrayed in his books, in his letters, in the memoirs of disciples and of enemies. Here are a child's memories, and they reveal humanity and kindliness, and softer, more generous traits of character which had quite escaped the mature associates and observers of the great pessimist.

So his life's story reads itself out. There is bitter irony in his choice of a snuff-box cover with horse-chestnuts painted on it. There is tragedy in his wistful outcry as he gazes on the picture of the saintly Trappist, Abbé Rancé. There is pathos in his words to his biographer Gwinner: "So life has strewn roses in my path too: to be sure only white roses." [20] The philosopher of pessimism was no hero, no saint, but his devotion to his philosophy reveals both heroism and saintliness. No one can question his right to inscribe on the title-page of his *Parerga* Juvenal's line: *Vitam impendere vero.* To stake one's life for the truth: it was the living motto of his life.

CHAPTER XI

GROUNDS AND LIMITS OF SCHOPENHAUER'S PESSIMISM

I

Schopenhauer compared his philosophy to Thebes with its hundred gates. Kuno Fischer sees only four gates: Kant, Plato, the Vedas, Buddha.[1] The main door is the Kantian; it is as the one and true heir to Kant's crown that Schopenhauer ever proclaims himself, in opposition to the other post-Kantians. To Rosenkranz he writes: "I have taken only one step beyond Kant, but not up in the air, as all the acrobats of my time, but on firm and solid ground." [2] His own chief claim as a technical philosopher was that he had solved Kant's problem of the thing-in-itself.

Schopenhauer's theory of knowledge accentuates Kant's phenomenalism. The world of our knowledge is a world in which the mind is at home, a world organized by the mind. No object without a subject; no subject without an object; the world is my idea. The naïve realist imagines that he sees, hears, smells, tastes, touches real, entirely extra-mental things, that he knows a world which exists as he knows it independently of his knowing it. Kant, admitting *that* things-in-themselves are, declares that we can never know *what* they are. All that we can know is experience in terms of space, time, causality.

This idealistic philosophy is in diametrical opposition to all substantialist metaphysics, materialistic or spiritualistic. 'Soul-substance,' to Kant, is hollow sound without meaning; and we can rightly regard Kant also as the true and final destroyer of materialistic dogmatism. Materialism, Schopenhauer says, is a persistent attempt to set up a system of physics without metaphysics, to make the phenomenon the thing-in-itself. But "nothing can be more clumsy than that, after the manner of all materialists, one should blindly take the objective as simply given in order to derive everything from it without paying any regard to the subjective, through which, however, nay, in which alone the former exists." [3] Man is the metaphysical animal. Physics is not metaphysics any more than indefinitely extended breadth is depth. "Those persons who believe that crucibles and retorts are the true and only source of all wisdom are in their own way just as perverse as were formerly their antipodes the Scholastics." [4] To be sure those who peel the husks of nature may imagine they are dissecting its kernel; all of them ostensibly suitors of Penelope, they yet sleep contentedly in the house of Odysseus, each by the side of his chosen maid-servant, banishing all thought of the sovereign mistress.

This express repudiation of materialism and its votaries should be kept in mind; it is in agreement with Schopenhauer's theory of experience and with his Kantian inheritance. Notwithstanding a misleading materialistic bias which is manifest in Schopenhauer's metaphysical account of the intellect, it is clear that with historical materialism, and especially with the materialism of his own time, Schopenhauer would have no part and lot. The references to Büchner in his correspondence should leave little doubt as to his own attitude towards materialism, which he repeatedly called a philosophy for barbers' and apothecaries' apprentices. When he quotes Cabanis, when he treats the intellect as a mere cerebral phenomenon, he is not to be confused with the materialist, any more than when he calls the brain parasitic, a pensioner of the body and its highest efflorescence. The difference between Schopenhauer and the materialist is radical: the latter would derive thought from matter, the immediately given from the mediately given, all the while forgetting that the matter of which he discourses is always necessarily object *of a subject.* But when Schopenhauer treats thought as a phenomenon of the brain, thought and brain, mind and body (themselves always correlative) must both be to him instruments and objectifications of *the* reality, which is the ultimate ground of them both and which transcends both subject and object.

We have now reached the point from which Schopenhauer would step beyond Kant. The thing-in-itself is neither matter nor mind, it is will. The world in its ultimate reality is not a system of intelligence nor a mechanical order of things; its inmost nature is best described by the analogy of our craving, driving, seeking character. Just as Hegel, conceiving of reality as the progressive self-organization of differences, and finding in the thought-process the most adequate and characteristic expression of this essential nature of all reality, chose "Thought" as his magic word, so Schopenhauer's radically different metaphysics leads him to call the ultimate reality "Will." That which sends the falling stone to the earth, the iron filings to the magnet, the sunflower towards the sun, the moth to the lighted candle is the same, and the same as that which sends the lover to the arms of his beloved. But this is nowise equivalent to "the insane opinion that the stone moves itself in accordance with a known motive, merely because this is the way in which will appears in man." [5]

Will is that which is most immediate in consciousness, and prior to the subject-object dualism; and like a magic spell, it unlocks to us the inmost being of all nature. It germinates in the plant; through it the crystal is formed and the magnetic needle turns to the North; it is manifest in chemical affinities, in repulsion and attraction, decomposition and combination, cohesion, gravitation. All these are different only in their phenomenal existence, but in their inner nature are identical. Organic or inorganic, conscious or unconscious, as the case may be, the will ever presses for its fulfilment, meeting impact with resistance, adapting means to end, responding to stimuli, seeking the gratification of instincts, acting on motives, on purpose, loving, hating, hoping, fearing, scorning, envying, enthusing, aspiring. Here is a teleology prior to and more ultimate than intelligence. "The bird builds the nest for the young which it does not yet know; the beaver constructs a dam the object of which is unknown to it; ants, marmots, and bees lay in provision for the winter they have never experienced; the spider and the ant-lion make snares, as if with deliberate cunning, for future unknown prey; insects deposit their eggs where the coming brood finds future nourishment. . . . The larva of the male stag-beetle . . . makes the hole in the wood for its metamorphosis as big again as the female does, in order to have room for its future horns." [6]

Gills, claws, teeth, fins, wings are all instruments of the will: the water pouch in the stomach of the camel, the sail of the nautilus, the eagle's far-seeing eye, the dog's keen nose. And likewise an instrument of the will is man's thinking power. Phenomenally, in terms of the subject-object dualism, the mind is the not-body; ultimately body and mind are objectifications and tools of the will-reality, elaborate means to attain its ends. What the snake does with its venom, the bird or the insect with its color mimicry, that man accomplishes with his deliberately thought-out method of attack and defense.

II

Ubiquitous and ever-active is the will—and it ever fails of final attainment. Eternal becoming and endless flux characterize its inmost nature; every attainment is only the beginning of a new pursuit. And right here is the seed sown of Schopenhauer's pessimism. For in man will is manifest as desire, and desire essentially insatiate. Will is want: its basis is need, deficiency; we want what we want, what we lack, and this consciousness of our lack is the kernel of suffering. "Pain," Schopenhauer wrote in 1817, "arises not from not-having, but from the desire to have, and yet not having." [7] This desire for what we lack, unsatisfied, is pain; the desire satisfied is pleasure, which quickly passes into another painful state of further desire, or else into a more general sense of desires gratified, which is tedium.

We can clearly see, then, that from Schopenhauer's point of view pleasure is the exception, pain the rule in human life. Pain is the fundamental, positive, and primary; pleasure is negative and secondary, the temporary alleviation of pain. "I know accordingly no greater absurdity than that of most metaphysical systems which explain evil as something negative, while it is exactly the positive which is making itself felt." [8] Ribot [9] observes that here also Schopenhauer has learned from Kant, except that what Kant mentions only in passing his disciple has developed into an important doctrine. Will is effort, is desire, is painful. "The desire lasts long, the demands are infinite; the satisfaction is short and scantily measured out"; [10] it is like the crust thrown to the beggar, that he may be hungry tomorrow also. In the plants there is no sensibility and no pain, but from the lowest animal life clear up the scale, as consciousness ascends, pain also increases: "He that increaseth knowledge increaseth sorrow." Not only is pleasure secondary and negative, impermanent: it is only a brief transition. Either the will reasserts itself in a new desire and a new pain, or life lapses into the dull sense of desires gratified, for desires that have been gratified are dust to him who can think of nothing further to spur him on. Life presents a more or less violent oscillation between pain and boredom. While the poor are ever battling with need, with pain, the rich are desperately at war with ennui. The illusory hope of real satisfaction sends rich and poor on the road, and the tramp meets the tourist. But on the road of craving desire no final satisfaction and no peace is to be found. "It is essentially all the same whether we pursue or flee, fear injury or seek enjoyment; the care for the constant demands of the will, in whatever form it may be, continually occupies and sways the consciousness; but without peace no true well-being is possible. The subject of willing is thus constantly stretched on the revolving wheel of Ixion, pours water into the sieve of the Danaids, is the ever-longing Tantalus." [11]

Even if the pleasures of life were real and permanent, even if life yielded a balance of pleasure over pain, still life would fall short of justification, for the evil remains: my present well-being cannot undo my past suffering or the present and past suffering of others. As Petrarch says:

A thousand joys don't make up for one torment.[12]

One beggar, one sick man, one corpse were enough for Gautama. But worse still: pleasure is mere froth and vapor, like the wine provided by Mephistopheles in Auerbach's cellar, "after every sensuous pleasure we also say:

And yet methought I were drinking wine." [13]

Life is a lie and it is a wicked lie. Man is a creature of desire, and thus normally selfish. Egoism is limitless; man is bent on attaining the utmost of pleasure; whatever is in his way rouses his hate and his ruthless opposition. Were each person to choose between his own destruction and that of all other men, who can doubt what the decision would be in most cases? Each man regards himself as the center of the world: "No sharper contrast can be imagined than that between the profound and exclusive attention which every person devotes to his own self, and the indifference with which, as a rule, all other people regard that self,—an indifference precisely like that with which he in turn looks upon them." [14]

Politeness is but a screen which men have adopted for hiding the shameful sight of their real motives. But the least pressure pushes the screen aside and reveals our naked selfishness. Well might we pray, "lead us not into temptation: let us not see what manner of persons we are." [15] A code of politeness is not enough; a corps of policemen is required to keep the peace. "The thousands that throng before our eyes, in peaceful intercourse each with the other, can only be regarded as so many tigers and wolves, whose teeth are secured by a strong muzzle." [16] *Homo homini lupus.*

With Hobbes, Schopenhauer describes life as a war of each against all. Strife only reveals that variance with itself which is essential to the will. "The will to live everywhere preys upon itself, and in different forms is its own nourishment, till finally the human race, because it subdues all the others, regards nature as a manufactory for its use." [17] Crystals in process of formation meet, cross, and disarrange each other. The young hydra, while still joined onto the old, fights with it for food. Cut the Australian bull-dog ant in two—head and tail rush into battle. In Java Junghuhn saw a plain as far as the eye could reach all covered with skeletons of large turtles, five feet long. On coming out of the sea to lay their eggs, they are attacked by wild dogs, which, by their united strength, turn over the turtles, strip off the small shell of their stomachs, and devour them alive. But often then a tiger pounces upon the dogs.[18] From this field of bones, turn to hundreds of other fields where some arch-fiend in the form of a conqueror has put hundreds of thousands of men opposite each other and said to them: "Shoot each other with guns and cannon!" [19] And they have done so. History is the recital of wars, the peaceful years are but pauses between the cat-fights.

Normal and universal is selfishness, but the wickedness, the suffering may reach staggering extremes. The egoist seeks his own advantage and is ever ready to strike down all who oppose him; but cruel spitefulness leads men to strike down others for the pure joy of seeing others suffer. Caligula wished the whole world had but one single neck, so that he could sever it all at one blow. From these two sources spring the vices of men, the bestial vices of egoism: greed, gluttony, lust, selfishness, avarice, covetousness, injustice, hardness of heart, pride, arrogance, etc.; the devilish vices of spitefulness: disaffection, envy, ill-will, malice, pleasure in seeing others suffer, prying curiosity, slander, insolence, petulance, hatred, anger, treachery, fraud, thirst for revenge, cruelty. "It is an array," Schopenhauer comments, "reminding one of the Princes of Darkness in Milton's Pandemonium." [20] Life's everyday sordidness and misery may not impress the callous spectator, "but one only needs to bring before his eyes the horrible suffering and misery in which even his own life is so clearly established, and the horror of it must certainly grip him: then indeed lead him through the infirmaries, military hospitals, and surgical chambers of torture, on through the prisons, through the Leads of Venice, the slave markets of Algiers, the torture chambers of the Inquisition, over the battlefields and through the judgment halls, unlock for him all the dark dwellings of misery where it creeps away from the gaze of cold curiosity, and finally from Dante read to him the death of Ugolino and his children from starvation in the tower and point out that this has really happened more than once," [21] and then this world will disclose itself to him for what it really is—the scene of tormented and agonized beings who exist by devouring each other, each ravenous beast the living grave of others. Where did Dante learn about his Inferno? Optimism, theodicies, and all prattle about this best of all possible worlds are idle, and they are wicked, cruel sneers at the endless and unspeakable miseries of man.

This is human life: a hospital for incurables. If there be any purpose in life, it seems to be suffering. "Work, torture, trouble, and need is certainly the lifelong lot of almost all men." [22] Men are like lambs gamboling in the meadow the while the butcher picks them over one by one. Life is as wretched as it is vile. Here is the blind mole, unweariedly digging with its shovel claws from birth to death: to what purpose? To eat enough to engender another blind digger. And here is a cotton spinner: a child of five he entered the factory and there has spent his life, performing the same mechanical labor, ten, twelve, fourteen hours a day, year in, year out: to what end is the satisfaction of drawing breath thus dearly purchased? Life is a wretched jest, as Voltaire called it, and wisdom, ancient and modern, has agreed with him. From Homer and Sophocles and Euripides to Shakespeare and Byron and Leopardi we hear the same sad refrain, and the old words of the Sage Bias still hold true: "Most men are bad." In all Homer Schopenhauer does not find one truly magnanimous character, although many are good and honest; and "in the whole of Shakespeare there may be perhaps a couple of noble, though by no means transcendently noble, characters to be found." [23] Abject selfishness, boundless avarice, well-concealed knavery, and also poisonous envy and fiendish delight in the misfortunes of others [24] are so universally prevalent that the slightest exception surprises us. But the optimist bids us: open your eyes and look at the world, how beautiful it is in the sunshine, with its mountains and valleys, streams, plants, animals, and so forth. "Is this world, then, a raree show?" [25] Schopenhauer exclaims. "The world is glorious to look at, but dreadful in reality." [26] Instead of inventing a hell in after-life, look about you: all the materials for hell are close at hand.

Past, present, and future are all one, progress is vain tedium. Life, essentially tragic, is in its details a sorry monotonous comedy: as in the dramas of Gozzi, the motives and incidents in each play are different, but the spirit is ever the same, and ever the same are the characters. "Pantaloon has become no more agile or generous, Tartaglia no more conscientious, Brighella no more courageous, and Columbine no more modest." [27] Life does not *have* evils, it *is* evil; as Calderon says:

> The greatest of man's sins
> Is that he was ever born.[28]

Life is a bankrupt, a business that does not pay expenses; the will is an effort which frustrates itself. The less of life, the better; its brevity is its only virtue. This is the wisdom of Hamlet's soliloquy: "Our state is so wretched that absolute annihilation would be decidedly preferable." [29] This, too, is Othello's judgment of life in his words to Iago:

> I'ld have thee live;
> For, in my sense, 'tis happiness to die.

So also Palmira to Mohammed in Voltaire's tragedy:

> The world is made for tyrants; live and reign! [30]

From all this torture is there no relief? Out of this dark cavern of illusion shines there no beacon light of enlightenment? From the craving weariness and the thirsty evil of life is there really no peace? We have heard the pessimistic verdict on life, wholesale and in detail: what is Schopenhauer's gospel of salvation?

III

Like Ulysses who in all his many trials never wept, but burst into tears on hearing his early heroic exploits sung in the palace of the Phaeacian king; or like that English client in court who wept as his case was set forth by his counsel and declared: "I never knew I had suffered half so much till I heard it here today," [31] so the reader is apt to turn away from Schopenhauer's portrayal of life with Hamlet's words on his lips:

> O that this too too solid flesh would melt,
> Thaw and resolve itself into a dew!
> Or that the Everlasting had not fixt
> His canon 'gainst self-slaughter! O God! God!
> How weary, stale, flat and unprofitable
> Seem to me all the uses of this world!
> Fie on't! Oh fie! . . .

But suicide is not the way out, for the ground of all woe is the insatiate will-to-live, self-asserting desire. This desire the man who takes his own life does not deny or destroy. He is full of it; precisely the vehemence with which he wills life and rebels against suffering brings him to the point of destroying himself. "Just because the suicide cannot give up willing, he gives up living " [32] But here is no salvation, for suicide registers the victory, not the defeat, of the tyrant will; the deliverance is altogether illusory, the will remains; only one of its individual manifestations has been destroyed. Deeper than individual life and death are the sources of woe in this world, and deeper and more radical the path of salvation. Not life is to be denied, but the will that is manifest in life, not the sufferings of existence, which the slave of desire finds intolerable, but its illusory joys are to be perceived and scorned and denied. In the midst of life, the desires of life and the will to live are to be curbed. Not death, cessation of life, but desireless peace, cessation of craving, is the blessed goal.

Here intelligence may come to our aid. Normally the intellect is a creature and tool of the will. In fact it is by virtue of his reason that man is the wicked animal: the brute's snarl is the response to an actual irritant, but man in revenge will harbor the evil resolve long after the original stirring of his wrath, will harbor it and with cold disdain will withstand the advances of tenderer emotions. So Mephistopheles speaks of man to whom the spark of divine light has been vouchsafed:

> He calls it reason, its use makes him free
> Far beastlier than any beast to be.[33]

Like a strong blind man, carrying on his shoulders the lame man who can see, even so are will and intellect. But in exceptional instances the intellect may gain so clear and so profound an insight into the nature of things that it may gain temporary, habitual, permanent emancipation from the craving will. The man who can see may check for a moment the strong blind man's headlong rush, may turn his course round about, may stop it altogether.

The first way out of the bondage of desire is in artistic contemplation. Raised by the power of the mind, a man may relinquish the common way of looking at things as related to each other and to his own will and advantage; he may so lose himself in the object as to lose sight for the moment of his own individuality and will; his mind as a clear mirror of the object may become one with it. "Then that which is so known is no longer the particular thing as such; but it is the *Idea*, the eternal form, the immediate objectivity of the will at this grade; and, therefore, he who is sunk in this perception is no longer individual, for in such perception the individual has lost himself; but he is *pure*, will-less, painless, timeless, *subject of knowledge*." [34] This is desireless contemplation, the aesthetic experience, the perception of the Platonic Ideas. Like the silent sunbeam that pierces through the rushing, aimless storm of craving passion is the steady glance of genius; the desire and the pursuit of particular things is like the rushing waterfall with its innumerable showering drops: the perception of art is like the rainbow gently resting on this raging torrent.

The intellect thus perceives clearly the world of will, itself being free for the moment from the miserable aims of self. The lofty dome embodies before his eyes the conflict between gravity and rigidity, burden and support: this is the essence of architecture. The beauty and grace of animal and human form is revealed in sculpture. In painting the rush and complexity of life is caught in a single moment of time, and the spirit that has stifled self-will and passion breathes, calm and gentle, from the picture of the saint. Poetry reveals the essential life and character of man, in all his efforts and actions. It utters itself directly in the lyric; but the most profound insight of the poet discloses the unspeakable wail and woe of human life, its essential infelicity, the strife of will with itself, the triumph of evil, the scornful mastery of chance. This is Tragedy, the summit of poetic art, and through the contemplation of it all the deeper insight is attained: not that there are evils in life, but that life is an evil thing that had better not be. Tragedy thus prepares the way for that curbing and quieting of the will-to-live which leads to the ultimate release.

But highest of all the arts is music, which expresses, not the manifestations of the will, but the will itself, its secret history and "all its emotions and strivings, with their manifold protractions, hindrances, and griefs." [35] The disquietudes of the heart, its desires and aversions, and its various degrees of relief are uttered in the alternate play of disquieting chords that rouse longing, and the more or less quieting and satisfying chords. Thus the major and the minor keys unlock to us the two basic moods of the soul, serenity, or at least healthiness, and sadness or depression.

This is the liberating work of art: when thus lifted out of the endless stream of willing, the mind observes things "without personal interest, without subjectivity, purely objectively, gives itself entirely up to them so far as they are ideas, but not in so far as they are motives. Then all at once the peace which we were always seeking, but which always fled from us on the former path of the desires, comes to us of its own accord, and it is well with us. It is the painless state which Epicurus prized as the highest good and as the state of the gods; for we are for the moment set free from the miserable striving of the will; we keep the Sabbath of the penal servitude of willing; the wheel of Ixion stands still." [36]

Alas for the impermanence of this salvation! "So near us always lies a sphere in which we escape from all our misery; but who has the strength to continue long in it? As soon as any single relation to our will, to our person, even of these objects of our pure contemplation, comes again into consciousness, the magic is at an end. . . ." [37] It is not enough to contemplate the inner nature of the will and woe: the momentary escape and relief from life is not enough; radical and permanent relief is needed. So art is to the man of insight, not a path out of life, but only an occasional consolation, "till his power, increased by this contemplation and at last tired of the play, lays hold on the real. The St. Cecilia of Raphael may be regarded as a representation of this transition." [38] It is the transition from art to morality and to asceticism, from beauty to virtue and to holiness.

IV

Schopenhauer found in Buddhism the religious version of his philosophy; and in no other respect is his reliance on Buddhism so thorough as in his moral gospel of deliverance from self. The self-centered life is illusory and wicked:

ignorance and misery spring from the same source. The Buddha who preached peace through enlightenment, the saint who has banished the lure of self, has pricked the bubble of individuality; his life is a life of love because his mind has been emancipated from the illusions that breed selfishness. This in brief is also Schopenhauer's theory of morals. The only real mark of acts truly moral is the absence of selfish motive; such deeds are actuated by interest in one's fellow beings, by pity for the suffering, sympathy with the cast down, justice and loving-kindness towards all. If the weal and woe of others affect my entire being so as to dominate my volition and motivate my deeds, then it is that compassion (*Mitleid*) enters, "the direct participation, independent of all ulterior considerations, in the sufferings of another, leading to sympathetic assistance in the effort to prevent or remove them." [39] The compassionate man is just, he does not shift onto the shoulders of others the burdens which life brings to us all; but loving-kindness moves him rather to relieve the heavy-laden and lighten their load.

The egoist, the malicious man, looks at all the world from the point of view of his own self-centered individuality. An impassable gulf separates him from his neighbor. But the compassionate man has more or less completely effaced the distinction between his own interests and those of others; beneath the multiplicity of this our world of shadow-shape existence he has perceived the more profound and ultimate reality. "No suffering is any longer strange to him. . . . It is no longer the changing joy and sorrow of his own person that he has in view, as is the case with him who is still involved in egoism. . . . He knows the whole, comprehends its nature, and finds that it consists in a constant passing away, vain striving, inward conflict, and continual suffering. . . . Why should he now, with such knowledge of the world, assert this very life through constant acts of will, and thereby bind himself ever more closely to it, press it ever more firmly to himself? . . . The will now turns away from life; it now shudders at the pleasures in which it recognizes the assertion of life. Man now attains to the state of voluntary renunciation, resignation, true indifference, and perfect willlessness." [40]

"To be just, noble, and benevolent is nothing else than to translate my metaphysics into action." [41] This is the ancient wisdom of the Upanishads: *Tat twam asi*, This thou art, and compassion is really the practical expression of an insight which passes understanding: ' Every purely benevolent act, all help entirely and genuinely unselfish, being, as such, exclusively inspired by another's distress, is, in fact, if we probe the matter to the bottom, a dark enigma, a piece of mysticism put into practice; inasmuch as it springs out of, and finds its only true explanation in, the same higher knowledge that constitutes the essence of whatever is mystical." [42]

Most rare and astounding is compassionate conduct, and profound are the experiences that may occasion it. Arnold von Winkelried, to open a way for his comrades, clasps in his arms as many hostile spears as he can grasp and rushes forward to his own death. Raymond Lully is admitted at last to the chamber of the fair lady he has long wooed, when she, opening her bodice, shows him her bosom frightfully eaten with cancer. From that moment, as if he had looked into hell, the passionate man goes to the desert to do penance. Suffering itself has sanctifying power; pain is the lye that purifies life. One path to salvation proceeds from perception and knowledge of the misery of life; a second path proceeds from great suffering itself.

"My whole philosophy," young Schopenhauer wrote, in 1817, "reduces itself to this: The world is the self-knowledge of the Will." [43] The keystone of all is resignation and denial of the will. Ethics and metaphysics are here one in a way radically different from Plato's. The denial of the will is the practical expression of the insight into the heart of reality which is ultimate philosophical wisdom. This is wisdom: to perceive the nothingness of value in the universe; for this is indeed the value of life, that it teaches us not to wish for it.

If we thus realize the metaphysical significance of compassion, we see that it leads beyond itself to something more thorough and final. Relieving the distress of life leads the moral saint to the resolve to relieve and be relieved of the essential distress, life itself. Thus compassion leads to asceticism. Just as the sexual passion is the supreme affirmation of the will-to-live, so voluntary chastity is its supreme renunciation. The man in the grip of sexual passion imagines that he is seeking his own highest fulfilment and gratification, and all the while he is but a tool of the will, fulfilling its end, the perpetuation of the species, the continuance of the wretched tragi-comedy of life. The ascetic has perceived the wretchedness of the tragi-comedy: he *will not play* any more, the will itself he has curbed within him, and its empire over him is at an end.

To such a profound insight into life, and to such heroic resolve, individual life or death are as indifferent as is life in general. Death is but the final payment of that debt which was contracted at conception and birth; and to each man death is a great reprimand: you have ever sought your own pleasure and advantage, but see, you are nothing lasting, you are nothing. From all the lusts of life the ascetic is free, a *contemptus mundi*, a supreme blessed indifference exalts him. "Everything is alike to me," Madame Guion writes, "I *cannot* will anything more: often I know not whether I exist or not." [44] A sublime melancholy is the ascetic's, which is also a joy ineffable, far more profound than any condition of desire. The man who has divorced life itself and espoused chastity, scorns his own meat and drink. His appetites are all renounced and death to him brings no reprimand: he does not struggle to avert it, nor does he violently seek it: voluntary starvation seals the denial which his every thought and act have signalized.

Before us is the thoroughgoing denial of all that is: "That constant strain and effort without end and without rest at all the grades of objectivity, in which and through which the world consists; the multifarious forms succeeding each other in gradation; the whole manifestation of the will; and, finally, also the universal forms of this manifestation, time and space, and also its last fundamental form, subject and object; all are abolished. No will: no idea, no world." [45]

Schopenhauer's answer is famous: "That we abhor annihilation so greatly, is simply another expression of the fact that we so strenuously will life, and are nothing but this will, and know nothing besides it. . . . What remains after the entire abolition of the will is for all those who are still full of will certainly nothing; but, conversely, to those in whom the will has turned and has denied itself, this our world, which is so real, with all its suns and milky-ways—is nothing." [46]

V

"If we admit that all is will, that all will is effort, that effort attains its aim only in exceptional cases, and that all frustrated effort is pain, that life, that is to say pain, does not end with death; it follows that there is only one possible remedy, to suppress pain by suppressing life, by suppressing the will. And as the body is the will made visible, to deny the body through asceticism is to deny the will. Just as procreation perpetuates life and woe, so the suppression of it in chastity is a suppression of the species. Consequently the ideal which Schopenhauer proposed to mankind is a suicide *en masse* by metaphysical means. In logic," Ribot concludes his summary, "all this is very well. In reality it is another matter." [47] It is the logic of the theory which we should first diagnose, for its well-being is only on the surface. Our first question may be stated bluntly: how can the will deny itself? Or it can be expressed more systematically, with reference to Schopenhauer's philosophy: in a system of thoroughgoing pessimism what room is there for a doctrine of salvation? Or yet conversely: is a world which admits of salvation, even though it be through utter resignation, a world of wholly negative value?

Already in the forties Schopenhauer's earliest followers,—Becker, Frauenstädt—were worrying over the difficulty of reconciling the denial of the will with the universal necessity of motivation. If character is unchangeable, how is the conversion to saintliness possible? If all that takes place is determined ultimately by the will-to-live, then how can negation of the will take place? If the will-to-live is universally dominant, how is the ascetic's choice of voluntary chastity to be explained? If the intellect is but the tool of the will, like claw or beak or venom, how can the saint, at the apex of intelligence, deny the will altogether? Should we not perhaps postulate, in opposition to the self-assertive will and its subservient intellect, a higher will-denying intelligence and also a higher Will? Schopenhauer does not minimize the difficulty, but he does not meet it. He relies here on Kant's doctrine of the empirical and the intelligible character: the former is, of course, always necessarily determined, Schopenhauer would say, by the self-assertive will-to-live. "But the entire will-act, which is the *intelligible* character, as it in itself and atemporally *wills*, may just as well *not will*,—instead of a *Velle*, it may just as well be a *Nolle*." [48] But is there no gradual attainment of saintly insight, a gradual approach to complete negation of the will? Schopenhauer replies: This growing insight prepares, but does not bring about gradually the will-denial. Only when intelligence has reached its apex of exaltation, its boiling point, does this entirely new phenomenon, the denial of the will, take place. A wanderer pursues his course, lantern in hand. Suddenly he sees that he is at the brink of an abyss, and turns about. The wanderer is the will, the lantern is the intellect. The wanderer does not turn a little to the right or to the left; he turns completely about, he abandons his former course altogether. The conversion is radical, and it is sudden, not gradual. The empirical, will-determined character has not been mended, but ended and given up altogether. There is mystery in this deliverance from the will: repeatedly Schopenhauer quotes the words of Malebranche: "Liberty is a mystery." The peace of God passeth all understanding.[49] This re-creation of man is what the Church calls a work of grace: we must be born anew. The natural man, the assertion of the will-to-live, is symbolized in Adam, but grace, the denial of the will, salvation, is in Christ, who is God incarnate. "Certainly the doctrine of original sin (assertion of the will) and of salvation (denial of the will) is the great truth which constitutes the essence of Christianity, while most of what remains is only the clothing of it, the husk or accessories." [50] Jesus Christ is thus to Schopenhauer the symbol or personification of the negation of the will-to-live.

But the Christian mystery is not to be compared to Schopenhauer's. The enigma of evil in Christianity concerns creation, finite existence: in a universe grounded in Perfect Goodness how can evil be permanent, and why should it be at all? Dismal as is its view of the phenomenal world (original sin), Christianity is essentially and ultimately optimistic. Perfect in wisdom and goodness and power is its ultimate reality, God, perfect and prevailing. But Schopenhauer's mystery, as we have seen, is a mystery of good, and its solution demands a thoroughgoing revision of his metaphysics and cosmology. Deeper and more ultimate than Schopenhauer's pessimism is his doctrine of salvation, deeper and more ultimate, and far more enlightening. The metaphysical significance of compassion and asceticism is more profound than Schopenhauer allowed: it reveals to us the more ultimate nature of the will-reality. "So then, behind the raw, unmoral will," we read in Volkelt, "a deeper will-kernel is hid; the morally significant will. . . . Now . . . we can perceive this will-to-live, which was proclaimed as the deepest and ultimate reality, that it is a shell, behind which lurks the Will as a morally momentous power." [51]

We are now on the way to perceive new meaning in the very contradictions of Schopenhauer's philosophy. The confusion in Schopenhauer's use of intelligence and will has been pointed out often enough. The will is blind, blundering, aimless, irrational, but it has manifested itself in and has for its tool purposive intelligence. But we should not be misled into mistaking confusion for final contradiction. Schopenhauer's philosophy is in many ways a drama of reality. Confused and discordant appear its characters at the outset; more and more fully are they revealed to us as we move to the climax. The four parts of Schopenhauer's *World as Will and Idea* are four acts of a drama—their order and sequence are not accidental and indifferent, nor are we moving on a plane. There is increasing depth and height, penetration and exaltation of insight as we proceed. Not only the audience or readers, the dramatist himself may learn about his characters, and it is poor criticism to abuse an author because his characters go their own way and do not follow his own projected course for them. Tolstoy's men and women do not always conform to his texts and sermons; they have characters of their own, and *Anna Karenina* is not the less great as a novel because Tolstoy finds Levin too real to manage. Enough if both author and reader, both dramatist and audience have been led to perceive new abysses in the human soul and in reality. All the greater is the novel or the drama because it has thus deepened our insight. Abstract consistency is not the sovereign virtue either in literature or in philosophy. Point out the discrepancy, the shift of viewpoints in the successive stages of Schopenhauer's philosophy, to be sure; but it were mere pedantry to rest satisfied with such criticism.

Consider the world of experience: is it not a phenomenal system of events in space and time, causally related and always involved in the subject-object dualism? But look more deeply: behind the phenomenal scheme, back of this Maya veil of experience is the blind, blundering, aimless Will; the rational shell holds an irrational kernel; intelligence is at the beck of desire; the will-driven soul is a slave of insatiate craving, miserable and wicked. This pessimistic metaphysics is not merely a substitute for the preceding idealistic theory of knowledge, not merely inconsistent with it: we witness here a grim expansion of thought, the dark recognition of the limitations of the phenomenal, the sense of unsounded, dismal depths, and profound despair. We are plunged in what seems impenetrable, whirling chaos that sweeps us resistlessly about, and there seems no way out of the whirlpool and no beacon-light ahead. But a beacon-light does appear, and a way out, not to firm ground that eye can see or hand or foot can touch, but surely out of the whirlpool of will-driven desire. There is momentary respite in art, there is the lasting quietism of compassion and chastity, and Nirvana. For one to whom the whirlpool has been all-in-all, the out-of-it, to be sure, is bodiless, without content, nothing. When Schopenhauer says "we freely acknowledge that what remains after the entire abolition of the will is for all those who are still full of will certainly nothing," [52] he is unconsciously criticising the finality of his own pessimism. For,—these are the concluding words of *The World as Will and*

Idea—"conversely, to those in whom the will has turned and has denied itself, this our world, which is so real, with all its suns and milky-ways—is nothing." And *nothing*, narrow and inadequate, is likewise the view of things as essentially and hopelessly will-driven and irrational. Not only the will is at peace in the sublime moment of aesthetic contemplation, not only the will is curbed and negated by the moral saint: *the pessimism of Schopenhauer is thereby also curbed and negated.* The world is not so worthless if it includes souls that are pessimistic about it, that condemn it, and that seek and find a way out, be this way the way to apparent nothingness. Condemnation is not only the reverse of esteem: it is also its obverse. Even on Schopenhauer's premises a world which includes a Buddha, a *Theologia Germanica,* a Schopenhauer is not a world that warrants absolute pessimism. Thus Schopenhauer's aesthetics and ethics, running counter as they do to his pessimism, may teach us what they have not taught him: wisdom more final than his pessimism. They serve to indicate the limits of his pessimism, and therefore demand its radical revision.

The world whose nature has been disclosed to us in the whole of Schopenhauer's philosophy is certainly not a world which warrants docile, complacent optimism. It demands a heroic, perhaps a Zoroastrian view. But absolute, hopeless gloom it does not demand nor warrant. Like Gautama, Schopenhauer had eyes to see darkness and a genius for gloom, but, like Gautama again, he sensed within himself enlightenment and the clear path of salvation. No philosopher has been more personal than Schopenhauer, according to Paulsen;[53] none since Pascal, according to Ruyssen.[54] Out of the roots of his heart's agonies have sprung the ashen shoots of his pessimism. But Schopenhauer's philosophy is not objectively personal: it does not take due account of itself. The man who condemned the world confronted it disdainfully, but not disdaining himself; he who preached the vanity and tedium of attainment never doubted the lasting value of his own work. In all this he was inconsistent: had his judgment of the world explicitly included himself, Goethe, Plato, Kant, Beethoven, Rossini, Buddha, Arnold von Winkelried, Abbé Rancé, Madame Guion, it would have been different in its finality. Is the laurel crown a crown of thorns covered with leaves? Small reason for despair here, if man *will* have laurel crowns at any cost. The sun rises and shines on an earth in which there is as yet no life: "I am the sun and must rise because I am the sun: look on me who can!" Beautiful, green, and blooming is the oasis, and it bewails its lonely charms, spent as they are on the desert-waste. But the desert answers: "Were I no waste, thou wert no oasis!" [55] Here are echoes from the agonies of Schopenhauer's own spirit, but they are not agonies of pure, absolute despair. The note of heroic worth is in them all.

The recognition of the personal element in Schopenhauer's view of life nowise justifies a treatment of his philosophy as a pathological phenomenon. With romantic intensity Schopenhauer perceived the tragic side of life, his own life affording him no lack of material. He could make no reasoned sense of the tragedy, and his irrationalism is more rightly to be regarded as a conclusion from its pessimism than as its premise. Keenly conscious of supreme worth, philosophic, aesthetic, moral-mystical, he yet saw it as wholly alien in this vale of woe, and demanding for its full utterance the renunciation of the world. Hence his nihilistic gospel of salvation. The paradox and the inconsistency in Schopenhauer are fundamentally religious. Not without reason did Tolstoy call Schopenhauer "the most gifted of men," and as late as 1890 retained Schopenhauer's picture and no other in his room.[56] Not without reason did Schopenhauer look to the opposite bank of the Main, to the house where five hundred years earlier a Frankfurter had written *Theologia Germanica*. For is not this the Christian truth also, only outwardly inconsistent and paradoxical: man is a sinner tainted and wholly bad, yet he is also the son of God. The self "will not admit that it *really* is what it is *in fact*." [57] His mind is a tool of the tyrant will, he is greed, lust, egoism, cruelty personified; but see, his is also disinterested, aesthetic contemplation, his is the pure intelligence that sees through the will, that curbs and denies the will, his the compassion, the chastity, the blessedness, the peace of the saint.

This paradox and mystery raise a still more ultimate one, which Schopenhauer recognizes, but renounces as wholly beyond his ken. *Why* this paradox and mystery? Whence is the great discord that permeates this world? If the roots of individuality go as deep as the assertion of the will-to-live, and are thus extirpated in the act of will-denial, then what would I be if I were not the will-to-live? Whence finally this will that may either assert itself or be denied altogether? These are questions to which no answer may be given. Our minds are unsuited to deal with them. "With our intellect, this mere tool of the will, we are everywhere striking upon insoluble problems, as against the walls of our prison." [58] A knowledge of the ground of the very inmost being-in-itself of things is thus unavailable, for it transcends the forms of knowledge and consciousness: "so much as to the limits of my philosophy, and indeed of all philosophy." [59]

"Whatever torch we may kindle, and whatever space it may light, our horizon will always remain bounded by profound night." [60] And at the conclusion of his lectures Schopenhauer quoted Lucretius:

> In what a gloom of life, in what dire perils
> Are spent our years, however few they be! [61]

The brighter the philosophical light that illumines the darkness of existence, the greater will the all-surrounding darkness disclose itself to be, and "the more intelligent a man is, the more keenly aware is he what darkness surrounds him, and just this stimulates him philosophically."[62] *Why* this world has so much evil that thwarts and resists the good, why it is thus and not otherwise: is thus no problem of ours? Goethe wrote in the album of a student, and Schopenhauer quoted to Adam von Doss: "The good Lord has indeed created the nut, but he has not also cracked it."[63] And well it is so.

CHAPTER XII

HARTMANN'S PHILOSOPHY OF THE UNCONSCIOUS

I

Twenty-five years after the publication of *The World as Will and Idea* Schopenhauer literally had to beg his publisher Brockhaus to try out a second enlarged edition of his masterpiece. Hartmann's publisher Heymons brought out seven editions of *The Philosophy of the Unconscious* in six years, to be followed by five more in Hartmann's life-time. That this was merely a publisher's triumph, Hartmann, of course, would have been the last one to admit. But in the preface to his seventh edition the thirty-two year old author speculates: Had Schopenhauer been fortunate enough to find a real publisher, had the thirty years of unrecognition been spared him, who can tell what his creative powers might not have given to the world, and how profoundly and how much earlier the entire course of nineteenth century philosophy might not have been affected thereby! We should not be overwhelmed by these regrets. No author doubts that there is a special pouch in hell for slothful publishers, but it would scarcely do to blame the House of Brockhaus for Germany's long neglect of Schopenhauer. When the master-pessimist first composed, Hegel was conducting the Symphony of the Absolute. It took thirty years before the pessimistic strain had a real chance in the concert of German thought, and it was precisely during that opportune season that Hartmann's violoncello stirred the public ear.

Karl Robert Eduard von Hartmann was born in 1842, the only son of a captain of artillery who later rose to the rank of major-general. Unlike Schopenhauer and Leopardi, he had a very happy childhood and in his memoirs speaks with feeling of his father's intelligent care and of his mother's tender affection. The early mental development of the child suffered from no neglect; his father directed the course of his studies, and in school he leaped years ahead of his comrades. He showed very early a preference for ploughing his furrow by himself, a distaste for the routine of school, and decided though not obstinate enthusiasms and aversions. Homer did not charm this boy, and Demosthenes left him unmoved, but the simple greatness of Thucydides captivated him, and he was profoundly affected by the *Apology* of Socrates and by Sophocles. The purely formal and technical sides of science, particularly of mathematics, did not interest him, but rather the philosophical significance of the ideas and processes. The religious school-instruction served to stimulate him philosophically, and he seems to have been something of a heretic from the very start. Besides his school-work he had special instruction in art and music, in both of which he showed technical skill and some original power. There is no evidence of early depression beyond the usual melancholy moments of a youth of unusual intelligence and gravity. The general early impressions are cheerful; cheerful and pleasant also on the whole are his reports of his teachers. All the same, he counts the day of his graduation from the gymnasium as perhaps the happiest in his life.

The university did not attract Hartmann: its schedules and its pedantry repelled him, and likewise the roughness and looseness of student life. The loftier tone of the younger officers in the army and his father's example inclined him towards a military career, and he entered upon it in the belief that only as a soldier could he live as a whole man.

But closer acquaintance with men in barracks disillusioned him: his comrades did not understand his high aspirations and he did not relish all their pleasures. One suspects that Hartmann would have reconsidered his choice of a career in any case, even had he not been compelled to do so. As it was, a severe contusion of the knee, which refused to heal and developed into grave rheumatism, finally settled the question of army life for him. He was now twenty-two, having, as he believed, "lived through and experienced more things, overcome more errors, stripped off more prejudices and seen through more illusions . . . than is vouchsafed to many educated people throughout their entire lives." [1] Such a man was bound to be a poet or a saviour of society, or, failing both, perhaps a vagrom philosopher. Hartmann tried art and music first, but he was a critic keen and honest enough to perceive that he was not meant to create lasting beauty. Wisdom was his last refuge: he undertook to solve the riddle of the universe. Towards the end of 1864 he began his first main work, *The Philosophy of the Unconscious*, finished it in two years, kept the manuscript in his desk another year, and when it appeared in November, 1868 (dated 1869, fifty years after Schopenhauer's *World as Will and Idea*) was, as he tells us, the most surprised man in Germany to find himself a world-famous philosopher before thirty.

The public was inclined to treat the young man's work as his final and completed philosophy, whereas he regarded it rather as a projected outline and Chapter I. He did not know what resting on his oars or laurels meant; he found himself the object of world-wide discussion, and wrote as much as all his critics put together. Hartmann's systematic works run to some sixteen thousand pages, on all the problems in the philosophical calendar, and then essays and articles without count on all things known, surmised, and unthinkable, in philosophical reviews, in monthlies, weeklies, dailies.

He composed music in his leisure, and had a drama, *Tristan und Isolde*, to his credit, or on his conscience.

He married twice. His first wife, Agnes Taubert, was an enthusiastic pessimist; her work, *Der Pessimismus und seine Gegner*, is considered in our next chapter. She died in 1877. Eighteen months later Hartmann married Alma Lorenz who made it the business of her life to safeguard her husband's energy, keep it from being dissipated in controversies, and direct it into systematic writing. The Hartmann home in Berlin was a nest of devotion and peace. The philosopher lived in and for his family, and he was a loyal friend. It became a proverb in the capital: "If you would like to see contented and cheerful faces, then go to the pessimists." [2] He died in 1906, at the age of sixty-four, in the forefront of German philosophers in spite of his being a free-lance without academic connections. Windelband characterized him,—rather too generously, I think,—as the author of one of the two "most significant systems of philosophy . . . of nineteenth century Germany." [3] In spite of protracted illness and pain, the invalid lived to see the philosophical plan of his youth realized in detail. His own life seemed an index of his philosophy of life: eudaemonological pessimism and teleological optimism,—life, on the whole unhappy, could yet realize its goal.

II

"Whoso brings much, will bring to many something." [4] One cannot read through Hartmann without being impressed with his high synthetic power. He is a system-builder in the classical manner. What he brings, therefore, he brings as a bee, not as an ant. An intelligent discussion of his pessimism may not ignore its relation to the rest of his philosophy. I have no desire to spread out unduly, however, and shall be as brief as I can in dealing with the setting of the stage on which the Tragedy of the Unconscious is being acted. First of all it will help us to get our cue right if we consider Hartmann's position in relation to his predecessors. Here we are not without expert guidance: no one has tried harder than Hartmann to define clearly his place in the history of philosophy.

Kant is the gate through which one enters into the nineteenth century, and it is natural for contemporary philosophers to look up their Kantian ancestry. The orthodox view, familiar to all readers of historical manuals of philosophy, traces the direct line of succession from Kant, through Fichte and Schelling, to Hegel, and the movement Kant-to-Hegel has been treated often enough as one integral process of thought. But Schopenhauer has not been without his champions upholding his claim as the only true heir and bearer of Kant's crown. Hartmann, when occasion demands it, is also apt and able to hunt up Kantian genealogies in his own behalf.[5] But he protests against the Kantomania, *Kantvergötterung*, in German philosophy,[6] and is more concerned to define his position with reference to Hegel, Schelling, and Schopenhauer, who provide him with his important philosophical alternatives.

The outstanding fact in the philosophy of Hartmann's day was the antithesis of Hegel and Schopenhauer. Hegelianism still dominated the academic lecture-hall; the standard aesthetics, protestant theology, philosophy of history and history of philosophy, all bore the Hegelian stamp. But Schopenhauer dominated the unanointed philosophy of the day. The two were antipodal all along the line. Schopenhauer built on the very elements in the Kantian philosophy (subjective idealism) which Hegel disavowed. Hegel's metaphysical principle is the capitalized Notion: the world is for him a spiritual system; the Real is the Rational; the universe makes sense, makes for sense, makes good sense. This is the optimism of the self-confident Logos: "The world-process is development, the development is logical, what is developed is the logical, and aside from it there is nothing." [7] Of all this Schopenhauer's system is an explicit and unqualified denial. The world is in reality irrational, blind striving, is essentially and irremediably miserable, a tragic blunder. On the one side, "the thinker with the most sublime genius for abstract speculation which the earth ever produced"; on the other an amazing master of keen perceptions "in each of which, Columbus-like, he stands an egg on end in the simplest way in the world." [8]

The pessimistic tenor of *The Philosophy of the Unconscious* very naturally led the casual reader to list the author with the disciples of Schopenhauer. Against this interpretation of his philosophy Hartmann protests vigorously and with good reason. Although being on the whole a Schopenhauerian in his estimate of the world-process, Hartmann finds Schopenhauer altogether one-sided in his ultimate explanation of the world. He objects to Schopenhauer's metaphysical dismissal of reason as mere phenomenon of the blind irrational will; within the realm of the phenomenal, he objects to Schopenhauer's subjective idealism; he perceives a covert materialism in Schopenhauer's account of the intellect, and regards it as inadequate and worthless. He opposes Schopenhauer's metaphysical estimate of mechanism and teleology. He regards the account of the origin and destiny of individuality in *The World as Will and Idea* as insufficient and self-contradictory. The distinction between empirical and intelligible character has corollaries which Schopenhauer has not thought out, and serves to raise the issue between monism and pluralism or monadism in metaphysics; regarding this issue Schopenhauer is very confused, as is exhibited perhaps most strikingly in his view of salvation through individual self-denial of the will. Even in his pessimism Hartmann, as we shall see, is no mere disciple of Schopenhauer, and his practical program is a rejection of Schopenhauer's quietism.

Hartmann's radical critique of Schopenhauer however does not constitute him a Hegelian. In method, in philosophical equipment and outlook, Hegel is free from most of Schopenhauer's vices, but he also lacks Schopenhauer's virtues. Shall we say that Hegel's world is like Athena, issued fully armed and complete from Zeus' head? Surely it shows how far the single strength of thought can go: how far short of the goal. In the world Hegel sees only spirit; he has no heart for nature; nature has no history, and ultimately reality is for him history, spiritual process. But even though reason be the hero of the play, yet it is after all not the whole play, nor yet its author. The play, the world-process, is history, but, Hartmann holds, it is natural history, which includes but is not exhausted by intelligence. The same observation would apply in axiology: the triumph of reason in our experience may justify a very relative, but surely not an absolute optimism.[9]

Methodologically, Hartmann rejects the Hegelian dialectic in favor of induction, but he is Hegelian enough to observe that, between two contradictories, the greater truth is in the middle. Precisely on Hegelian grounds the issue cannot be: either Hegel or Schopenhauer. Hegel's own philosophy is not the final synthesis of thought; it also becomes thesis in its turn, involves an antithesis, demands a more ultimate synthesis. The Hegelian pantheism of the Idea, *panlogism,* is the thesis; the Schopenhauerian pantheism of the Will, *panthelism,* is the antithesis. The problem of problems imposed by the situation in philosophy as Hartmann conceived it was to find the synthesis of this dialectical triad. This he undertook to do, and he found his guide in Schelling; not only in the Schelling of the Jena days, known to us as the second step from Kant to Hegel, but also and more particularly in the Schelling of the forties.

Schelling is the most variously fertile of German philosophers. Hegel's dependence on him is familiar to all students of the history of philosophy. What is not so familiar, however, is the fact, pointed out by Hartmann, that Schopenhauer's central doctrine may be read out of Schelling ten, twenty years before the publication of *The World as Will and Idea* (1819). "The source of self-consciousness is will (1797). . . . There is finally and preëminently no other Being but will. The will is primary Being and to it alone are applicable all its predicates: groundlessness, eternity, independence of time, self-assertion (1809)." [10] Schelling, doing his thinking in public as Hegel sarcastically observed, did not perhaps see life steadily and see it whole, but he did see it a good many times, and saw a good many sides of it well. The philosophies which he thus served to stimulate or else anticipated, he was also later instrumental in reconciling. This was the outcome of his positive philosophy, the last of the four or five systems through which he ran in his one lifetime.

The truth about reality, then, as Hartmann following Schelling sees it, lies between Hegel and Schopenhauer. They are both right in recognizing one ultimate aspect of the real, wrong in ignoring or depreciating the reality of the other ultimate aspect. Schopenhauer treats intelligence as a by-product or tool of the Will-to-live. Hegel treats will as a subordinate moment in the ultimately logical process. But Schopenhauer's blind will-to-live cannot account for the intelligence which it is supposed to generate, nor can the logical significance of Hegel's world by itself explain its own actuality, its coming to be. If we use the terminology of Spinoza, we may say that both Hegel and Schopenhauer are in the similarly grave embarrassment of treating an attribute as the substance, and trying to derive the other attribute from it.[11] Will and Idea, creativeness and intelligence, drive and significance, are both attributes, incommensurable and complementary. Neither can be derived from the other; they are the two ultimate moments of the real. These two factors are involved in the world-process throughout: the one making activity possible, the other determining the nature of the activity. We see here for instance the two elements which go to make causality possible: "That in general anything comes to pass, that the effect *follows*, depends on the Will; that the effect, *if* it follows, follows *with necessity as this and no other*, depends on the Logical. . . . *That* things be, is determined by the alogical Will; *what* things are, is determined by the logical Idea." [12]

Schopenhauer had compared will and intelligence to a strong blind man carrying on his shoulders a cripple who can see. Hartmann corrects the picture: "It is not a blind man who carries a lame one showing the way, but it is a single whole and sound one, that certainly, however, cannot see with the legs and walk with the eyes." [13] The ultimate of ultimates is neither Will nor Idea: that is, neither one to the exclusion of the other. Schelling called it ± A;[14] Hartmann calls it the Unconscious, Absolute Substance, Absolute Subject or Spirit. It is the source, the core, the goal of reality. The progressive recognition of it in German philosophy marks its progress. "Schelling in his Philosophy of Identity showed the right road by recognizing the absolute as the eternally unconscious; Hegel advanced along the side of the unconscious Idea, and Schopenhauer along the side of the unconscious, alogical Will; both of which sides were reunited in Schelling's last system in the principle of Absolute Spirit." [15] What Schelling had perceived in principle, Hartmann now undertakes to understand and, more important for our purpose, to estimate in detail. It is the main theme of *The Philosophy of the Unconscious.*[16]

III

Hartmann compares the sphere of the Unconscious to the well-cultivated vine-clad hill that has yielded fine fruit and crops but not the long-expected hidden treasure. He proposes to seek the golden store "in the noble ores of its rocky beds, rather than on the surface of the fruitful earth." [17] The subsoil of consciousness, however, is not brute matter. Hartmann's survey of nature leads him to reject a mechanistic for a teleological view of it; but the teleology of nature is unconscious teleology. That mere mechanics or mere chance can explain, for instance, eyesight, he regards as outside the bounds of probability. By mathematical calculations of his own he undertakes to show that this probability is less than fifteen per ten million.[18] But it is not by such ingenious reckoning that he would persuade himself of the claims of unconscious teleology in nature. He surveys bodily and mental life and finds in both manifestations of the Unconscious. The slightest bodily movement presupposes the unconscious idea of the position of the corresponding nerve-endings in the brain and the unconscious will to stimulate them. Instinct is purposive action without consciousness of the purpose. "Instinct is not the result of conscious reflection—not a consequence of bodily organization—not mere result of a mechanism founded in the organization of the brain—not the effect of a dead, and essentially foreign mechanism, externally adhering to the mind—but the individual's *own* activity, springing from his inmost nature and character." [19] The Unconscious is manifested as the dominant factor in reflex action and in the reparative power of nature; materialism is incapable of accounting for numberless facts of everyday experience. The action of mind on body is in the end inexplicable except by means of an unconscious will. If bodily activity points beyond chance and mechanism to teleology, mental life points beneath consciousness to the underlying Unconscious.

Hartmann examines instinct in the human mind, devoting particular attention in a long chapter to the Unconscious in sexual love, which recalls but does not match Schopenhauer's famous chapter in the second edition of *The World as Will and Idea.* "Where one is conscious of no will in the satisfaction of which an existing pleasure or displeasure could exist, this will is an unconscious one. . . . The obscure, ineffable, inexpressible in feeling lies in the unconsciousness of the accompanying ideas." [20] Character and morality, aesthetic judgment and production, language, thought, sense-perception, all hark back, beyond consciousness, to an unconscious direction. "The laboratory of volition is hidden in the Unconscious." [21]

Neither eighteenth century 'design in nature' nor Darwinism can explain the beauty of the peacock's tail; the conscious feeling and the idea of the beautiful point in the end to the unconscious processes. Thought leans on intuition; all real philosophy is, in the first and in the last chapters at least, mystical: witness Spinoza, "flower of philosophical mysticism." [22] In history the struggle between lower and higher races does not proceed by conscious plan; a power beyond our conscious projects moves resistlessly, eradicating the inferior. To retard or try to check this process in the interests of alleged mercy is to cut off a dog's tail kindly, that is, gradually, inch by inch.[23]

Consciousness and material existence both require for their ultimate explanation the recognition of the unconscious. In this world-process, what is the precise status of consciousness; what is its origin and its final cosmic rôle?

According to Hartmann, the initial possibility of existence is due to the unaccountable will-activities of the metalogical Unconscious. These will activities are alogical; opposing each other, they clash and recoil, and are thus confronted with the amazing fact of externality. Thus arises consciousness: it is "the stupefaction of the will at the *existence* of the idea *not willed and yet sensibly felt by it.*" [24] "The *World* consists only of a sum of activities or will-acts of the Unconscious, and the ego consists of another sum of activities or will-acts of the Unconscious. Only so far as the former activities intersect the latter does the world become *sensible* to me; only so far as the latter intersect the former do I become sensible to myself." [25] The mind, which for Hartmann is prior to consciousness, has, according to its own nature, the ideas which it wills and which form the contents of its will. This self-contained peace of the Unconscious is disturbed by organized matter; sensation takes place, not self-evoked but received from without. The unconscious mind is now conscious. As Hartmann expresses it, in an outburst of eloquence, "the great revolution has come to pass, the first step to the world's redemption taken; the idea has been rent from the will, to confront it in future as an independent power, in order to bring under subjection to itself its former lord. This amazement of the will at the rebellion against its previously acknowledged sway, this sensation which the interloping idea produces in the Unconscious, this is *Consciousness.*" [26]

Observe now in this drama of world-redemption that it is to be a tragedy, a redemption through woe. In the very origin of consciousness pain is involved: "The breaking of the will on the resistance of a foreign will crossing it, or the centripetal rebound, is *sensation,* and moreover, as non-satisfaction of the will, *pain*-sensation." [27] And the increase of knowledge is increase of sorrow: to the experience of pain is added and superadded the clear perception of evil and of apparently stupid guilt. Consciousness has involved unconscious mind in pain and dissatisfaction, has raised the problem which only the intelligent mind can meet and solve. We have now approached Hartmann's account of experience as on the whole miserable and his program of salvation through negation of the cosmic will.

IV

"It is related of an ancient Brahmin that he was so affected with astonishment at the sight of an insect-capturing plant, that, forgetful of meat and drink, he remained seated before it till the end of his life." [28] The inerrant fitness of the activity of the Unconscious has a similarly hypnotic effect on us: we find in nature infallible, unhesitating adaptation of means to ends, not only in the general scheme, but in the least detail. The absolute clairvoyance of the Unconscious, its ever-suitable direction of all data, its ceaseless and most appropriate intervention at every step of the process dazzle us and hold us spellbound. We proclaim this world the best possible of worlds, God's own world, and therefore a good and a happy world. This is the conclusion which the theist is apt to draw from his recognition of teleology in nature.

Here Hartmann advises us to proceed with caution and watch our step. The infallibility of the infinite omniscient Unconscious does involve the conclusion that this is the *best possible world—under the circumstances of there being a world at all!* But to call this world the best possible in the sense of perfect, altogether good and faultless, a bower of bliss in which all evil is somehow good, merely the shadow in the lovely picture: to proceed to such optimistic conclusions is to be guilty of bad logic and poor observation of the facts of life. This world may be the best possible world and may yet be a world of woeful experience, the tragedy of which is intensified by the ideal values which intelligence strives to realize in it. Indeed it may be the best possible world in that it points to its own extinction.[29] The sharp distinction between the evaluation of the world in hedonistic-eudaemonological and in teleological-evolutionistic terms is regarded by Hartmann as his own contribution to axiology. He regards this distinction as essential to all true morality and all intelligent religion. It is well to keep this point in mind, and not to confuse Hartmann's philosophy with absolute pessimism or *Weltschmerz* or miserabilism: a confusion against which he tirelessly protests.

Evaluation may be in logical or in alogical terms. In the logical scale we consider knowledge-values, aesthetic, moral, redemption-values; likewise developmental and teleological values; in the alogical scale we have will-values and pleasure-pain values.[30]

The epistemological pessimist (sceptic, agnostic) doubts the possibility of real knowledge and regards the alleged knowledge-values as illusory. Against him we cannot maintain that our knowledge is either complete or adequate. While we may be optimistic regarding the ultimate perfection of attainable knowledge, its present state demands a much more modest estimate. But even this more modest "epistemological bonism" does not justify us in regarding knowledge-values as of intrinsic or absolute worth. What is good knowledge is not on that account *good;* what is known well it may yet be a pity to know. The fact is that science is indifferent to worth.

In the realm of aesthetic values, a similar conclusion holds. Beauty is not the ultimate standard or the last word in axiology, as some aesthetes would have it. The world might be a misbegotten hell, but to the artist it would still have its appropriate beauty. A thing of beauty need not be a joy forever. The universe as a whole is neither beautiful nor ugly.

The universe as a whole is also neither good nor evil. Moral values are as relative as aesthetic values; they are real only in the experiences and judgments of moral agents. We find in this world virtue and vice; our judgment of the balance between them may lead us to ethical optimism or to pessimism, but a sound philosophy cannot lead to despair or to jubilation; its task, as Spinoza told us, is to understand. Ethical optimism, if at all possible, is always only in prospect. The present is even less likely to yield us moral than scientific or aesthetic satisfaction. The values in the logical scale are realized in development and aspiration. This is particularly true of the redemption-values of the religious life: salvation is possible only in a tragic world, in a world recognized as essentially tragic, a world in the tragedy of which one is moved to play or to share a hero's part.

Confidence in evolution-values is a postulate of epistemological, moral, and religious optimism. A developing world is a moving not a stagnant world; seemingly a circle, it is really a spiral. Faith in evolution-values is faith in the reality of growth, of cultural progress, of advance towards some goal. It is an insurance against the blight of dead monotony. Evolutionistic optimism thus finds its completion in teleological optimism of which, in fact, the other varieties are to be regarded as special aspects. Teleological optimism is conviction that the world makes sense, has an end, is intelligible. An anti-teleological optimist is an unthinkable contradiction: unthinkable, but not extinct.

In the alogical scale, as far as will-values are concerned, any kind of world is better than no-world, and while we have here no basis for distinguishing better or best, any world whatever is indifferently good. The pleasure-pain values are logically inexplicable facts of feeling which reason may not ignore and which philosophy must reckon with, for they are of prime importance in all axiology. Is the attainment of happiness the prime purpose of creation? Then it were impious to doubt that life yields a positive balance of pleasure. But should life yield a balance of pain, then, if there be any purpose and goal, it will have to be sought elsewhere than in pleasure. "The measurement of cosmic value in hedonistic terms is thus neither below the dignity of science nor is it indirectly disposed of by measurements in other than hedonistic terms. . . . In the pursuit of this investigation, *Wertlehre* becomes *Wägungslehre;* for the pleasure value in existence is positive or negative, depending upon this, which of the two, pleasure or pain, *outweighs* the other." [31] Aside from our own individual attitude, whether it be one of *Weltschmerz* or of imperturbable personal cheerfulness, this question regarding the pleasure-pain balance in life admits of an objective study and a scientific answer. Is this balance positive, negative, or a zero of indifference? Pessimism in this field may be a purely theoretical doctrine, as little of a depressed state itself as a biological doctrine is a living organism, or the science of opiates is itself a narcotic.

Turning thus to eudaemonological axiology or weighing of the balance of pleasure in life, Hartmann surveys the various possible standpoints. In a spirit of negative dogmatism, we may declare the problem absurd: pleasure and pain being incommensurable, there being no real compensation and accordingly no 'balance.' Or else, while admitting that an absolute intelligence might cope with the problem ("God knows how!") we may declare it to be past our mortal ken. Or we may be sceptics, doubting whether we can solve the problem. Or again, in a positively dogmatic manner, we may assert that the balance of pleasure over pain, or of pain over pleasure, is a maximum, holding to superlative eudaemonological optimism and pessimism respectively. Or still once more we may declare that pleasure and pain match and compensate each other in a balance of indifference. Or finally, in a critical spirit, we may reckon the pleasure-pain balance as relative, as inclining to pleasure (meliorism), or to pain (peiorism), or else perhaps, while admitting the actuality of the balance, regard it as indefinite and infinitesimal, past reliable reckoning. Of these three varieties of a critical view, Hartmann's theory is the second. His conclusion is peioristic: life is on the whole more painful than pleasant; but he is much better informed about the painfulness.

The empirical-inductive survey of everyday life is a melancholy recital. If we take a cross-section of life, we find unmixed evil, but scarcely unmixed good. All along the line pain, fear, countless ills, ruinous labor, disappointment sway the balance. Trace the average man's career from birth to death: how dim is the light, how dark the shadows in the picture! In this art of dolorous recital Schopenhauer has made it very difficult for anyone to approach him. What Hartmann lacks in brilliant insight, he makes up in comprehensiveness and detail of observation. One example will illustrate his procedure: here is Hartmann's account of the home life in which the average man seeks assured happiness in this sorry world. The reader will remember that Hartmann himself was happily married.

"Family happiness is even in normal circumstances uncertain. Either husband or wife is not of much account, or they are not quite suited to each other, or the marriage is childless, or else yields so rich a crop of children that daily care visits the home, or efforts to prevent too many births poison conjugal happiness, or the illnesses of parents or children cast a shadow over the home, or the parents must need bewail the loss of the very children who seem dearest, or else the worry over some blind, deaf-mute, imbecile, epileptic, or otherwise sickly or invalid child embitters their joy in the others. If the children grow up, then the school-worries over lazy or ungifted children weigh over the parents more than over the children, and perhaps there is a light-minded, good-for-nothing among them. Should the children all fare well, then suddenly the mother dies, and leaves her husband to worry how with strange help he can bring up the children, or else the father himself passes from the home circle and leaves the family in sudden need. . . ." [32] A paragraph immediately following this retails with equal impartiality of detail the trials and tribulations of the unmarried folk.

The joys and blessings of the 'higher life' are likewise mixed and uncertain. The thinker's joy is known to few, but arduous futile labor is the lot of the many who set out on the path of knowledge. This is even truer in the life of art: how exceptional the success, the joy of creation, genuine understanding and recognition,—how common the bitter futility of untalented endeavor, the still more bitter and futile struggle with stupid apathy! Here, in science and art, pure joy is indeed to be found; alas that it is so rare! The moral life does yield attainment of worth; of this Hartmann has no doubt, but he doubts that happiness marks the attainment of virtue. Peace of heart, a neutral state, is all that the moral hero can expect. And religion, far from being a source of happiness, is rather designed to cure man of his predilection for it.

This general conclusion from experience is supported by detailed psychological observations, by reasoning, and by demonstrations as to how and why pain preponderates over pleasure. An instance or two must suffice. "Pain is (apart from the complete blunting of the nerves by great pain) the more painful, pleasure the more indifferent and cloying, the longer it lasts." [33] Concomitant pleasures weaken each other, but concomitant pains enhance each other; one chance unpleasantness can ruin the happiest day, but the day of misery is scarcely relieved by an incidental pleasure.

Hartmann does not subscribe to Schopenhauer's doctrine that pain is primary and positive, and pleasure only negative, the temporary alleviation of pain. It is true that, owing to the fact that there is far more pain than pleasure in life, most pleasure does follow the remission of pain, but this does not affect the truth in principle that pure positive pleasure is to be had. Examples may be found, not only in intellectual and aesthetic experience, but also in the sensual life. Hartmann, however, shares Schopenhauer's general conclusion that man's hope of a lasting balance of happiness in this life is doomed to disappointment.

The pathetic expectation of a balance of happiness in this life is called by Hartmann the first stage of man's illusion. "Happiness is considered as having been actually attained at the present stage of the world's development, accordingly attainable by the individual of today in his earthly life." [34] The progress of intelligence lays bare this illusion: even in the realm of most intense desires and passions,—hunger, love, ambition, to mention only three,—the pains of the unsatisfied far exceed in frequency and in intensity the pleasures of satisfaction. The supreme attainable felicity is painless contentment: a dreamless sleep. Hartmann's elevenfold dolorous inventory of life exhibits it as a losing business.

Disappointed in his expectations here and now, man turns his hopes to the hereafter, and now conceives happiness as attainable by the individual in a transcendent life after death. In the life of the individual the transition from the first to this second stage of the great illusion corresponds to the passage from the blithe trust of innocent childhood to the wistful yearning of adolescence. Representing it in the history of the race is the succession of Greek-Roman-Jewish antiquity by Christianity. On the extreme weariness of life in the ancient world falls the ray of the Christian hope of personal immortality, a hope the brighter because of the dark despair and disdain of the present life. Hartmann misses no opportunity to brand this hope as not only illusory but also pernicious: illusory because reflecting belief in the eternal reality of the empirical self, and pernicious because springing from self-centeredness and egoism. How could there be any individual happiness in the hereafter? Even if we overlooked for the moment the overwhelming empirical evidence of the dependence of our self-consciousness on the bodily organism and the consequent illusoriness of the belief in personal existence after death, even if we ventured to speculate on mere suppositions, what happiness could we predicate of life beyond death, however conceived? The view of reincarnation could only regard the soul as involved repeatedly in the same sorry round of bodily existence, whether on this earth or elsewhere. The hope that our soul may be reborn in a happier world rests on the supposition that our earth is the stepchild of the Absolute. But what justifies us in regarding our unhappy globe as the drudge or the wretched experimental station of an otherwise blissful universe? All analogy is against such fancies.[35] The conception of disembodied existence precludes consciousness, feeling, memory, precludes also any discussion of pleasure-pain. The desire for immortality arises from egoism, and the relinquishing of this desire and hope is a prime condition of genuine morality and true religion. This second illusion man must dispel; in dispelling it, he renounces utterly the quest of happiness along the lines of individual satisfaction.

This is genuine advance, but it is not enough. For a third stage of the illusion of happiness must now be transcended: this is the belief in social progress, so characteristic of our modern age. Happiness is relegated to and sought in the future of the world. But what justifies this sublime faith in progress? How is progress to bring us real felicity?[36] Civilization brings forth new diseases to match the advance of medicine, and even if medicine does win the race with disease, "cheerful youth will always form only a fraction of mankind, and the other part be composed of morose old age."[37] Death will always be with us, and in life, domination of one man by another, and discontent, and with the increase of knowledge, increased doubt and dismay. "With the advance of culture, demands increase always more rapidly than the means for their general satisfaction." [38] He who rests his hopes of happiness on civilization and progress should consider the world as he has it: are the most civilized people the most or the least contented? The progress of human culture is of value, but why? Because it releases for mental exertion human energies which at lower levels of existence have been employed in the satisfaction of elemental needs. Man has thus more opportunity to understand the futility of life's quest of happiness, to tear the veils of illusion, to see the truth and find the way out of the misery of life. That is to say, in savage life Eduard von Hartmann would have had to hunt and fish and grub to keep alive, and his sixteen thousand pages of gray wisdom would have been left unwritten.

So the progress of intelligence gradually brings humanity to the realization that self-centeredness is as stupid as it is futile and pernicious, and that the quest of happiness is doomed to defeat. "After the three stages of illusion of the hope of a positive happiness it has finally seen the *folly* of its endeavor; it finally foregoes all *positive* happiness, and longs only for *absolute painlessness,* for nothingness, Nirvana." [39]

Hartmann's Nirvana should not be confused with the Buddhist or the Schopenhauerian quietist goal of individual self-renunciation. Schopenhauer's doctrine is open to the serious objection which we considered in the previous chapter and which Hartmann presses vigorously: "How should it be possible for the individual to negate his individual will as a whole, not merely theoretically but also practically, as his individual volition is only a ray of the Only Will?" [40] But even supposing that the impossible were to happen; suppose that through asceticism, eremite vigils, and voluntary starvation, one certain egoistic will has been denied, one self-engrossed individual extinguished, what would that signify? Simply that one man has died: "To the Only Will the consequences would have been the same if a tile had killed that man; it continues after, as before, with unenfeebled energy, with undiminished avidity." [41] And even if all men were to turn ascetics, and mankind were to die out gradually by sexual continence, the remedy would be no more radical than before. Nature, the Unconscious, would evolve some new type to replace man, and the sorry tragi-comedy of existence would go on.

In *The Philosophy of the Unconscious* Hartmann regards the ascetic endeavor after individual negation as "an aberration only in procedure, not in *aim.*" [42] In his later work, *Das sittliche Bewusstsein,* he offers a less favorable diagnosis: "The goal of the denial of the will is clearly here also decidedly *egoistic.*" [43] Morality and religion demand the utter uprooting of selfishness; redemption is not redemption of self but redemption from self. The denial of the will is not to be individual in any sense, and nowise partial. It should be universal and final, and should register the extinction of the entire world-process.

We have come now to the climax of Hartmann's philosophy: a fantastic eschatology which has aroused amazement and ridicule, and which Hartmann himself, never explicitly abandoning, has yet in his later writings subjected to revision and higher criticism. Instead of ascetic withdrawal from life, he advocates provisionally the affirmation of the will-to-live, not in the sense of egoism, but in the sense of complete devotion to life and its pains, active participation in the business of living, in the advancement of culture and progress. All this is to be provisional, a preparation for the grand finale of cosmic will-negation. The progress of culture and intelligence will disclose to men in increasing numbers and in increasing measure the essential infelicity of life. The largest part of the Unconscious Spirit manifests itself in humanity and exceeds the will objectified in organic and inorganic nature. When, as a result of progressive pessimistic enlightenment, humanity's will-denying power comes to outweigh the world-affirming power objectified in unenlightened nature, and when furthermore the consciousness of mankind has been completely awakened to the folly of volition and the misery of existence, and has conceived a resistless yearning for the peace and painlessness of non-existence, and when, as a third condition, perfected communication between the peoples of the earth has made a simultaneous common resolve possible, humanity will be able, by one universal act of will-denial at the proper moment, to vote the world out of being.

V

The boldness of this young recruit's strategy roused general amazement; the more so as it was intended to crown a philosophy of "speculative results according to the inductive method of physical science." The assumption involved in Hartmann's first condition that the world-negating willpower of disillusioned humanity should exceed the world-affirming will-power of the rest of the cosmos was regarded as one "belonging to the region of airiest fancy." [44] Even Mainländer, boldly credulous in his own speculations, found in Hartmann's Cosmic Extinction Vote good occasion for satire: "From all parts of the world arrive telegrams. . . . You burst out in a cry of joy and rush forthwith to the Französische Strasse and there, let us say, you wire ten thousand dispatches to this effect: 'World-redemption tomorrow noon twelve o'clock sharp. All to commit suicide simultaneously, weapons optional.' . . . Immediately thereafter the Twilight of the Gods begins." [45] Hartmann stated at the outset that by cosmic will-denial he did not mean a mere suicide of humanity *en masse.* Already in 1874, when only thirty-two, he was characterizing his first *magnum opus* as "a work of youth, with its characteristic merits and defects." [46] In a note written some twenty years after the first publication of *The Philosophy of the Unconscious,* he 'explained' his meaning: universal will-denial and the end of the world-process, he said, should be regarded, not naturalistically, but as a supernatural act "by which the Cosmic Being withdraws itself from its former will-manifestations and gives up, along with the phenomenal world, also its laws and its apparent substance (matter)." [47]

On this hyperphysical interpretation of cosmic extinction, the third condition, mentioned above, of "a sufficient communication between the peoples of the earth" by "the perfection and more dexterous application of technical discoveries . . . to allow of a *simultaneous common resolve*" [48] should have to be ruled out. It is in fact not only neglected but explicitly omitted by Hartmann in his later writings.[49]

Hartmann's eschatology has been the object of as particular attention on the part of his critics as his 'doctrine of creation.' The Universal World-Extinction Congress, the praise of this best of all possible worlds because it admits of being voted out of existence, and in particular Hartmann's comforting description of this miserable world as "a painful mustard plaster which the cosmic One-and-All applies to itself, in order to draw out an inner pain and thus to eliminate it," [50] have led many to share the judgment of Kurt that "a more muddled chaos of philosophical fancies . . . is indeed very difficult to conceive." [51] But it is not enough to cite page and line, and laugh in scorn at this "mustard-plaster metaphysics." When a philosopher explains that 'he could not possibly have meant' this or that passage written twenty, thirty years earlier, it is much less to the point to confront him with his rejected early words than to understand the full significance of his rejection of them. Hartmann's later explanation of the cosmic will-extinction vote is very significant: it serves to indicate an important shift in his axiology, a shift in emphasis which we may observe generally in all his writings. It is scarcely a shift from pessimism to optimism, but it is a shift from general negation towards partial affirmation. The hedonistic pessimist holds his ground to the end and does not retreat beyond the ramparts of peiorism. But instead of proceeding from hedonistic pessimism to a cosmic threnody, as he did in his youth, the mature Hartmann keeps increasingly in view the reality of the non-hedonic values of life.

John Stuart Mill's radical revision of Bentham did not save him from continuing to believe himself to the end a utilitarian. Hartmann's radical and increasing departure not only from the letter but also from the spirit and the flavor of Schopenhauer's axiology leaves him in similar confusion regarding the full meaning of his own procedure. The present exposition of Hartmann's account of value has relied mainly on his first and on one of his last works. It is to be trusted that the lack of uniformity which this double source lends to an exposition of Hartmann's philosophy of life has not been unduly accentuated. Should we boldly confront the *Grundriss der Axiologie* with the latter part of the *Philosophy of the Unconscious*, evidence would be abundant of the real change in Hartmann's emphasis. Should we further make use of the guidance which Hartmann himself provides in the *Grundriss der Axiologie* by his copious references to his earlier works, we would see that the shift is not sudden but gradual and characterizes the entire course of Hartmann's philosophical writings.

In what sense is Hartmann's thought as it progressively utters itself, a philosophy of negation? Hartmann negates the reality of pleasure-capital in life; he would disclose the illusion of eudaemonological hopes; he points at this hope and craving as feeders of egoism, and denounces egoism as the hidden spring of all spurious morals. This is the first and the last word of his capital work, *Das sittliche Bewusstsein*. Be the eudaemonistic pseudo-ethics positive or negative, individual or social, earthly-empirical or transcendent, it is alike unavailing. Morality demands the emancipation from the preoccupation with happiness, and it culminates in the ethics of redemption: "Real existence is the incarnation of the Deity, the world-process records the passion of God incarnate and at the same time the road to the redemption of the one crucified in the flesh; *while morality is the coöperation in the shortening of this pain and of the path of redemption.*" In these closing words of *Das sittliche Bewusstsein*, Hartmann's philosophy of religion is forecast. The fundamental postulate of religion as of morality is "pessimism in its broadest scope": [52] not the pessimism of the Gospels, which Hartmann calls *Entrüstungspessimismus*, that is, pessimism springing largely from the intolerable sense of present miserable conditions, as due to man's frailty and sin,[53] but a metaphysical pessimism more nearly allied to the Buddhist, leading to the emancipation from self-engrossment and its illusions—a pessimism more precisely with regard to the attainability or the importance of happiness.

Egoistic craving is "the root of all evil striving." [54] But the world is not only in need of redemption, it is also capable of being redeemed. To be sure, nothing *is* except God's will, and in this sense God wills the evil in the world. But he wills it "not . . . as something that should exist and last, but as something that must be overcome, which exists just in order to be negated." [55] Evil may thus be of value and significance to morality as a spur to resistance. "Evil is the pike in the fish-pond of the moral world-order, which keeps the good carp from becoming too lazy and the pond from turning stagnant through their peaceful inactivity." [56] This *kakodicy,* as Hartmann calls it, or teleological justification of evil, is in no sense an everlasting Yea to actuality; it is the grim recognition that life is a life of toil and combat, and that these are the conditions for the attainment of any moral values. The justification of evil, we should keep in mind, is teleological, not eudaemonological.[57]

The world-process is thus "a unique great tragedy,"—"the world-tragedy of the divine spirit." [58] The world-process is "the means of God's self-redemption from that in him which should not be." [59] "God's redemption consists in the universal denial of the will which is to be attained through the redemption of the world, *i.e.,* in the return of the will from a state of actuality to one of potentiality." [60] In this work of redemption, man, emancipated from egoistic craving, can participate, and is thus lifted up to over-individuality. "Thus God can redeem the world only in so far as he himself is redeemed thereby; he cannot redeem the world as such without redeeming himself. Just as little can God redeem me as individual personality. . . . But I can indeed redeem God, *i.e.,* I can coöperate positively in the world-process which is to bring about his redemption." [61]

This idea is central and climacteric in Hartmann's "autosoteric, autonomous, cosmotragic, immanent religion of the Absolute Spirit." [62] Hartmann contrasts his eschatology with the Christian. The Christian theologians look forward to the last day when the world will be no more and God will again be all in all: but on one condition: "*They* must then *still be there so as to share* in the bliss of God's undimmed glory." [63] It is this subtle egoism which requires eradication. Is this world a vale of sorrows,—and what true Christian can contest this charge?—then surely the extinction of the cosmos, the return from the actuality of existence to the pure potentiality of the Absolute, is not an irreligious notion, nor does it involve metaphysical nihilism. The denial of the world-process is the affirmation of pure potentiality, and *vice versa:* each of these is the negation of the other: which of the two is preferred depends on our axiology. An extinguished cosmos is to us Nothing, but as Schopenhauer told us, for those of us who have denied the will, this our seemingly so real world, with all its suns and milky ways—is nothing. Pessimism leads us to universalize our choice between the reality of the willed cosmos and the willed no-cosmos. And this sublime coöperation of man with God in the redemption-extinction of the cosmos is to be accomplished precisely through the gradual spread of pessimism, through the emancipation of the human spirit from the gay or wistful illusion of hedonistic egoistic optimism.[64]

Certain initial difficulties confront us here. How is Hartmann's Unconscious to function as God, and what can be the meaning of the divine self-redemption? Hartmann has carefully and very elaborately disposed of theism; his God is not personal, and if we speak of 'Him,' it is only for convenience in expression. But how is Hartmann's "concrete monism" to include the character which he ascribes to God; how can he write that "love is the Absolute's highest form of moral manifestation?"[65] What love does the Absolute Unconscious have to reveal? Well does Sommer point out: "The Absolute has nothing to reveal, its essence consists only in an inexpressible composition of blind Will and logical Idea; individuals are utterly devoid of love, for their essence is engrossed in egoism and inbred impulses and instincts of the loveless Unconscious; love is quite groundless in this cheerless and desolate view of the world."[66] As a matter of fact, however, Hartmann's view of life is not cheerless; he does conceive the world-process as one of divine redemption through self-emancipated love and through cultural progress in the world. Certainly if we hold Hartmann to his early text, his redemption is not possible, and his critics are right in treating his doctrine of redemption as a grotesque pendant to the fantastic eschatology of *The Philosophy of the Unconscious.* But Hartmann's later axiology does serve to indicate the necessary revision of his earlier metaphysics. This revision is not executed by Hartmann in explicit terms; instead, he endeavors to fit and adjust, or pours new wine into old bottles.

Some of his critics have rated him an important philosopher not because but in spite of his pessimism, or have regarded the latter merely as Hartmann's personal reflection of the *Zeitgeist:* the young German of the fifties and sixties writes of this misbegotten cosmos; the man of later and more hopeful days is the evolutionary optimist.[67] Certainly we may note a decided change in Hartmann's procedure. The philosopher who had condemned the whole world-process because it did not yield to man a balance of pleasure, is also the philosopher who advocates the overcoming of eudaemonism, theoretical and practical, as the prime condition of true ethics and religion. He is not merely a eudaemonological pessimist; he is also an evolutionistic-teleological optimist. Even with regard to pleasure his later designation of his view is not superlative, but only comparative pessimism or peiorism. With regard to the non-hedonic values of life he inclines to optimism.

Hartmann's later philosophy of life is an example of what real devotion to values is still open to one who has renounced and discarded the quest of pleasure-values. This world of ours, as he views it, is not a bower of happiness, but in it intelligence may aspire to the attainment of genuine values and, as we have seen, its very evils may well be a challenge to our spirit to negate them, be it for that purpose necessary to negate the world-process itself. This negation of the world-process, again, comes to mean, not a solemn world-congress to vote the world out of existence, nor anything literally or allegorically catastrophic. Even if it were possible for united humanity to put a full stop to the present world-process, would the redemption so conceived be final? The absolute Unconscious cannot be extinguished; it may once again become manifested in a world-process; opposed alogical will-activities may once again collide and recoil, giving rise to consciousness, and raising the curtain on another cosmic tragedy. Be the actors in that tragedy as pessimistically enlightened and as brave as ourselves, their cosmic extinction vote may, in turn, prove no more final than ours. Hartmann to be sure reasoned that the chances of such a repetition of the world-cycle are at worst even, and the probability $\frac{1}{2}$. "That an indefinitely large number of such epochs of actual existence (Buddhist kalpas) should proceed from God's eternal being, is extremely improbable (for *n* number of epochs, the probability would be $\frac{1}{2n}$)." [68] Hartmann insists on the validity of this reasoning and adheres to his initial judgment that the chances of world-redemption diminish progressively and "the probability $\frac{1}{2n}$ becomes so small that it is practically sufficient for consolation." [69] The comfort and the logic of this reasoning seem alike dubious.

But we should not allow Hartmann's use of allegorical-liturgical speech in his philosophy of religion to confuse us regarding the changed meaning of his ideal of redemption-through-negation. This ideal in his pessimistic philosophy comes to mean the continuous resistance to evil, characteristic of man's higher spiritual life. Within the frame of his own concrete monism, Hartmann is entertaining an idea that corresponds to that of the denial of worldliness in the theism of the Christian gospel of salvation. So Paul Christ observes that "Whatever is true, beautiful, and good in Hartmann's ethics is derived, not from his pessimism, but from an antagonistic and ineradicable idealism, an unconscious

Christianity."[70] "Whosoever shall seek to gain his life shall lose it, but whosoever shall lose his life shall preserve it."[71]

Our value scale is not completely applicable to the Absolute. The Absolute does not know; for it there is no beauty nor ugliness, no good nor evil. Even as the object of religious worship, it is only as within-the-world that we conceive the Absolute as God, and then we conceive of his world-woe as a postulate of religion. But world-woe does not signify a meaningless, valueless world: "The teleological scale and that of pleasure-pain are nowise conflicting in the Absolute. In the Absolute eudaemonology and teleology coincide."[72] All this to be sure is hypothetical; and while phenomenal comparative pessimism or peiorism remains even if we reject the doctrine of the Absolute as unwarranted speculation, the evolutionistic-teleological optimism does require for its full justification the axiology of the Absolute. Hartmann's bold venture in absolutism is thus seen to concern his vindication of the positive values and his teleological optimism.

His use of the term 'God' does not imply a belief in an absolute consciousness or personal world-author or director. In his *Grundriss der Metaphysik*[73] he lists eleven arguments in favor of an absolute consciousness, only to criticize them all in turn and to advance eighteen against the belief, to his mind an adequate assortment. The spiritual activity of Hartmann's God is unconscious and this should be kept in mind in all our discussion of his account of God's world-woe, divine grace and divine redemption goal. These are all to be taken in a decidedly Pickwickian sense. The very use of the term *Erlösung*, redemption, in Hartmann's philosophy has been regarded as an impertinence, "a hopeless offspring of pessimism";[74] thus Steffes insists that "Hartmann teaches desperation and absolute resignation, not true redemption."[75]

Hartmann opposes teleological pessimism as firmly if not as repeatedly as eudaemonological optimism. That the world is aimless he denies as vigorously as that its aim is the attainment of pleasure. The hopeless view of life without a goal is to him intolerable: suicide would be the normal corollary of such a philosophy. He rejects such a view even when it restricts itself to a phenomenalistic form and proceeds to quietism. If teleological pessimism is hopeless desperation, hedonistic optimism makes for weakness, softness, cowardice in the presence of pain; it is a check to heroic endeavor and a bar to cultural advance. A bower of happiness may prove more intolerable than our poor world with all its troubles. Hartmann quotes Schiller:

> Some fear and some hope and some sorrow:
> Else how live from today till tomorrow—
> Else how bear the dull load of a life
> Unrelieved by some change or by strife? [76]

But man is too weak a creature to cope with a world which he believes to be one of unmitigated woe. Such a dismal view may also lead to suicide. Between the two extremes Hartmann proposes his comparative pessimism or peiorism with regard to happiness: it discourages softness and hardens man into a heroic mould. Thus Hartmann is led to his "most auspicious constellation": a cheerful temper with a theoretical peiorism; and thus also we reach his practical vindication of his view of life; not miserabilism, not *Weltschmerz* or desperation, but, with no disdain and little hope of happiness, firm devotion to the pursuit of the higher aims and values that ennoble life and redeem the world by overcoming evil and defying frustration. The worth of life, "eudaemonologically disintegrated, is teleologically once more restored." [77]

Particular interest attaches to the fact that Hartmann, pessimist though he is regarding the attainability of positive happiness, and rather lukewarm and grudging in his affirmation of attained moral, aesthetic, or religious values, never hesitates on the reality of teleological value: the reality of aims, goals in the universe which render our present activity significant. In thus emphasizing real purposiveness in the world, he is inconsistent; for what purpose, what end or aim or teleology could the Unconscious have? That he insists notwithstanding on his teleological optimism is doubly significant: despite his pessimism and alongside his alogical Absolute is this reality of the reach after value, this purposiveness and self-transcendence essential to value which he recognizes clearly in the world-process, even if he is unable to provide adequately for them in his metaphysics.

A very enlightening process of development is thus to be observed in Hartmann's thought. It manifests the inadequacy of eudaemonistic axiology. But it does more. It show aesthetics, ethics, and religion as necessarily resting on the metaphysical affirmation of value, on teleological optimism; it shows that Hartmann, as he recognizes more intimately the reality of the higher values, shifts the pessimistic emphasis in his estimate of the world. Schopenhauer's utter despair of the world is rejected by Hartmann, but while sharing the teleological-evolutionistic optimism of the Hegelians, he would point out to them that this sort of optimism does not preclude hedonistic pessimism. Hegel himself, Hartmann maintains, is virtually, if not in outspoken terms, a eudaemonological pessimist: not outspoken because of his extreme rationalism and his preoccupation with the eulogy of the Absolute Idea.[78] More alive than Hegel to the actuality of the irrational in the universe, more systematic and logical and less impressionistic a mind than Schopenhauer, Hartmann gives us a philosophy of life which, if it lacks the opposite virtues of the one or the other, escapes in its middle course also some of their main defects.

The change in the architect's plan revealed in the progressive erection of this immense philosophical structure is as instructive as it is sometimes exasperating. Itself the record of an axiology gradually modified to meet the demands of ethics, aesthetics, and philosophy of religion, Hartmann's system reveals, altogether in spite of its author's intentions, but perhaps better than any other system of thought, the limitations of pessimism. In this particular respect it is even more instructive than the philosophy of Schopenhauer. The progressive revision of its negations is a delineation of the character and scope of the different values which our judgment of the world discloses to us. The serious embarrassments in which Hartmann is involved in his ethics and philosophy of religion are due to his insistence on gathering grapes and figs from his thorns and thistles, or rather he finds figs and grapes on his alleged thistles and thorns, and would have the full benefit of his crop without allowing his trees the better names which they have earned for themselves. This metaphysical ungraciousness need not mislead us. The positive statement of theory of values in Hartmann's philosophy is the more informing because it proceeds from an initial attitude of negation, and the delineation of the values is perhaps the more vindicating just because it has been, as it were, exacted and delivered only on demand.

CHAPTER XIII

A GERMAN SLOUGH OF DESPOND

I

We have noted already the conglomerate character of Schopenhauer's system, which even his genius was not able to fuse into a unitary whole. There is a sort of dramatic unity in the action of Schopenhauer's philosophical tragedy, but it has not been articulated logically, and those whom it most moved to thought set their minds to overcome its dilemmas. Schopenhauer's correspondence records his consuming desire for expert and ardent disciples, letter-perfect and loyal to the letter of his doctrine. But, for all his 'apostles' and 'evangelists,' and notwithstanding the broad and sustained popular interest in his philosophy,—an interest in which Kant alone among his German predecessors excells him,—Schopenhauer did not inaugurate a definite and lasting philosophical tradition. Who are the competent orthodox followers of Schopenhauer? The Schopenhauerians are mostly 'of the left,' and differ from each other in the parts of their common master's doctrine which they deny or neglect in order to bear down on some other parts or aspects. We need only to consider the outstanding features of "this system, constructed mosaic-like from *a priori aperçus:*" [1] its ultra-Kantian subjective idealism, the individualistic leanings of its monistic metaphysics, its irrationalistic voluntarism, and its near-Platonic objective idealism, its partial and very misleading materialistic bias, and its dominant pessimistic tone,—and we should not be surprised at the great variety of possible revised versions which speculative zeal has evolved.

It is instructive to note that even the most intimate and perhaps on the whole the most loyal of Schopenhauer's immediate disciples, Julius Frauenstädt, his literary executor and the first editor of his Works, departs not inconsiderably from the teachings of the master. This is due not so much to his early Hegelianism, which he did his best to forget,[2] but rather to his desire to achieve a logically consistent Schopenhauerianism. His principle of method is the following: "Where a philosopher makes two contradictory assertions, both cannot be accepted for his real and true meaning, but only one of them, and the other must then be regarded as abandoned by his true meaning." [3] Frauenstädt would thus deliberately ignore the plurality of conflicting motives in Schopenhauer's philosophy, all genuine, and requiring for a true synthesis more than the use of a blue pencil. His procedure is thus radically different from Hartmann's, who rightly takes him to task for making Schopenhauer's thought less inconsistent but also "emptier and more meager." [4]

While Mainländer and Bahnsen, as we shall see, develop Schopenhauer's doctrine of the will into a pluralistic metaphysics, Frauenstädt on the whole adheres to the dominantly monistic tone of *The World as Will and Idea.* But, in distinction from the determined pessimism of these two, Frauenstädt departs so far from his master as to fight shy of the very term 'pessimism.' He resists the near-Brahmanic illusionism of Schopenhauer's subjective-idealistic theory of knowledge, and with his more serious trust in knowledge is to be found a more positive estimate of the world-process. Like Schopenhauer he champions compassion, but his ethics does not point to a nihilistic finale; he tones down decidedly his master's threnody.

In order to proceed from Schopenhauer towards a philosophic affirmation, one needs a different method and a different attitude towards Schopenhauer than is evidenced in Frauenstädt's attempted revision of his master's philosophy. Carl Du Prel proposes an idea, fertile with possibilities which are not adequately worked out. He would welcome suffering as a discipline of the individual will that should bring it to renunciation; his Nirvana, however, is not one of annihilation but "the transcendental order of things, which is also not attained by quietism, but rather by restless activity on the battlefield. . . . Not in itself, therefore, should the will-to-live be renounced, though indeed every stage of progress attained by it should be renounced, not in favor of the nothing, but in favor of a higher stage, and that this may happen have we placed ourselves in this world of preponderating suffering."[5] More instructive in our study of the aftermath of Schopenhauer is the vaster and more critical undertaking of Eduard von Hartmann discussed in our last chapter. We shall now turn to examine briefly two really amazing developments of Schopenhauerian will-metaphysics: Mainländer's individualistic salvation-philosophy of the Will-to-die, and Bahnsen's dialectical irrational pluralism, the philosophy of irreducible cosmic contradiction and conflict. To offset and to set off the heroic speculative irresponsibility of these two, a briefer mention will first be made of a more moderate apologist for pessimism, Agnes Taubert.

II

Agnes Taubert's father was, like Hartmann's, a general of artillery. The friendship of the parents brought the young people together, and from the very first Eduard and Agnes shared a common attitude towards life and a common purpose. They married in 1871. Agnes was not only a devoted wife and mother, but also an effective champion of pessimism on her own account. How effective and how independent, may be judged from the fact that her little book of 164 pages, *Der Pessimismus und seine Gegner*, which appeared in 1873, four years before her death, won for her a distinct, if modest, place in the history of nineteenth century pessimism. While writing explicitly in answer to some eight critics of Hartmann, she did not write as Hartmann's wife; the initial *A.* Taubert on the title-page hid her identity from those not intimate with Hartmann's family, and he did not go out of his way to reveal it, so that for years writers referred to her as a man. It has been suggested that Agnes Taubert did wield a masculine pen. She wrote more clearly and more vigorously than Hartmann; Heymons, their publisher, thought that she influenced her husband's writing for the better by making it more direct and to the point. Hartmann declared that she first set the pessimistic issue on the scientific path.

Taubert eschews romancing, metaphysical or other flights, and keeps resolutely to experience. The question of the value of life she would answer by surveying the alleged sources of it. The question is considered in explicitly hedonistic terms: "Is life worth living?" means "Does life yield positive happiness?" She counts her many blessings one by one, and finds them mostly misnomers. Youth, health, freedom, prosperity, love and benevolence, enjoyment of nature, aesthetic and moral satisfaction, the joys of the hereafter, social progress: these leave the balance of happiness decidedly negative. Taubert's survey is more objective than that of her betters; she does not gloat miserably over this miserable world, and she is not grudging in her recognition of weal wherever she finds it. No optimist could desire a more eloquent account of the improvement in the everyday life of the European masses during the last two centuries than is to be found in her tenth chapter. Progress is a reality; living conditions are astonishingly better. But they have not made men happier. As Schopenhauer told us, the pleasure-bent will is insatiate; our racing desires outstrip our satisfactions through social progress, and leave us increasingly discontented.

It is precisely the optimistic delusion which sends people in futile pursuit of happiness and dooms them to disappointment and discontent. Pessimism, far from being a cheerless philosophy of life, is rather the source of true consolation in such a world as ours. For is not this, after all, the one important question: "How are we, the disillusioned, to live on?" To one who has truly perceived the futility of the pleasure-hunt, life can bring no disenchantment. Freed from their ignoble attachment to pleasure, the true moral worth and meaning and dignity of life, in friendship, science, and art, can express themselves and be realized. Without illusions and, if not gaily, at least cheerfully, men can devote their energies to the repression of selfishness and the alleviation of crying needs and flagrant miseries; even the available pleasures in life are doubly cherished in their dark frame, and no petulant discontent poisons and degrades human life. To disillusioned and deliberate intelligence pessimism is thus not only a gospel of peace but a call to noble activity. According to Taubert, pessimism "stimulates us most effectively not only to endure life, but to live it to the full in a manner truly worthy of man." [6]

Hartmann criticized this hopefulness: "Taubert will not hear of a negative goal of evolution, but rather finds the immanent aim of the culture-process in the alleviation of suffering, and thus admits . . . a certain harmony between the common weal and the development of civilization, in decided contrast to my view of the antinomy between these two." [7] All the same we are bound to note the cheerful strain which comes occasionally, and rather reluctantly, from Hartmann's violoncello, and we may wonder whether, in the relation of Eduard von Hartmann and Agnes Taubert, the man's view of life was brightened or the woman's darkened. In Sully's judgment, "Taubert reads very much like an optimist who has made a mistake by stumbling into a system of pessimistic philosophy, and who vainly strives to extricate himself from the treacherous bog." [8]

III

Schopenhauer's attempted revision and completion of Kant's philosophy involved him, as we have seen, in serious difficulties. If the world of our experience is merely phenomenal, appearance, and our intelligence merely the tool of the one universal will-to-live which alone is ultimately real, if accordingly no change in character through enlightenment is conceivable, then how could we ever explain or admit the possibility of salvation through individual will-denial?

A reverent disciple of Kant and 'standing on Schopenhauer's shoulders,' but proceeding in a different direction from Hartmann, Philipp Batz (1841–1876), who wrote under the name of Mainländer, endeavors to provide a sound philosophical basis for his unwavering confidence in the reality and finality of self-salvation. Here is a profound pessimist profoundly convinced that there is a way out. The individual will is real; it can change its character through enlightenment and attain redemption—redemption through final self-extinction! This philosophy, as fantastic a fabric as speculative gloom perhaps ever spun out, is a metaphysical system of voluntaristic pluralism of the *Will-to-die.* Mainländer entitled his work *The Philosophy of Redemption.*

He sets out from the indisputable reality of the individual will. My own reality is alone axiomatic to me; the reality of all else is for me an inference, a conclusion, a conjecture, possibly an illusion. And when I say, I alone am indisputably real, I do not mean my body, my mind, my world: I mean the individual will which constitutes the ultimate reality and inmost kernel of my being. This, Mainländer holds, is the great truth; Kant and the Buddha approach it from different directions: Kant, by proving that all I can know, the world and myself in it, is phenomenal appearance; Buddha, by completing this truth with the doctrine of Karma: real alone is Karma, the individual will-to-live. This last, in Mainländer's judgment, based exclusively upon his own peculiar interpretation of Spence Hardy's two works, *Manual of Buddhism* and *Eastern Monachism*, is the first axiom of esoteric Buddhism. He asks us also to believe that it is likewise the first truth of esoteric Christianity. Though Christ taught the reality of the external world, which Buddha denied, the central truth of both is the same: in Buddha, the inexpugnable reality of his karmic will; in Christ, the incarnation of God in him, God's only begotten Son. When Christ teaches, "Heaven and Earth shall pass away, but my words shall not pass away," he, like Buddha, is teaching absolute individualism: "I and the Father are one"—"I, Buddha, am God." The same axiom is uttered in a dark passage in the Upanishads, which is quoted by Schopenhauer: *Hae omnes creaturae in totum ego sum, et praeter me aliud ens non est.*[9]

So then we are told: for each individual there is only one indubitable reality: his own will. Gautama, to himself alone real, is to Mainländer perhaps a phantom; and to me now, writing at my desk, they are both phantoms, and my poor essay about them likewise a phantom; but indubitably real is my own self, my will: indubitably real to myself, but, in its turn, a phantom to you, gentle reader! Is this philosophical madness? Mainländer answers: "This is not an insane standpoint, but only one that could *drive one to insanity.*" [10] It is the standpoint of the mystics. So Angelus Silesius:

> I know that, but for me, God would not last a wink:
> Were I no more, He too must desolately sink! [11]

The essential egoism of the individual will, its self-engrossment and self-centeredness, is thus clearly accounted for. If we assume the reality of others, it is in order to make clear to ourselves the reality of our own will-efforts and will-conflicts. Buddha's view of others as really in need of redemption was essential to his own self-redemption. Thus Mainländer would reconcile what he calls esoteric and exoteric Buddhism. We begin with the indisputable reality of our own individual will, and we proceed to the assumption of other real individual wills.

But whence is this universe of coëxisting individual wills? Mainländer's answer to this question explains both his pessimism and his doctrine of salvation. He recognizes in the universe only clashing individual wills, and no God; his philosophy, as he tells us in the very preface to his work, is atheism. But it is also theism. While there *is* no God, in or out of the world, there *was* a God. This pluralistic world, which excludes the present reality of God, demands the assumption of God's pre-cosmic reality, as a condition of its coming into being.

We come now to Genesis I in Mainländer's philosophy and religion. "In the beginning was the Act," was Faust's version. It is also Mainländer's version. In the beginning was the act, the deed of God. What God—what deed? We can describe this pre-cosmic God as simple infinite unity. Its one single deed was to will its extinction, *Nichtsein.* As simple unity, however, God simply could not pass away. The accomplishment of this task required the disintegration or splitting up of the pre-cosmic divine unity into a multiplicity of individuals. This immense manifold world, then, has come into being in order that in and through it God's *Will-to-die* might be realized. So the first and last thing God ever did was to die: the cosmos is the instrumentality and the process of God's extinction: "God died, and his death was the life of the World." One is reminded of the destiny of Pan Ku, in old Chinese mythology. His death initiated the creation of the world. "His breath became the wind; his voice, the thunder; his left eye, the sun; his right eye, the moon; his blood flowed in rivers; his hair grew into trees and plants; his flesh became the soil; his sweat descended as rain; while the parasites which infested his body were the origin of the human race." [12]

What is an individual will, then? Ostensibly a will-to-live, unconscious or conscious drive or desire for self-preservation and self-enhancement; really, however, it is a striving for self-extinction, a will-to-die. This will-to-die, which Mainländer recognizes even in gases, fluids, and inorganic solids, is exhibited ever more clearly as we rise in the scale of being. In place of the law of the conservation of energy, he holds that energy is ever diminished and becomes extinct. The working out of the pre-cosmic God's expiration is manifest most completely in human life. Insatiate desire, ever luring us on the hunt for pleasure, and ever disclosing its futility, war and cruel industrial oppression of man by man, poverty, sickness, failure, old age, "the heartaches and the thousand natural shocks that flesh is heir to," all goad us into a realization of the essential infelicity of common sensual life. On the other hand, the occasional blessedness of whole-hearted benevolence, the bliss of the saint, the exquisite joy of aesthetic creation and contemplation, the pure perception of truth in science, the generous struggle for the emancipation of man from political and economic oppression: these all serve to fill us with a wistful sense of what life would be, were it not futile individual craving. Our very joys, even the noblest, serve to confirm us in our essential will-to-die; they show us what is better than insatiate desire, and thereby disclose to us what is best of all and alone good in the end.

"He that increaseth knowledge increaseth sorrow," wrote Ecclesiastes, and Mainländer's estimate of the course of human culture sustains his view. "The principal law of civilization is pain; the will is thus weakened and spirit is enhanced. It continually educates man, and makes him ever more susceptible to pain. . . . Civilization . . . kills. As bleached bones mark the road through the desert, so the monuments of collapsed culture-realms, indicating the death of millions, mark the course of civilization." The cultural and spiritual perfection of man is a preparation for the rejection of life: "To be a philosopher, means to learn to die: this is the last conclusion of wisdom." [13] The eyes of the sage incline towards the grave. So, in the poem *Lázaro* of the Colombian poet José Asuncion Silva, the dead Lazarus weeps for joy when Jesus brings him back to life, but four weeks later find him wandering among the tombs of the old cemetery, wishing he were there again.

A pessimist is a man who is ripe for death. Through enlightenment he has been emancipated from the egoistic insatiate greed; his will has thus been transformed, and moral enthusiasm has possessed his being. This complete change of character, as Mainländer maintains against his master Schopenhauer, is not only possible, but is an outstanding fact essential to morality and religion. This utter penetration and possession of the will by the truth that life is an evil and that it were better not to be: this is the philosophical denial of the individual will-to-live. [14] And as man perceives unmistakably the essential evil of life, so he also sees clearly the way out. The "great sad voice" from the dark pulpit of James Thomson's *City of Dreadful Night* has a word of grim cheer:

O Brothers of sad lives! they are so brief;
A few short years must bring us all relief:

> Can we not bear these years of labouring breath?
> But if you would not this poor life fulfill,
> Lo, you are free to end it when you will,
> Without the fear of waking after death.

Mainländer does not agree with Schopenhauer regarding suicide. He would not bar the exit which even the Stoic left open to overtaxed misery. But, while he rejects Schopenhauer's idea that the individual life is only a phenomenon and that the cosmic will survives the act of suicide, and holds against his master that the individual will is real and that it does find final end of all its sorrows in death, Mainländer points to a higher path out of the stinking morass of life. For how can I seek extinction for myself when I leave others after me in the bog? Indeed only the childless one is really extinguished in suicide, for the others continue their wretched careers in their children. The suicide deprives himself of the chance of teaching others the true gospel. To end life really, we must end its perpetuation. This is Mainländer's sovereign remedy: complete continence, and he becomes the avowed arch-apostle of virginity as supreme and final virtue. The hour of destiny is not the hour of death, but the hour when man faces the question: shall I or shall I not become responsible for the beginning of another life, for the forging of another link in the wretched chain of individual existence? The eulogy of virginity he finds in the gospel of Buddha and of Christ, of all great and true religion, and the wisest of men have recognized it, even while admitting their own failure to attain unto the lofty practice. He quotes to this effect a striking page from Humboldt's memoirs. Complete chastity delivers us from "the bond that binds us most firmly to the world": [15] and his one gratitude is that he has been enabled in word and deed to share and to answer the call of Orestes, in Goethe's *Iphigenia aus Tauris*, which he uses as the motto for the metaphysical sections in his philosophy:

> I thank you, O ye gods,
> That you have destined me in childlessness
> To die my death.—And hearken thou to me,
> Love not the sun nor yet the stars too dearly.
> Come, down with me to the dark realm descend. . . .
> Come, childless, guiltless follow me, descend! [16]

Mainländer, ranking with Goethe the poet of *Parzival*, which he calls the most profound poem in the world, would revive the Order of the Holy Grail, consecrated to the pursuit of the four cardinal virtues: love of country, justice, lovingkindness, and chastity, the last being the summit of perfection:

> If the Grail's sign thou wouldst bear,
> Woman's love thou must forswear. [17]

He urges the virgin soul, man or woman, to prize its unflecked purity above all else in life: he counsels those who are already parents at least to direct their children into the path of childless salvation. He does not advocate the hermit's life for all. "One will withdraw completely from the world, will escape into solitude and will mortify himself like a religious penitent, convinced that only a constantly humbled will can persist in renunciation; another one will keep on with his calling; a third will, just as before, dry the tears of the unfortunate with word and deed; a fourth will fight for his nation or for all mankind, will invest his utterly disdained life in the work of hastening the attainment of the ideal state in which alone the redemption of all can take place." [18]

So Mainländer, in the prophet's seat, surveys the future. Socialism, as it brings ever nearer economic justice and universal education, will bring men ever nearer the light. A time will come when all men will freely enter into the world of Shakespeare and Goethe, will understand Kant and Schopenhauer, will learn the truth of life from Buddha and Christ. A time will come when men and women will live together as brothers and sisters, in pure intellectual union without any carnal stain, working side by side, or else in solitude, for the hastening of the great extinction for which the whole creation groans. And in the death of everyone that dies chaste, the pre-cosmic God's will-to-die will have attained unto fulfillment. Thus ever nearer on the horizon gleams the New Jerusalem of esoteric Christianity, gleams the Buddhist Nirvana, the City of Peace in Extinction. "In the heart of things, the immanent Philosopher sees in the entire cosmos only the deepest longing for complete extinction; it is as if he heard clearly the call that pierces all the celestial spheres: Redemption! Redemption! Death to our Life! and the cheering reply: you *all* will find extinction and will be redeemed!" [19]

I have been content to give in brief outline the pessimistic philosophy of salvation of one who has not been sure even of a sentence in the histories of philosophy. Its fantastic quality and its speculative unrestraint lend it a certain exotic interest, and, despite its frequently warped versions of philosophic and religious commonplaces, it as frequently manifests keen and revealing insight. Mainländer's book needs wide margins, for the reader who is not carried away by the author's ardent style is bound to register serious objections. Why proceed from the declaration of the ultimate reality of the individual wills to the assumption of a pre-cosmic simple divine unity; and what can be the metaphysical status of a reality whose entire career is chronicled in the one statement that it willed its own extinction? What basis in fact is there in this "scientifically established atheism and pessimism" for the doctrine of the gradual diminution of energy and for the pessimistic-salvational exploitation of this doctrine? Should one criticize, or should one merely state, without comment, Mainländer's version of esoteric Christianity as cosmotheistic atheism? In the Doctrine of the Trinity he makes a "small grammatical substitution":

Athanasius taught: "God is, the Christ is, the Holy Ghost is." Mainländer: "God *was;* Christ is (=this World); the Holy Ghost is—God's Way to Extinction!"[20] Or should one take any notice of the fantastic if somewhat shamefaced Utopianism of Mainländer's esoteric evangel? The reign of God the Father lasted about 4000 years, and the reign of Christ about half as long, 2000 years: therefore the reign of the Holy Ghost should be half of that or about 1000 years, at the end of which time all mankind is to be saved through extinction! Mainländer informs us further that, after mankind's cessation through complete continence, animal life and plant life will follow in the path of extinction, and then the lower forms of being, until all that is shall lapse into non-being, absolute void, *nihil negativum. "It is finished!"* [21]

With regard to Mainländer's sovereign remedy, Hartmann has observed, much to the point, that, if it is precisely through enlightenment that one is led to recognize and to embrace the ideal of complete chastity, this ideal will be embraced, at least at the outset, only by a select enlightened minority. Should these select few die childless, it would only mean that generation after generation the utterly unredeemed sensual majority of mankind will survive and reproduce itself, so that, instead of leading to the salvation of mankind, Mainländer's plan, if followed, would "simply serve to make humanity more and more animal, would contribute to the ascendency of stupidity and brutality over intelligence and morality." [22] Hartmann has likewise pointed out Mainländer's failure to reconcile his two moral principles of egoism, necessary expression of the genuinely real individual will, and the individual's whole-hearted devotion to the common weal, to the Whole: the reconciliation of the endeavor after self-redemption with the struggle for universal redemption thus remains unachieved.[23]

The peculiar significance and interest of Mainländer's

views are due to his fundamental attitude expressed in the very title of his work, *Die Philosophie der Erlösung*. He is a pessimistic salvationist. He begins with Schopenhauer's gospel of deliverance from the will-to-live, and to this end endeavors to revise and reconstruct the metaphysical groundwork of his master. Becker, Frauenstädt, and other disciples of Schopenhauer speculated how the cosmic will could be really curbed and denied; Mainländer asked: Since the will does really curb and extinguish itself, what sort of a will is it? His individualistic metaphysics is the answer. Salvationism is the central note of Mainländer's thought, and this salvationism leads him occasionally to vacillate in his pessimism. Even aside from the fact that he confessed his own happiness in his pessimistic chaste apostolate, and as late as one month before his death wrote of his "peaceful solitude" in which he was "so unutterably happy," [24] his objective estimate of human life is not as pessimistic as either Schopenhauer's or Hartmann's. In his critique of the latter,—an attack abounding in clean hits, but marred by bitter sarcasm and invective,—he challenges Hartmann's 'first stage of illusion.' Not all alleged happiness is illusory, he tells the philosopher of the Unconscious: "You treat the pleasures of art and science as illusory; here I must decidedly dissent. These pleasures are so pure and fine that, if man could abide in them *forever*, life would be the highest good."[25] But Mainländer looks forward with assurance to the day when every workingman will know his Goethe and his Kant, and he firmly holds the will to be capable of transformation through enlightenment. If art and science and the higher spiritual life generally can be made the increasingly universal possession of man, and if in them are pure bliss and beauty, then how could, or why should the progressively enlightened will reject life? Instead of willing the cessation of high spiritual endeavor in order to end the coarse miseries of life, may it not, should it not rather, at whatever cost of pain or apparent outward defeat, cherish and cleave to the higher values of life, and because of them bless life for the gold despite the dross?

These hints of possible lines of criticism may serve to indicate the almost bewildered sense of cosmological and axiological confusion with which the reader of Mainländer is left. Particularly striking here is the significant feature of philosophies of despair to which we cannot too often call attention, for the further study of it may well lead us to the very heart of our problem. Pessimism is in Mainländer's case a sort of devotion. He cherishes so passionately the higher values that to see them contaminated by the coarse fabric of life drives him to black despair; while on the other hand, his perception of his own ability to understand and to reject the polluted evil business of living gives him a grim sense of exaltation, akin to religious fervor, which has a sustaining quality of its own. On Mainländer's altar of nothingness the flame of pessimistic devotion burns so ardently that the spectator ponders and pities, but remains unconvinced regarding the finality of the philosophy of despair.

IV

Julius Frauenstädt modifies and mollifies the pessimism of his master Schopenhauer; but Julius Bahnsen departs from Schopenhauer's letter only in order to emphasize the asperity of his spirit. Towards the end of his life Schopenhauer assumed a pontifical manner: in Bahnsen he certainly had a disciple 'more Catholic than the Pope.'[26] Yet this ultra-Schopenhauerian was brought up on Hegelianism, and, at least formally, undertakes the same technical task which engaged Hartmann: a synthesis of Hegel and Schopenhauer. A comparison of the radically different ways in which this task is accomplished by Bahnsen and by Hartmann would exhibit the essential opposition between the two and would be of added interest owing to the fact that Bahnsen was stimulated in the delineation of his theory by his contact with Hartmann.

Hartmann, as we have observed, regards Hegel's Idea and Schopenhauer's Will as the two aspects or attributes of the one substantial metalogical Unconscious. In his own philosophy, he believes, Hegel and Schopenhauer correct and complete each other. Bahnsen, however, would revise Hegel by capitalizing the irrational or Schopenhauerian moment in the Hegelian dialectic, and he would complete Schopenhauer by excising from his philosophy the last vestiges of rationalism. The Hegelian dialectic, as we know, is a process in which the essentially rational character of reality is progressively elicited. This logical character of the dialectic Hartmann accentuates and adopts as one fundamental character of his Unconscious. This logical character precisely is what Bahnsen repudiates: the dialectic of the world-process, according to him, is not a logical dialectic, explicitly or implicitly; the ultimate reality is Will, and it is not logical in any ultimate sense. The dialectic of the world-process is the clash of Will with itself, an irrational and irremediable conflict; it is a dialectic of Will and actuality. Bahnsen calls it a *Realdialektik,* to distinguish it from the mere concept-dialectic of the Hegelians. Thus he would out-Hegel Hegel in the interests of his master Schopenhauer.[27]

The essential doctrine of Bahnsen affirms the clash and contradiction in the Will-Reality of the world, and negates its fundamentally logical character. His main work is entitled *Der Widerspruch im Wissen und Wesen der Welt,* and its first volume begins with this quotation from Shakespeare's *Troilus and Cressida;*

> O madness of discourse,
> That cause sets up with and against itself!
> Bifold authority! where reason can revolt

> Without perdition, and loss assume all reason
> Without revolt: this is and is not. . . .
> . . . that a thing inseparate
> Divides more wider than the sky and earth.[28]

There is no meaning in the world-process, no far-off divine event, no real teleology of whatever sort. Hartmann's evolutionary optimism is thus entirely rejected by Bahnsen. We cannot speak of development or purpose or final goal in the universe: the world is not a cosmos but a chaos of clashing will-strains, an "inextricable tangle of contradictions of the most tragic negativity." [29]

The thoroughgoing irrationalism of Bahnsen leads him even beyond his master. He casts aside the Kantian idealism and the monism of Schopenhauer. The Will-Reality is not one, and manifests in its activity no unity of character. The Will eternally tears itself in self-partition (*Selbstentzweiung*); reality is eternally at war with itself. "The logically impossible is actual fact, and the logically necessary is in actuality ruled out." [30] Schopenhauer's picture of history as an endless cat-fight (*Katzbalgerei*) is here elaborated into a metaphysic: "a pluralistic, anti-logical, real-dialectical individualism." [31]

Irrational atheistic individualism, a world-view of the meaningless eternally self-tormenting and self-rending chaos of will-forces: a dismal view of a woeful and futile world: miserabilism is a mild name for it. "The primal mystery of the Will consists in this, that it finds peace nowhere except in the unrest of ever-impetuous striving despite all frustration." [32] Here at last is unblushing and unreluctant pessimism; it repudiates the notion of development as a vestige of optimism, and would put no trust in salvation through hope in progress or even through self-denial. Salvation through art and science is likewise disdained as illusory: these are no higher or deeper visions into the nature of reality; in an irrational world they are vain phantoms, and the thought of their ultimate futility only deepens the woe as it poisons the initial joy of the enlightened mind. Even morality, compassion, denial of the will are no final goals, nor do they avail to save us from the irremediably self-centered and self-conflicting Will, "The law and the prophets demand that I love my neighbor *as myself:* so much of selfishness must needs remain in all benevolence." [33] To Hartmann's three stages of illusion Bahnsen adds a fourth: the illusory hope of any kind of redemption, whether through individual or cosmic will-denial, here or hereafter, eudaemonologically or teleologically: all these are vain, adolescent dreams of an awakening from the nightmare of existence. The perversity of the world is congenital and beyond repair. You may observe and delineate it: redeem it you cannot. "The goal of all ideal striving is, essentially, the metaphysically impossible." [34]

Bahnsen's pessimistic individualism very naturally directed his attention to characterology, in which he attained some distinction. His character studies, and in particular his sketches of Shakespeare's women, exhibit a Schopenhauerian eye for the dark sides of human life, but without Schopenhauer's clarity or force of expression. Bahnsen writes aphorisms burdened with parentheses and manifold illustrations and asides; his style has the vices without the virtues of Nietzsche's. It is gloomy writing, and the author vainly protests his personal cheerfulness. His intellectual autobiography, *Wie ich wurde, was ich ward,* is a record of disappointments personal, domestic, patriotic, literary, academic: brief cantos of an unmelodious epic of tribulation and woe. A devoted Schleswiger, he was forced to submit to detested Prussian dominion; his wife, whom he worshipped, died seventeen months after their marriage, and his second marriage was unhappy. A Tübingen doctor of philosophy, he hoped in vain for an academic career. "Bahnsen, Bahnsen, where are your chances?" [35] his comrades would call to him, and he lived and died a miserably paid, snubbed and maltreated school-teacher, the victim of small-town intrigues and petty tyrannies. He lived to see Hartmann rise to fame by betraying, as he believed, the cause of true pessimism and by dubious self-advertising practices, while his own books either did not get published, or did not get reviewed, or did not sell, or came out inopportunely, or collapsed through the bankruptcy of the publisher.

He admits that his tongue, when occasion demanded it, could be ruthlessly cutting,[36] but he insists that his pessimism is not merely the expression of a sour mood, but a soundly established philosophy of life. The systematic criticism of his doctrine has been a particular object of Hartmann. Are the "henads," as Bahnsen calls the clashing individual will-forces, mere results of the self-partition of the Cosmic Will, which, for all its self-rending, remains ultimately one? Or are the henads ultimate in their own right, that is, monads? All the difficulties in which Leibniz's monadism is involved confront us here, plus the prime difficulty of Bahnsen's essential irrationalism. If the henads have aseity, the doctrine of their conflict and the primal Will's self-partition require serious revision; if the henads are but individual functionings of the one primal Will, then Bahnsen's pluralism loses metaphysical status.[37]

But, one may ask, how can such dilemmas affect a philosopher who begins by disclaiming any rhyme or reason in the universe? Of more concern to our study of Bahnsen's pessimism than his henadism would be the essential irrationalism of the doctrine. It is of interest to observe, and it is a point that requires further attention, that the more pronounced the irrationalism of a pessimist is, the more unqualified seems to be his pessimism: witness Hartmann—Schopenhauer—Bahnsen. Certainly no real value can be expected from a world conceived as utterly irrational and meaningless. This is James Thomson's "sense more tragic than defeat and blight," in *The City of Dreadful Night:*

> The sense that every struggle brings defeat
> Because Fate holds no prize to crown success;
> That all the oracles are dumb or cheat
> Because they have no secret to express;
> That none can pierce the vast black veil uncertain
> Because there is no light beyond the curtain;
> That all is vanity and nothingness.

Bahnsen's philosophy is a dolorous elaboration of his first epigram written at the age of seventeen, in 1847, "the year of his birth as a philosopher": "Man is only a self-conscious Nothing." [38] Huber calls this nihilistic philosophy "the utmost extreme to which pessimism has gone, or for that matter could go." [39] Bahnsen himself, in his character-study of Lady Macbeth, quotes Shakespeare's words which he calls "an instinctive paraphrase of abstract nihilism": [40]

> Life's but a walking shadow. . . .
> . . . It is a tale
> Told by an idiot, full of sound and fury,
> Signifying nothing.

In such a world of self-rending, meaningless actuality, how is one to live his life? Bahnsen answers: "Not to despair is the surest mark of spiritual might: without hope, to live as if one still hoped, . . ." [41] and furthermore, to smile at one's futile fortitude. The only pessimism worthy of the name is a pessimism tragically earnest and at the same time grimly humorous: I am a puppet in the hands of Infinite Perversity, and there is absolutely no way out of it, but I know it, and so take the puppet-play in which I take a part with a sense of humor; I laugh at the puller of the strings,—and this is my revenge.[42] But in a world of hopeless irrationality what would justify Bahnsen's high estimate of this tragic-humorous attitude, or the preference for any attitude over any other? In the meaningless puppet-play of existence, has any puppet's philosophy any meaning, or any puppet's reaction any value?

CHAPTER XIV

A GRADATIONAL VIEW OF THE NATURE OF EVIL

I

It is a sound principle of criticism that a philosophy of life, however large the body of particular evidence on which it bases its conclusions, however close the abstract consistency of its principles, yet falls short of adequacy so long as it cannot account for itself. On this reef many a philosophical system is shipwrecked: consistent materialism, for instance. The materialistic account of the world involves the exclusion of intelligence and its values as ultimate aspects of reality. In a world thus conceived, all theory and all truth would be so much 'weather,' and therefore materialistic philosophy and its claim to truth would become either meaningless or self-contradictory.

As our survey of the philosophies of disdain and despair has repeatedly shown, this sort of self-refutation is flagrantly manifested in unqualified pessimism. The pessimist cannot assume the 'naturalistic' actualism and indifference to alleged values in which the materialist is apt to seek refuge. His is a tragic philosophy, and the more dismal his account of the crowding evils of life, the more intense his disgust with wretched existence, the more unreserved his negation of the reality of good,—the more amazing should his own philosophy appear to himself. For what is more assuredly admirable than noble disdain and worthy resistance? As we have observed more than once, an utterly worthless world would not admit of being condemned, and the world is not devoid of real value, at any rate not so long as it includes upright and forthright contemners of itself.

Schopenhauer, Hartmann, Mainländer, Bahnsen, and all the gray cloud of witnesses thus unwittingly and to a greater or less extent point elsewhere than they intend. Were all the facts of life as dark as the pessimistic survey portrays them, and were all men bovine in their dull response, the world might perhaps deserve the pessimist's stern verdict. But that stern verdict itself, manifesting as it does a sense and a standard of worth higher than bovine dullness, is a fact which compels reconsideration of the case. Even if no other reason were available, pessimistic philosophy itself, in so far as it is a reasoned protest and more than a mere moan and troubled weather, would alone refute the extreme pessimistic condemnation of life. This is of course the ancient paradox of scepticism. The sceptic's only refuge is in being passively non-committal: the first word he utters in advocacy of his doctrine, his own defense of it serves to disprove it. For it is the assertion of no mean degree of knowledge, to affirm than no knowledge is to be had. Utter and aggressive nihilism in the field of value, whether theoretical or practical, in consistency negates itself.

Again and again in our previous discussion, and now once more at the beginning of this concluding chapter, attention has been called to this aspect and implication of pessimistic philosophy. It were sorry pedantry, however, if we were to remain satisfied with the exhibition of this pessimistic paradox. Reasoned dissatisfaction with life does reveal one variety of heroic reaction which, in resisting evil, reaffirms positive worth and the tragic dignity of life; but shall we deny that it also reveals wellnigh insurmountable obstacles to positive worth which it were dull complacency to ignore? Not so easily is pessimism reasoned out of court. If its own noble disdain disproves the finality of its verdict, yet even more clearly does it disclose the shallowness of the ostrich philosophy of placid or stubborn contentment, the pitiable sense of security of a head buried in the sands of dogmatism and eyes closed to the grim actualities of existence. This double wisdom pessimism and tragedy teach us: thus imposing on us the weight of the world's woe and the problems that it raises, cosmological, ethical, religious.

II

The affirmation of the illusoriness or the mere finitude of evil may be dictated by various motives and may reflect different and even partly conflicting spiritual moods: a theologian's jealousy for the spotless character of his one omnipotent God, a pantheist's mystical disdain of what eyes can see when open, an insistent absolutist or quasi-aesthetic demand for the harmonious and perfect finality of the cosmos, a complacent or a neurotic persistence in pronouncing reality fundamentally and ultimately good and all alleged evil mere appearance and error.

The theological predicament issues from the necessity of recognizing and indeed emphasizing evil, the misery and sin of unredeemed man, while at the same time holding the Creator all-perfect and blameless. An explicit imputation of sin and an intense consciousness of our evil state is indispensable to a religion of salvation. "Wretched man that I am!" St. Paul exclaims, setting the tone of a hundred saints' lamentations. But the more extreme the saint's abhorrence of sin and of 'the World,' the more resolute is his insistence that God is nowise responsible for evil.

The intellectual and moral perplexity resulting from this duality of conviction directs theology in different ways. Piety may seek an escape from its embarrassment in virtual or in explicit dualism. So the Zoroastrian, holding fast to the antithesis of good and evil, refusing to admit that these two could have the same source and ground, and regarding Ahura-Mazda as infinitely good and the creator of good, postulated a counter creative power, Ahriman, to account for the presence of evil in the world. So Manicheanism, combining Persian with Greek ideas, assailed and left lasting scars in Christian theology, capitalizing the Christian disdain of the flesh and 'the World' into a dualistic doctrine of God and Matter. But, while theological dualism, referring good and evil to opposed cosmic sources, would thus safeguard the moral reputation of God, in the end it also allows monism to prevail. Evil is real, it is alien to God and opposed to God, but it does not deserve to be real and it will not prevail. In the end Ahura-Mazda's hosts will utterly destroy Ahriman's band; the world will be purged of all evil, and only pure good will remain. If a grim sense of the moral struggle dictated a dualist theology to the Zoroastrian, a confident meliorism enabled him to look forward to a monistic finale.

The aggressive monism of Augustinian and Calvinist Christianity is involved in serious dilemmas. In branding human free will as the real cause of evil in the world, this sort of theology may treat man as having cosmic initiative, thus showing only imperfect emancipation from dualism or pluralism. Or else it may rely on the explanation of evil as mere privation of the good, in order to secure an antithesis between good and evil serious enough to serve the purposes of a solemn doctrine of salvation, but without incriminating God or jeopardizing the essential monism of the system. This and subsidiary perplexities, and the disposal of them, engage theologians Catholic and Protestant, and the number of alternative solutions is scarcely exhausted. If one group of apologists seem to deserve Job's ironical designation, advocates for God, another group, growing of late, appear to be touched with Job's own tragic concern for moral integrity, the more tragic owing to the vastly increased range of human existence and accountability in Christian as distinguished from Jewish vistas. Do the facts of life easily rule out undeserved suffering? Is the world's course really a pageant of Divine Providence and steady justice? Are storms, earthquakes, hurricanes and pestilence and the thousand less lurid but no less ruthless blights that afflict and destroy human life explained away so readily as just consequences of man's first disobedience and the fruit of that forbidden tree? Does Eternal Loving Justice, lovingly electing some undeserving children of Adam to grace, justly allow multitudes of other undeserving children of Adam to expiate in person the inherited consequences of Adam's alleged free will in which they themselves had no part and lot?

The moral enormities which these questions challenge have led some modern minds, in their reaction particularly against Calvinist rigidity, to manifest readiness for radical departures in theology. This world of ours impressed William James as too various to allow of being summed up, either as to substance or character, in any monistic formula. In this world real good is to be found, and flagrant evil, one as real as the other, and likewise a vast region of manifold gray indifference, the realm of non-committal actual nature. In this multiverse evil is not to be argued out of existence; it is real enough and calls for real opposition, else the moral struggle is superfluous and the tragedy of life a farce in wretched taste. "It *feels* like a real fight,—as if there were something really wild in the Universe which we, with all our idealities and faithfulnesses are needed to redeem." [1] The best we have a right to hope, is that the struggle, real and hard enough, is yet not futile, that possibly and in ways at present unknown to us this half-wild and half-saved Universe is ever more truly being redeemed. In this process of redemption grace is no divine gift of which we are the passive recipients, but "God himself . . . may draw vital strength and increase of very being from our fidelity." [2]

Without the rigid cosmogony of Zoroastrian dualism, this frankly and flexibly pluralistic conception of a Finite Deity represents a certain interesting strain in modern religious thought: the tendency to safeguard and justify moral heroism by heroic sacrifices in monistic theology. Infinity, omnipotence, creationism, all have to go, that in the end God may remain the first and chief upholder of an order that is worthy to prevail. Yet even James needs more assurance than he is prepared to claim: the assurance, for instance, that the natural order of physical science is "not ultimate but . . . the external staging of a many-storied universe in which spiritual forces have the last word and are eternal." [3] Act on this assurance, he counsels us, and your very act serves to justify the assurance.

James' heroic doctrine is explicitly not the terminus but a signpost of cosmic speculation. Does it point to no more than half-hesitant half-trustful meliorism? Can it lead to a demand for fuller vindication of that deserved and prevailing dominance of spiritual forces to which it hopefully aspires? Can it secure the more flexible frame of pluralistic cosmology without lapsing into the vagaries of polytheism? These questions suggest a more ultimate systematic point: Is the notion of a finite god the sole residuary legatee in the alleged liquidation of the monistic estate in theology? Or may it not be that the collapse of philosophical and theological absolutism calls for a radical revision of monism in more concrete and explicitly dynamic terms rather than for its abandonment in favor of nondescript pluralism? Even he who, with good reason, holds to this second alternative should not fail to acknowledge the wholesome emphasis which the modern pluralist has put on this variously real, concrete world of experience, and the pluralist's refusal to call black white or to abuse the moral vocabulary.

III

The conviction that our day-by-day life is beset with evil assumes a radically different meaning in absolutist minds. Recognize the sphere and range of evil, we are advised; it is in and of the day-by-day, it is a characteristic of finite experience and limited to it. Evil is essentially finitude; in the infinite perfection of Ultimate Reality it is somehow absorbed and transcended. Whether in the ancient form of Brahmanic pantheism or in its more modern absolutist versions, this sort of philosophy has been led by the very errors and evils that embroil our finite world to depreciate the reality of the finite. The world in which errors and evils abound is itself an error, an illusion, Maya. Transcending and sublimating it is the infinite and perfect Absolute. That even a monadistic philosophy like that of Leibniz yielded to the lure of this sort of theodicy only indicates the wide range of its influence.

This view has already caused us grave misgivings. The description of evil as essentially imperfection or limitation of finite being, the reduction of the antithesis good-evil to infinite-finite, replacing as it does a moral by a metaphysical distinction, virtually dismisses all the moral or value-aspects of the problem. If 'evil' in the end is merely finitude, then 'good' presumably is but infinitude, and it is hard to see how the Infinite is really *good:* a serious matter for theology; but, more serious for philosophy, it is hard to see what room is left for the recognition of any value or what meaning attaches to the very 'perfection' of the Absolute, to assure which all finite evidence has been so loftily ruled out of court. Absolutism, setting out religiously to exalt God, is thus apt to find itself, after all its pious renunciations of our unworthy world, forced at last to face a stark actualism in which things simply are, finite or infinite, with nothing really worthy or unworthy. Thus is Gospel judgment visited on him who would know and exalt infinite God and begins by ignoring his finite brother.

To be sure, we may, with Spinoza, confront and accept reality as that which simply *is*, inviting analysis of its structure and contemplation of its infinity, but ultimately precluding evaluation in terms of good and evil, terms strictly human in reference and connotation. But in that case our deep appreciation of Spinoza's noble ethics will be sustained only if we neglect the metaphysics on which it is supposed to rest. If we interpret Spinoza to mean that values "while relative to men . . . are founded in the nature of things and are not arbitrary," [4] it is hard to see why they are not ultimately in and of the nature of things. But if we explicitly treat values as human inventions, then we may reflect that the perfection of rationality, as it leads us to see all things under the pattern of eternity, finally points to a consummation in which reason, completely emancipated from partiality and mere finitude, reaches, beyond good and evil, to the vision of Substance as it is and simply *is*, Eternal Actuality.

If we hold to this sort of metaphysics, a further difficulty confronts us, itself twofold in character. Whatever their real cosmic status, good-evil are convincingly real in so-called finite experience. Pronounce them partly or wholly illusory: if you propose in their place a view of reality that precludes worth in the distinctive sense of the term, that concentrates on analysis and explanation and dismisses evaluation, what ground do you have for urging your view as true and thus as worthy of being preferred to the view which you would abandon? So in the end evaluation in some sense persists even in the most determined 'naturalism.'

Another side of this difficulty is even more disturbing. Calling a thing 'merely finite' or illusory does not really dispose of it. What is the relation of this merely finite manifestation to the Ultimate Reality that is thus distortedly and illusorily manifested? Is it really alien to the essential character of the Absolute that it manifests itself in such an illusory manner? This difficulty is the more embarrassing the more pronounced our disgust with mere finitude and yet the more decidedly religious our attitude and procedure with respect to the Absolute. So Brahmanism was reluctant to deal with the problem, why the one universal Brahman should have become manifested in this Maya world of wretched particularity.

Some modern systems of absolutism have sought a monistic conclusion, not by the disdainful utter erasure of the finite or its mystic absorption in the Infinite, but by the more concrete relating of the two. In this attempted rapprochement idealistic systems of thought reveal varying degrees of respect for finite individuality and its values, from pronounced championship of personal-social categories as essential to a spiritual view of Reality, to a point of view from which "both the world of the intelligence and that of morality, both truth and goodness, turn into phenomenal appearances, that is, into things which manage to exist without being real, and which in becoming real and passing into the Absolute cease to exist."[5] But must value, in reaching its apogee, find also its extinction in the Perfection of the Absolute?

A caricature may sometimes bring out certain characteristic features of a physiognomy more effectively than a portrait. So some of the features of absolutism which we have been criticizing are exhibited flagrantly and without the balancing influence of a disciplined logic in the reckless and confused body of assertions and denials that constitutes the 'philosophy' of Christian Science. The alleged originality of Mrs. Eddy, no longer a tenable alternative after the publication of *The Quimby Manuscripts*,[6] is of no interest to us here. What interests us is the peculiar design of illusionism which

Mrs. Eddy adopted and embroidered as the thought-texture of her faith, in so far as it concerns the problems before us. Christian Science would solve the problem of evil by pronouncing our ills illusory, an error of 'mortal mind.' The evidence of experience to the contrary is rejected, since forsooth "health is not a condition of matter but of Mind; nor can the material senses bear reliable testimony on the subject of health." [7] Such error may be far-spread, as stubborn as it is pernicious, but when enlightened by the Truth man can overcome and transcend the illusion. We may labor under grievous delusions, as the founder-mother did when she wrote to Dr. Quimby about her "spinal inflammation and its train of sufferings gastric and bilious;" [8] but insight and illumination will show us as it showed her that disease is but error, and that, for instance, arsenic is poisonous only because of men's general delusion that it is a poison.

There is confusion at the outset here. If pain and sickness are but errors of mortal mind, then the alleged healing is a misnomer, and in the reported 'cures' the accounts of grievous ailments should most charitably be taken as concessions to the conventional speech of 'mortal mind.' [9] But the real trouble is deeper. Grant, as we readily do, the real service of Christian Science in calling general attention to the imaginary (but none the less evil!) psychopathic character of certain illnesses, overlook discrepancy or extravagance of statement, pass over the flagrant rejection of the testimony of immediate experience, strain credulity to the limit regarding fact and theory alike, and, notwithstanding all evidence or judgment to the contrary, affirm that suffering, disease, and other evils are mere error. All the same, does this view justify the complacent optimism in which it issues in theology or in social philosophy?

If the evils of life are but illusion, is this illusion aught but evil? That life should have real evils calling for real resistance, this man can understand and can gird up his loins. But, here is God's own world, really perfect, a very paradise did man but know it; and yet in this bower of bliss man labors under grievous illusions of harrowing alleged diseases, to his sorrow believing that arsenic is a poison, tortured apparently by the seeming suffering and decease of those he loves, and in the end like all men before him succumbing to the fixed delusion that he is dead. To entertain this view of the world as a diabolic deception of man, and, precisely by believing this doctrine, to be suave and complacent, cosmically and in practical social relations: this is surely a disclosure of the amazing illogical capacities of the human mind that a pessimist could well feature in his dismal exhibit.

To this variety of confused and reckless theodicy by fiat one may answer with the words of Galileo, *E pur se muove:* facts are not so easily argued out of existence. Or one may suggest the appropriateness of canonizing Bottom the Weaver for his proposal to notify the timorous ladies of *Midsummer Night's Dream* that the lion in his tragedy was no real lion but only Snug the Joiner in disguise. Or perhaps one may recommend, as further food for complacent enlightenment, Maupassant's little classic, *The Necklace,* the story of how Mathilde Loisel loses a diamond necklace borrowed from a friend, is kept by pride from confessing the loss, but instead borrows with her husband thirty-six thousand francs to purchase its duplicate, and is aged and broken by ten years' hard labor in paying back the money, only to learn, when in the end she tells her friend about it, that the original necklace was of paste diamonds, worth five hundred francs at most, and that the tragedy of its loss was only an error of mortal mind!

IV

If absolutism looks disdainfully over and beyond the troublous world of weekday experience to contemplate the Sabbath peace and perfection of the Eternal, hedonistic empiricism is wedded to the particular and reduces the problem of evil and of the worth of the cosmos to a question of pleasure-pain balance. Whether life is worth living, and whether one is to incline towards the Everlasting Yea or the Everlasting Nay, is judged to depend on this, whether pleasure outweighs pain or pain pleasure. So the philosophy of value turns out to be simply a matter of hedonistic metrics or bookkeeping.

Leaving out of account for the moment the ethical adequacy of the hedonistic calculus as a test of the worth of human life, and considering only the calculus itself, it promises more than it seems likely to deliver. The phrase 'pleasure-pain balance' suggests a claim to statistical precision, a standard of measure, reliable reckoning of amounts or units of pleasure and pain. Does our life actually allow of such a hedonistic audit and inventory?

It is clear that in such an attempted judgment on life lengthy jeremiads cannot be allowed to take the place of statistical reports. Human existence is vastly complex and various and may provide dismal exhibits to suit the most confirmed pessimist. Schopenhauer and Hartmann have shown us how much evil together with how little good can be crowded into a composite biography of Man. To him who needs no conviction the pessimistic account may seem conclusive, but to another, perhaps Matthew Arnold's, in *Empedocles on Etna:*

> Shall we, with temper spoil'd,
> Health sapp'd by living ill,
> And judgment all embroil'd
> By sadness and self-will,
> Shall *we* judge what for man is not true bliss or is?
>
> Is it so small a thing
> To have enjoy'd the sun,
> To have lived light in the spring,

> To have loved, to have thought, to have done;
> To have advanced true friends, and beat down baffling foes?

A 'scientific' statistical settlement of this issue seems unlikely. How unlikely, Paulsen intimated in his proposal, instead of judging human life wholesale, to estimate the hedonic balance of a man's single day's experiences: "A. Receipts in Pleasure: 1. Slept well—equal so many units; 2. Enjoyed my breakfast—; 3. Read a chapter from a good book—; 4. Received a letter from a friend—; etc. B. Pain: 1. Read a disagreeable story in the paper—; 2. Disturbed by a neighbor's piano—; 3. Received a tiresome visit—; 4. Ate burnt soup—; etc.—The philosopher is requested to insert the amounts in the proper places." [10] If you cannot enter the separate items, how can you be so sure about the totals, and is not your final estimate of the balance but a general impression, inadequately supported and unduly bilious, or else perhaps too sanguine? Petrarch's line, and the opposite which it suggests, should prove disturbing to hedonistic reckoning:

> A thousand joys don't make up for one torment.[11]

Hedonistic calculation is further complicated, as all critical readers of Jeremy Bentham know, by the fact that a man's estimate of a pleasure or a pain varies: it is different when anticipated, when actually experienced, when remembered. Shall we judge each experience on its merits, moment by moment? But moment by moment consciousness may be exhausted or dominated by an intense experience of pleasure or pain leaving little or no occasion for comparison or calculus. Or shall we rely on our cooler judgment in the matter? But what is it, and, even though it shows our erstwhile honey to be but wormwood in retrospect, can it alter the actual record of the former experience? And is it really wormwood even in retrospect?

> How sad and bad and mad it was,
> But then, how it was sweet! [12]

Or again, shall we let the impartial spectator judge for us? But who is he to be? Shall we choose a Hartmann, agreeing with him that if, despite the countless miseries of human life, men still live on contentedly, the reason is that they are too stupid to recognize their wretchedness? Or shall we rather select him or her who opined that the inner side of every cloud is bright and shining and so wore clouds inside out to show the lining?

Ruling out the probability of reaching a reliable computation of pleasure-pain units in our experience, Sully undertook to show that we may arrive at a fair notion respecting the pleasure-value of our life, thus "transforming the question 'Does pleasure exceed pain?' into the other question, 'Is happiness attainable?'" [13] But this shift of the question does not evade the difficulty raised by Hartmann's reflection just cited. Men are not intelligent enough to realize how unhappy they are, the pessimist declares, and the optimist maintains the very opposite. Hedonistic reckoning is thus complicated by the demand that in certain circumstances men ought to be (that is, if they were intelligent, would be) unhappy—or happy. Pessimist and optimist differ in their judgment of the merits of a particular case, and in the counsel of wisdom which they offer, but they both employ in the end standards other than actual experienced pleasure and pain.

The hedonistic calculus fails to provide a true criterion of the value of life, not only and not mainly because it falls short of precision, but because of its inadequacy and even irrelevance. That men live disconsolate and dreary lives, blindly groping for a happiness which is actually theirs for the asking, is a fact as common as it is pitiable. So Goethe teaches us homely wisdom:

> Wilt thou roaming e'er importune?
> See, the good it lies so near.
> Only learn to grasp thy fortune,
> For thy fortune's always here.[14]

On a loftier plane Epictetus pleads for a recognition of true happiness in virtue: "Show me a man that is sick—and happy; in danger—and happy; on his death-bed—and happy; an exile—and happy; in evil report—and happy! Show me him, I ask again. So help me Heaven, I long to see *one* Stoic!" [15] Thus the pity of it is not so much that men are unhappy as that they do not know where to seek and find true and worthy happiness.

Contrariwise, few things are as depressing and disgusting as men's actual toleration or even enjoyment of ignoble conditions and ways of life. The old proverb quoted by St. Peter is to the point: "The dog turning to his own vomit again; and the sow that had washed, to wallowing in the mire." [16] More tragic than disgusting is the state of countless multitudes the world over, living lives of squalor and daily indignity to their human nature. Shall we say that their apparent acquiescence and cheerfulness constitute their lives blessed? Indeed rebellious discontent would be the first bright gleam in their existence. In Tolstoy's study of the masses submerged in the Moscow slums, nothing was more disquieting than the dull and sometimes gay contentment of countless dwellers in the gutters of life. Tolstoy in his mission of redemption was actually more unhappy than those he was trying to save from poverty and filth of body and soul. Shall we pronounce Tolstoy worse off than his paupers?

Man may be happy not realizing the indignity of his life, or he may be miserable because of his petulance and his incapacity to perceive the precious values within his reach; or again he may be oppressed by a tragic infelicity, the result of high desires in a sordid and unresponsive world. "In respect of this better aspect of my life," Royce wrote, "I suffer because of the very depth and magnitude of my meanings." [17] In all these cases the pleasure-pain balance discloses its inadequacy and irrelevance. The reckless hedonist would do well to remember John Stuart Mill's words: "It is better to be a human being dissatisfied than a pig satisfied; better to be Socrates dissatisfied than a fool satisfied. And if the fool, or the pig, is of a different opinion, it is because they only know their own side of the question. The other party to the comparison knows both sides." [18]

We have seen that an estimate of the value of life in terms of experienced pleasure and pain is not only statistically unavailable but really of no avail. No one can contest that happiness is one of the elements of a worthwhile life; but the final judgment of a man, and of human life generally, is not in terms of actual pleasure and pain that may be had but in terms of the worthiness of the pleasure or pain in question. Hedonism fails through axiological insufficiency: a standard other than pleasure-pain is needed if pleasure and pain are to be tested, graded and so integrated with the other values of life. To ignore the demand for such a standard is to give up the essential task of evaluation. Happiness itself has been defined as "the harmonious and steady development of all our capacities in their order of excellence." [19] The important question, after all, is not, Are men happy or unhappy? but rather this, Is it well that men are thus and thus happy or unhappy? So hedonism, optimistic or pessimistic, points beyond itself to some more adequate type of evaluation.

V

The advocacy in modern utilitarianism of the principle, the greatest happiness of the greatest number, and the general advance from egoistic to universalistic hedonism, imply the virtual adoption of a criterion no more adequate than the hedonistic: that the good and the evil in life are measurable in terms of benevolence and egoism.

One of the standing problems in ethical and religious thought has concerned this issue between self-assertion and self-denial. Buddhism found in self-centeredness the source of all evil, and sought salvation through the extinction of self. Likewise we read in the *Theologia Germanica:* "Be simply and wholly bereft of Self. . . . Put off thine own will, and there will be no hell." So again Pascal: "The selfish bent is the beginning of all disorder." [20] Theological ethics has characteristically, though not always as explicitly as here, taken the same position: to attain moral perfection, man must radically overcome his native selfishness.

Hobbes outraged respectable England with his doctrine that man could organize a morally satisfactory state on the basis of egoism. Against Hobbes, Shaftesbury and Hutcheson maintained that man is not a selfish anarch by nature, and sought moral-social perfection in the normal balance between selfish and benevolent impulses, that is to say, a balance which inclined towards benevolence. But, while the Hobbist view was wholly impious in the theologian's eyes, this view of the natural benevolence of man seemed also unchristian in its pagan assumption that mere once-born man could attain moral perfection. The note of denial is so strong in Christian thought ancient and modern just because the theologian had found avarice, lust and greed, in a word, self-assertion, dominant in the life of unregenerate man. Even the Golden Rule and similar maxims insist at best only on a reconciliation through sympathy: I am imaginatively to put myself in the place of others and do as I would be done by. It is assumed, then, that in all my activities and relations my concern for self is to be the standard. Self-regard is recognized, and also the disparity between self-regard and benevolence: to overcome this disparity, the magic of sympathy is invoked. But it is a magic that only the grace of God can fully work in the life of a man.

Three secular efforts to trace the path of moral perfection out of the narrow confines of selfishness deserve particular notice. Hedonism, in emphasizing the pursuit of pleasure and happiness, inclines at first to exclusiveness, impressed as it seems by the thought that the pursuer of pleasure must necessarily pursue the pleasure which he knows directly, namely his own. Bentham, while recognizing in his hedonistic calculus the factor of extent, and while insisting on the principle of impartiality (everyone to count for one and no one for more than one), yet finds the motive for benevolent action in one's own vicarious enjoyment of the pleasures of others. John Stuart Mill's utilitarianism is genuinely altruistic in its intentions; but how are self-sacrifice, the Golden Rule, the individual's pursuit of the greatest happiness of the greatest number, to be justified on hedonistic grounds? Here, as also in his doctrine of different kinds or grades of pleasure, Mill really goes beyond the frame of strict hedonism. Sidgwick, in his plea for the disinterested pursuit of happiness, whether my own or my neighbor's, seems to overlook the fact that happiness is bound up with interest and is immediately known to me only as experienced by myself. The pleasures of others are, after all, only hearsay pleasures to me: what hedonistic motive can I have for preferring them to my own?

How, then, can I espouse and pursue what runs counter to my desires? Kant and his followers seek an answer to this question by a distinction between the empirical and the moral will, the lower and the higher self. The law to which one submits despite his desires is not a law imposed from without, but the law of the self's moral reason.

A third line of argument proceeds from evolutionary grounds. Spencer would show that exclusive egoism defeats its end as surely as pure altruism. Reconciliation and compromise are to be attained through the increasingly better adapted relations of man to man, which will make sympathy more normal and the purposes and ends of men less conflicting.

The view that man is self-assertive by nature led Schopenhauer, as we have seen, to the radical view that normal human conduct is evil, that morality consists in compassion alone, and that moral perfection points to the negation of the will-to-live. This doctrine invited the sharp reaction of Nietzsche: if healthy man is by nature self-assertive, why seek moral perfection in the denial of the will-to-power? Why not rather disdain weak pity and ruthlessly press for the nobler strength of Superman?

The issue thus becomes accentuated in modern discussion. Contemporary moralists try to prove that the self is essentially social, and that the true interests of self and society do not conflict, but what constitutes true interest in this sense is not clearly brought out, and in the face of actual conflict between ourselves and others, we are ordinarily urged to develop altruistic zeal for reasons not explicitly stated, or else are left to make our own ethics as we go.

The main idea to guide the revision of this confused chapter in ethical theory is set forth in Green's *Prolegomena to Ethics*, and we may use Green's doctrine of shareable goods in order to sketch a possible settlement of the old issue between egoism and altruism.

We are instructed in different ethical theories to seek moral perfection in benevolence and active sympathy, or else in aggressive self-assertion, or else in some sort of compromise between the two. Let us test the adequacy of these views and formulas by considering some undisputed examples of excellence and saintliness and some cases of obvious and flagrant vice. We are told that, of the things that abide, love is the greatest. Behold Dante's love of Beatrice, Tennyson's love of Hallam, Father Damien's love for the Hawaiian lepers, the devotion of a hundred saints to God: can we convey the true spirit of this love and devotion in terms of egoism or of altruism, or of any compromise whatever between the two? The devotion of man to woman, of man to man, of man to men, of man to God is seen to involve utter surrender and oblivion of self, but also enhancement in self-expression and self-affirmation. It is a paltry miser's idea of philanthropy to confuse it with mere self-denial; nothing would so easily repel love as the note of almsgiving in the bestowal; and how must the good God be regarding the near-saints who love him in a spirit of self-sacrifice? At the apex of moral perfection, the issue between self-assertion and self-denial evidently loses meaning: what we admire here cannot be stated either in egoistic or in altruistic terms, for here is utter self-denial together with complete self-affirmation.

At the other end of the moral scale, consider a libertine, a miser, a cruel brute or tyrant, a traitor. Here are men corrupting, exploiting, oppressing, torturing their fellows and doing all this, we are told, for their own self-gratification and self-aggrandisement. But, if we examine the matter more closely, we see flagrant self-neglect and self-destruction here. Don Juan, Scrooge, Richard the Third, Judas have really 'forgotten themselves' in the blind pursuit of some outlaw passion; in a very true sense of the word, their lives are lives of self-negation and self-destruction.

The assertion of one self means the denial of another, and what we condemn in the vicious man of whatever variety is not his self-assertion but rather the sort of self he has chosen to affirm and the sort of self he has chosen to deny. If now we consider that the term 'self' signifies aims chosen, objects of pursuit or devotion, in a word values, we may render our discussion clearer by distinguishing the main objectives of action, in so far as one's assertion or one's denial of them involves the assertion or the denial of them by others and thus the so-called conflict between egoism and altruism.

Of the values or goods which we pursue, some cannot be shared, some can be shared, and some must be shared to be attained at all. Two men starving hungry and food only for one; two men meeting on a bridge just broad enough for one: these are familiar examples of situations involving conflicting interests, competition and combat. So long as we are concerned in the pursuit of material goods and advantages we are enmeshed in conflict and the issue of egoism and altruism is bound to vex us: shall we press for our own advantage, shall we draw back and yield the gain to others? Even here, of course, I may be instructed that my neighbor's gain is not necessarily my loss, that employer and employee do not necessarily have opposed interests, that capital and labor need not be at daggers drawn. All the same, on the level where material goods are sought competition prevails and self-satisfaction is not clearly compatible with the satisfaction of others.

On a somewhat higher plane of endeavor we pursue goods which are social in character, can be shared, and are not diminished in being shared. Even material prosperity may possess this character. The rise or fall of prosperity in Europe may well condition similar rise and fall in the United States. Success and satisfaction in personal relations, in the pursuit of career or ambition, need not involve conflict; men may find themselves partners in enterprises in which they need not feel that they are always grasping for each other's share.

But what we observe as we proceed to the highest levels of human endeavor is that the end pursued must be shared to be attained at all. A scientist has discovered a new truth, a law which will revolutionize his science. Shall he keep it as his own private possession? Unless he share it with others it cannot be a vital truth in his science: to have the full measure of it himself, it must be in the thought of others. Or here is another scientist who has discovered a cure for a dread malady. This treasure he literally does not have, it is not a *cure,* until he has given it to the world. The poet's song, the artist's vision, the composer's harmony are doubly attained in being shared:

> He does not write at all whose poems no one reads, [21]

as Martial has it in one of his epigrams. My moral perfection demands the eliciting of moral perfection in others. Morally I cannot possibly gain except as others gain with me and through me. Hosea's effort to reclaim his faithless wife serves to transfigure morally his own interests and outlook on life and makes him a tragic prophet of the Lord. The wisdom of religion is that to gain our life we must lose it, for we truly keep only what we have shared and bestowed.

Not only the moral aristocracy of life serves to reveal this truth; the homely nobility of everyday life exhibits it on all sides. Consider the spiritual solidarity of parent and child, brother and sister in every real home; the devotion of men and women to some 'Cause' that dominates as it also expresses their individuality. Nothing so surely cures us of ethical snobbery as a fair-minded perception of the range of generous 'disinterested' interest in the lives of 'common' people, cheerful self-identification with the lot and interests of others due to the dominance of the self by the zest for higher values. This is not to be confused with mere gregariousness. Furthermore, the sensual mutuality of voluptuaries is not to be cited as an objection to this view. Lust as distinguished from love involves mutual exploitation: two barterers each one convinced he is making a fine trade, each using the other as a means. This is the very reverse of mutual respect and generous devotion.

Moral downfall does not proceed from altruism to selfishness, but involves a degradation in the values that are pursued by the agent. Just as soon as spiritual goods are, as we say, commercialized and regarded as sources of material advantage, the spirit of man topples down into the market-place and once more he is holding tight to his purse: the scientist is now thinking of priority of publication, the inventor of patent-rights, poet and artist of copyrights, royalties, and laurels, and even the near-saint is worrying over his order and place in the heavenly procession. In the scientist as scientist, in the poet as poet, in the saint as saint the issue between self and not-self does not arise, but it flares up the moment they descend to the view of their values as sources of material advantage.

The difference between low and high in morals is thus not the difference between selfish and unselfish; it is the difference between the peddler and the poet. The peddler's soul cannot understand the generous objectivity and impersonality of the sage, the singer, or the saint. These seem so blind to their own interests, so impractical and 'innocent.' The peddler calls the philosopher a visionary, the poet mad, the saint a world-denying ascetic. It is useless to teach the peddler altruism; on the level on which he lives, to teach him altruism would be to run counter to the 'healthy forces of life.' But as he rises above the peddler's level he gradually warms to the pursuit of higher goods, of goods that not only can but must be shared to be attained at all. So the rise to moral perfection may be viewed as an advance from conflict to community of interest, not through the abstract denial of the self, but through its enrichment and exaltation. A more concrete view of the moral self enables us to recognize that the issue between egoism and altruism, apparently insoluble at lower levels of conduct, is at the highest levels meaningless, and all along the line artificial as far as a genuine understanding of the moral situation is concerned, or an estimate of the value of life.

VI

Our survey of the problem of evil and of the alternative proposed solutions has revealed several sources of confusion. The endeavor to recognize and to clear up these confusions has suggested a better way out. The theory which is now presented in conclusion makes no presumptuous claims to originality or novelty: enough if it preserve the sound elements of other doctrines and avoid their confusion of issues, unwarranted preconceptions, insufficient respect for fact, and undue complacency or depression.

One thing seems clear at the very outset: this is a world of good *and* evil, however we may have to define the two. Wholesale and unqualified condemnation of the world, and likewise suave dismissal of evil as unreal are plainly at variance with the facts of life, are indeed self-refuting views. Value, whatever its more adequate definition, has this essential character of bipolarity: it is positive or negative, in whatever field we may examine it. Truth implies and is meaningless apart from error; virtue is similarly related and opposed to vice, beauty and justice and happiness to their respective opposites. "In the scale of existence," Dean Inge writes, "there are no minus signs. . . . But . . . the moral standard is essentially dualistic, and the dualism cannot be transcended without transcending the standpoint of morality." [22] Using the terms good and evil in the broadest sense to designate value positive and negative, we are bound to say that, if either is admissible, both must be. We have them both on our hands, both actual. Our problem is to understand the relation between them, and the essential character of the world which the perception of their relation serves to reveal. So axiology and cosmology may contribute to each other.

The attempted reduction of evil to finitude is a virtual rejection of the clear point with which we start, and, as we have seen, leads not to the solution but to the abandonment of the problem of evil. The reduction of good and evil to pleasure and pain ignores the variety and complexity of value, and, instead of simplifying our problem, serves only to confuse it. The reduction of good and evil to self-denial and self-assertion narrows the range of value unduly and even in this narrow range is disclosed as artificial and as dictated by theological and other preconceptions rather than as warranted by experience.

The essential defects of the theories just reviewed are two. First, the outright dismissal of evil or its reduction to finitude involves an evasion of the characteristic problem of value and, in particular, by reducing moral to metaphysical evil, rules out ethics. Second, the proposed equating of good and evil with pleasure and pain, or with self-denial and self-assertion, mistakenly looks for sheep and goats in the world, treating good and evil as distinct things or aspects or qualities, as if we could say of *x* that it is and remains good and the good, and of *y* that it is evil and the evil in the world.

The realm of value is too vast and complex to be thus forced in the frame of any such *x* and *y*. This undue simplification of the problem of evil, furthermore, overlooks the fact that truth, for instance, has no status in isolation but is always relative to a context, and not only may but characteristically does lose, in another context, its truth character and is disclosed as an error. And likewise with the other values. The value-character of reality, in other words, is not to be sought in individual things or aspects or qualities that stay put, that can be isolated and exhibited for praise or execration. Good and evil, truth and error, beauty and justice and the rest are what they are always in relation, in certain contexts, and in different contexts and relations may and do disclose a metamorphosis: the sheep turn out to be also goats! Yet even if philosophy of value could be formulated with offhand simplicity in terms of pleasure-pain or benevolence-selfishness, the real problem of theodicy would still remain: How are we to estimate a world in which sheep and goats have thus been picked out and opposed to each other?

Value positive or negative is not to be located in certain areas of existence but is a fundamental and ultimate character of all existence. No thing *is* value, but in all things value of some sort may be sought, recognized, enhanced, frustrated. The value-character of reality is a character which is postulated, and in being postulated involves a demand for its realization or a demand for its negation, and in both demands a fundamental recognition of higher and lower and an incipient or determined preference. Valuation is thus bound up with conative experience; it implies a moving world in which interest stimulates will-activity, in which intelligence is not a mere passive recipient of the factual, but an active participant, preferring, demanding, resisting. The true is what we should believe and maintain; the beautiful is what we should enjoy and cherish; the good is what we should pursue, do, love, and uphold; and so with the other values, and in all these cases the chosen value is the preferred claimant setting us in opposition to rival invasions of interest.[23]

The world discloses value only in and to personal experience. Values are personal in reference and connotation. This main principle, which commands weighty support, has found classical expression in Green's formula: Values are always "relative to value for, of, or in a person." [24] Some of the reasons for upholding this view have been stated in the last chapter of my work, *The Problem of Immortality*, and perhaps need not be rehearsed.

This principle of the relation of value and personality, however, is liable to a certain grave misinterpretation. It may be expressed in the doctrine that value is *merely* personal, that nature is indifferent to value, that value of whatever sort is merely read into nature by persons, is as it were a poetic fiction of reality. In support of this opinion is cited the mere factuality of existence as physical science deals with it. But does the physical-scientific view of nature exhaust reality? Is not scientific activity itself, and the possibility of physical *science*, an indication that the range of reality transcends factual-mechanistic categories? What would be the chemical formulae of a true and of an untrue chemical theory? Nature, in the full and only proper sense of the word, is not merely factual and indifferent to value, for nature includes human nature, includes scientific, logical activity and its standards, aesthetic creation and contemplation, moral endeavor and ideals, religious worship. These are all in and of nature, quite as real certainly as atoms, electrons, positive and negative charges. An utterly impersonal universe would not allow of value or valuation, but the universe is not wholly impersonal. That values are essentially bound up with personality is thus nowise a reflection on their reality; indeed, quite the contrary, if we only consider the range of being that is exemplified in personality. Value is personal; its range and roots are the range and roots of personality, and these, after all, reach over all nature. To ignore this last is to ignore the problem "how a universe without mind or value could produce mind and value." [25]

Personal activity may not be as common as mechanical process, but this observation is neither surprising nor relevant to the reflection it is intended to convey. The apex of the pyramid is not any the less apex because it covers less area than the base. Was there a long time during which there was neither man nor man's thinking and valuation in nature? All the more clearly, then, should we recognize that nature among its other capacities had and has the making of human nature in it. The lower we perceive the sub-human range of nature to extend, the clearer evidence should we find, in nature's attainment unto personality, of its essentially dynamic, upward-reaching character. So John Keats wrote words of wisdom which Bernard Bosanquet was to interpret and develop: "The world is the vale of soul-making." [26] But we should also recognize the arduousness of this attainment. We should be on our guard not to oversimplify our cosmology either in the manner of the subjective idealist or in the manner of the materialist.

Personality and valuation serve to exhibit more adequately and as it were in fuller maturity characteristics and capacities which reality manifests less adequately and in germ and bud at lower levels of existence. The clear perception of the values of life evident to critical intelligence may enable us, without any anthropomorphism or mythology, to perceive the promise of them all along the line. So far is nature from being indifferent to worth.

VII

It is the essence and nature of everything, Spinoza told us, to endeavor to persist in its own being. In a world of things and processes different in character, difference and conflict-in-relation are just what we should expect. It is of the essence of fire to set the green wood aflame, and it is of the essence of the moisture and the sap in the wood to delay flaming and to extinguish the fire. It is the nature of the invading horde of germs to take hold, multiply and take possession of the organism, and it is the nature of the organism to resist the infection which threatens its health and life. It is as natural for a dog's ravenous hunger to cause it to snap the bone out of another dog's mouth as it is for our social sense and reason to control appetite. The 'flesh' and the 'spirit' are both 'nature,' each in its sphere persisting, each in relation to the other and overarching to dominate the other. Our life, and the world we live in, may be conceived as a vast concourse of activities self-persisting, counteracting, conflicting.

But this cosmic concourse is a scale or hierarchy of activities. Things are not indifferently on a par; the difference among them is gradational. What the specific order of gradation is, in different fields of experience, constitutes the special problem of the philosophy of value in its various branches, logical, aesthetic, ethical. The meaning of the terms 'higher' and 'lower' is itself ever-expanding: signifying difference in complexity and range of categories, enhanced self-realization and self-judgment. The hierarchy points from mechanism to life and consciousness, from unconscious and nonrational to self-conscious and rational activity, from law-conforming process to action on principle and in pursuit of ideal ends.

That there is some sort of hierarchy, however, that there is higher and lower in the world, is not a conclusion of valuation but its prime presupposition. Its very outlook is gradational. The first axiom of the philosophy of value is: there is a hierarchy of being, or there is higher and lower in the world, some things are preferable, better, worthier than others. Grant this way of looking at the world, for unless we do the problems of value not only cannot be solved but cannot even arise: what, from such a point of view, is evil?

In this gradational view of things, evil is literally *degradation,* the surrender of the higher to the lower in the scale of being, the effective down-pulling incursion of the lower against the higher. This definition of evil would apply irrespective of the judgment as to what in any specific case is higher or lower, for such difference of judgment would involve a corresponding difference of judgment as to what in the circumstances is evil, and would reaffirm this fundamental conception of the nature of evil.

The perception of the cosmic process as gradational in character and the personal response to this perception find expression in the various categories of the philosophy of value. Thus the self-maintenance of the higher and its reaching to ever fuller realization and enhancement is progress, whether cosmic, biologic or human-social. Man's degrading surrender to a lower incursion involves him in varieties of vice. His effective resistance to the baser invasion is virtue. His self-satisfaction at any stage of advancement is complacency and marks stagnation: this we may call the sin against the Holy Ghost. His sense of inability to maintain himself on high ground or to attain ground still higher, if due to the conviction that the universe is callous or hostile to the enhancement of worth, gives rise to a consciousness of frustration, the tragic sense of life.

If we survey 'normal' valuation in different fields of experience, this definition of evil finds substantial warrant and illustration. So disease involves the actual or the impending or threatened disorganization and degradation of bodily structure, the breakdown of highly complex and articulated tissue into tissue cruder or more elementary, like a riot or rebellious chaos upsetting the well-ordered state: deformation and growing together of joints, atrophy of muscle or bone, purulent effusion; filling up of air-cells with a viscid mass of amorphous exudation, coagulating and consolidating the lungs; wasting away of cells and organs into a caseous pulp; degeneration of highly specialized brain-structure and perversion of cerebro-neural activity; inflammation, suppuration, lesions, necrosis, paralysis partial or general, cessation of functions essential to continued life; death, disintegration and putrefaction of tissues,—dust and ashes. The career of microbes and bacteria are in their own way as natural as ours: what is evil is rather their ascendency, in disease, over the higher course and career of man. So Pascal's and Leopardi's and Dostoyevsky's illnesses, and Keats' premature death, and Lenau's and Schumann's mental eclipse sadden and perplex us. We resent these rude jests of matter at the expense of mind. But this invasion may and does stir man to worthy resistance, stimulating medical intelligence in the cure and prevention of disease and in the alleviation of pain. There are no doubt limits to this resistance; as Petrarch put it, only death can keep a young man from old age.[27] But whether or not faced with insurmountable obstacles, man here develops vigor and insight in resistance, and heroism even in defeat. Pascal has shown us, against Ecclesiastes, that man does have preëminence above the beasts, that he does not die as a beast dies.

In the field of the higher values evil manifests itself similarly, as degradation, perversion, frustration. Error and fallacy result from the failure of the mind to maintain itself on the intelligent level. Prejudice, dogmatism, partisanship, emotional bias, hasty generalization, confusion, tautology, irrelevance, self-contradiction: in all these logical evils intelligence is perverted and clouded; its rôle is usurped by lower faculties, and it fails to attain the truth-value of ideas or, as Professor Fite would put it, "the fullness of critical imagination." [28]

In the realm of art, beauty and ugliness are always relative to a certain development of taste and spiritual heritage, culture, and refinement. Plato's *Symposium* is the classical vision of the sublime career open to man in his rise to higher and higher perception and love of Beauty: the sublime career and also its hazards and responsibilities. What normally satisfies a crude primitive taste may prove wearisome or repulsive to a more cultivated nature, and enjoyable to it only when itself becomes depraved. So jazz is good music—for savages, but not for the heirs of Bach and Beethoven.

In the economic life, and particularly in modern industry, evil is flagrantly manifest in the mechanization of human energy and human life. Is not this the radical evil in the economic system, the treatment of human labor as goods, as something to be bought and sold, exploited and discarded when worn out: man regarded as a cog in the machine, as so much productive material, as merely an economic agent to be replaced in part or altogether by more perfected machinery or more effective manipulation? This system is evil in that it registers the actual or threatened defeat of human by brute material factors. Modern civilization in utilizing the resources of nature may show 'natural piety,' restraint and responsibility to later generations, or it may wastefully squander and exhaust the means to its own effective future activity. In applying science to the demands of modern industry, man may use the forces of nature as levers for the upbuilding of the higher values, and in this sense even 'brute' nature may be as it were vicariously humanized; or it may and it does drag human life to the level of crude matter. It all depends on the objectives that dictate the course and direction of our technically expert society.

So again we may view the flagrant evil of war in the life of modern humanity. The rise of man from savagery and barbarism to civilization has made his life increasingly international. This actual international life—industrial, intellectual, social—demands of man a corresponding cosmopolitan morality that should enter and dominate international relations: through arbitration, world-coöperation, and appeal to the judgment of a world-conscience. This is the path upward, leading to peace, to the higher and fuller life of mankind. Modern war, on the contrary, is the dragging down of civilized nations to the levels and methods of barbarism and savagery.

In the moral field more narrowly conceived, the same principle holds true. That which is natural to the beast may well be a vice in man. In fact the beast is never beastly. Beastliness is not mere animality; it is degradation of the human to the brutish level, a level natural to the beast but unnatural to man. So we read in Dante:

> Consider of what origin ye are,
> You were not made to live as do the brutes,
> But to seek virtue and to learn the truth.[29]

When man forgets his human distinctiveness, his characteristic rôle and career in nature, to tread the jungle-track of beastliness, his vices are just this, *degrading*. The finest example of this truth in tragedy that comes to mind is in Hamlet's scene with his mother:

> Look here upon this picture, and on this,
> The counterfeit presentment of two brothers: . . .
> This was your husband. . . . Look you now what follows.
> Here is your husband. . . . Have you eyes?
> . . . What Judgment
> Would step from this, to this?

This is the evil: Hamlet's uncle was no fit mate for Queen Gertrude. Replacing her former worthy husband by this "mildewed ear"

> Calls virtue hypocrite, takes off the rose
> From the fair forehead of an innocent love,
> And sets a blister there. . . .
> . . . Such an act
> As from the body of contraction plucks
> The very soul, and sweet religion makes
> A rhapsody of words. . . .

This idea of vice as essentially self-degradation St. Augustine has expressed in words of profound insight which will bear repeating: "When the will abandons the higher, and turns to what is lower, it becomes evil, not because that is evil to which it turns, but because the turning itself is perverse.—Cum enim se voluntas relicto superiore ad inferiora convertit, efficitur mala: non quia malum est, quo se convertit, sed quia perversa est ipsa conversio." [30]

The view of existence which is here developed recognizes unflinchingly the actuality of evil, but is not on that account plunged in pessimistic despair. It is nowise to be mistaken for the complacent theory of evil as the mere shadow in the picture or the discord swelling the larger harmony. Evil is not 'somehow good,' any more than sinking is somehow rising. Evil is evil and the opposite of good, contrary in course and direction. But it is a fact that what at a lower level and from a lower point of view passes for good and at that level is good discloses from a higher point of view its insufficiency, and adherence to it at the higher level becomes evil. So again St. Augustine writes: "He who inordinately loves the good which any nature possesses, even though he obtain it, himself becomes evil in the good, and wretched because deprived of a greater good." [31] In that sense, but in that sense only, we could well say that all good is somehow evil. So far at any rate is the view here advocated removed from complacency.

Thus it is the destiny of every good theory to open up vistas of inquiry, realms of evidence, new problems which in the end indicate the shortcomings of the theory and cause it to be replaced by one more adequate. It is the destiny of every truth in the end to help prove itself an error and itself again an element in a higher truth. In the entire realm of value every solution is but the better setting of a new problem, every achievement but the clearer recognition of a greater task. Spinoza's principle which we recognized is only one half of the truth; our dynamic universe requires also the other half, which Unamuno has expressed so eloquently in his disturbed and disturbing book, *The Tragic Sense of Life:* "Every created being not only tends to preserve itself in itself, but to perpetuate itself, and, moreover, to invade all other beings, to be others without ceasing to be itself, to extend its limits to the infinite but without breaking them." [32] Not bare identity of structure, nor yet change and bare sequence of discretes, but growth, unfolding and genuine enhancement of perfection, active, arduous, and inexhaustible, characterize the world-process.

The vaster the field of attainment and advance, the greater is the range of possible error and frustration. Indeed the perception of a certain value as in some respects inadequate and unworthy is the first step in the attainment of the higher and worthier value. The criticism and the collapse of the lower truth are the birth-pangs of the new truth; remorse and repentance, the thresholds to saintliness. Life does not lose but gains in tragic hazard as it gains in prospect and in dignity. Not self-sufficiency and bland placidity, but vigilant aspiration marks the heroic soul: its ideals are always in the van and its march to higher values never ceases. Far from content to accept the adulation of those with lower standards, it is ever keenly aware of the vast unattained and, by it judging its own attainment, finds itself ever short of the mark. Didn't James Martineau write somewhere: "The blessings of a satisfied conscience are least experienced where they are most deserved"? So we read of Leonardo da Vinci: "What to others appears perfection is to him teeming with error." [33] So Socrates' high conception of knowledge led him to count himself ignorant. So Jesus: "Why callest thou me good?" [34]

It is of the essence of value, then, that it recognizes no final terminus or conclusion. The target, to borrow a phrase from Professor Boodin,[35] is a moving target. Perfection has its base, of course, but its base is always a springboard.

Perfection is perfectibility. All along the line of human endeavor this truth is demonstrated, and on the higher peaks of achievement it stands out most clearly. Theology, to be sure, has demanded a conception of God in terms of absolute perfection, a perfection all past perfect or present absolute, without prospect or problems. But, as we have endeavored to indicate elsewhere,[36] this conception of divine perfection carries over inappropriate mechanistic notions of completeness and plenitude into the realm of value. If we conceive of God as the Apogee of Value, then God's perfection must be dynamic: it is not the alleged terminus of perfectibility, but its cosmic course, its heart and soul. Matthew Arnold wrote of "the enduring power not ourselves which *makes for* righteousness." [37] The core of reality is this eternal perfectibility: the heavens declare it; evolution cosmic, biologic, or human-social discloses it; man's logical, aesthetic, and moral activity reveals its sublime range. Man's idea of God is his gesture towards the dizzy utmost of value, the infinite reach and endless span of it. When our vigor fails and our lot seems hopeless, and the abyss wells up to engulf us and our ideals, when wild Nature seems to mock our helpless dignity, and dull scepticism whispers harsh doubts of the reality of value, and all that is worthy in our world is 'scientifically' exhibited as ephemeral and episodic, then the very tragedy which the cosmos thus reënacts in our experience serves to save us from despair: in our own loyal aspiration after values we find our conviction that they are in and of Reality and abiding. And this conviction of the ultimate reality, conservation, enhancement of value is man's faith in God.

In God is no stagnant plenitude but plenitude of ideal activity, no dull placidity but ever-heroic redemption of the world from the hazard of settling back. "My Father worketh hitherto, and I work." [38] Not less than myself but more is God thus resistant to the evil tug of the downpulling and the inert and the complacent. For just this upward-urging, ever more perfectly active character of the cosmos is what we can intelligently mean by God. And the evil tug is not outside of God or alien to the divine nature, but just as in finite beings so in the cosmic system of them, in God, it is the negative moment, the obverse of positive enhancement and ideal activity. For there can be no higher without its corresponding lower.

There is accordingly no coming to terms with evil, not ever. Only he straightforwardly 'accepts the universe' who accepts it unreservedly as a battleground of achievement, only he who in thus accepting it is clearly aware of evils to be resisted and overcome. It has been said that the way to understand best the articles of the Creed is to keep clearly in mind the heresies which they were meant to combat. So the pursuit of truth is through the clearance of error, and virtue is in resistance to vice, and beauty is won through the refusal of ugliness. But this does not mean that error or vice or ugliness are accepted as any the less evil because they are conditions of good: they *are—to be resisted.* The only view of the world that might justify pessimistic despair would be a view that perceived no evil in it, nothing perverse, nothing lower to surmount or overcome, and therefore nothing higher to challenge our endeavor: no problem, no task, no hazard of defeat or frustration: dull, placid monotony! There is a reported saying of Machiavelli: "The worst misfortune in life is not sickness, nor poverty, nor grief; but tediousness." [39] Pessimistic philosophy, as we have seen, may have the reverse effect of that intended by the pessimist: it may be a goad to the sluggish. Evil and the perception of it are conditions for heroic recognition and pursuit of value, be it truth, beauty, goodness; for "powers subjected to no strain. . . atrophy and eventually disappear." [40] In this sense evil is always only relative to good; but, paradoxically, if we refuse to perceive and resist it as evil, then it becomes evil absolute and utterly damns the very man who makes his peace with it.

This is the outlook for a world that admits of valuation: this contest, contact and conflict, of higher and lower, ever persisting, each achievement opening new prospects, raising new problems, imposing new duties, facing new hazards. There is a grim element in this idea; we can apply to our purpose words which Plato wrote in the *Theaetetus:* "Evils . . . can never pass away; for there must always remain something which is antagonistic to good." [41] But another version of this truth, and one more inspiriting, is Emerson's: "Within every man's thought is a higher thought: within the character he exhibits today, a higher character." [42] Good and evil are not distinct realities and have no status in isolation; they are always relative to each other. Evil is that ever-present side or factor in the actual world, by resistance to which a possible worthier side or nature affirms itself and gains reality through attainment. This contest is at the heart of things; it has neither beginning nor end, and it makes our world significant and stirring. The gradational theory of the nature of evil thus expresses essential characteristics of our logical, aesthetic, and moral activity, does justice to the complexity and dynamic hierarchy of nature, and points to an idea of perfection which does not nullify the fundamental character of value of which perfection is rightly conceived as the apogee.

NOTES

CHAPTER I. THE PROBLEM OF EVIL IN THE GREAT RELIGIONS

1. Cf. Tsanoff, *The Problem of Immortality*, 1924, Chapters III and XII.
2. *Prolegomena to Ethics*, 5. edition, p. 210.
3. William James, *Varieties of Religious Experience*, p. 83.
4. Quoted from James, *Varieties of Religious Experience*, p. 83.
5. "Walt Whitman," *Leaves of Grass*, McKay edition, pp. 62 f.
6. *Maitri Upanishad*, 1:4, transl. in R. E. Hume, *The Thirteen Principal Upanishads*, 1921, pp. 413 f.
7. *Chandogya Upanishad*, 6:9 ff., transl. in R. E. Hume, *op. cit.*, pp. 246 ff.
8. *The Problem of Immortality*, pp. 215 f.
9. Cf. Schopenhauer's Supplement to his *World as Will and Idea*, Chap. XLVI, *ad fin.;* cf. also Johannes Huber, *Der Pessimismus*, 1876, pp. 12 f., 20 ff.
10. *Iliad* XVII, 446 f.; XXIV, 525 f.; transl. by Lang, Leaf, and Myers.
11. Cf. Otto Pfleiderer, *The Philosophy of Religion*, transl. by Allan Menzies, Vol. IV, pp. 3 f.
12. *Prometheus Bound*, transl. by Lewis Campbell, first soliloquy.
13. Cf. Huber, *Der Pessimismus*, pp. 13 f.
14. *Iliad* VI, 146 ff.; transl. by Lang, Leaf, and Myers.
15. *Agamemnon*, 1326 ff.; transl. by Lewis Campbell.
16. *Oedipus Rex*, 1186 ff.; transl. by Lewis Campbell.
17. Transl. by A. S. Way.
18. *Libation-Bearers*, 1016 ff.; transl. by Morshead.
19. *Philoctetes*, 440 ff.; transl. by Lewis Campbell.
20. *Religion in Greek Literature*, 1898, p. 285.
21. *Ibid.*, p. 304.
22. *Republic*, 380, 381; cf. 379, 391; Jowett's translation of Plato is quoted.
23. *Republic*, 380.
24. *Timaeus*, 42.
25. *Phaedrus*, 246.
26. *Phaedo*, 79.

27. *Republic*, 610.
28. *Statesman*, 272 f.
29. *Discourses of Epictetus* (Arrian), I: 14, 1–6 (H. Crossley's translation in *The Golden Sayings of Epictetus*).
30. *Meditations*, IV: 19, transl. by Casaubon.
31. Lucretius, *On the Nature of Things*, II, 180 f.; transl. by Cyril Bailey.
32. *History of Philosophy*, transl. by J. H. Tufts, 2. edition, p. 87.
33. *Theaetetus*, 176.
34. *De Providentia*, quoted here from Jules Martin, *Philon*, 1907, p. 100.
35. Émile Bréhier, *Les idées philosophiques et religieuses de Philon d'Alexandrie*, 1908, p. 274.
36. *Enneads*, III: ii: 14; the translation quoted in these pages, unless otherwise indicated, is Stephen MacKenna's.
37. *Enneads*, II: ix: 13.
38. *Enneads*, II: ix: 13.
39. W. R. Inge, *The Philosophy of Plotinus*, Vol. I, p. 257.
40. *Enneads*, III: viii: 4; translation in Inge, *op. cit.*, Vol. I, p. 152.
41. "Walt Whitman," *Leaves of Grass*, McKay edition, pp. 47, 62.
42. B. A. G. Fuller, *The Problem of Evil in Plotinus*, 1912, p. 130.
43. Cf. Eduard von Hartmann, "Plotin's Axiologie," in *Zur Geschichte und Begründung des Pessimismus*, 2. edition, pp. 29–63, esp. pp. 62 f.
44. *Grundriss der Geschichte der griechischen Philosophie*, 1883, p. 290.
45. *Op. cit.*, Vol. I, p. 135.
46. Thomas Whittaker, *The Neo-Platonists*, 2. edition, p. 68.
47. Cf. his edition and translation of Plotinus, Paris, 1924, Vol. I, p. 111.
48. *Enneads*, I: viii: 5, 8.
49. *Enneads*, I: viii: 11.
50. *Enneads*, I: viii: 7.
51. J. E. Boodin, *Cosmic Evolution*, 1925, p. 41.
52. *Winter's Tale*, IV: iv: 89 ff.; cf. Boodin, *Cosmic Evolution*, p. 75.
53. *The Philosophy of Religion*, Vol. IV, pp. 10 f.
54. R. T. Flewelling, *Christ and the Dramas of Doubt*, pp. 78 f.
55. Job, iv: 7.
56. Job, xii: 6.
57. Job, iii: 25.
58. Genung, *The Epic of the Inner Life*, 1900, p. 20.
59. Ecclesiastes, i: 2, 14, 9.
60. L. W. Batten, *Good and Evil: A Study in Biblical Theology*, 1918, p. 101.
61. Ecclesiastes, iii: 19 f.

CHAPTER II. THE CHRISTIAN-MEDIEVAL TRADITION

1. I Cor., xv: 22.
2. Romans, vii: 24.
3. Romans, viii: 38 f.
4. II Timothy, i: 12.
5. St. Augustine, *Contra Faustum Manichaeum,* VI: 4; English translation of St. Augustine's *Works,* edited by Marcus Dods, Vol. V, pp. 173 f.
6. Cf. O. Plümacher, *Der Pessimismus in Vergangenheit und Gegenwart,* 2. edition, p. 54.
7. *Confess.* X: xxxiii (50); *Works,* Vol. XIV, pp. 272, 273.
8. *Confess.* I: iii; *Works,* Vol. XIV, p. 3.
9. *Contra Epistolam Manichaei,* XXXIII; *Works,* Vol. V, p. 133.
10. *De Civitate Dei,* XII: 6; *Works,* Vol. I, pp. 488 f. (Translation slightly revised).
11. *De Gratia Christi et de Peccato Originali,* II: 46; *Works,* Vol. XII, p. 89; cf. in this connection *De Civitate Dei,* XII: 3 sqq.; *Contra Epistolam Manichaei,* XXV (39); *Contra Faustum Manichaeum,* VI: 8; XXI: 14; *Confess.* VII: xvi (22); *Works,* Vol. I, pp. 484 ff.; Vol. II, pp. 4 f., 25 f.; Vol. V, pp. 136, 181, 395; Vol. XIV, p. 162.
12. *De Civitate Dei,* XII: 8; *Works,* Vol. I, p. 491.
13. *Contra Julianum Pelagianum,* III: iii (9); cf. Jules Martin, *Saint Augustin,* 1901, p. 190.
14. *Contra duas Epistolas Pelagianorum,* II: ii (2–3); *Works,* Vol. XV, pp. 271 ff.: St. Augustine's skillfully drawn series of contrasts between the Pelagians and the Manicheans.
15. *De Gratia Christi,* XXXV (38); *Works,* Vol. XII, p. 35.
16. *De Civitate Dei,* XIX: 4; *Works,* Vol. II, pp. 302, 306.
17. *De Correptione et Gratia,* XI (31); *Works,* Vol. XV, pp. 99 f.
18. *De Correptione et Gratia,* XII (37); *Works,* Vol. XV, p. 106.
19. Quoted here from Joseph McCabe's *St. Augustine and His Age,* p. 384, Note. McCabe would amend the passage to read: "*except* to a theological microscope," and informs us that he was once the happy possessor of such an instrument.
20. *De Spiritu et Littera,* XXX (52); *Contra duas Epistolas Pelagianorum,* I: iv (8); II: ii (2); *Works,* Vol. IV, p. 211; Vol. XV, pp. 243, 272.
21. *De Gratia Christi,* XXVI (27); *De Gratia et Libero Arbitrio,* VI (13), IX (21); *De Praedestinatione Sanctorum,* II (3); *Works,* Vol. XII, p. 27; Vol. XV, pp. 27, 34 f., 122.

22. *De Correptione et Gratia*, VI (10); *Works*, Vol. XV, p. 78.
23. *De Praedestinatione Sanctorum*, VIII (16); *De Dono Perseverantiae*, IX (21); *Works*, Vol. XV, pp. 139, 187.
24. *De Correptione et Gratia*, VIII (19); *Works*, Vol. XV, p. 87.
25. *De Correptione et Gratia*, XIII (40); *Works*, Vol. XV, pp. 108 f.
26. Philippians, ii: 12.
27. *The Philosophy of Religion*, Vol. IV, p. 19.
28. *De Gratia et Libero Arbitrio*, XXII (44); *Works*, Vol. XV, p. 63.
29. *De Peccatorum Meritis et Remissione*, I: xvi (21); *Works*, Vol. IV, p. 21.
30. Quoted from Nourrisson, *La philosophie de St. Augustin*, 1866, Vol. II, p. 373.
31. Cf. C. H. C. Pirie-Gordon, *Innocent the Great*, 1907, p. 19.
32. *De Contemptu Mundi, sive De Miseria Conditionis Humanae Libri Tres*, Migne, *Patrologia Latina*, Vol. CCXVII, Paris, 1889, Columns 701–746.
33. *Ibid.*, I: 1.
34. *Ibid.*, I: 2, 3, 6, 7.
35. *Ibid.*, I: 9, 11.
36. *Ibid.*, I: 13, 21, 29.
37. *Ibid.*, II: 1.
38. *Ibid.*, III: 1, 17.
39. E. Gilson, *Saint Thomas D'Aquin*, 4. edition, p. 11.
40. A.-D. Sertillanges, *La philosophie morale de St. Thomas D'Aquin*, 2. edition, p. 8.
41. *Summa Theologica, Prima Secundae* (I–II), *Q.* III, *Art.* 8.
42. *Summa Theologica*, I–II, *Q.* LXXIII, *Art.* 3; transl. by Fathers of the English Dominican Province, Vol. VII, p. 298; cf. *Summa Theologica*, I–II, *Q.* LXXXVII, *Art.* 4; II–II, *Q.* XX, *Art.* 1.
43. Sertillanges, *St. Thomas D'Aquin*, 4. edition, Vol. I, p. 321; cf. pp. 322 f.
44. *Ibid.*, Vol. I, pp. 326, 327.
45. *Op. cit.*, p. 6.
46. *Of the Imitation of Christ*, transl. published in "The World's Classics," I: 1, 3.
47. *Ibid.*, III: 48; I: 22; II: 1; cf. III: 27.
48. *Ibid.*, III: 55.
49. *Ibid.*, II: 11; III: 3, 21.
50. *Ibid.*, III: 47, 8.
51. *Circe*, transl. by H. Layng, London, 1744, p. 18.
52. *Ibid.*, pp. 164, 145.

53. *Ibid.*, p. 188.
54. *Ibid.*, pp. 249 f.

CHAPTER III. PASCAL'S DESPAIR OF REASON

1. *Oeuvres complètes*, Paris, Garnier, Vol. II, p. 313.
2. Cf. Pascal, *Oeuvres*, *Grands Écrivains* ed., Vol. XI, pp. 133 ff.; F. Strowski, *Pascal et son temps*, 4. edition, Vol. III, pp. 34 ff.
3. *Port-Royal*, 8. edition, Vol. III, p. 48, Note.
4. *Oeuvres*, Vol. VI, p. 41.
5. *Oeuvres*, Vol. XII, p. xxvii; Vol. XIV, p. 343.
6. Cf. V. Giraud's introduction to the edition of the *Pensées* in the *Collection Gallia*, p. xxv; cf. also Giraud, *La vie héroïque de Blaise Pascal*, p. 155.
7. *Pascal et son temps*, Vol. III, p. 313.
8. *Oeuvres*, Vol. X, pp. 4 f.; cf. Vol. XII, p. 13.
9. *Oeuvres*, Vol. XII, p. 78.
10. *Port-Royal*, Vol. II, p. 412.
11. Cf. *Oeuvres*, Vol. XIII, pp. 214, 216.
12. *Oeuvres*, Vol. XIII, p. 139; cf. pp. 13, 132.
13. *Oeuvres*, Vol. XIII, pp. 126 f.
14. Lucien Lévy-Bruhl, *History of Modern Philosophy in France*, Engl. transl., Chicago, 1899, p. 92.
15. *Oeuvres*, Vol. XIV, pp. 230 ff.; cf. Strowski, *op. cit.*, Vol. II, pp. 290 ff.
16. Cf. in this connection Strowski, *op. cit.*, Vol. III, pp. 292 ff.; Jacques Chevalier, *Pascal*, 9. edition, pp. 195 ff.; Sully Prudhomme, "La méthode de Pascal," in the *Revue de Paris*, Sept. 1, 1894; J. Laporte, "Le coeur et la raison selon Pascal," in the *Revue philosophique*, Vol. CIII, 1927.
17. *Oeuvres*, Vol. XIII, p. 440; cf. Vol. XII, p. lxxxvii.
18. *Oeuvres*, Vol. XIII, p. 318.
19. *Oeuvres*, Vol. XIII, pp. 198 f., 201.
20. Cf. Boutroux, *Pascal*, 6. edition, pp. 178 f.
21. *Oeuvres*, Vol. XIII, p. 145.
22. *Oeuvres*, Vol. XIII, p. 146.
23. *Loc. cit.*
24. *Oeuvres*, Vol. XIII, p. 154; cf. p. 271.
25. *Oeuvres*, Vol. XIII, p. 154.
26. II. Timothy, i: 12.
27. *Le scepticisme: Aenesidème-Pascal-Kant*, 1865, p. 329; cf. p. 327.

28. *Oeuvres*, Vol. XIII, p. 438.
29. James Thomson, "Parallel between Pascal and Leopardi," in his translation of *Essays, Dialogues, and Thoughts of Giacomo Leopardi*, p. 91; cf. Prévost-Paradol, *Études sur les moralistes français*, 1913, pp. 136 f.
30. *Oeuvres*, Vol. XIII, pp. 261 ff.; transl. by Albert Guérard in his *Reflections on the Napoleonic Legend*, p. 268; cf. *Oeuvres*, Vol. XIII, pp. 303 f., 314 f.

CHAPTER IV. SCEPTICISM AND THEODICY

1. Cf. Ludwig Feuerbach, *Pierre Bayle*, in his *Sämmtliche Werke*, 1905, Vol. V, pp. 123 ff.
2. Bayle, *Dictionnaire historique et critique*, 1780, Vol. III, pp. 305b, 306a.
3. Cf., W. Bolin, *Bayle*, in Feuerbach, *op. cit.*, p. 3.
4. Lactantius, *De Ira Dei*, 12; Bayle, *Dict.*, Vol. III, p. 625b; English translation quoted from William King's *Essay on the Origin of Evil*, 1731, p. 294.
5. *Dict.*, Vol. III, p. 625b.
6. Cf. *Dict.*, Vol. III, p. 626a: "Paulician answer" to Lactantius; *Dict.*, Vol. III, p. 306a: "Continuons de faire parler Zoroaster"; *Dict.*, Vol. III, p. 542: "Voyons ce qu'un Manichéen pourrait repondre à ce discours d'un Origéniste"; cf. also Feuerbach, *op. cit.*, pp. 219–226: Bayle's list of seven propositions in favor of orthodoxy and nineteen against.
7. Cf. *Dict.*, Vol. III, pp. 544a, 627 ff.; cf. *Réponse aux questions d'un provincial*, in *Oeuvres diverses*, Hague, 1737, Vol. III, pp. 662 f., 817 f., 869 ff.; also Otto Lempp, *Das Problem der Theodicee in der Philosophie und Litteratur des 18. Jahrhunderts*, 1910, pp. 24 f.
8. Feuerbach, *op. cit.*, pp. 242, 244, 245. Cf. *Oeuvres diverses*, Vol. III, pp. 652a, 796, 809 ff., 814.
9. *Dict.*, Vol. III, pp. 318 f.; *Oeuvres diverses*, Vol. III, pp. 662a, 666, 682. Cf. Bayle, *Réponse aux questions d'un provincial*, Vol. II, 1706, p. 134.
10. *Dict.*, Vol. III, pp. 631b, 629a.
11. *Dict.*, Vol. III, p. 733a.
12. *Dict.*, Vol. III, pp. 634b, cf. pp. 306b, 625a, 627a; *Oeuvres diverses*, Vol. III, p. 832b.
13. *Dict.*, Vol. IV, p. 635; cf. Vol. III, pp. 626b, 544b, 627, 629, 631b, 636a.
14. *Dict.*, Vol. III, p. 733b.

15. *Dict.*, Vol. IV, pp. 617 ff.; cf., Feuerbach, *op. cit.*, p. 183, quoting further from Bayle.
16. *Dict.*, Vol. IV, p. 619.
17. *Op. cit.*, p. 272.
18. Feuerbach, *Darstellung, Entwicklung und Kritik der Leibniz'schen Philosophie*, in his *Sämmtliche Werke*, 1905, Vol. IV, p. 108.
19. *Leibniz's System*, 1902, p. 474.
20. Eckhart: Leibniz "spoke well of everybody, and made the best of everything, er kehrte alles zum Besten"; *The Monadology, and Other Philosophical Writings*, transl. by Robert Latta, 1898, p. 17.
21. Leibniz, *Opera Philosophica Omnia*, ed. Erdmann, 1840, p. 470.
22. Clodius Piat, *Leibniz*, p. 248; cf. Nourrisson, *La philosophie de Leibniz*, 1860, pp. 273 f.
23. Cf. Leibniz's *Discourse on Metaphysics, Correspondence with Arnauld, and Monadology*, transl. by Montgomery, pp. 118, 119; *Opera*, ed. Erdmann, pp. 519, 521; cf. p. 669: "Libertas est spontaneitas intelligentis"; *Monadology*, etc., transl. Latta, p. 146; *Opera*, ed. Erdmann, p. 669: "Omnes tamen actiones sunt determinatae et nunquam indifferentes, quia semper datur ratio inclinans quidem non tamen necessitans, ut sic potius, quam aliter fiat. Nihil fit sine ratione."
24. Bertrand Russell, *A Critical Exposition of the Philosophy of Leibniz*, 1900, p. 172: "A monism is necessarily pantheistic, and a monadism, when it is logical, is as necessarily atheistic."
25. This traditional designation of Leibniz's God, according to Bertrand Russell, is not to be found in Leibniz's works (*op. cit.*, p. 187).
26. Otto Lempp, *Das Problem der Theodicee*, p. 50; cf. pp. 49 ff.
27. *Opera*, ed. Erdmann, pp. 509 f.
28. *Ibid.*, pp. 507, 548.
29. *Monadologie*, 89; transl. by Latta, p. 269.
30. *Opera*, ed. Erdmann, p. 261; transl. by A. G. Langley, *New Essays concerning Human Understanding*, 1896, p. 201.
31. *Opera*, ed. Erdmann, p. 472.
32. *Ibid.*, pp. 548 f.; cf. p. 538.
33. Gerhardt, *Die Philosophische Schriften von G. W. Leibniz*, Vol. III, p. 33; quoted here from Bertrand Russell, *op. cit.*, p. 296.
34. *Opera*, ed. Erdmann, p. 510.
35. *Op. cit.*, p. 189; cf. *Monadologie*, sections 40–41.
36. *The Philosophical Works of Leibniz*, transl. by G. M. Duncan, 2. edition, p. 286.

37. *De Origine Mali*, 1702; English translation, with notes, 1731, p. 73.
38. Bayle adds: "On ne sauroit comprendre qu'il ait pu s'imaginer que le bien moral surpasse le mal moral; ce seroit une fausseté trop manifeste," *Oeuvres diverses*, Vol. III, p. 653; cf., Bayle's extended critique of King, *ibid.*, pp. 650 ff.; King, *Origin of Evil*, pp. 78, 273 ff.
39. *Origin of Evil*, pp. 285 f.
40. *Ibid.*, p. 80; cf. pp. 52 ff.
41. *Ibid.*, pp. 81, 93 f., 299.
42. *Ibid.*, p. 134; cf., pp. 116 ff., 125, 130 ff., 142 ff., 191, 232.
43. *Ibid.*, pp. 181, 185 ff., 197 ff., 223.
44. *Ibid.*, p. 316.
45. *Ibid.*, pp. 296 ff.

CHAPTER V. EIGHTEENTH CENTURY OPTIMISM

1. Cf. Otto Lempp, *Das Problem der Theodicee*, p. 79, Note.
2. *The Moralists*, in *Characteristics*, ed. by J. M. Robertson, Vol. II, pp. 64 f.
3. *Ibid.*, p. 108; cf. p. 65.
4. *Ibid.*, pp. 22, 23, 107.
5. *Ibid.*, pp. 57 ff.
6. *Ibid.*, p. 107.
7. *Ibid.*, p. 109.
8. *History of English Thought in the Eighteenth Century*, 3. edition, Vol. II, p. 33.
9. *A System of Moral Philosophy*, Vol. I, p. 215.
10. *Theory of Moral Sentiments*, Part VI, Section ii, Chap. 3.
11. *Ibid.*, Part I, Section iii, Chap. 1.
12. *Works*, Oxford edition, Vol. I, p. 54.
13. Tsanoff, *The Problem of Immortality*, p. 252.
14. *Observations on Man*, Vol. III, p. xi.
15. *Ibid.*, Vol. I, pp. 35, 419, 426, 430, 437.
16. *Ibid.*, Vol. I, p. 420; Vol. II, pp. 15, 16, 23 f.
17. *Ibid.*, Vol. I, p. 83; Vol. II, pp. 28, 29; Sully, *Pessimism*, 1877, p. 58.
18. *History of English Thought in the Eighteenth Century*, Vol. II, p. 66.
19. *Observations on Man*, Vol. III, pp. 479, 485; Vol. II, p. 491.
20. *The Light of Nature Pursued*, 1768–1774, Vol. II, p. 165; Vol. III, pp. 223 f., 226, 231, 233, 178.
21. *Ibid.*, Vol. III, pp. 234 ff., 239, 236, 257; Vol. IV, pp. 304, 430.
22. Quoted from Sully's *Pessimism*, p. 59.

23. *Philosophical Works*, 1754, Vol. IV, p. 296.
24. *Ibid.*, Vol. IV, pp. 323, 335, 297 ff., 357; Vol. I, pp. 67 f.; Vol. V, pp. 37, 45; Otto Lempp, *Das Problem der Theodicee*, p. 130.
25. Cf., however, Walter Sichel, *Bolingbroke and His Times: The Sequel*, p. 426: "The real problem raised is as old as the Book of Job: Why should the righteous suffer? and Bolingbroke's answer remains at bottom the Scripture's: Is God a man?"
26. "Pope ein Metaphysiker!" written in collaboration with Mendelssohn, in Lessing's *Werke*, ed. Georg Witkowski, in Meyers Klassiker, Vol. III, p. 329.
27. Leslie Stephen, *History of English Thought in the Eighteenth Century*, Vol. II, p. 350.
28. *Essay on Man*, IV, 35 ff.; III, 27; I, 240 f., 279 f.; IV, 49 ff.
29. *Ibid.*, IV, 123 ff.; I, 57 ff.; II, 1 f.; III, 316 f.; I, 155 ff., 289 ff.
30. *Works*, Vol. II, 1871, p. 333.
31. Job, xiii: 7 ff.
32. Cf. in this connection, particularly with regard to Reimarus, Lempp, *op. cit.*, pp. 149–170.
33. *Philosophisches Lexicon*, 4. edition, enlarged by J. C. Hennings,1775, Vol. I, pp. 457, 458, Article "Böse," pp. 460, 461.
34. *Ibid.*, Vol. I, p. 463; Vol. II, p. 1528; Vol. I, pp. 470, 1406.
35. *Ibid.*, Vol. II, p. 1528.
36. *Oeuvres*, Lyons, 1756, Vol. I, p. 193.
37. *Ibid.*, Vol. I, pp. 202, 208.
38. *Ibid.*, Vol. I, p. 252.
39. David Strauss, quoted here from Ludwig Fulda's edition of Brockes' poems, in the *Deutsche National-Litteratur* series, hereafter cited as *D. N. L.*, Vol. XXXIX, p. 288; Walter Raleigh, *Milton*, p. 255.
40. Der Schöpfer der Vergissmeinnicht selbst spricht:
    Vergiss mein nicht!
    (*D. N. L.*, Vol. XXXIX, p. 351).
41. Sind auch in Wölfen viele Dinge zu unserm Nutzen noch zu finden.
    Wir haben nicht nur ihrer Bälge im scharfen Frost uns zu erfreuen,
    Es dienen ihrer Glieder viele zu grossem Nutz in Arzeneien.
    (*Ibid.*, p. 378).
42. Für die Schwindsucht ist ihr Unschlitt, fürs Gesicht die Galle gut;
    Gemsenfleisch ist gut zu essen, und den Schwindel heilt ihr Blut;

Auch die Haut dient uns nicht minder; strahlet nicht aus diesem Thier,
Nebst die Weisheit und der Allmacht auch des Schöpfers Lieb herfür?
(Quoted here from H. Hettner's *Litteraturgeschichte des achtzehnten Jahrhunderts*, Part III, Book I, 4. edition, p. 312).

43. Ein wohlgesetzt Gemüht kan Galle süsse machen,
Da ein verwehnter Sinn auf alles Wermuth streut.
(*D. N. L.*, Vol. XLI–2, p. 17).

44. Zweideutig Mittelding von Engeln und von Vieh. . . .
. . . Vielleicht ist unsre Welt, die wie ein Körnlein Sand
Im Meer der Himmel schwimmt, des Übels Vaterland! . . .
Und dieses Punkt der Welt von minder Trefflichkeit
Dient in dem grossen All zu der Vollkommenheit. . . .
. . . Wann du der Thaten Grund uns würdigest zu lehren,
Dann werden alle dich, o Vater! recht verehren.
(*Ibid.*, pp. 34, 92, 93, 95, 103, 104)

45. Es öffnet Leibniz mir des Schicksals Heiligtum,
Und Licht bezeichnet seine Pfade.
(*D. N. L.*, Vol. XLV–2, p. 54).

46. So schwindet nach und nach das Uebel aus der Welt,
Das jetzt die Ordnung stört und unser Glück vergällt;
So wird die Zukunft erst des Schöpfers Güte preisen.
Dann löst sich alles auf. . . .
Wer jetzt im Dunkeln tappt, wird dann im Lichtmeer schwimmen,
Und jeder Misston rein, zum Klang der Sphären stimmen. . . .
(*Werke*, Goschen ed., 1856, Vol. XXV, pp. 136 f.).

47. Cf. F. B. Kaye's edition of *The Fable of the Bees*, 1924, Vol. I, p. xlviii.
48. *Ibid.*, p. 36.
49. Leslie Stephen, *op. cit.*, Vol. II, p. 372.
50. Quoted here from T. O. Wedel's article, "On the Philosophical Background of *Gulliver's Travels*," in *Studies in Philology*, October, 1926, p. 437.
51. "Day of Judgment," quoted here from Leslie Stephen, *op. cit.*, Vol. II, p. 373.
52. *Dialogues concerning Natural Religion*, in Green and Grose's edition of Hume's *Treatise of Human Nature*, Vol. II, p. 381.

53. *Ibid.*, pp. 382, 391, 397.
54. *Ibid.*, pp. 413, 414.
55. *Ibid.*, pp. 436, 437, 438.
56. *Night Thoughts*, I, 14; V, 88, 99; VII, 151, 180; IX, 255.

CHAPTER VI. THE DESPAIR OF CIVILIZATION

1. *Oeuvres complètes*, ed. Moland, Vol. XXII, p. 405.
2. *Deuxième discours de la liberté, Oeuvres*, Vol. IX, pp. 390 f.
3. *Remarques sur les Pensées de Pascal, Oeuvres*, Vol. XXII, p. 44.
4. *Traité de métaphysique*, 1734, *Oeuvres*, Vol. XXII, p. 201.
5. *Essai sur les moeurs*, Chap. IX; *Oeuvres*, Vol. XI, p. 235; transl. in John Morley, *Voltaire*, p. 322.
6. *Oeuvres*, Vol. IX, p. 475; cf. p. 471.
7. *Oeuvres*, Vol. IX, p. 476.
8. *Oeuvres*, Vol. XVII, p. 584.
9. *Oeuvres*, Vol. XXI, p. 218.
10. *Oeuvres*, Vol. XXI, p. 217.
11. Gerhard Gran, *Jean Jacques Rousseau*, Engl. transl., pp. 314 f.
12. Second Letter to Malesherbes, translation quoted from Morley, *Rousseau*, Vol. I, pp. 133 f.
13. Morley, *Rousseau*, Vol. I, p. 135.
14. Rousseau, *Oeuvres complètes*, 1835, Vol. I, pp. 470, 475.
15. *Oeuvres*, Vol. I, p. 491; quoted here from Jules Lemaître, *Jean Jacques Rousseau*, Engl. transl., pp. 92 f.
16. *Oeuvres*, Vol. I, p. 551; transl. in Morley, *Rousseau*, Vol. I, pp. 167 f.
17. Cf. Gerhard Gran, *Jean Jacques Rousseau*, p. 347.
18. Reply to Bordes; *Oeuvres*, Vol. I, p. 499, Notes; quoted from Lemaître, *op. cit.*, pp. 93 f.
19. Arthur Chuquet, *J.-J. Rousseau*, 4. edition, p. 32.
20. *Oeuvres*, Vol. IV, 1836, p. 224.
21. *Oeuvres*, Vol. IV, pp. 239 ff., 244, 246.
22. Morley, *Rousseau*, Vol. I, p. 311.
23. Quoted from Morley, *Voltaire*, p. 16.
24. Höffding, *Rousseau und seine Philosophie*, 1897, p. 74.
25. *Ibid.*, pp. 106 ff., 126.
26. *Oeuvres*, Vol. I, p. 558; quoted from Lemaître, *op. cit.*, p. 113. Cf. Petrarch's different turn to a similar reflection: "You have not the speed of the horse, but he gallops for you." (*Entretiens sur la bonne et mauvaise fortune*, 1673, Vol. II, p. 396).
27. Third Letter to Malesherbes; *Oeuvres*, Vol. I, p. 397.

28. Cf. *Diaries of Leo Tolstoy: Youth, 1847–1852*, transl. by C. J. Hogarth and A. Sirnis, p. 141 (March 29, 1852).
29. Cf. L. N. Tolstoy, *Pysma* (*Letters*), edited by P. A. Sergeyenko, Vol. I, 1910, p. 132 (Letter to N. N. Strakhov, March 9, 1879).
30. Cf. *Pysma*, Vol. I, p. 121 (Letter to Strakhov, Nov. 13, 1876).
31. Cf. Pascal's Life, written by his sister, in his *Oeuvres*, Vol. I, pp. 66 ff.
32. Cf. Letter to M. S. Dudtchenko, December 10, 1903, reporting conversation with W. J. Bryan, *Pysma*, Vol. I, p. 282.
33. *Pysma*, Vol. II, 1911, p. 57 (Letter to A. A. Fet, September 28, 1879); translation quoted from Aylmer Maude, *Life of Tolstoy: Later Years*, p. 10.
34. *Pysma*, Vol. I, pp. 142 ff.; transl. in Havelock Ellis, *The New Spirit*, 1890, p. 225.
35. *The World and the Individual*, Vol. II, p. 340.
36. *Pysma*, Vol. II, pp. 155 ff. (Letter to an English editor, December 15, 1894).

CHAPTER VII. THE DEVIL IN MODERN POETRY

1. *History of English Thought in the Eighteenth Century*, 3. edition, Vol. II, p. 352.
2. Quoted from Gerhard Gran, *Jean Jacques Rousseau*, Engl. transl., 1912, p. 97.
3. *Inferno*, IX, 61 ff.:

   O voi che avette gl' intelletti sani,
   Mirate la dottrina che s'asconde
   Sotto il velame dei versi strani.

   (Johnson's translation quoted in the text).
4. *Paradise Lost*, V, 572 ff.
5. *Paradise Lost*, V, 772.
6. *Ibid.*, III, 130 ff.
7. *Ibid.*, III, 214 ff.
8. *Ibid.*, II, 190 f.; I, 105 ff., 254 ff.; IX, 171 ff.; *Paradise Regained*, III, 209 ff.; *Paradise Lost*, I, 159 ff.; IV, 75 ff., 91 f.
9. *Paradise Regained*, IV, 145; *Paradise Lost*, VI, 178 ff.; XI, 515 ff.; *Lycidas*, 119; cf., Saurat, *Milton: Man and Thinker*, 1925, pp. 19 f.
10. *Paradise Regained*, III, 85 f.; *Paradise Lost*, XII, 587; VII, 613 ff.
11. A. H. Gilbert, "The Problem of Evil in Paradise Lost," *Journal of English and Germanic Philology*, Vol. XXII, p. 181.
12. *Paradise Lost*, I, 217 ff.

13. *Cain*, Act I, Scene i, lines 64 ff.
14. *Cain*, I, i, 144 ff.
15. *Byron*, p. 146.
16. *Cain*, I, i, 167 f., 174 ff., 189 ff.
17. *Cain*, I, i, 465 f., 518 f., 519 f., 522 ff., 213 ff.
18. *Cain*, II, ii, 414 ff.
19. *Cain*, II, i, 80 ff.
20. *Cain*, III, i, 303 f., 460 ff., 547 ff.
21. Quoted from Byron's *Works, Poetry*, Vol. V, editor E. H. Coleridge, p. 204.
22. Richard Ackermann, *Lord Byron*, 1901, p. 127.
23. *Cain*, I, i, 138 ff.; II, ii, 237 f.; III, i, 371 ff., 500 f.
24. *Cain*, I, i, 45.
25. Byron's letter to Moore, Nov. 3, 1821, quoted here from the Globe edition of his *Works*, p. 791, Note.
26. *Cain*, II, ii, 459 ff.
27. *Childe Harold*, III, xlii.
28. S. C. Chew, Jr., *The Dramas of Lord Byron*, 1915, p. 81.
29. *Manfred*, II, iv, 53 ff.; III, iv, 129 ff.; I, ii, 36 ff.
30. Ai-je dit à l'argile inerte: Souffre et pleure!
    Auprès de la défense ai-je mit le désir?
    L'ardent attrait d'un bien impossible à saisir,
    Et le songe immortel dans le néant de l'heure?
    Ai-je dit de vouloir et puni d'obéir?

    O misère! Ai-je dit à l'implacable Maître,
    Au Jaloux, tourmenteur du monde et des vivants,
    Qui gronde dans la foudre et chevauche les vents:
    La vie assurément est bonne, je veux naître!
    Que m'importait la vie au prix où tu la vends?
31. A. L. Guérard, *French Prophets of Yesterday*, p. 200.
32. Translation by N. Jarintzov, in her *Russian Poets and Poems*, 1917.
33. Die immer fliegt und fliegend springt
    Und gleich im Gras ihr altes Liedchen singt.
    (*Prolog im Himmel*). The translation quoted in the text is Bayard Taylor's, hereafter cited as *B. T.*
34. Cf. David Masson, *The Three Devils*, 1874, pp. 41 ff.
35. Ich bin der Geist der stets verneint!
    Und das mit Recht; denn alles was entsteht,
    Ist wert dass es zu Grunde geht.
    (*Erster Theil: Studierzimmer; B. T.*, Vol. I, p. 54).

36. So ist denn alles was ihr Sünde,
Zerstörung, kurz das Böse nennt,
Mein eigeintliches Element.
(*Ibid.*, *B. T.*, Vol. I, p. 55).

37. *B. T.*, Vol. II, p. 299.

38. Du siehst, mit diesem Trank im Leibe,
Bald Helenen in jedem Weibe.
(*Erster Theil: Hexenküche; B. T.*, Vol. I, p. 112).

39. *B. T.*, Vol. I, p. 203.

40. Versinke denn! Ich könnt' auch sagen: steige!
's ist einerlei.
(*Zweiter Theil: Finstere Galerie; B. T.*, Vol. II, p. 68).

41. Vorbei und reines Nicht, vollkommnes Einerlei!
Was soll uns denn das ew'ge Schaffen?
Geschaffenes zu nichts hinwegzuraffen!
"Da ist's vorbei." Was is daran zu lesen?
Es ist so gut, als wär' es nicht gewesen.
Und treibt sich doch im Kreis, als wenn es wäre.
Ich liebte mir dafür das Ewig-Leere.
(*Zweiter Theil: Grosser Vorhof des Palasts; B. T.*, Vol. II, pp. 295 f.).

42. Staub soll er fressen, und mit Lust (*Prolog im Himmel; B. T.*, Vol. I, p. 15).

43. Werd ich zum Augenblicke sagen:
Verweile doch! du bist so schön!
Dann magst du mich in Fesseln schlagen,
Dann will ich gern zu Grunde gehn!
(*Erster Theil: Studierzimmer; B. T.*, Vol. I, p. 68).

44. *Schopenhauer, Hamlet, Mephistopheles*, 3. edition, p. 214.

45. Ein Theil von jener Kraft,
Die stets das Böse will, und stets das Gute schafft.
(*Erster Theil: Studierzimmer; B. T.*, Vol. I, p. 54).

46. Ein guter Mensch, in seinem dunklen Drange,
Ist sich des rechten Weges wohl bewusst.
(*Prolog im Himmel; B. T.*, Vol. I, p. 14).

47. Des Menschen Tätigkeit kann allzu leicht erschlaffen,
Er liebt sich bald die unbedingte Ruh;
Drum geb ich gern ihm den Gesellen zu,
Der reizt und wirkt und muss als Teufel schaffen.
(*Ibid.; B. T.*, Vol. I, p. 15).

48. Im Innern hier ein paradiesich Land,
Da rase draussen Flut bis auf zum Rand,
Und wie sie nascht, gewaltsam einzuschiessen,
Gemeindrang eilt, die Lücke zu verschliessen.
Ja! diesem Sinne bin ich ganz ergeben,
Das ist der Weisheit letzter Schluss:
Nur der verdient sich Freiheit wie das Leben,
Der täglich sie erobern muss.
(*Zweiter Theil: Grosser Vorhof des Palasts; B. T.*, Vol. II, p. 294).

49. Es irrt der Mensch, so lang er strebt.
(*Prolog im Himmel; B. T.*, Vol. I, p. 14).

50. Wer immer strebend sich bemüht,
Den können wir erlösen.
(*Zweiter Theil: Bergschluchten, Wald, Fels, Einöde; B. T.*, Vol. II, p. 459).

51. June, 1831; quoted here from *B. T.*, Vol. II, p. 459.
52. Cf. *B. T.*, Vol. I, pp. 345 f., Note.
53. Heine calls it "ein geniales Meisterwerk," *Sämmtliche Werke*, Meyers Klassiker edition, Vol. VI, p. 502.
54. Tucker Brooke's edition, Oxford, lines 81 f.
55. Lines 312 ff., 547, 1019, 1328 f.
56. Cf. Lessing's *Werke*, in *Deutsche National-Litteratur*, Vol. LX-ii, pp. 160–174; Vol. LXIV, pp. 196 ff.
57. Cf. William Hamilton, *Metaphysics*, Lecture I, citing an array of similar views from Aristotle to Jean Paul Richter; cf. also W. R. Inge, *The Philosophy of Plotinus*, Vol. II, p. 239.
58. Grillparzer, *Sämmtliche Werke*, Moritz Necker edition, Vol. X, p. 179.
59. *Sämmtliche Werke*, Meyers Klassiker edition, Vol. VI, p. 506.
60. *Ibid.*, Vol. VI, p. 490.
61. *Mosaiken und Silhouetten*, 1877, p. 166.
62. Ich schaue durch die steinern harten Rinden
Der Menschenhäuser und der Menschenherzen,
Und schau' in beiden Lug und Trug und Elend.
Auf den Gesichtern les' ich die Gednaken,
Viel schlimmer. In der Jungfrau Schamerröten
Seh' ich geheime Lust begehrlich zittern,
Auf dem begeistert stolzen Jünglingshaupt
Seh' ich die lachend bunte Schellenkappe;
Und Fratzenbilder nur und sieche Schatten

Seh' ich auf dieser Erde, und ich weiss nicht,
Ist sie ein Tollhaus oder Krankenhaus.

(*Die Heimkehr: Götterdämmerung;* translation by Louis Untermeyer, in *Poems of Heinrich Heine*, revised edition, 1923).

63. Ich schrieb bei nächtlicher Lampe
Den Jammer, der mich traf;
Er ist bei Hoffmann und Campe
Erschienen in Klein-Oktav.

(Quoted here from Plümacher, *Der Pessimismus*, 2. edition, p. 115).

64. *Werke*, edited by Castle, Vol. V, p. 150.

65. Ich bin kein *delirischer* sondern ein lyrischer Dichter.

(*Werke*, Meyers Klassiker edition, Vol. I, p. xciii).

66. Ich will Ihm gegenüber treten,
Beglücken kann mich nur ein Wissen
Das mein ist und von seinem lossgerissen.
Ich will mich immer als mich selber fühlen.

(*Faust: Die Verschreibung*).

67. Dann lass ich rings um ihn mein Feuer brennen,
Er wird im Glutring hierhin, dorthin rennen,
Ein Skorpion sein eignes Ich erstechen.

(*Faust: Der Teufel.* The frequency of this scorpion-simile in romantic poetry is significant; we find it in Byron, in Vigny, in Shelley, in Coleridge; cf. S. C. Chew, Jr., *The Dramas of Lord Byron*, p. 68, Note).

68. Verderbend mich als Gegenschöpfer fühlen.

(*Faust: Der Teufel*).

69. Mein Faust, ich will dir einen Tempel bauen,
Wo dein Gedanke ist als Gott zu schauen.
Du sollst in eine Felsenhalle treten
Und dort zu deinem eignen Wesen beten.

(*Faust: Das Waldgespräch*).

70. Niemanden hörig mehr und unterthan,
Verfolg ich in mich einwärts meine Bahn.

(*Ibid.*).

71. *Werke*, edited by Castle, Vol. IV, p. 234.

72. Mein Ich! das höhle, finstre, karge,
Umschauert mich gleich einem Sarge.
Im Starrkampf wilder Eigensucht
Warf mich der Teufel in die Schlucht.

Lebendig in den Grabesfinsternissen,
Hab ich, erwacht, die Augen aufgerissen,
Und ich begann mit unermess 'nen Klagen
Mich selber anzunagen.
Ich habe nur gesprengt die dumpfe Haft;
Mit doppelt heisser Leidenschaft
Streck' ich die Arme wieder aus
Nach Gott und Welt aus meinem Totenhaus.
Nach Gott!—doch nein!—der Kummer ist es nur:
Könnt ich vergessen, dass ich Kreatur!

(*Faust: Fausts Tod*).

73. Ich bin ein Traum mit Lust und Schuld und Schmerz,
Und träume mir das Messer in das Herz. (*Ibid.*).

74. Der Gott der Freuden ist ein Gott der Schranken.
(*Werke*, Meyers Klassiker edition, Vol. II, p. 431).

75. Die eine hält in derber Liebeslust
Sich an die Welt mit klammernden Organen;
Die andre hebt gewaltsam sich vom Dust
Zu den Gefilden hoher Ahnen.
(*Erster Theil: Vor dem Tor; B. T.*, Vol. I, p. 45).

76. Grabbe, *Werke*, Vol. II, p. 136.

77. Wozu übermenschlich,
Wenn du ein Mensch bleibst?
Wozu Mensch,
Wenn du nach übermenschlichem nicht strebst?
(*Don Juan und Faust*, Act III, Scene iii).

78. Ich spann'
Die Segel wieder, fahr' mit neuem Winde!
(Act IV, Scene iv).

79. Und *wen* sie auch im Arme hält,
Ein andrer ist's als den sie meint.
(*Don Juan: Don Juan und Isabella*).

80. *Don Juan und Faust*, Act II, Scene ii.

81. Nein, nein!
Es ist kein Gott! Zu seinem Ehre
Will ich das glauben.
(*Herzog Theodor von Gothland;* quoted here from Huber, *Der Pessimismus*, p. 56).

82. Es gab einst einen *Gott*, der war
Zerschlagen—wir sind seine Stücke.
(Act IV, Scene iii).

CHAPTER VIII. LEOPARDI'S LYRICAL PESSIMISM

1. *Epistolario di Giacomo Leopardi*, edited by Prospero Viani, with new material by G. Piergili, 3 volumes, 1925, Vol. I, p. 88.
2. *Epistolario*, Vol. I, pp. 86 f.
3. Giovanni Mestica, *Studi Leopardiani*, 1901, p. 3.
4. *Epistolario*, Vol. III, p. 475.
5. Sainte-Beuve, *Portraits contemporains*, Vol. IV, 1870, p. 367.
6. Leopardi, *Scritti letterari*, edited by Mestica, Vol. II, 1899, pp. 89 ff. Regarding Leopardi's early studies, cf. also Paul Hazard, *Giacomo Leopardi*, 1913, pp. 9 ff., 23 ff.
7. E che pensieri immensi,
   Che dolci sogni mi spirò la vista
   Di quel lontano mar, quei monti azzurri,
   Che di qua scopro, e che varcare un giorno
   Io mi pensava, arcani mondi, arcana
   Felicità fingendo al viver mio!
   (*Le ricordanze*).
8. G. A. Cesareo, *La vita di Giacomo Leopardi*, 1902, pp. 25 ff.
9. *Lettere a Marianna ed Anna Brighenti*, 1887, quoted here from Hazard, *op. cit.*, p. 21.
10. Edited by Carducci and published under the title *Pensieri di varia filosofia e di bella letteratura*, in seven volumes. Quotations are from the 3. impression of Vol. I, and from the 2. impression of the other six volumes (cited hereafter as *Zibaldone*); Vol. I, pp. 411 f.
11. Qui passo gli anni, abbandonato, occulto,
    Senz 'amor, senza vita; ed aspro a forza
    Tra lo stuol de' malevoli divengo:
    Qui di pietà mi spoglio e di virtudi,
    E sprezzator degli uomini mi rendo,
    Per la greggia ch' ho appresso: e intanto vola
    Il caro tempo giovanil; piú caro
    Che la fama e l'allor, piú che la pura
    Luce del giorno, e lo spirar: ti perdo
    Senza un diletto, inutilmente, in questo
    Soggiorno disumano, intra gli affanni,
    O dell 'arida vita unico fiore.
    (*The Poems of Leopardi*, edited with Introduction and Notes and a Verse-Translation in the Metres of the Original, by Geoffrey L. Bickersteth, Cambridge University Press, 1923).

12. Sento che va languendo entro mio petto
La vital fiamma, e 'ntorno guardo, e al mondo
Sol per me veggo il funeral mio letto.
E sento del pensier l' immenso pondo,
Sí che vo 'l labbro muto e 'l viso smorto
E quasi mio dolor piú non ascondo.
(*Appressamento della morte*): Quoted from Bickersteth, *op. cit.*, p. 11.
13. *Epistolario*, Vol. I, p. 57.
14. Cf. *Epistolario*, Vol. III, p. 95.
15. *Epistolario*, Vol. I, p. 217; translation from Bickersteth, *op. cit.*, p. 17.
16. *Epistolario*, Vol. I, p. 338.
17. *Epistolario*, Vol. I, p. 362.
18. *Epistolario*, Vol. II, pp. 31 f.
19. *Epistolario*, Vol. II, pp. 304, 336 f.
20. *Epistolario*, Vol. II, pp. 356 ff.
21. *Epistolario*, Vol. II, pp. 404, 405.
22. Cf. "Gli amori di Giacomo Leopardi," in Mestica, *Studi Leopardiani*, pp. 55–190.
23. Ranieri, *Sette anni di sodalizio con Giacomo Leopardi*.
24. *Epistolario*, Vol. II, p. 479; cf. Hjalmar Hahl, *Les tendances morales dans l'oeuvre de Giacomo Leopardi*, Helsingfors, 1896, p. 14.
25. *Studi Leopardiani*, p. 45.
26. *Zibaldone*, Vol. I, p. 195.
27. *Opere*, edited by G. Mestica, 1906, Vol. II, p. 386; *Zibaldone*, Vol. IV, pp. 388 ff.
28. Volgiti indietro, e guarda, o patria mia,
Quella schiera infinita d' immortali,
E piangi e di te stessa ti disdegna.
(*Sopra il monumento di Dante*).
29. Cf. *Zibaldone*, Vol. V, pp. 228 ff.; Vol. II, pp. 53 ff.; Vol. IV, p. 376.
30. Cf. *Zibaldone*, Vol. V, p. 298; Vol. II, pp. 232 ff., 246; Vol. IV, pp. 270 ff.
31. To this point Leopardi returns repeatedly: cf. *Zibaldone*, Vol. I, p. 223; Vol. II, p. 91; Vol. IV, pp. 251 f.; *Opere*, Vol. II, pp. 373 f.
32. Il garzoncel, come inesperto amante,
La sua vita ingannevole vagheggia.
(*Le ricordanze*).
33. Cf. *Epistolario*, Vol. I, p. 291; *Zibaldone*, Vol. IV, pp. 289 f.

34. *Operette morali, Opere,* Vol. II, p. 19; transl. in *Essays, Dialogues and Thoughts of Giacomo Leopardi,* by James Thomson ('B.V.'), London, Routledge, p. 106.
35. *Opere,* Vol. II, p. 238; Thomson's transl., p. 261.
36. Cf. *Zibaldone,* Vol. I, p. 165; Vol. VII, p. 60.
37. Fantasmi, intendo,
Son la gloria e l' onor; diletti e beni
Mero desio; non ha la vita un frutto,
Inutile miseria.
(*Le ricordanze*).
38. Cf. *Zibaldone,* Vol. II, p. 393; Vol. III, p. 422; Vol. VI, pp. 270 f., 359; Romualdo Giani, *L'Estetica nei "Pensieri" di Giacomo Leopardi,* 1904.
39. *Zibaldone,* Vol. I, p. 181; Vol. IV, pp. 391 f.; cf. Vol. I, p. 439; Vol. II, pp. 105 f.; Vol. VII, pp. 66 f., 108 f., 238 f.
40. Cf. *Zibaldone,* Vol. III, pp. 269 ff.; Vol. VII, pp. 29 f., 191 ff.; cf. also Mestica, *Studi Leopardiani,* pp. 452 ff.; A. Graf, *Foscolo, Manzoni, Leopardi,* 1914, pp. 251 ff.; G. A. Levi, *Storia del Pensiero di Giacomo Leopardi,* 1911, pp. 122 ff. Cicero speaks of nature as our stepmother, and both St. Augustine and Bayle quote him with approval: Bayle, *Dictionnaire,* Article "Ovid," Remarque *E;* cf. T. O. Wedel, "On the Philosophical Background of *Gulliver's Travels,*" *Studies in Philology,* October, 1926, p. 443.
41. Arcano è tutto,
Fuor che il nostro dolor.
(*Ultimo canto di Saffo*).
42. *Opere,* Vol. II, p. 107; Thomson's transl., p. 170; cf. *Zibaldone,* Vol. VII, pp. 198 ff.
43. Cf. *Zibaldone,* Vol. II, pp. 461 f.
44. Sovente in queste rive,
Che, desolate, a bruno
Veste il flutto indurato, e par che ondeggi,
Seggo la notte; e su la mesta landa
In purissimo azzurro
Veggo dall' alto fiammeggiar le stelle,
Cui di lontan fa specchio
Il mare, e tutto di scintille in giro
Per lo vòto seren brillare il mondo.
E poi che gli occhi a quelle luci appunto,
Ch' a lor sembrano un punto,
E sono immense, in guisa

Che un punto a petto a lor son terra e mare
Veracemente; a cui
L' uomo non pur, ma questo
Globo ove l' uomo è nulla
Sconosciuto è del tutto; e quando miro
Quegli ancor piú senz' alcun fin remoti
No di quasi di stelle
Ch' a noi paion qual nebbia, a cui non l' uomo
E non la terra sol, ma tutte in uno,
Del numero infinite e della mole,
Con l' aureo sole insiem, le nostre stelle
O sono ignote, o cosí paion come
Essi alla terra, un punto
Di luce nebulosa; al pensier mio
Che sembri allora, o prole
Dell' uomo? E rimembrando
Il tuo stato quaggiú, di cui fa segno
Il suol ch' io premo; e poi dall' altra parte,
Che te signora e fine
Credi tu data al Tutto, e quante volte
Favoleggiar ti piacque, in questo oscuro
Granel di sabbia, il qual di terra ha nome,
Per tua cagion, dell' universe cose
Scender gli autori, e conversar sovente
Co' tuoi piacevolmente, e che i derisi
Sogni rinnovellando, ai saggi insulta
Fin la presente età, che in conoscenza
Ed in civil costume
Sembra tutte avanzar; qual moto allora,
Mortal prole infelice, o qual pensiero
Verso te finalmente il cor m'assale?
Non so se il riso o la pietà prevale.

(*La ginestra*).

45. *Degli spiriti e delle forme nella poesia di Giacomo Leopardi*, 1898, p. 38.
46. Cf. Francesco de Sanctis, *Studio su Giacomo Leopardi*, 7. edition, p. 279; F. A. Aulard, *Poésies et oeuvres morales de Leopardi*, 1880, Vol. I, pp. 35–40.
47. *Opere*, Vol. II, pp. 168, 339; Thomson's transl., pp. 215, 346.
48. Non val cosa nessuna
I moti tuoi, né di sospiri è degna

La terra. Amaro e noia
La vita, altro mai nulla; e fango è il mondo.
T' acqueta omai. Dispera
L' ultima volta. Al gener nostro il fato
Non donò che il morire. Omai disprezza
Te, la natura, il brutto
Poter che, ascoso, a comun danno impera,
E l' infinita vanità del tutto.

(*A se stesso*).

49. Re delle cose, autor del mondo, arcana
Malvagità, sommo potere e somma
Intelligenza, eterno
Dator de' mali e reggitor del moto. . . .

Cf. Cesareo, *op. cit.*, p. 149; the translation of this passage in the text is by the present writer.

50. *Zibaldone*, Vol. VII, pp. 104 f.

51. *Zibaldone*, Vol. I, p. 183.

52. O greggia mia che posi, oh te beata,
Che la miseria tua, credo, non sai!
Quanta invidia ti porto!

(*Canto notturno*).

53. E piegherai
Sotto il fascio mortal non renitente
Il tuo capo innocente:
Ma non piegato insino allora indarno
Codardamente supplicando innanzi
Al futuro oppressor; ma non eretto
Con forsennato orgoglio inver le stelle,
Né sul deserto, dove
E la sede e i natali
Non per voler ma per fortuna avesti;
Ma piú saggia, ma tanto
Meno inferma dell' uom, quanto le frali
Tue stirpi non credesti
O dal fato o da te fatte immortali.

(*La ginestra*).

54. *Zibaldone*, Vol. VII, pp. 106 f.; cf., *Opere*, Vol. II, p. 85; Thomson's transl., pp. 153 f.

55. *Epistolario*, Vol. I, p. 556; *Odyssey*, XI, 539; cf., Sainte-Beuve, *op. cit.*, p. 415; Carducci, *op. cit.*, p. 121.

56. *Opere*, Vol. II, p. 291; Thomson's transl., p. 300; cf., *Zibaldone*,

Vol. II, pp. 101 ff.; cf. also Tsanoff, *The Problem of Immortality*, pp. 303–310.

57. *Op. cit.*, p. 166.
58. Cf. *Zibaldone*, Vol. I, p. 177; Vol. VI, p. 419; Vol. V, p. 50.
59. *Opere*, Vol. II, p. 276; Thomson's transl., p. 290.
60. E già nel primo giovanil tumulto
 Di contenti, d' angosce e di desio
 Morte chiamai piú volte, e lungamente
 Mi sedetti colà su la fontana
 Pensoso di cessar dentro quell' acque
 La speme e il dolor mio.
61. *Zibaldone*, Vol. III, pp. 473 ff.; cf. Vol. I, pp. 176, 177, 183; Vol. IV, pp. 124, 219 f., 272, 302 ff.
62. Quando gl' infausti giorni
 Virile alma recusa,
 Riede natura, e il non suo dardo accusa?
63. Morremo. Il velo indegno a terra sparto
 Rifuggirà l'ignudo animo a Dite,
 E il crudo fallo emenderà del cieco
 Dispensator de' casi.
64. *Zibaldone*, Vol. III, pp. 396, 397.
65. *Zibaldone*, Vol. I, pp. 349 f.; transl. in Bickersteth, *op. cit.*, p. 104.
66. Sempre caro mi fu quest' ermo colle,
 E questa siepe, che da tanta parte
 Dell' ultimo orizzonte il guardo esclude.
 Ma sedendo e mirando, interminati
 Spazi di là da quella, e sovrumani
 Silenzi, e profondissima quiete
 Io nel pensier mi fingo; ove per poco
 Il cor non si spaura. E come il vento
 Odo stormir tra queste piante, io quello
 Infinito silenzio a questa voce
 Vo comparando: e mi sovvien l' eterno,
 E le morte stagioni, e la presente
 E viva, e il suon di lei. Cosí tra questa
 Immensità s'annega il pensier mio:
 E il naufragar m' è dolce in questo mare.
67. Fra cotanto dolore
 Quanto all' umana età propose il fato,
 Se vera e quale il mio pensier ti pinge,

Alcun t' amasse in terra, a lui pur fora
Questo viver beato.

68. *Zibaldone*, Vol. V, p. 223; cf. Vol. IV, pp. 224 ff., 318; *Opere*, Vol. II, p. 55; Thomson's transl., p. 131; Pascal, *Oeuvres*, Vol. XIII, pp. 261 ff.; cf. Gentile's *Proemio* to his edition of the *Operette morali*, 1925, pp. xlvii f.
69. *Zibaldone*, Vol. IV, p. 213.
70. Natura umana, or come,
Se frale in tutto e vile,
Se polve ed ombra sei, tant' alto senti?
Se in parte anco gentile,
Come i piú degni tuoi moti e pensieri
Son cosí di leggeri
Da sí basse cagioni e desti e spenti?
(*Sopra il ritratto di una bella donna*).
71. Levi, *op. cit.*, p. 158.
72. Sempre i codardi, e l' alme
Ingenerose, abiette
Ebbi in dispregio.
(*Il pensiero dominante*).
73. *Zibaldone*, Vol. III, p. 478; Vol. IV, p. 292.
74. *Op. cit.*, pp. 330 f.
75. *Zibaldone*, Vol. I, pp. 184 f.; Vol. III, p. 383.
76. Carducci, *op. cit.*, pp. 14 ff.
77. *Epistolario*, Vol. I, p. 454.
78. *Zibaldone*, Vol. VI, p. 421.
79. *Zibaldone*, Vol. I, p. 351.
80. *Opere*, Vol. II, p. 362; Thomson's transl, p. 365.
81. *Zibaldone*, Vol. VII, pp. 361 f.
82. *Op. cit.*, p. 113.
83. Nobil natura è quella
Che a sollevar s'ardisce
Gli occhi mortali incontra
Al comun fato, e che con franca lingua,
Nulla al ver detraendo,
Confessa il mal che ci fu dato in sorte,
E il basso stato e frale;
Quella che grande e forte
Mostra se nel soffrir, né gli odii e l' ire
Fraterne, ancor piú gravi
D' ogni altro danno, accresce

Alle miserie sue, l' uomo incolpando
Del suo dolor, ma dà la colpa a quella
Che veramente è rea, che de' mortali
Madre è di parto e di voler matrigna.

84. *Epistolario*, Vol. I, pp. 454 f.
85. *Saggi critici*, 30. edition, pp. 297 f.
86. *Zibaldone*, Vol. I, p. 322.

CHAPTER IX. ARISTOCRACY WITHOUT ILLUSIONS: ALFRED DE VIGNY

1. Vigny, *Journal d'un poète*, Entry for the year 1843.
2. Cf. Richard Huber, *Alfred de Vigny als Philosoph*, Marburg Diss., 1913, pp. 89 ff.
3. Cf. N. Serban, *Alfred de Vigny et Frédéric II: Étude d'influence littéraire*, Paris, 1920.
4. Cf. Otto G. Harlander, "Alfred de Vignys pessimistische Weltanschauung," in *Romanische Forschungen*, XXIX, 1910, p. 414.
5. Cf. Émile Montégut, *Nos morts contemporains*, Première série, Paris, 1883, p. 345.
6. "Alfred de Vigny," in *Revue des deux mondes*, 1891, p. 691.
7. Léon Séché, *Alfred de Vigny et son temps*, p. 87.
8. *Servitude et grandeur militaires*, Baldensperger edition, p. 143.
9. *Correspondance*, 1816–1863, 2. edition by Emma Sakellaridès, p. 245.
10. Edmond Estève, *Alfred de Vigny, sa pensée et son art*, Paris, 1923, p. 19.
11. Cf. É. Charavay, *Alfred de Vigny et Charles Baudelaire, Candidats à l'Académie Française*, Paris, 1879.
12. *Journal d'un poète*, December, 1837.
13. *Ibid.*, 1834, near the beginning.
14. Moi-même, crédule à ma joie,
    J'enivre mon coeur, je me noie
    Aux torrents d'un riant orgueil;
    Mais le Malheur devant ma face
    A passé: le rire s'efface,
    Et mon front a repris son deuil.
    (*Le malheur*).
15. O Seigneur! j'ai vécu puissant et solitaire,
    Laissez-moi m'endormir du sommeil de la terre!
    (*Moïse*).
16. *Stello*, Baldensperger edition, p. 205.

17. Mais le ciel reste noir, et Dieu ne répond pas.
(*Le Mont des Oliviers*).
18. *Stello*, p. 192.
19. *Op. cit.*, pp. 292 ff.
20. Albert L. Guérard, *French Prophets of Yesterday*, pp. 183 f.; cf. Marc Citoleux, *Alfred de Vigny*, pp. 240 ff.
21. Quoted here from Baldensperger's edition of Vigny's *Poëmes*, p. 414.
22. Tiens toujours tes regards plus haut que sur la Terre;
La mort de l'Innocence est pour l'homme un mystère;
Ne t'en étonne pas, n'y porte pas tes yeux;
La pitié du mortel n'est point celle des Cieux.
Dieu ne fait point de pacte avec la race humaine:
Qui créa sans amour fera périr sans haine.
(*Le déluge*).
23. —Ton père ne vient pas; nous seront donc punis?
—Sans doute après la mort nous serons réunis.
24. Je n'en veux pas; j'y trouverais des chaînes.
(*La prison*).
25. *Journal*, 1834, *ad fin*.
26. Je n'entends ni vos cris ni vos soupirs; à peine
Je sens passer sur moi la comédie humaine
Qui cherche en vain au ciel ses muets spectateurs. . . .
On me dit une mère, et je suis une tombe.
Mon hiver prend vos morts comme son hécatombe,
Mon printemps ne sent pas vos adorations!
(*La maison du berger*).
27. Je ne sais d'assurés, dans le chaos du sort,
Que deux points seulement: *La souffrance et la mort.*
(*Paris*).
28. *Journal*, 1835.
29. F. Baldensperger, *Alfred de Vigny*, *Contribution à sa biographie intellectuelle*, Paris, 1912, p. 24.
30. Comment on doit quitter la vie et tous ses maux,
Ce vous qui le savez, sublimes animaux!
A voir ce que l'on fut sur terre et ce qu'on laisse,
Seul le silence est grand; tout le reste est faiblesse. . . .
Gémir, pleurer, prier est également lâche.
Fais énergiquement ta longue et lourde tâche,
Dans la voie où le Sort a volu t'appeler.
Puis après, comme moi, souffre et meurs sans parler.
(*La mort du loup*).

31. S'il est vrai qu'au Jardin sacré des Écritures,
Le Fils de l'homme ait dit ce qu'on voit rapporté;
Muet, aveugle et sourd au cri des créatures,
Si le Ciel nous laissa comme une monde avorté,
Le juste opposera le dédain à l'absence
Et ne répondra plus que par un froid silence
Au silence éternel de la Divinité.

32. Vivez, froide Nature, et revivez sans cesse
Sur nos pieds, sur nos fronts, puisque c'est votre loi;
Vivez, et dédaignez, si vous êtes déesse,
L'Homme, humble passager, qui dût vous être un Roi;
Plus que tout votre règne et que ses splendeurs vaines
J'aime la majesté des souffrances humaines:
Vous ne recevrez pas un cri d'amour de moi.
(*La maison du berger*).

33. *Journal*, 1844.
34. *Ibid.*, 1834.
35. *Servitude et grandeur militaires*, p. 200.
36. *Ibid.*, p. 248; *Journal*, 1835, beginning.
37. *Servitude et grandeur militaires*, p. 248.
38. *Journal*, 1836, near the beginning.
39. *Stello*, p. 426.
40. *Servitude et grandeur militaires*, p. 222.
41. *Journal*, 1834, *ad fin.*
42. *Loc. cit.*
43. *Ibid.*, 1830, *ad fin.*
44. Marc Citoleux, *Alfred de Vigny*, p. 1; cf. pp. 23, 63, 303 ff.
45. Cf. *Journal*, 1842.
46. Elle dit, en fondant chaque neuve cité,
"Vous m'appelez la Loi, je suis la Liberté."

47. Le vrai Dieu, le Dieu fort est le Dieu des idées!
Sur nos fronts où le germe est jeté par le sort,
Répandons le savoir en fécondes ondées,
Puis, recueillant le fruit tel que de l'âme il sort,
Tout empreint du parfum des saintes solitudes,
Jetons l'oeuvre à la mer, la mer des multitudes:
—Dieu la prendra du doigt pour la conduire au port.

48. Du corps et non de l'âme accusons l'indigence.
Des organes mauvais servent l'intelligence. . . .
En traducteurs grossiers de quelque auteur céleste
Ils parlent. . . .

49. Tous sont morts en laissant son nom sans auréole,
Mais sur le Livre d'or voilà qu'il est écrit,
Disant: "Ici passaient deux races de la Gaule
Dont le dernier vivant monte au temple et s'inscrit,
Non sur l'obscur amas des vieux noms inutiles,
Des orgueilleux méchants et des riches futiles,
Mais sur le pur tableau des titres de l'*esprit.*

50. *XIXe Siècle*, p. 133.
51. *Journal*, 1835.
52. Cf. Ernest Dupuy, *Alfred de Vigny: Ses amitiés, son rôle littéraire,* Vol. I, pp. 300 ff.; Vol. II, pp. 36 ff.
53. *Journal*, 1862.
54. Estève, *Op. cit.*, p. 31.
55. *Daphné*, Delagrave edition, p. 10.

CHAPTER X. THE WARP OF SCHOPENHAUER

1. Translated by Susanna Winkworth, Golden Treasury Series, pp. 67, 73, 122.
2. *Sämmtliche Werke*, edited by Paul Deussen, Vol. II, p. 693; Haldane and Kemp's translation of *The World as Will and Idea*, 6. edition, Vol. III, p. 423. (Cited hereafter as *Werke* and *H.-K.*).
3. *Arthur Schopenhauer's handschriftlicher Nachlass*, edited by Eduard Grisebach, Vol. IV, p. 260.
4. Cf. P. J. Möbius, *Ueber Schopenhauer*, 1899, pp. 7 ff.
5. *Arthur Schopenhauers Briefwechsel und andere Dokumente*, edited by Max Brahn, 1911, p. 7.
6. O Wollust, o Hölle,
O Sinne, o Liebe,
Nicht zu befriedgen
Und nicht zu besiegen!
Aus Höhen des Himmels
Hast du mich gezogen
Und hin mich geworfen
In Staub dieser Erde. . . .

(*Briefwechsel*, p. 8).

Was wäre wünschenswerter wohl,
Als ganz zu siegen
Über das leere und so arme Leben,

Was keinen Wunsch uns je erfüllen kann,
Ob Sehnsucht gleich uns auch das Herz zersprengt.
Wie wär es schön, mit leichtem leisen Schritte
Das wüste Erdenleben zu durchwandeln,
Dass nirgends je der Fuss im Staube hafte,
Das Auge nicht vom Himmel ab sich wende.

(*Briefwechsel*, p. 9).

7. *Briefwechsel*, p. 19.
8. *Schopenhauer's Gespräche und Selbstgespräche*, edited by Eduard Grisebach, 1902, p. 11.
9. W. Gwinner, *Schopenhauer's Leben*, 2. edition, p. 143.
10. *Werke*, Vol. XI, p. 46; translation quoted from Wallace, *Life of Arthur Schopenhauer*, pp. 95 f.
11. *Briefwechsel*, p. 61.
12. *Briefwechsel*, p. 73.
13. Gwinner, *op. cit.*, p. 283.
14. *Geschichte der neueren Philosophie*, 3. edition, Vol. II, p. 354.
15. *Schopenhauer's Gespräche und Selbstgespräche*, pp. 133 f.
16. Kuno Fischer, *Schopenhauers Leben, Werke und Lehre*, 3. edition, p. 133.
17. J. Frauenstädt, *Memorabilien, Briefe und Nachlassstücke* (published together with E. O. Lindner's *Arthur Schopenhauer. Von ihm. Ueber ihn*), 1863, p. 336.
18. *Ibid.*, p. 510.
19. *Siebentes Jahrbuch der Schopenhauer-Gesellschaft*, 1918, p. 31.
20. H. Frommann, *Arthur Schopenhauer*, 1872, p. 6.

CHAPTER XI. GROUNDS AND LIMITS OF SCHOPENHAUER'S PESSIMISM

1. *Op. cit.*, p. 338.
2. *Schopenhauer-Briefe*, edited by Ludwig Schemann, 1893, p. 198.
3. *Werke*, Vol. II, p. 196; *H.-K.*, Vol. II, p. 381.
4. *Werke*, Vol. II, p. 198; *H.-K.*, Vol. II, p. 383.
5. *Werke*, Vol. I, p. 126; *H.-K.*, Vol. I, p. 137.
6. *Werke*, Vol. I, pp. 191, 192; *H.-K.*, Vol. I, p. 210.
7. *Werke*, Vol. XI, p. 530.
8. *Werke*, Vol. V, pp. 317 f.
9. *La philosophie de Schopenhauer*, 13. edition, p. 134.
10. *Werke*, Vol. I, p. 231; *H.-K.*, Vol. I, p. 253.
11. *Werke*, Vol. I, p. 231; *H.-K.*, Vol. I, p. 254.

12. Mille piacer' non vagliono un tormento.
(Sonetto 195); cf. *Werke*, Vol. II, p. 659; *H.-K.*, Vol. III, p. 386.
13. Mir deuchte doch, als tränk' ich Wein.
(*Werke*, Vol. II, p. 571; *H.-K.*, Vol. III, p. 297).
14. *Werke*, Vol. III, p. 667; cf. p. 666; *The Basis of Morality*, translated by A. B. Bullock, p. 152; cf. p. 151.
15. *Werke*, Vol. I, p. 433; *H.-K.*, Vol. I, p. 474.
16. *Werke*, Vol. III, p. 664; *Bas. of Mor.*, p. 147.
17. *Werke*, Vol. I, p. 175; *H.-K.*, Vol. I, p. 192.
18. *Werke*, Vol. II, p. 405; *H.-K.*, Vol. III, p. 112.
19. *Werke*, Vol. II, p. 661; *H.-K.*, Vol. III, p. 388.
20. *Werke*, Vol. III, p. 671; *Bas. of Mor.*, p. 158.
21. *Werke*, Vol. X, pp. 442 f.; cf. *Werke*, Vol. I, p. 383; *H.-K.*, Vol. I, p. 419.
22. *Werke*, Vol. V, p. 319.
23. *Werke*, Vol. II, p. 497; *H.-K.*, Vol. III, p. 217.
24. *Werke*, Vol. II, p. 733; *H.-K.*, Vol. III, p. 466.
25. *Werke*, Vol. II, p. 665; *H.-K.*, Vol. III, p. 392.
26. *Werke*, Vol. IV, p. 529; *Counsels and Maxims*, translated by T. Bailey Saunders, p. 130.
27. *Werke*, Vol. I, p. 216; *H.-K.*, Vol. I, p. 237.
28. *Werke*, Vol. I, p. 300; *H.-K.*, Vol. I, p. 328 (Calderon, *Life Is a Dream*, Act I, Scene I).
29. *Werke*, Vol. I, p. 383; *H.-K.*, Vol. I, p. 418.
30. Tu dois régner; le monde est fait pour les tyrans.
(Act V, Scene iv); cf. Kuno Fischer, *op. cit.*, p. 381.
31. *Werke*, Vol. II, p. 678; *H.-K.*, Vol. III, p. 406.
32. *Werke*, Vol. II, p. 472; *H.-K.*, Vol. III, p. 516.
33. Er nennt's Vernunft, und braucht's allein
Nur tierischer als jedes Tier zu sein.
(*Faust, Prolog im Himmel*); cf. *Werke*, Vol. XI, p. 41.
34. *Werke*, Vol. I, pp. 210 f.; *H.-K.*, Vol. I, p. 231.
35. *Werke*, Vol. II, p. 514; *H.-K.*, Vol. III, p. 237.
36. *Werke*, Vol. I, p. 231; *H.-K.*, Vol. I, p. 254.
37. *Werke*, Vol. I, p. 233; *H.-K.*, Vol. I, p. 256.
38. *Werke*, Vol. I, p. 316; *H.-K.*, Vol. I, p. 346.
39. *Werke*, Vol. III, p. 678; *Bas. of Mor.*, p. 170.
40. *Werke*, Vol. I, pp. 447 f.; *H.-K.*, Vol. I, pp. 489 f.
41. *Werke*, Vol. II, p. 688; *H.-K.*, Vol. III, p. 417.
42. *Werke*, Vol. III, pp. 742 f.; *Bas. of Mor.*, p. 278.
43. *Werke*, Vol. XI, p. 504.

44. *Werke*, Vol. I, p. 462; *H.-K.*, Vol. I, p. 505.
45. *Werke*, Vol. I, p. 486; *H.-K.*, Vol. I, pp. 530 f.
46. *Werke*, Vol. I, pp. 486, 487; *H.-K.*, Vol. I, pp. 531, 532.
47. *Op. cit.*, p. 140.
48. *Schopenhauer's Briefe*, edited by Grisebach, p. 93.
49. Cf. Paul Deussen, *The Elements of Metaphysics*, transl. by C. M. Duff, 1894, p. 316.
50. *Werke*, Vol. I, p. 480; *H.-K.*, Vol. I, p. 524.
51. *Arthur Schopenhauer. Seine Persönlichkeit, seine Lehre, sein Glaube*, 4. edition, p. 279.
52. *Werke*, Vol. I, p. 487; *H.-K.*, Vol. I, p. 532.
53. *Schopenhauer, Hamlet, Mephistopheles*, 3. edition, p. 53.
54. *Schopenhauer*, p. 84.
55. *Werke*, Vol. V, pp. 714 f.; cf. the *Theologia Germanica*, p. 96.
56. Richard Gebhard, "Schopenhauer und Tolstoi," in *Erstes Jahrbuch der Schopenhauer-Gesellschaft*, p. 25; Kuno Fischer, *op. cit.*, p. 247.
57. Bernard Bosanquet, *The Value and Destiny of the Individual*, p. 247.
58. *Werke*, Vol. II, p. 735; *H.-K.*, Vol. III, p. 469.
59. *Werke*, Vol. II, p. 736; *H.-K.*, Vol. III, p. 471.
60. *Werke*, Vol. II, p. 206; *H.-K.*, Vol. II, p. 392.
61. Qualibus in tenebris vitae quantisque periclis
    Degitur hoc aevi quodcumquest!
    (*De rerum natura*, II, 15 sq.); cf. *Werke*, Vol. X, p. 583.
62. *Werke*, Vol. X, p. 584.
63. *Schopenhauer's Briefe*, edited by Grisebach, p. 357.

CHAPTER XII. HARTMANN'S PHILOSOPHY OF THE UNCONSCIOUS

1. "Mein Entwicklungsgang," *Gesammelte Studien und Aufsätze gemeinverständlichen Inhalts* (cited hereafter as *G. S. A.*), 3. edition, p. 30.
2. Otto Braun, *Eduard von Hartmann*, 1909, p. 22.
3. *Allgemeine Geschichte der Philosophie* (in *Kultur der Gegenwart*), 2. edition, p. 577.
4. "Wer vieles bringt, wird manchem etwas bringen." *Faust*, "Vorspiel."
5. Hartmann undertakes to show that Kant, not Schopenhauer, was the true father of modern pessimism, as resulting from an objective estimate of the world and of human life rather than springing

from personal depression or quietist-ascetic temper. Cf. Hartmann, *Zur Geschichte und Begründung des Pessimismus*, 2. edition, Chapter IV; *Philosophische Fragen der Gegenwart*, 1885, pp. 112 ff.).

6. *Neukantianismus, Schopenhauerianismus und Hegelianismus, in ihrer Stellung zu den philosophischen Aufgaben der Gegenwart*, 3. edition, p. 25.
7. *G. S. A.*, p. 604.
8. *G. S. A.*, pp. 575, 569 f.
9. *Kritische Wanderungen durch die Philosophie der Gegenwart*, 1890, pp. 64 f.
10. Schelling, *Werke*, I: i: 401; I: vii: 350; quoted in *G. S. A.*, p. 681.
11. *Philosophische Fragen der Gegenwart*, p. 51.
12. *Philosophie des Unbewussten*, 12. edition, Vol. II, p. 449; *The Philosophy of the Unconscious*, transl. by Coupland, Vol. III, p. 186 (cited hereafter as *Phil. Unbew*, and *Coupl.*); *G. S. A.*, p. 673. Cf. Ludwig Feuerbach, *Darstellung, Entwicklung und Kritik der Leibniz'schen Philosophie* (*Werke*, Vol. IV), p. 116: "Mit dem Willen ist die Existenz gegeben, mit der Vernunft das Wesen."
13. *Phil. Unbew.*, Vol. II, p. 454; *Coupl.*, Vol. III, p. 191.
14. *G. S. A.*, p. 705.
15. *G. S. A.*, pp. 723 f.; cf. Schopenhauer, *Werke*, Vol. II, p. 736; *H.-K.*, Vol. III, p. 470: "The inner being in itself of things is nothing that knows, no intellect, but an unconscious. . . ."
16. Regarding Hartmann's estimates of his predecessors, see also his *Geschichte der Metaphysik*, in *Ausgewählte Werke*, Vols. XI–XII, 1899–1900, especially Part II, pp. 89–128, 167–246, 289–305, and also *Phil. Unbew.*, Vol. I, pp. 13 ff.; *Coupl.*, Vol. I, pp. 16 ff.
17. *Phil. Unbew.*, Vol. I, p. 1; *Coupl.*, Vol. I, p. 2.
18. *Phil. Unbew.*, Vol. I, p. 43; *Coupl.*, Vol. I, p. 51.
19. *Phil. Unbew.*, Vol. I, p. 97; *Coupl.*, Vol. I, p. 113.
20. *Phil. Unbew.*, Vol. I, p. 217; *Coupl.*, Vol. I, p. 251.
21. *Phil. Unbew.*, Vol. I, p. 228; *Coupl.*, Vol. I, p. 263.
22. *Phil. Unbew.*, Vol. I, p. 320; *Coupl.*, Vol. I, p. 371.
23. *Phil. Unbew.*, Vol. I, p. 331; *Coupl.*, Vol. II, p. 12.
24. *Phil. Unbew.*, Vol. II, p. 33; *Coupl.*, Vol. II, p. 83.
25. *Phil. Unbew.*, Vol. II, p. 172; *Coupl.*, Vol. II, p. 242.
26. *Phil. Unbew.*, Vol. II, p. 34; *Coupl.*, Vol. II, p. 84.
27. *Phil. Unbew.*, Vol. II, p. 38; *Coupl.*, Vol. II, p. 88.
28. *Phil. Unbew.*, Vol. II, p. 273; *Coupl.*, Vol. II, p. 356.
29. Thus Drews regards Hartmann as combining in one formula the

optimism of Leibniz and the pessimism of Schopenhauer (*Eduard von Hartmanns philosophisches System im Grundriss*, p. 332).

30. "Erkenntniswert, Schönheitswert, Sittlichkeitswert, Erlösungswert, Entwickelungswert, Zweckmässigkeitswert, Willenswert, Lustwert." This part of the exposition of Hartmann follows in the main his *Grundriss der Axiologie oder Wertwägungslehre* (*System der Philosophie im Grundriss*, Vol. V) and the *Philosophy of the Unconscious*.
31. *Grundr. d. Axiol.*, p. 31.
32. *Ibid.*, p. 59.
33. *Phil. Unbew.*, Vol. II, p. 296; *Coupl.*, Vol. III, p. 13.
34. *Phil. Unbew.*, Vol. II, p. 295; *Coupl.*, Vol. III, p. 12.
35. *Zur Gesch. u. Begr. des Pessimismus*, p. 255.
36. *Grundr. d. Axiol.*, pp. 64 ff.
37. *Phil. Unbew.*, Vol. II, p. 376; *Coupl.*, Vol. III, p. 103.
38. *Zur Gesch. u. Begr. des Pessimismus*, p. 253.
39. *Phil. Unbew.*, Vol. II, p. 389; *Coupl.*, Vol. III, pp. 117 f.
40. *Phil. Unbew.*, Vol. II, p. 398; *Coupl.*, Vol. III, p. 128.
41. *Phil. Unbew.*, Vol. II, p. 399; *Coupl.*, Vol. III, p. 129.
42. *Phil. Unbew.*, Vol. II, p. 399; *Coupl.*, Vol. III, p. 129.
43. *Das sittliche Bewusstsein*, in *Ausgewählte Werke*, Vol. II, 2. edition, p. 51.
44. Volkelt, *Das Unbewusste und der Pessimismus*, 1873, p. 266.
45. *Die Philosophie der Erlösung*, 2. edition, Vol. II, pp. 640 f.
46. *G. S. A.*, p. 39.
47. *Phil. Unbew.*, Vol. II, p. 561.
48. *Phil. Unbew.*, Vol. II, p. 408; *Coupl.*, Vol. III, p. 139.
49. Cf. *Kategorienlehre*, 1896, p. 495, Note; cf. also Note of 1904 to *Phil. Unbew.*, Vol. II, p. 571.
50. *Das sittliche Bewusstsein*, p. 684.
51. *Wahrheit und Dichtung in den Hauptlehren Eduard von Hartmann's*, 1894, p. 24.
52. *Die Religion des Geistes*, 3. edition, p. 185.
53. Cf. *Das Christenthum des Neuen Testaments*, 1905, p. 86.
54. *Die Religion des Geistes*, p. 192.
55. *Ibid.*, p. 189.
56. *Das sittliche Bewusstsein*, p. 591.
57. Cf. *Zur Gesch. u. Begr. d. Pess.*, pp. 327 ff., 359 ff., 370: "Die Bedeutung des Leides."
58. *Die Religion des Geistes*, p. 259; *Das religiöse Bewusstsein der Menschheit*, 2. edition, (*Ausgewählte Werke*, Vol. V), p. 615.

59. *Grundr. d. Religionsphilosophie*, p. 79.
60. *Die Religion des Geistes*, p. 267.
61. *Das sittliche Bewusstsein*, p. 688.
62. *Das religiöse Bewusstsein der Menschheit*, p. 625.
63. *Phil. Unbew.*, Vol. II, p. 577.
64. Cf. Hugo Sommer, *Die Religion des Pessimismus*, 1884, p. 21.
65. *Das sittliche Bewusstsein*, p. 246.
66. *Der Pessimismus und die Sittenlehre*, 2. edition, p. 125.
67. Braun, *op. cit.*, pp. 149 f.
68. *Die Religion des Geistes*, pp. 247 f., Note; cf. *Phil. Unbew.*, Vol. II, pp. 438 f.; *Coupl.*, Vol. III, pp. 172 f.; *Grundriss der Metaphysik*, p. 102.
69. *Phil. Unbew.*, Vol. II, p. 439; *Coupl.* Vol. III, p. 173.
70. *Der Pessimismus und die Sittenlehre*, pp. 180 f.
71. Luke, xvii:33; *Das sittliche Bewusstsein*, p. 477.
72. *Grundr. d. Axiol.*, p. 162; cf. pp. 141, 148.
73. Pp. 110 ff.
74. Sommer, *Die Religion des Pessimismus*, p. 14.
75. *Eduard von Hartmanns Religionsphilosophie des Unbewussten*, 1921, p. 550.
76. *Das sittliche Bewusstsein*, p. 474; cf. Bahnsen, *Der Widerspruch im Wissen und Wesen der Welt*, Vol. I, pp. 177 f.:

    Etwas fürchten und hoffen und sorgen
    Muss der Mensch für den kommenden Morgen,
    Dass er die Schwere des Daseins ertrage
    Und das ermüdende Gleichmass der Tage.
    (*Die Braut von Messina*, Act I).
77. *Grundr. d. Axiol.*, p. 194; cf. pp. 166, 167, 181.
78. Cf. *Kritische Wanderungen durch die Philosophie der Gegenwart*, pp. 64 f.

CHAPTER XIII. A GERMAN SLOUGH OF DESPOND

1. Hartmann, *Philosophische Fragen der Gegenwart*, p. 39; cf. pp. 38–57: "Die Schopenhauer'sche Schule."
2. Cf. in this connection his *Studien und Kritiken zur Theologie und Philosophie*, a work of his pre-Schopenhauerian days.
3. *Neue Briefe über die Schopenhauer'sche Philosophie*, quoted here from Hartmann, *Neukantianismus, Schopenhauerianismus und Hegelianismus*, 3. edition, p. 119.
4. *Neukantianismus*, p. 120; cf. Hartmann's critique of Frauenstädt, *ibid.*, pp. 28 ff., 115–165.

5. *The Philosophy of Mysticism*, II:ii:6; transl. by Massey, Vol. II, pp. 308, 309.
6. *Der Pessimismus und seine Gegner*, pp. 122, 132.
7. *Philosophische Fragen der Gegenwart*, pp. 52 f.
8. *Pessimism*, 1877, p. 109.
9. *Die Philosophie der Erlösung*, Vol. II, 2. edition, p. 84; cf. pp. 191 ff.
10. *Phil. d. Erl.*, Vol. II, p. 89.
11. Ich weiss dass ohne mich Gott nicht ein Nu kann leben:
    Werd' ich zu nicht, er muss von Noth den Geist aufgeben.
    (*Cherubinischer Wandersmann*).
12. *Phil. d. Erl.*, Vol. I, 3. edition, p. 108; cf. H. A. Giles, *Religions of Ancient China*, 1918, p. 8.
13. *Phil. d. Erl.*, Vol. I, pp. 242, 261; Vol. II, p. 251.
14. *Phil. d. Erl.*, Vol. I, pp. 189 ff., 196 ff., 218.
15. *Phil. d. Erl.*, Vol. II, p. 448; cf. Vol. I, pp. 209 f., 219 f.
16. Ich danke, Götter,
    Dass ihr mich ohne Kinder auszurotten
    Beschlossen habt.—Und lass dir rathen habe
    Die Sonne nicht zu lieb und nicht die Sterne.
    Komm', folge mir ins dunkle Reich hinab. . . .
    Komm' kinderlos und schuldlos mit hinab!
    (*Iphigenia auf Tauris*, Act III, Scene I); cf. *Phil. d. Erl.*, Vol. I, p. 317.
17. Frauenminne muss verschwören
    Wer zur Gralsschaar will gehören.
    Cf. *Phil. d. Erl.*, Vol. II, pp. 268, 254, 427 ff.
18. *Phil. d. Erl.*, Vol. I, p. 221.
19. *Phil. d. Erl.*, Vol. I, p. 335; cf. Vol. II, p. 333.
20. *Phil. d. Erl.*, Vol. II, pp. 202, 203.
21. *Phil. d. Erl.*, Vol. I, p. 345; cf. Vol. I, p. 312; Vol. II, p. 205.
22. *Das sittliche Bewusstsein*, p. 549.
23. *Geschichte der Metaphysik*, Vol. II, p. 530.
24. *Phil. d. Erl.*, Vol. II, p. 341.
25. *Phil. d. Erl.*, Vol. II, p. 630.
26. Cf. Bahnsen's correspondence with Schopenhauer, in Ludwig Schemann's edition of *Schopenhauer-Briefe*, 1893, pp. 347–362, and also pp. 449–454 for biographical and bibliographical details.
27. Cf. *Zur Philosophie der Geschichte;* Hartmann, *Neukantianismus*, pp. 10 ff., 166 ff.; *Geschichte der Metaphysik*, Vol. II, pp. 510 ff.; *Philosophische Fragen*, pp. 261 ff.; O. Plümacher, *Der Kampf ums Unbewusste*, pp. 9 ff.

28. *Troilus and Cressida*, Act V, Scene ii.
29. *Das Tragische als Weltgesetz und der Humor als ästhetische Gestalt des Metaphysischen*, 1877, p. 28; cf. *Der Widerspruch im Wissen und Wesen der Welt*, 1880–1882, Vol. I, p. 204; Vol. II, p. 331.
30. Cf. O. Plümacher, *Der Pessimismus in Vergangenheit und Gegenwart*, 2. edition, p. 163.
31. Hartmann, *Geschichte der Metaphysik*, Vol. II, p. 511.
32. *Widerspruch*, Vol. I, p. 51.
33. *Mosaiken und Silhouetten*, 1877, p. 7; cf. *Beiträge zur Charakterologie*, Vol. I, pp. 105 f., 340.
34. *Widerspruch*, Vol. II, p. 206; cf. Vol. I, p. 50: "Widerspruchsverwirklichung begleitet jedes Wesen vom Augenblick des Erzeugtwerdens bis zu dem des Sterbens."
35. *Wie ich wurde*, edited by R. Louis, 1905, p. 41.
36. *Ibid.*, p. 127.
37. Cf. Hartmann, *Philosophische Fragen*, pp. 295 ff.; *Gesch. d. Metaphysik*, Vol. II, pp. 521 ff.
38. *Wie ich wurde*, pp. xxxvii, 161; cf. *Widerspruch*, Vol. II, p. 454.
39. *Der Pessimismus*, p. 80.
40. *Wie ich wurde*, p. 199.
41. *Das Tragische als Weltgesetz*, p. 13.
42. Cf. A. Burdeau in the *Revue philosophique*, Vol. V, 1878, p. 588.

CHAPTER XIV. A GRADATIONAL VIEW OF THE NATURE OF EVIL

1. "Is Life Worth Living?" in *The Will to Believe*, p. 61.
2. *Loc. cit.*
3. *Ibid.*, p. 56.
4. S. Alexander, "Naturalism and Value," in *The Personalist*, October, 1928, p. 246.
5. Sir Henry Jones, *A Faith that Enquires*, p. 44, criticizing absolutism.
6. Edited by H. W. Dresser, New York, Crowell, 1921.
7. *Science and Health*, p. 120.
8. *The Quimby Manuscripts*, Appended facsimile letter, p. i.
9. Cf. G. G. Atkins, *Modern Religious Cults and Movements*, pp. 157 ff.
10. *A System of Ethics*, transl. by Frank Thilly, pp. 289 f.
11. Mille piacer' non vagliono un tormento.
    (Sonetto 195; cf. Schopenhauer's *Werke*, Deussen edition, Vol. II, p. 659).

12. Browning, "Confessions," in *Dramatis Personae.*
13. *Pessimism*, 1877, p. 279.
14. Willst du immer weiter schweifen?
    Sieh, das Gute liegt so nah.
    Lerne nur das Glück ergreifen,
    Denn das Glück ist immer da.
    (*Erinnerung*).
15. H. Crossley's translation, *The Golden Sayings of Epictetus*, p. 68.
16. II Peter, ii: 22.
17. *The World and the Individual*, Vol. II, p. 406.
18. *Utilitarianism*, Douglas' edition, *The Ethics of John Stuart Mill*, p. 97.
19. Paul Janet, *Philosophie du bonheur*, 1863, p. 19.
20. *Theologia Germanica*, transl. Susanna Winkworth, Golden Treasury Series, pp. 73, 122; Pascal, *Pensées, Oeuvres*, Vol. XIII, p. 385; cf. Ernest Naville, *Le problème du mal*, 1868, pp. 74, 204.
21. Non scribit, cujus carmina nemo legit.
    (Martial, *Epigr.* III, ix; transl. by W. C. A. Ker, in the Loeb Classical Library). The notice of this line I owe to the interest of Mr. Donald Mugridge.
22. *The Philosophy of Plotinus*, Vol. I, p. 133.
23. Cf. Urban, *Valuation*, pp. 54, 63, and also Professor Urban's articles on Value in the *Journal of Philosophy*, Vols. XIII, XIV; Sorley, *Moral Values and the Idea of God*, pp. 54–131, 134, 498. Cf. also A. P. Brogan, "The Implication of Meliorism concerning the Relation between Value and Existence," in the *Proceedings of the Sixth International Congress of Philosophy*, pp. 308 ff.
24. *Prolegomena to Ethics*, Section 184.
25. E. S. Brightman, *Religious Values*, p. 135.
26. Cf. Bosanquet, *The Value and Destiny of the Individual*, pp. 63 ff.
27. *Entretiens sur la bonne et mauvaise fortune*, Paris, 1673, Vol. I, p. 6.
28. *Moral Philosophy; The Critical View of Life*, p. 268.
29. Considerate la vostra semenza,
    Fatti non foste a viver come bruti,
    Ma per seguir virtute e conoscenza.
    (*Inferno*, XXVI, 118 ff.; Johnson's translation quoted in the text).
30. *De Civitate Dei*, XII, section 6.
31. *Ibid.*, XII; English translation of Augustine's *Works*, Vol. I, p. 491.
32. *The Tragic Sense of Life*, p. 208.
33. Merejkovsky, *The Romance of Leonardo da Vinci*, transl. by Herbert

Trench, Vol. I, p. 211. Cf. Carl Hilty, *Happiness*, transl. by F. G. Peabody, 1903, p. 107: "My impression is that there is not one of us who has ever, even for a single day, done his whole duty."

34. Matthew, xix: 16.
35. *Cosmic Evolution*, p. 45.
36. *The Problem of Immortality*, pp. 345 ff.
37. *Literature and Dogma*, Chapter I.
38. John, v: 17.
39. Merejkovsky, *The Romance of Leonardo da Vinci*, Book XIII, Chap. x.
40. E. C. Wilm, *The Problem of Religion*, p. 172; cf. Émile Lasbax, *Le problème du mal*, 1919, p. 372.
41. *Theaetetus*, 176.
42. Quoted from McComb, *The Future Life in the Light of Modern Inquiry*, p. 94.

INDEX